◆ ◆ ◆ ◆ ◆ ◆ ◆ ◆ ◆ ◆ ◆ ◆ ◆ ◆ ◆ ◆ ◆ ◆ ◆ ◆

Presented to

———————————————————————

From

———————————————————————

on the occasion of

———————————————————————

———————————————————————

◆ ◆ ◆ ◆ ◆ ◆ ◆ ◆ ◆ ◆ ◆ ◆ ◆ ◆ ◆ ◆ ◆ ◆ ◆ ◆

THE NEW
AMERICAN
BIBLE

REVISED EDITION

THE NEW AMERICAN

BIBLE

REVISED EDITION

Translated From the Original Languages
With Critical Use of All the Ancient Sources
Authorized by the Board of Trustees of the
Confraternity of Christian Doctrine
And Approved by the Administrative Committee
of the United States Conference of Catholic Bishops

NEW TESTAMENT

Nihil Obstat:
Stephen J Hardegen, OFM, LSS
Censor Deputatus

Imprimatur:
+James A. Hickey, STD, JCD
Archbishop of Washington
August 27, 1986

OLD TESTAMENT

Rescript

In accord with canon 825 §1 of the *Code of Canon Law*, the United States Conference of Catholic Bishops hereby approves for publication *The New American Bible, Revised Old Testament*, a translation of the Sacred Scriptures authorized by the Confraternity of Christian Doctrine, Inc.

The translation was approved by the Administrative Committee of the United States Conference of Catholic Bishops in November 2008 and September 2010. It is permitted by the undersigned for private use and study.
Given in the city of Washington, the District of Columbia, on the Feast of Saint Jerome, Priest and Doctor of the Church, the 30th day of September, in the year of our Lord 2010.

Francis Cardinal George, OMI
Archbishop of Chicago
President, USCCB

Published by the United States Conference of Catholic Bishops, Washington, DC.

Maps © 2015 Lucidity Information Design, LLC.

First printing, September 2015

ISBN (Paperback) 978-1-60137-484-4
ISBN (Personal Edition) 978-1-60137-485-1
ISBN (Gift Edition) 978-1-60137-486-8

Collaborators on the Old Testament
of the New American Bible 1970
Bishops' Committee of the Confraternity of Christian Doctrine

Most Rev. Charles P. Greco, D.D.,
Chairman
Most Rev. Joseph T. McGucken, S.T.D.

Most Rev. Vincent S. Waters, D.D.
Most Rev. Romeo Blanchette, D.D.
Most Rev. Christopher J. Weldon, D.D.

Editors in Chief

Rev. Louis F. Hartman, C.SS.R., S.S.L.,
LING. OR. L., Chairman
Rev. Msgr. Patrick W. Skehan, S.T.D., LL.D.,
Vice-Chairman

Rev. Stephen J. Hartdegen, O.F.M., S.S.L.,
Secretary

Associate Editors and Translators

Rev. Edward P. Arbez, S.S., S.T.D.
Rev. Msgr. Edward J. Byrne, PH.D., S.T.D.
Rev. Edward A. Cerny, S.S., S.T.D.
Rev. James E. Coleran, S.J., S.T.L., S.S.L.
Rev. John J. Collins, S.J., M.A., S.S.L.
Sr. M. Emmanuel Collins, O.S.F., PH.D.
Prof. Frank M. Cross Jr., PH.D.
Rev. Patrick Cummins, O.S.B., S.T.D.
Rev. Antonine A. DeGuglielmo, O.F.M.,
S.T.D., S.S.L., S.S.LECT. Gen.
Rev. Alexander A. Di Lella, O.F.M., S.T.L.,
S.S.L., PH.D.
Most Rev. John J. Dougherty, S.T.L., S.S.D.
Rev. William A. Dowd, S.J., S.T.D., S.S.L.
Prof. David Noel Freedman, PH.D.
Rev. Michael J. Fruenthaner, S.J., S.T.D.,
S.S.D.
Rev. Msgr. Maurice A. Hofer, S.S.L.
Rev. Justin Krellner, O.S.B., S.T.D.
Rev. Joseph L. Lilly, C.M., S.T.D., S.S.L.
Rev. Roderick F. MacKenzie, S.J., M.A.,
S.S.D.
Rev. Edward A. Mangan, C.SS.R., S.S.L.

Rev. Daniel W. Martin, C.M., S.T.L., S.S.L.
Rev. William H. McClellan, S.J.
Rev. James McGlinchey, C.M., S.T.D.
Rev. Frederick Moriarty, S.J., S.S.L., S.T.D.
Rev. Richard T. Murphy, O.P., S.T.D., S.S.D.
Rev. Roland E. Murphy, O. Carm., M.A.,
S.T.D., S.S.L.
Rev. Msgr. William R. Newton, M.S., S.S.D.
Rev. Everhard Olinger, O.S.B.
Rev. Charles H. Pickar, O.S.A., S.T.L., S.S.L.
Rev. Christopher Rehwinkel, O.F.M.,
S.T.D., S.S. LECT. GEN.
Rev. Msgr. John R. Rowan, S.T.D., S.S.L.,
Prof. J.A. Sanders, PH.D.
Rev. Edward F. Siegman, C.PP.S., S.T.D.,
S.S.L.
Rev. Msgr. Matthew P. Stapleton, S.T.D.,
S.S.L.
Rev. Msgr. John E. Steinmueller, S.T.D.,
S.S.L.
Rev. John Ujlaki, O.S.B., LITT.D.
Rev. Bruce Vawter, C.M., S.T.L., S.S.D.
Rev. John B. Weisengoff, S.T.D., S.S.L.

Collaborators on the Revised Psalms
of the New American Bible 1991
Bishops' Ad Hoc Committee

Most Rev. Enrique San Pedro, S.J.
Most Rev. Richard Sklba, D.D.
Most Rev. Donald W. Trautman, S.T.D.,
S.S.L.

Most Rev. Emil A. Wcela
Most Rev. John F. Whealon, S.S.L.,
Chairman

Board of Editors

Rev. Richard Clifford, S.J.
Br. Aloysius Fitzgerald, F.S.C.
Rev. Joseph Jensen, O.S.B.

Rev. Roland Murphy, O.Carm.
Sr. Irene Nowell, O.S.B.
Dr. Judith Sanderson

Revisers

Prof. Gary Anderson
Rev. Michael L. Barré, S.S.
Rev. Christopher T. Begg
Dr. Joseph Blenkinsopp
Rev. Anthony R. Ceresko, O.S.F.S.

Rev. Richard J. Clifford, S.J.
Rev. Aelred Cody, O.S.B.
Prof. Michael D. Coogan
Rev. Alexander A. Di Lella, O.F.M.
Dr. Robert A. Di Vito

Br. Aloysius Fitzgerald, F.S.C.
Rev. Michael D. Guinan, O.F.M.
Rev. William L. Holladay
Rev. William Irwin, C.S.B.
Rev. Joseph Jensen, O.S.B.
Rev. John S. Kselman
Rev. Leo Laberge, O.M.I.
Dr. Conrad E. L'Heureux
Dr. Paul G. Mosca
Rev. Dr. Roland E. Murphy, O.Carm.

Dr. Michael Patrick O'Connor
Rev. Brian J. Peckham, S.J.
Prof. Jimmy J. Roberts
Sr. Eileen M. Schuller, O.S.U.
Dr. Byron E. Shafer
Prof. Mark S. Smith
Prof. Matitiahu Tesvat
Dr. Eugene C. Ulrich
Prof. James C. VanderKam
Rev. Jerome T. Walsh

English Consultants

Dr. Catherine Dunn

Br. Daniel Burke, F.S.C.

Business Manager

Charles A. Buggé

Collaborators on the Revised New Testament of the New American Bible 1986

Bishops' Ad Hoc Committee

Most Rev. Theodore E. McCarrick, D.D.
Most Rev. Richard J. Sklba, D.D.
Most Rev. J. Francis Stafford, D.D.

Most Rev. John F. Whealon, D.D., Chairman

Board of Editors

Rev. Msgr. Myles M. Bourke
Rev. Francis T. Gignac, S.J., Chairman

Rev. Stephen J. Hartdegen, O.F.M., Secretary
Rev. John H. Reumann

Revisers

Rev. Msgr. Myles M. Bourke
Rev. Frederick W. Danker
Rev. Alexander A. Di Lella, O.F.M.
Rev. Charles H. Giblin, S.J.
Rev. Francis T. Gignac, S.J.
Rev. Stephen J. Hartdegen, O.F.M.
Dr. Maurya P. Horgan

Rev. John R. Keating, S.J.
Rev. John Knox
Dr. Paul J. Kobelski
Dr. J. Rebecca Lyman
Br. Elliott C. Maloney, O.S.B.
Dr. Janet A. Timbie

Consultants

Rev. Joseph Jensen, O.S.B.
Rev. Aidan Kavanagh, O.S.B.

Dr. Marianne Sawicki

Business Manager

Charles A. Buggé

Word Processor

Suzanna Jordan

Collaborators on the Old Testament of the New American Bible 2010

Bishops' Committee on Doctrine
Subcommittee on the Translation of Scripture Text

Most Rev. Arthur J. Serratelli, Chairman
Justin Cardinal Rigali
Most Rev. Blase J. Cupich

Most Rev. Richard J. Sklba
Most Rev. Anthony B. Taylor

Contents

OLD TESTAMENT

NEW TESTAMENT

BIBLICAL BOOKS IN ALPHABETICAL ORDER

OLD
TESTAMENT

· · · · · · · · · · · · · · · · · ·

PREFACE TO THE REVISED NEW AMERICAN BIBLE OLD TESTAMENT

The first step in the genesis of the *New American Bible* was taken in 1936 when His Excellency, the Most Reverend Edwin V. O'Hara, D.D., chairman of the Episcopal Committee of the Confraternity of Christian Doctrine, invited a group of Catholic Scripture scholars to plan for a revised edition of the Challoner-Rheims New Testament, primarily on the basis of the Vulgate; the plans soon expanded to include the revision of the Old Testament. Archbishop O'Hara's initiative resulted in the formation of the Catholic Biblical Association, whose principal activity in its early years was this work of revision and translation. (For information on the work done on the New Testament, see the "Preface to the *New American Bible*: First Edition of the New Testament" and "Preface to the Revised Edition.") In 1943 His Holiness Pope Pius XII issued the encyclical *Divino afflante spiritu*, which encouraged Scripture scholars to translate the Scriptures from the original languages. He wrote: "We ought to explain the original text which was written by the inspired author himself and has more authority and greater weight than any, even the very best, translation whether ancient or modern. This can be done all the more easily and fruitfully if to the knowledge of languages be joined a real skill in literary criticism of the same text." Although at this point work on almost twenty of the Old Testament books was completed or near completion, that work was abandoned and the new project of translating from the Hebrew, Greek, and Aramaic was undertaken.

The completed books of the Old Testament were initially published, as they became available, in four volumes: Genesis–Ruth (1952), Job–Sirach (1955), Isaiah–Malachi (1961), and Samuel–Maccabees (1969). Some fifty scholars collaborated on this project; these were mainly Catholics, but, in accord with the suggestion of Vatican II that "with the approval of the church authority, these translations be produced in cooperation with separated brothers" so that "all Christians may be able to use them" (*Dei Verbum*, No. 22), non-Catholics also participated in the work. To this point the translation had been known under the name of the "Confraternity of Christian Doctrine" or CCD for short, but when these parts of the Old Testament were combined with the New Testament in a single volume, it was given the name "*New American Bible*," in part to reflect its ecumenical character. In producing the new volume certain changes were made from the original four volumes: a retranslation of the Book of Genesis, cross-references, new and expanded exegetical notes.

New translations and revision of existing translations are required from time to time for various reasons. For example, it is important to keep pace with the discovery and publication of new and better ancient manuscripts (e.g., the Dead Sea scrolls) so that the best possible textual tradition will be followed, as required by *Divino afflante spiritu*. There are advances in linguistics of the biblical languages which make possible a better understanding and more accurate translation of

4

the original languages. And there are changes and developments in vocabulary and the cultural background of the receptor language. An obvious example of this is the abandonment in English of the second person singular (use of "thee," "thou," "sayest," "hearest"), which had a major impact on Bible translations. Other changes are less obvious but are nevertheless present. There have been changes in vocabulary; for example, the term "holocaust" is now normally reserved for the sacrilegious attempt to destroy the Jewish people by the Third Reich. Concerns such as these are reflected in what Pope John Paul II spoke of as the "three pillars" of good biblical translation: "A good translation is based on three pillars that must contemporaneously support the entire work. First, there must be a deep knowledge of the language and the cultural world at the point of origin. Next, there must be a good familiarity with the language and cultural context at the point where the work will arrive. Lastly, to crown the work with success, there must be an adequate mastery of the contents and meaning of what one is translating"— and he praised the translation that "utilizes the vocabulary and idioms of everyday speech" ("le parole e le forme della lingua di tutti i giorni"). (From an address to the United Bible Societies, November 26, 2001.)

This new edition is a thorough revision of the already excellent *New American Bible* Old Testament of 1970. Work on most books of the Old Testament, begun in 1994 and completed in 2001, was done by forty revisers and a board of eight editors. The 1991 revision of the Psalter, the work of thirty revisers and six editors, was further revised by seven revisers and two editors between 2009 and 2010. As suggested in the comments above, the revision aimed at making use of the best manuscript traditions available (see next), translating as accurately as possible, and

rendering the result in good contemporary English. In many ways it is a more literal translation than the original *NAB* and has attempted to be more consistent in rendering Hebrew (or Greek) words and idioms, especially in technical contexts, such as regulations for sacrifices. In translating the Psalter special effort was made to provide a smooth, rhythmic translation for easy singing or recitation, and to retain the concrete imagery of the Hebrew.

Where the Old Testament translation supposes the received text— Hebrew, Aramaic, or Greek, as the case may be—ordinarily contained in the best-known editions, as the original or the oldest extant form, no additional remarks are necessary. Where the translators have departed from those received texts, e.g., by following the Septuagint rather than the Masoretic text, accepting a reading of what is judged to be a better textual tradition, as from a Qumran manuscript, or by emending a reading apparently corrupted in transmission, such changes are recorded in the revised edition of the *Textual Notes on the New American Bible*. Additional information on the textual tradition for some books may be found in the introduction to the book in the same *Textual Notes*.

In particular, important manuscripts from Cave 4 of Qumran, as well as the most useful recensions of the Septuagint, have been consulted in the preparation of 1 and 2 Samuel. Fragments of the lost Book of Tobit in Aramaic and in Hebrew, recovered from Cave 4 of Qumran, are in substantial agreement with the Sinaiticus Greek recension used for the translation of this book. The lost original Hebrew text of 1 Maccabees is replaced by its oldest extant form in Greek. Judith, 2 Maccabees, and parts of Esther are also translated from the Greek. The translation of The Wisdom of Ben Sira is based on the original Hebrew as far as it is preserved, with corrections from the ancient versions; otherwise, the Greek of the Septuagint is followed. In the Book of Baruch the basic text is the Greek of the Septuagint, with some readings derived from an underlying Hebrew form no longer extant. In the deuterocanonical sections of Daniel (3:24–90; 13:1–14:42), the basic text is the Greek text of so-called Theodotion, occasionally revised according to the Greek text of the Septuagint. ✠

THE PENTATEUCH

The Pentateuch (Greek for "five books") designates the first five books of the Jewish and Christian Bible (Genesis, Exodus, Leviticus, Numbers, and Deuteronomy). Jewish tradition calls the five books Torah (Teaching, Law) because of the centrality of the Sinai covenant and legislation mediated through Moses.

The unity of the Pentateuch comes from the single story it tells. God creates the world and destines human beings for the blessings of progeny and land possession (Gn 1–3). As the human race expands, its evil conduct provokes God to send the flood to wipe out all but righteous Noah's family. After the flood, the world is repopulated from his three sons, Ham, Shem, and Japheth (Gn 4–9). From them are descended the seventy nations of the civilized world whose offense this time (building a city rather than taking their assigned lands, Gn 10–11) provokes God to elect one family from the rest. Abraham and his wife, Sarah, landless and childless, are promised a child and the land of Canaan. Amid trials and fresh promises, a son (Isaac) is born to them and Abraham takes title to a sliver of Canaanite land, a kind of down payment for later possession (Gn 12–25). Gn 25–36 tells how their descendant Jacob becomes the father of twelve sons (because of which he is called "Israel"), and Gn 37–50 tells how the rejected brother Joseph saves the family from famine and brings them to Egypt.

In Egypt, a pharaoh who knew not Joseph subjects "the seventy sons of Jacob" ("the Hebrews") to hard labor, keeping them from their land and destroying their male progeny (Ex 1). Moses is commissioned to lead the people out of Egypt to their own land (Ex 2–6). In ten plagues, the Lord defeats Pharaoh. Free at last, the Hebrews leave Egypt and journey to Mount Sinai (Ex 7–18), where they enter into a covenant to be the people of the Lord and be shaped by the Ten Commandments and other laws (Ex 19–24). Though the people commit apostasy when Moses goes back to the mountain for the plans of the dwelling (tabernacle), Moses' intercession prevents the abrogation of the covenant by God (Ex 32–34). A principle has been established, however: even the people's apostasy need not end their relationship with God. The book ends with the cloud and the glory taking possession of the tent of meeting (Ex 36:34–38). "The sons of Israel" in Ex 1:1 are the actual sons of Jacob/Israel the patriarch, but at the end of the book they are the nation Israel, for all the elements of nationhood in antiquity have been granted: a god (and temple), a leader, a land, and an authoritative tradition.

Israel remains at the holy mountain for almost a year. The entire block of material from Ex 19:1 to Nm 10:11 is situated at Sinai. The rituals of Leviticus and Numbers are delivered to Moses at the holy mountain, showing that Israel's worship was instituted by God and part of the very fabric of the people's life. Priestly material in the Book of Exodus (chaps. 25–31, 35–40) describes the basic institutions of Israelite worship (the tabernacle, its furniture, and priestly vestments). Leviticus, aptly called in rabbinic tradition the Priests' Manual, lays down the role of priests to teach Israel the distinction between clean and unclean and to see to their holiness. In Nm 10:11–22:1, the journey is resumed, this time from Sinai through the wilderness to

Transjordan; Nm 22:2–36:13 tells of events and laws in the plains of Moab.

The final book of the Pentateuch, Deuteronomy, consists of four speeches by Moses to the people who have arrived at the plains of Moab, ready to conquer the land: 1:1–4:43; 4:44–28:68; 29:1–32:52; 33:1–34:12. Each speech is introduced by the formula "This is the law/words/blessing."

The Priestly editor used literary formulas. The formula "These are the generations (the wording can vary) of . . ." occurs five times in the primordial history (Gn 2:4a; 5:1; 6:9; 10:1; 11:10) and five times in the ancestral history (11:27; 25:12; 25:19; 36:1 [v. 9 is secondary]; 37:2). In Exodus and Numbers the formula (with slight variations) "They departed from (place name) and encamped at (place name)" occurs in two groups of six: A. Ex 12:37a; 13:20; 14:1–2; 15:22a; 16:1; 17:1a; and B. 19:2; Nm 10:12; 20:1a; 20:22; 21:10–11; 22:1.

Who wrote the Pentateuch, and when? Up to the seventeenth century, the virtually unanimous answer of Jews and Christians was "Moses." Moses wrote the Pentateuch as David wrote the Psalter and Solomon wrote the wisdom literature. Though scholars had noted inconsistencies (compare Ishmael's age in Gn 16:16 and 21:5, 14) and duplications (Gn 12, 20, and 26), they assumed Mosaic authorship because of the prevalent theory of inspiration: God inspired authors while they wrote. With the rise of historical criticism, scholars began to use the doublets and inconsistencies as clues to different authors and traditions.

By the late nineteenth century, one theory of the sources of the Pentateuch had been worked out that proved acceptable in its main lines to the majority of scholars (apart from Christian and Jewish conservatives) then and now. It can be quickly sketched. In the premonarchic period of the Judges (ca. 1220–1020 B.C.), the twelve tribes had an oral form of their story from creation to the taking of the land. With the beginnings of monarchy in the late eleventh and tenth centuries, the oral material was written down, being known as the Yahwist account (from its use of the divine name Yhwh). Its abbreviation, "J," comes from the German spelling of the divine name. In the following century, another account took shape in the Northern Kingdom (called E after its use of Elohim as a divine name); some believe the E source is simply a supplement to J. After the fall of the Northern Kingdom in 722/721 B.C., the E version was taken to Jerusalem where it was combined with the J version to produce J-E. During the exile (conventionally dated 587–539 B.C.) or thereafter, an editor recast J-E to make it relevant for the exiled population. This editor is conventionally known as P (=Priestly) because of the chronological and ritual interests apparent in the work. P can also designate archival material and chronological notices. The audience for the Priestly edition no longer lived in the land and was deeply concerned about its survival and its claim on the land.

Deuteronomy (=D) stands alone in style, genre (preaching rather than narrative), and content. How did it come to be the fifth book of the Pentateuch? The J-E narrative actually ends in Numbers, when Israel arrives at the plains of Moab. Many scholars believe that Deuteronomy was secondarily attached to Numbers by moving the account of Moses' death from its original place in the J-E version in Numbers to the end of Deuteronomy (chap. 34). Deuteronomy was attached to Genesis–Numbers to link it to another great work, the Deuteronomistic History (Joshua to Kings). Deuteronomy is now the fifth book of the Pentateuch and the first book of the Deuteronomistic History.

In the last three decades, the above consensus on the composition of the

Pentateuch has come under attack. Some critics are extremely skeptical about the historical value of the so-called early traditions, and a few doubt there ever was a preexilic monarchy of any substance. For such scholars, the Pentateuch is a retrojection from the fourth or third centuries B.C. Other scholars postulate a different sequence of sources, or understand the sources differently.

How should a modern religiously minded person read the Pentateuch? First, readers have before them the most significant thing, the text of the Pentateuch. It is accurately preserved, reasonably well understood, and capable of touching audiences of every age. Take and read! Second, the controversies are about the sources of the Pentateuch, especially their antiquity and character. Many details will never be known, for the evidence is scanty. Indeed, the origin of many great literary works is obscure.

The Pentateuch witnesses to a coherent story that begins with the creation of the world and ends with Israel taking its land. The same story is in the historical Ps 44, 77, 78, 80, 105, 114, and 149, and in the confessions Dt 26:5–9, Jos 24:2–13, and 1 Sm 12:7–13. Though the narrative enthralls and entertains, as all great literature does, it is well to remember that it is a theopolitical charter as well, meant to establish how and why descendants of the patriarchs are a uniquely holy people among the world's nations.

The destruction of the Jerusalem Temple and deportation of Israelites in the sixth century B.C. seemed to invalidate the charter, for Israel no longer possessed its land in any real sense. The last chapter of the ancient narrative—Israel dwelling securely in its land—no longer held true. The story had to be reinterpreted, and the Priestly editor is often credited with doing so. A preface (Gn 1) was added, emphasizing God's intent that human beings continue in existence through their progeny and possess their own land. Good news, surely, to a devastated people wondering whether they would survive and repossess their ancestral land. The ending of the old story was changed to depict Israel at the threshold of the promised land (the plains of Moab) rather than in it. Henceforth, Israel would be a people oriented toward the land rather than possessing it. The revised ending could not be more suitable for Jews and Christians alike. Both peoples can imagine themselves on the threshold of the promised land, listening to the word of God in order to be able to enter it in the future. For Christians particularly, the Pentateuch portrays the pilgrim people waiting for the full realization of the kingdom of God. ✠

THE BOOK OF GENESIS

Introduction

Genesis is the first book of the Pentateuch (Genesis, Exodus, Leviticus, Numbers, Deuteronomy), the first section of the Jewish and the Christian Scriptures. Its title in English, "Genesis," comes from the Greek of Gn 2:4, literally, "the book of the generation (*genesis*) of the heavens and earth." Its title in the Jewish Scriptures is the opening Hebrew word, *Bereshit*, "in the beginning."

The book has two major sections—the creation and expansion of the human race (2:4–11:9), and the story of Abraham and his descendants (11:10–50:26). The first section deals with God and the nations, and the second deals with God and a particular nation, Israel. The opening creation account (1:1–2:3) lifts up two themes that play major roles in each section—the divine command to the first couple (standing for the whole race) to produce offspring and to possess land (1:28). In the first section, progeny and land appear in the form of births and genealogies (chaps. 2–9) and allotment of land (chaps. 10–11), and in the second, progeny and land appear in the form of promises of descendants and land to the ancestors. Another indication of editing is the formulaic introduction, "this is the story; these are the descendants" (Hebrew *tōledôt*), which occurs five times in Section I (2:4; 5:1; 6:9; 10:1; 10:31) and five times in Section II (11:10; 25:12, 19; 36:1 [v. 9 is an addition]; 37:2).

The Composition of the Book. For the literary sources of Genesis, see Introduction to the Pentateuch. As far as the sources of Genesis are concerned, contemporary readers can reasonably assume that ancient traditions (J and E) were edited in the sixth or fifth century B.C. for a Jewish audience that had suffered the effects of the exile and was now largely living outside of Palestine. The editor highlighted themes of vital concern to this audience: God intends that every nation have posterity and land; the ancestors of Israel are models for their descendants who also live in hope rather than in full possession of what has been promised; the ancient covenant with God is eternal, remaining valid even when the human party has been unfaithful. By highlighting such concerns, the editor addressed the worries of exiled Israel and indeed of contemporary Jews and Christians.

Genesis 1–11. The seven-day creation account in Gn 1:1–2:3 tells of a God whose mere word creates a beautiful universe in which human beings are an integral and important part. Though Gn 2:4–3:24 is often regarded as "the second creation story," the text suggests that the whole of 2:4–11:9 tells one story. The plot of Gn 2–11 (creation, the flood, renewed creation) has been borrowed from creation-flood stories attested in Mesopotamian literature of the second and early first millennia. In the Mesopotamian creation-flood stories, the gods created the human race as slaves whose task it was to manage the universe for them—giving them food, clothing, and honor in temple ceremonies. In an unforeseen development, however, the human race grew so numerous and noisy that the gods could not sleep. Deeply angered, the gods decided to destroy the race by a universal flood. One man and his family, however, secretly warned of the flood by his patron god, built a boat and survived. Soon regretting their impetuous decision, the gods created a revised version of humankind. The new race was created mortal so they would never again grow numerous and bother the gods. The authors of Genesis adapted the creation-flood story in accord with their views of God and humanity. For example, they attributed the fault to human sin rather than to divine miscalculation (6:5–7) and had God reaffirm without change the original creation (9:1–7). In the biblical version God is just, powerful, and not needy.

How should modern readers interpret the creation-flood story in Gn 2–11? The stories are neither history nor myth. "Myth" is an unsuitable term, for it has several different meanings and connotes untruth in popular English. "History" is equally misleading, for it suggests that the events actually took place. The best term is creation-flood story. Ancient Near Eastern thinkers did not have our methods of exploring serious questions. Instead, they used narratives for issues that we would call philosophical and theological. They added and subtracted narrative details and varied the plot as they sought meaning in the ancient stories. Their stories reveal a privileged time, when divine decisions were made that determined the future of the human race. The origin of something was thought to explain its present meaning, e.g., how God acts with justice and generosity, why human beings are rebellious, the nature of sexual attraction and marriage, why there are many peoples and languages. Though the stories may initially strike us as primitive and naive, they are in fact told with skill, compression, and subtlety. They provide profound answers to perennial questions about God and human beings.

Genesis 11–50. One Jewish tradition suggests that God, having been rebuffed in the attempt to forge a relationship with the nations, decided to concentrate on one nation in the hope that it would eventually bring in all the nations. The migration of Abraham's family (11:26–31) is part of the general movement of the human race to take possession of their lands (see 10:32–11:9). Abraham, however, must come into possession of his land in a manner different from the nations, for he will not immediately possess it nor will he have descendants in the manner of the nations, for he is old and his wife is childless (12:1–9). Abraham and Sarah have to live with their God in trust and obedience until at last Isaac is born to them and they manage to buy a sliver of the land (the burial cave at Machpelah, chap. 23). Abraham's humanity and faith offer a wonderful example to the exilic generation.

The historicity of the ancestral stories has been much discussed. Scholars have traditionally dated them sometime in the first half of the second millennium, though a few regard them as late (sixth or fifth century B.C.) and purely fictional. There is unfortunately no direct extra-biblical evidence confirming (or disproving) the stories. The ancestral stories have affinities, however, to late second-millennium stories of childless ancestors, and their proper names fit linguistic patterns attested in the second millennium. Given the lack of decisive evidence, it is reasonable to accept the Bible's own chronology that the patriarchs were the ancestors of Israel and that they lived well before the exodus that is generally dated in the thirteenth century.

Gn 25:19–35:43 are about Jacob and his twelve sons. The stories are united by a geographical frame: Jacob lives in Canaan until his theft of the right of the firstborn from his brother Esau forces him to flee to Paddan-Aram (alternately Aram-Naharaim). There his uncle Laban tricks him as he earlier tricked his brother. But Jacob is blessed with wealth and sons. He returns to Canaan to receive the final blessing, land, and on the way is reconciled with his brother Esau. As the sons have reached the number of twelve, the patriarch can be given the name Israel (32:28; 35:10). The blessings given to Abraham are reaffirmed to Isaac and to Jacob.

The last cycle of ancestor stories is about Jacob's son Joseph (37:1–50:26, though in chaps. 48–49 the focus swings back to Jacob). The Joseph stories are sophisticated in theme, deftly plotted, and show keen interest in the psychology of the characters. Jacob's favoring of Joseph, the son of his beloved wife Rachel, provokes his brothers to kill him. Joseph escapes death through the intercession of Reuben, the eldest, and of Judah, but is sold into slavery in Egypt. In the immediately following chap. 38, Judah undergoes experiences similar to Joseph's. Joseph, endowed by God with wisdom, becomes second only to Pharaoh in Egypt. From that powerful position, he encounters his unsuspecting brothers who have come to Egypt because of the famine, and tests them to see if they have repented. Joseph learns that they have given up their hatred because of their love for Israel, their father. Judah, who seems to have inherited the mantle of the failed oldest brother Reuben, expresses the brothers' new and profound appreciation of their father and Joseph (chap. 44). At the end of Genesis, the entire family of Jacob/Israel is in Egypt, which prepares for the events in the Book of Exodus.

Genesis in Later Biblical Books. The historical and prophetic books constantly refer to the covenant with the ancestors Abraham, Isaac, and Jacob. Hos 10 sees the traits of Jacob in the behavior of the Israel of his own day. Is 51:2 cites Abraham and Sarah as a model for his dispirited community, for though only a couple, they became a great nation. Jn 1, "In the beginning was the word," alludes to Gn 1:1 (and Prv 8:22) to show that Jesus is creating a new world. St. Paul interprets Jesus as the New Adam in Rom 5:14 and 1 Cor 15:22, 24, whose obedience brings life just as the Old Adam's disobedience brought death. In Rom 4, Paul cites Abraham as someone who was righteous in God's eyes centuries before the Law was given at Sinai.

Outline of Genesis

PREAMBLE. THE CREATION OF THE WORLD

CHAPTER 1

The Story of Creation.* **¹**In the beginning, when God created the heavens and the earth*ᵃ*—**²**†and the earth was without form or shape, with darkness over the abyss and a mighty wind sweeping over the waters—*ᵇ*

³Then God said: Let there be light, and there was light.*ᶜ* **⁴**God saw that the light was good. God then separated the light from the darkness. **⁵**God called the light "day," and the darkness

he called "night." Evening came, and morning followed—the first day.‡

⁶Then God said: Let there be a dome in the middle of the waters, to separate one body of water from the other. **⁷**God made the dome,§ and it separated the water below the dome from the water above the dome. And so it happened.*ᵈ* **⁸**God called the dome "sky." Evening came, and morning followed—the second day.

⁹Then God said: Let the water under the sky be gathered into a single basin, so that the dry land may appear. And so it happened: the water under the sky was gathered into its basin, and the dry land appeared.*ᵉ* **¹⁰**God called the dry land "earth," and the basin of water he called "sea." God saw that it was good. **¹¹***ᶠ*Then God said: Let the earth bring forth vegetation: every kind of plant that bears seed and every kind of fruit tree on earth that bears fruit with its seed in it. And so it happened: **¹²**the earth brought forth vegetation: every kind of plant that bears seed and every kind of fruit tree that bears fruit with its seed in it. God saw that it was good. **¹³**Evening came, and morning followed—the third day.

¹⁴Then God said: Let there be lights in the dome of the sky, to separate day from night. Let them mark the seasons, the days and the years,*ᵍ* **¹⁵**and serve as lights in the dome of the sky, to illuminate the earth. And so it happened: **¹⁶**God made the two great lights, the greater one to govern the day, and the lesser one to govern the night, and the stars.*ʰ* **¹⁷**God set them in the dome of the sky, to illuminate the earth, **¹⁸**to govern the day and the night, and to separate the light from the darkness. God

---

* [1:1–2:3] This section, from the Priestly source, functions as an introduction, as ancient stories of the origin of the world (cosmogonies) often did. It introduces the primordial story (2:4–11:26), the stories of the ancestors (11:27–50:26), and indeed the whole Pentateuch. The chapter highlights the goodness of creation and the divine desire that human beings share in that goodness. God brings an orderly universe out of primordial chaos merely by uttering a word. In the literary structure of six days, the creation events in the first three days are related to those in the second three.

1. light (day)/darkness (night) = 4. sun/moon
2. arrangement of water = 5. fish + birds from waters
3. a) dry land = 6. a) animals
   b) vegetation   b) human beings: male/female

The seventh day, on which God rests, the climax of the account, falls outside the six-day structure.

Until modern times the first line was always translated, "In the beginning God created the heavens and the earth." Several comparable ancient cosmogonies, discovered in recent times, have a "when . . . then" construction, confirming the translation "when . . . then" here as well. "When" introduces the pre-creation state and "then" introduces the creative act affecting that state. The traditional translation, "In the beginning," does not reflect the Hebrew syntax of the clause.

† [1:2] This verse is parenthetical, describing in three phases the pre-creation state symbolized by the chaos out of which God brings order: "earth," hidden beneath the encompassing cosmic waters, could not be seen, and thus had no "form"; there was only darkness; turbulent wind swept over the waters. Commencing with the last-named elements (darkness and water), vv. 3–10 describe the rearrangement of this chaos: light is made (first day) and the water is divided into water above and water below the earth so that the earth appears and is no longer "without outline." **The abyss**: the primordial ocean according to the ancient Semitic cosmogony. After God's creative activity, part of this vast body forms the salt-water seas (vv. 9–10); part of it is the fresh water under the earth (Ps 33:7; Ez 31:4), which wells forth on the earth as springs and fountains (Gn 7:11; 8:2; Prv 3:20). Part of it, "the upper water" (Ps 148:4; Dn 3:60), is held up by the dome of the sky (vv. 6–7), from which rain descends on the earth (Gn 7:11; 2 Kgs 7:2, 19; Ps 104:13). **A mighty wind**: literally, "spirit or breath [*ruah*] of God"; cf. Gn 8:1.

‡ [1:5] In ancient Israel a day was considered to begin at sunset.

§ [1:7] **The dome**: the Hebrew word suggests a gigantic metal dome. It was inserted into the middle of the single body of water to form dry space within which the earth could emerge. The Latin Vulgate translation *firmamentum*, "means of support (for the upper waters); firmament," provided the traditional English rendering.

a. [1:1] Gn 2:1, 4; 2 Mc 7:28; Ps 8:4; 33:6; 89:12; 90:2; Wis 11:17; Sir 16:24; Jer 10:12; Acts 14:15; Col 1:16–17; Heb 1:2–3; 3:4; 11:3; Rev 4:11.
b. [1:2] Jer 4:23.
c. [1:3] 2 Cor 4:6.
d. [1:7] Prv 8:27–28; 2 Pt 3:5.
e. [1:9] Jb 38:8; Ps 33:7; Jer 5:22.
f. [1:11] Ps 104:14.
g. [1:14] Jb 26:10; Ps 19:2–3; Bar 3:33.
h. [1:16] Dt 4:19; Ps 136:7–9; Wis 13:2–4; Jer 31:35.

saw that it was good. [19]Evening came, and morning followed—the fourth day. [20i]Then God said: Let the water teem with an abundance of living creatures, and on the earth let birds fly beneath the dome of the sky. [21]God created the great sea monsters and all kinds of crawling living creatures with which the water teems, and all kinds of winged birds. God saw that it was good, [22]and God blessed them, saying: Be fertile, multiply, and fill the water of the seas; and let the birds multiply on the earth.[j] [23]Evening came, and morning followed—the fifth day.

[24k]Then God said: Let the earth bring forth every kind of living creature: tame animals, crawling things, and every kind of wild animal. And so it happened: [25]God made every kind of wild animal, every kind of tame animal, and every kind of thing that crawls on the ground. God saw that it was good. [26l]Then God said: Let us make* human beings in our image, after our likeness. Let them have dominion over the fish of the sea, the birds of the air, the tame animals, all the wild animals, and all the creatures that crawl on the earth.

[27]God created mankind in his
   image;
   in the image of God he created
      them;
   male and female[†] he created
      them.

[28]God blessed them and God said to them: Be fertile and multiply; fill the earth and subdue it.[‡] Have dominion over the fish of the sea, the birds of the air, and all the living things that crawl on the earth.[m] [29§n]God also said: See, I give you every seed-bearing plant on all the earth and every tree that has seed-bearing fruit on it to be your food; [30]and to all the wild animals, all the birds of the air, and all the living creatures that crawl on the earth, I give all the green plants for food. And so it happened. [31]God looked at everything he had made, and found it very good. Evening came, and morning followed—the sixth day.[o]

CHAPTER 2

[1]Thus the heavens and the earth and all their array were completed.[a] [2¶]On the seventh day God completed the work he had been doing; he rested on

---

‡ [1:28] **Fill the earth and subdue it:** the object of the verb "subdue" may be not the earth as such but earth as the territory each nation must take for itself (chaps. 10–11), just as Israel will later do (see Nm 32:22, 29; Jos 18:1). The two divine commands define the basic tasks of the human race—to continue in existence through generation and to take possession of one's God-given territory. The dual command would have had special meaning when Israel was in exile and deeply anxious about whether they would continue as a nation and return to their ancient territory. **Have dominion:** the whole human race is made in the "image" and "likeness" of God and has "dominion." Comparable literature of the time used these words of kings rather than of human beings in general; human beings were invariably thought of as slaves of the gods created to provide menial service for the divine world. The royal language here does not, however, give human beings unlimited power, for kings in the Bible had limited dominion and were subject to prophetic critique.

§ [1:29] According to the Priestly tradition, the human race was originally intended to live on plants and fruits as were the animals (see v. 30), an arrangement that God will later change (9:3) in view of the human inclination to violence.

¶ [2:2] The mention of the seventh day, repeated in v. 3, is outside the series of six days and is thus the climax of the account. The focus of the account is God. The text does not actually institute the practice of keeping the Sabbath, for it would have been anachronistic to establish at this point a custom that was distinctively Israelite (Ex 31:13, 16, 17), but it lays the foundation for the later practice. Similarly, ancient creation accounts often ended with the construction of a temple where the newly created human race provided service to the gods who created them, but no temple is mentioned in this account. As was the case with the Sabbath, it would have been anachronistic to institute the temple at this point, for Israel did not yet exist. In Ex 25–31 and 35–40, Israel builds the tabernacle, which is the precursor of the Temple of Solomon.

---

* [1:26] **Let us make:** in the ancient Near East, and sometimes in the Bible, God was imagined as presiding over an assembly of heavenly beings who deliberated and decided about matters on earth (1 Kgs 22:19–22; Is 6:8; Ps 29:1–2; 82; 89:6–7; Jb 1:6; 2:1; 38:7). This scene accounts for the plural form here and in Gn 11:7 ("Let us go down . . ."). Israel's God was always considered "Most High" over the heavenly beings. **Human beings:** Hebrew *'ādām* is here the generic term for humankind; in the first five chapters of Genesis it is the proper name Adam only at 4:25 and 5:1–5. **In our image, after our likeness:** "image" and "likeness" (virtually synonyms) express the worth of human beings who have value in themselves (human blood may not be shed in 9:6 because of this image of God) and in their task, dominion (1:28), which promotes the rule of God over the universe.

† [1:27] **Male and female:** as God provided the plants with seeds (vv. 11, 12) and commanded the animals to be fertile and multiply (v. 22), so God gives sexuality to human beings as their means to continue in existence.

---

i. [1:20] Jb 12:7–10.
j. [1:22] Gn 8:17.
k. [1:24] Sir 16:27–28.
l. [1:26–27] Gn 5:1, 3; 9:6; Ps 8:5–6; Wis 2:23; 10:2; Sir 17:1, 3–4; Mt 19:4; Mk 10:6; Jas 3:7; Eph 4:24; Col 3:10.

m. [1:28] Gn 8:17; 9:1; Ps 8:6–9; 115:16; Wis 9:2.
n. [1:29–30] Gn 9:3; Ps 104:14–15.
o. [1:31] 1 Tm 4:4.

a. [2:1] Is 45:12; Jn 1:3.

GN

the seventh day from all the work he had undertaken.[b] [3]God blessed the seventh day and made it holy, because on it he rested from all the work he had done in creation.[c]

I. THE STORY OF THE NATIONS

The Garden of Eden. [4]This is the story of the heavens and the earth at their creation. When the LORD God made the earth and the heavens— [5]there was no field shrub on earth and no grass of the field had sprouted, for the LORD God had sent no rain upon the earth and there was no man[†] to till the ground, [6]but a stream[‡] was welling up out of the earth and watering all the surface of the ground—[7]then the LORD God formed the man[§] out of the dust of the ground and blew into his

nostrils the breath of life, and the man became a living being.[d]

[8]The LORD God planted a garden in Eden, in the east,[¶] and placed there the man whom he had formed.[e] [9]"Out of the ground the LORD God made grow every tree that was delightful to look at and good for food, with the tree of life in the middle of the garden and the tree of the knowledge of good and evil.[f]

[10]A river rises in Eden[††] to water the garden; beyond there it divides and becomes four branches. [11]The name

---

* [2:4] **This is the story**: the distinctive Priestly formula introduces older traditions, belonging to the tradition called Yahwist, and gives them a new setting. In the first part of Genesis, the formula "this is the story" (or a similar phrase) occurs five times (2:4; 5:1; 6:9; 10:1; 11:10), which corresponds to the five occurrences of the formula in the second part of Genesis (11:27; 25:12, 19; 36:1[9]; 37:2). Some interpret the formula here as retrospective ("Such is the story"), referring back to chap. 1, but all its other occurrences introduce rather than summarize. It is introductory here; the Priestly source would hardly use the formula to introduce its own material in chap. 1.

  The cosmogony that begins in v. 4 is concerned with the nature of human beings, narrating the story of the essential institutions and limits of the human race through their first ancestors. This cosmogony, like 1:1–3 (see note there), uses the "when . . . then" construction common in ancient cosmogonies. The account is generally attributed to the Yahwist, who prefers the divine name "Yhwh" (here rendered LORD) for God. God in this story is called "the LORD God" (except in 3:1–5); "LORD" is to be expected in a Yahwist account but the additional word "God" is puzzling.

† [2:5] **Man**: the Hebrew word 'adam is a generic term meaning "human being." In chaps. 2–3, however, the archetypal human being is understood to be male (Adam), so the word 'adam is translated "man" here.

‡ [2:6] **Stream**: the water wells up from the vast flood below the earth. The account seems to presuppose that only the garden of God was irrigated at this point. From this one source of all the fertilizing water on the earth, water will be channeled through the garden of God over the entire earth. It is the source of the four rivers mentioned in vv. 10–14. Later, with rain and cultivation, the fertility of the garden of God will appear in all parts of the world.

§ [2:7] God is portrayed as a potter molding the human body out of earth. There is a play on words in Hebrew between 'adam ("human being," "man") and 'adama ("ground"). It is not enough to make the body from earth; God must also breathe into the man's nostrils. A similar picture of divine breath imparted to human beings in order for them to live is found in Ez 37:5, 9–10; Jn 20:22. The Israelites did not think in the (Greek) categories of body and soul.

¶ [2:8] **Eden, in the east**: the place names in vv. 8–14 are mostly derived from Mesopotamian geography (see note on vv. 10–14). Eden may be the name of a region in southern Mesopotamia (modern Iraq), the term derived from the Sumerian word eden, "fertile plain." A similar-sounding Hebrew word means "delight," which may lie behind the Greek translation, "The Lord God planted a paradise [= pleasure park] in Eden." It should be noted, however, that the garden was not intended as a paradise for the human race, but as a pleasure park for God; the man tended it for God. The story is not about "paradise lost."

  The garden in the precincts of Solomon's Temple in Jerusalem seems to symbolize the garden of God (like gardens in other temples); it is apparently alluded to in Ps 1:3; 80:10; 92:14; Ez 47:7–12; Rev 22:1–2.

** [2:9] The second tree, the tree of life, is mentioned here and at the end of the story (3:22, 24). It is identified with Wisdom in Prv 3:18; 11:30; 13:12; 15:4, where the pursuit of wisdom gives back to human beings the life that is made inaccessible to them in Gn 3:24. In the new creation described in the Book of Revelation, the tree of life is once again made available to human beings (Rev 2:7; 22:2, 14, 19). **Knowledge of good and evil**: the meaning is disputed. According to some, it signifies moral autonomy, control over morality (symbolized by "good and evil"), which would be inappropriate for mere human beings; the phrase would thus mean refusal to accept the human condition and finite freedom that God gives them. According to others, it is more broadly the knowledge of what is helpful and harmful to humankind, suggesting that the attainment of adult experience and responsibility inevitably means the loss of a life of simple subordination to God.

†† [2:10–14] **A river rises in Eden**: the stream of water mentioned in v. 6, the source of all water upon earth, comes to the surface in the garden of God and from there flows out over the entire earth. In comparable religious literature, the dwelling of god is the source of fertilizing waters. The four rivers represent universality, as in the phrase "the four quarters of the earth." In Ez 47:1–12; Zec 14:8; Rev 22:1–2, the waters that irrigate the earth arise in the temple or city of God. The place names in vv. 11–14 are mainly from southern Mesopotamia (modern Iraq), where Mesopotamian literature placed the original garden of God. The Tigris and the Euphrates, the two great rivers in that part of the world, both emptied into the Persian Gulf. Gihon is the modest stream issuing from Jerusalem (2 Sm 5:8; 1 Kgs 1:9–10; 2 Chr 32:4), but is here regarded as one of the four great world rivers and linked to Mesopotamia, for Cush here seems to be the territory of the Kassites (a people of Mesopotamia) as in Gn 10:8. The word Pishon is otherwise unknown but is probably formed in imitation of Gihon. Havilah seems, according to Gn 10:7 and 1 Chr 1:9, to be in Cush in southern Mesopotamia though other locations have been suggested.

---

b. [2:2] Ex 20:9–11; 31:17; Heb 4:4, 10.
c. [2:3] Ex 20:11; Dt 5:14; Neh 9:14.

d. [2:7] Gn 3:19; 18:27; Tb 8:6; Jb 34:15; Ps 103:14; 104:29; Eccl 3:20; 12:7; Wis 7:1; Sir 33:10; 1 Cor 15:45.
e. [2:8] Is 51:3; Ez 31:9.
f. [2:9] Gn 3:22; Prv 3:18; Rev 2:7; 22:2, 14.

of the first is the Pishon; it is the one that winds through the whole land of Havilah, where there is gold. ¹²The gold of that land is good; bdellium and lapis lazuli are also there. ¹³The name of the second river is the Gihon; it is the one that winds all through the land of Cush.ᵍ ¹⁴The name of the third river is the Tigris; it is the one that flows east of Asshur. The fourth river is the Euphrates.

¹⁵The LORD God then took the man and settled him in the garden of Eden, to cultivate and care for it.ʰ ¹⁶The LORD God gave the man this order: You are free to eat from any of the trees of the gardenⁱ ¹⁷except the tree of knowledge of good and evil. From that tree you shall not eat; when you eat from it you shall die.*ʲ

¹⁸The LORD God said: It is not good for the man to be alone. I will make a helper suited to him.†ᵏ ¹⁹So the LORD God formed out of the ground all the wild animals and all the birds of the air, and he brought them to the man to see what he would call them; whatever the man called each living creature was then its name. ²⁰The man gave names to all the tame animals, all the birds of the air, and all the wild animals; but none proved to be a helper suited to the man.

²¹So the LORD God cast a deep sleep on the man, and while he was asleep, he took out one of his ribs and closed up its place with flesh.ˡ ²²The LORD God then built the rib that he had taken from the man into a woman. When he brought her to the man, ²³the man said:

"This one, at last, is bone of my bones
    and flesh of my flesh;
This one shall be called 'woman,'
    for out of man this one has been taken."‡

²⁴ᵐ That is why a man leaves his father and mother and clings to his wife, and the two of them become one body.§

²⁵The man and his wife were both naked, yet they felt no shame.¶

CHAPTER 3

Expulsion from Eden. ¹Now the snake was the most cunning** of all the wild animals that the LORD God had made. He asked the woman, "Did God really say, 'You shall not eat from any of the trees in the garden'?" ²The woman answered the snake: "We may eat of the fruit of the trees in the garden; ³ᵃit is only about the fruit of the tree in the middle of the garden that God said, 'You shall not eat it or even touch it, or else you will die.'" ⁴But the snake said to the woman: "You certainly will not die!ᵇ ⁵God knows well that when you eat of it your eyes will be opened and you will be like gods, who know†† good and evil." ⁶The woman saw that the tree was good for food and pleasing to the eyes, and the tree was desirable for gaining wisdom. So she took some of its fruit and ate it; and she also gave some to her husband, who was with her, and he ate it.ᶜ ⁷Then the eyes of

---

‡ [2:23] The man recognizes an affinity with the woman God has brought him. Unlike the animals who were made from the ground, she is made from his very self. There is a play on the similar-sounding Hebrew words *'ishsha* ("woman," "wife") and *'ish* ("man," "husband").

§ [2:24] One body: lit., "one flesh." The covenant of marriage establishes kinship bonds of the first rank between the partners.

¶ [2:25] They felt no shame: marks a new stage in the drama, for the reader knows that only young children know no shame. This draws the reader into the next episode, where the couple's disobedience results in their loss of innocence.

** [3:1] Cunning: there is a play on the words for "naked" (2:25) and "cunning/wise" (Heb. *'arum*). The couple seek to be "wise" but end up knowing that they are "naked."

†† [3:5] Like gods, who know: or "like God who knows."

---

* [2:17] You shall die: since they do not die as soon as they eat from the forbidden tree, the meaning seems to be that human beings have become mortal, destined to die by virtue of being human.

† [2:18] Helper suited to him: lit., "a helper in accord with him." "Helper" need not imply subordination, for God is called a helper (Dt 33:7; Ps 46:2). The language suggests a profound affinity between the man and the woman and a relationship that is supportive and nurturing.

g. [2:13] Sir 24:25.
h. [2:15] Sir 7:15.
i. [2:16] Ps 104:14–15.
j. [2:17] Gn 3:2–3; Rom 6:23.
k. [2:18] Tb 8:6; Sir 36:24; 1 Cor 11:9; 1 Tm 2:13.
l. [2:21] Sir 17:1; 1 Cor 11:8–9; 1 Tm 2:13.

m. [2:24] Mt 19:5; Mk 10:7; 1 Cor 7:10–11; Eph 5:31.

a. [3:3] Gn 2:17; Rom 6:23.
b. [3:4–5] Wis 2:24; Sir 25:14; Is 14:14; Jn 8:44; 2 Cor 11:3.
c. [3:6] Gn 3:22; 1 Tm 2:14.

both of them were opened, and they knew that they were naked; so they sewed fig leaves together and made loincloths for themselves.

⁸When they heard the sound of the LORD God walking about in the garden at the breezy time of the day,* the man and his wife hid themselves from the LORD God among the trees of the garden.ᵈ ⁹The LORD God then called to the man and asked him: Where are you? ¹⁰He answered, "I heard you in the garden; but I was afraid, because I was naked, so I hid." ¹¹Then God asked: Who told you that you were naked? Have you eaten from the tree of which I had forbidden you to eat? ¹²The man replied, "The woman whom you put here with me—she gave me fruit from the tree, so I ate it." ¹³The LORD God then asked the woman: What is this you have done? The woman answered, "The snake tricked me, so I ate it."ᵉ

¹⁴Then the LORD God said to the snake:

Because you have done this,
    cursed are you
        among all the animals, tame or
        wild;
On your belly you shall crawl,
    and dust you shall eat
        all the days of your life.†ᶠ
¹⁵I will put enmity between you
    and the woman,
        and between your offspring and
        hers;
They will strike at your head,

while you strike at their heel.‡ᵍ

¹⁶To the woman he said:

I will intensify your toil in
    childbearing;
    in pain§ you shall bring forth
    children.
Yet your urge shall be for your
    husband,
    and he shall rule over you.

¹⁷To the man he said: Because you listened to your wife and ate from the tree about which I commanded you, You shall not eat from it,

Cursed is the ground¶ because of
    you!
    In toil you shall eat its yield
    all the days of your life.ʰ
¹⁸Thorns and thistles it shall bear
    for you,
    and you shall eat the grass of the
    field.
¹⁹By the sweat of your brow
    you shall eat bread,
Until you return to the ground,
    from which you were taken;
For you are dust,
    and to dust you shall return.ⁱ

---

‡ [3:15] **They will strike . . . at their heel**: the antecedent for "they" and "their" is the collective noun "offspring," i.e., all the descendants of the woman. Christian tradition has seen in this passage, however, more than unending hostility between snakes and human beings. The snake was identified with the devil (Wis 2:24; Jn 8:44; Rev 12:9; 20:2), whose eventual defeat seemed implied in the verse. Because "the Son of God was revealed to destroy the works of the devil" (1 Jn 3:8), the passage was understood as the first promise of a redeemer for fallen humankind, the protoevangelium. Irenaeus of Lyons (ca. A.D. 130–200), in his *Against Heresies* 5.21.1, followed by several other Fathers of the Church, interpreted the verse as referring to Christ, and cited Gal 3:19 and 4:4 to support the reference. Another interpretive translation is *ipsa*, "she," and is reflected in Jerome's Vulgate. "She" was thought to refer to Mary, the mother of the messiah. In Christian art Mary is sometimes depicted with her foot on the head of the serpent.

§ [3:16] **Toil . . . pain**: the punishment affects the woman directly by increasing the toil and pain of having children. **He shall rule over you**: the punishment also affects the woman's relationship with her husband. A tension is set up in which her urge (either sexual urge or, more generally, dependence for sustenance) is for her husband but he rules over her. But see Sg 7:11.

¶ [3:17–19] **Cursed is the ground**: the punishment affects the man's relationship to the ground (*'adam* and *'adamah*). **You are dust**: the punishment also affects the man directly insofar as he is now mortal.

---

* [3:8] **The breezy time of the day**: lit., "the wind of the day." Probably shortly before sunset.
† [3:14] Each of the three punishments (the snake, the woman, the man) has a double aspect, one affecting the individual and the other affecting a basic relationship. The snake previously stood upright, enjoyed a reputation for being shrewder than other creatures, and could converse with human beings as in vv. 1–5. It must now move on its belly, is more cursed than any creature, and inspires revulsion in human beings (v. 15).

d. [3:8] Jer 23:24.
e. [3:13] 2 Cor 11:3.
f. [3:14] Is 65:25; Mi 7:17; Rev 12:9.

g. [3:15] Rom 16:20; 1 Jn 3:8; Rev 12:17.
h. [3:17] Gn 5:29; Rom 5:12; 8:20; Heb 6:8.
i. [3:19] Gn 2:7; Jb 10:9; 34:15; Ps 90:3; 103:14; Eccl 3:20; 12:7; Wis 15:8; Sir 10:9; 17:2; Rom 5:12; 1 Cor 15:21; Heb 9:27.

20The man gave his wife the name "Eve," because she was the mother of all the living.*

21The LORD God made for the man and his wife garments of skin, with which he clothed them. **22**Then the LORD God said: See! The man has become like one of us, knowing good and evil! Now, what if he also reaches out his hand to take fruit from the tree of life, and eats of it and lives forever?*j* **23**The LORD God therefore banished him from the garden of Eden, to till the ground from which he had been taken. **24**He expelled the man, stationing the cherubim and the fiery revolving sword east of the garden of Eden, to guard the way to the tree of life.

CHAPTER 4

Cain and Abel. **1**The man had intercourse with his wife Eve, and she conceived and gave birth to Cain, saying, "I have produced a male child with the help of the LORD."† **2**Next she gave birth to his brother Abel. Abel became a herder of flocks, and Cain a tiller of the ground.‡ **3**In the course of time Cain brought an offering to the LORD from the fruit of the ground, **4**while Abel, for his part, brought the fatty portion§ of the firstlings of his flock.*a* The LORD looked with favor on Abel

and his offering, **5**but on Cain and his offering he did not look with favor. So Cain was very angry and dejected. **6**Then the LORD said to Cain: Why are you angry? Why are you dejected? **7**If you act rightly, you will be accepted;¶ but if not, sin lies in wait at the door: its urge is for you, yet you can rule over it.*b*

8Cain said to his brother Abel, "Let us go out in the field."** When they were in the field, Cain attacked his brother Abel and killed him.*c* **9**Then the LORD asked Cain, Where is your brother Abel? He answered, "I do not know. Am I my brother's keeper?" **10**God then said: What have you done? Your brother's blood cries out to me from the ground! **11**Now you are banned from the ground†† that opened its mouth to receive your brother's blood from your hand.*d* **12**If you till the ground, it shall no longer give you its produce. You shall become a constant wanderer on the earth. **13**Cain said to the LORD: "My punishment is too great to bear. **14**Look, you have now banished me from the ground. I must avoid you and be a constant wanderer on the earth. Anyone may kill me at sight." **15**Not so! the LORD said to him. If anyone kills Cain, Cain shall be avenged seven times. So the LORD put a mark‡‡ on Cain, so that

---

* [3:20] The man gives his wife a more specific name than "woman" (2:23). The Hebrew name *hawwa* ("Eve") is related to the Hebrew word *hay* ("living"); "mother of all the living" points forward to the next episode involving her sons Cain and Abel.

† [4:1] The Hebrew name *qayin* ("Cain") and the term *qaniti* ("I have produced") present a wordplay that refers to metalworking; such wordplays are frequent in Genesis.

‡ [4:2] Some suggest the story reflects traditional strife between the farmer (Cain) and the nomad (Abel), with preference for the latter reflecting the alleged nomadic ideal of the Bible. But there is no disparagement of farming here, for Adam was created to till the soil. The story is about two brothers (the word "brother" occurs seven times) and God's unexplained preference for one, which provokes the first murder. The motif of the preferred younger brother will occur time and again in the Bible, e.g., Isaac, Jacob, Joseph, and David (1 Sm 16:1–13).

§ [4:4] **Fatty portion**: it was standard practice to offer the fat portions of animals. Others render, less satisfactorily, "the choicest of the firstlings." The point is not that Abel gave a more valuable gift than Cain, but that God, for reasons not given in the text, accepts the offering of Abel and rejects that of Cain.

¶ [4:7] **You will be accepted**: the text is extraordinarily condensed and unclear. "You will be accepted" is a paraphrase of one Hebrew word, "lifting." God gives a friendly warning to Cain that his right conduct will bring "lifting," which could refer to acceptance (*lifting*) of his future offerings or of himself (as in the Hebrew idiom "*lifting* of the face") or *lifting* up of his head in honor (cf. note on 40:13), whereas wicked conduct will make him vulnerable to sin, which is personified as a force ready to attack. In any case, Cain has the ability to do the right thing. **Lies in wait**: sin is personified as a power that "lies in wait" (Heb. *robes*) at a place. In Mesopotamian religion, a related word (*rabisu*) refers to a malevolent god who attacks human beings in particular places like roofs or canals.

** [4:8] **Let us go out in the field**: to avoid detection. The verse presumes a sizeable population which Genesis does not otherwise explain.

†† [4:11] **Banned from the ground**: lit., "cursed." The verse refers back to 3:17 where the ground was cursed so that it yields its produce only with great effort. Cain has polluted the soil with his brother's blood and it will no longer yield any of its produce to him.

‡‡ [4:15] **A mark**: probably a tattoo to mark Cain as protected by God. The use of tattooing for tribal marks has always been common among the Bedouin of the Near Eastern deserts.

---

j. [3:22] Gn 2:9; Rev 22:2, 14.

a. [4:4] Ex 34:19; Heb 11:4.

b. [4:7] Sir 7:1; Jude 11.

c. [4:8] Wis 10:3; Mt 23:35; Lk 11:51; 1 Jn 3:12; Jude 11.

d. [4:11] Dt 27:24.

GN

no one would kill him at sight. [16]Cain then left the Lord's presence and settled in the land of Nod,* east of Eden.

Descendants of Cain and Seth.

[17†]Cain had intercourse with his wife, and she conceived and bore Enoch. Cain also became the founder of a city, which he named after his son Enoch. [18]To Enoch was born Irad, and Irad became the father of Mehujael; Mehujael became the father of Methusael, and Methusael became the father of Lamech. [19]Lamech took two wives; the name of the first was Adah, and the name of the second Zillah. [20]Adah gave birth to Jabal, who became the ancestor of those who dwell in tents and keep livestock. [21]His brother's name was Jubal, who became the ancestor of all who play the lyre and the reed pipe. [22]Zillah, on her part, gave birth to Tubalcain, the ancestor of all who forge instruments of bronze and iron. The sister of Tubalcain was Naamah. [23‡]Lamech said to his wives:

> "Adah and Zillah, hear my voice;
>   wives of Lamech, listen to my
>   utterance:
> I have killed a man for wounding
>   me,
>   a young man for bruising me.
> [24]If Cain is avenged seven times,
>   then Lamech seventy-seven
>   times."

[25§]Adam again had intercourse with his wife, and she gave birth to a son whom she called Seth. "God has granted me another offspring in place of Abel," she said, "because Cain killed him." [26]To Seth, in turn, a son was born, and he named him Enosh.

At that time people began to invoke the Lord by name.[e]

CHAPTER 5

Generations: Adam to Noah.¶

[1a]This is the record of the descendants of Adam. When God created human beings, he made them in the likeness of God; [2]he created them male and female. When they were created, he blessed them and named them humankind.

[3b]Adam was one hundred and thirty years old when he begot a son

---

§ [4:25–26] The third and climactic birth story in the chapter, showing that this birth, unlike the other two, will have good results. The name Seth (from the Hebrew verb *shat*, "to place, replace") shows that God has replaced Abel with a worthy successor. From this favored line Enosh ("human being/humankind"), a synonym of Adam, authentic religion began with the worship of Yhwh; this divine name is rendered as "the LORD" in this translation. The Yahwist source employs the name Yhwh long before the time of Moses. Another ancient source, the Elohist (from its use of the term *Elohim*, "God," instead of *Yhwh*, "LORD," for the pre-Mosaic period), makes Moses the first to use Yhwh as the proper name of Israel's God, previously known by other names as well; cf. Ex 3:13–15.

¶ [5:1–32] The second of the five Priestly formulas in Part I ("This is the record of the descendants . . ."; see 2:4a; 6:9; 10:1; 11:10) introduces the second of the three linear genealogies in Gn 1–11 (4:17–24 and 11:10–26). In each, a list of individuals (six in 4:17–24, ten in 5:1–32, or nine in 11:10–26) ends in three people who initiate action. Linear genealogies (father to son) in ancient societies had a communicative function, grounding the authority or claim of the last-named individual in the first-named. Here, the genealogy has a literary function as well, advancing the story by showing the expansion of the human race after Adam, as well as the transmission to his descendant Noah of the divine image given to Adam. Correcting the impression one might get from the genealogy in 4:17–24, this genealogy traces the line through Seth rather than through Cain. Most of the names in the series are the same as the names in Cain's line in 4:17–19 (Enosh, Enoch, Lamech) or spelled with variant spellings (Mahalalel, Jared, Methuselah). The genealogy itself and its placement before the flood shows the influence of ancient Mesopotamian literature, which contains lists of cities and kings before and after the flood. Before the flood, the ages of the kings ranged from 18,600 to 36,000 years, but after it were reduced to between 140 and 1,200 years. The biblical numbers are much smaller. There are some differences in the numbers in the Hebrew and Greek manuscripts.

---

* [4:16] **The land of Nod**: a symbolic name (derived from the verb *nûd*, to wander) rather than a definite geographic region.

† [4:17–24] Cain is the first in a seven-member linear genealogy ending in three individuals who initiate action (Jabal, Jubal, and Tubalcain). Other Genesis genealogies also end in three individuals initiating action (5:32 and 11:26). The purpose of this genealogy is to explain the origin of culture and crafts among human beings. The names in this genealogy are the same (some with different spellings) as those in the ten-member genealogy (ending with Noah), which has a slightly different function. See note on 5:1–32.

‡ [4:23–24] Lamech's boast shows that the violence of Cain continues with his son and has actually increased. The question is posed to the reader: how will God's creation be renewed?

---

e. [4:26] 1 Chr 1:1; Lk 3:38.

a. [5:1] Gn 1:27; Wis 2:23; Sir 17:1; Jas 3:9.
b. [5:3–32] 1 Chr 1:1–4; Lk 3:36–38.

in his likeness, after his image; and he named him Seth.*c* **4**Adam lived eight hundred years after he begot Seth, and he had other sons and daughters. **5**The whole lifetime of Adam was nine hundred and thirty years; then he died.

6When Seth was one hundred and five years old, he begot Enosh. **7**Seth lived eight hundred and seven years after he begot Enosh, and he had other sons and daughters. **8**The whole lifetime of Seth was nine hundred and twelve years; then he died.

9When Enosh was ninety years old, he begot Kenan. **10**Enosh lived eight hundred and fifteen years after he begot Kenan, and he had other sons and daughters. **11**The whole lifetime of Enosh was nine hundred and five years; then he died.

12When Kenan was seventy years old, he begot Mahalalel. **13**Kenan lived eight hundred and forty years after he begot Mahalalel, and he had other sons and daughters. **14**The whole lifetime of Kenan was nine hundred and ten years; then he died.

15When Mahalalel was sixty-five years old, he begot Jared. **16**Mahalalel lived eight hundred and thirty years after he begot Jared, and he had other sons and daughters. **17**The whole lifetime of Mahalalel was eight hundred and ninety-five years; then he died.

18When Jared was one hundred and sixty-two years old, he begot Enoch. **19**Jared lived eight hundred years after he begot Enoch, and he had other sons and daughters. **20**The whole lifetime of Jared was nine hundred and sixty-two years; then he died.

21When Enoch was sixty-five years old, he begot Methuselah. **22**Enoch walked with God after he begot Methuselah for three hundred years, and he had other sons and daughters. **23**The whole lifetime of Enoch

was three hundred and sixty-five years. **24**Enoch walked with God,* and he was no longer here, for God took him.*d*

25When Methuselah was one hundred and eighty-seven years old, he begot Lamech. **26**Methuselah lived seven hundred and eighty-two years after he begot Lamech, and he had other sons and daughters. **27**The whole lifetime of Methuselah was nine hundred and sixty-nine years; then he died.

28When Lamech was one hundred and eighty-two years old, he begot a son **29**e*and named him Noah, saying, "This one shall bring us relief from our work and the toil of our hands, out of the very ground that the LORD has put under a curse."† **30**Lamech lived five hundred and ninety-five years after he begot Noah, and he had other sons and daughters. **31**The whole lifetime of Lamech was seven hundred and seventy-seven years; then he died.

32When Noah was five hundred years old, he begot Shem, Ham, and Japheth.‡f

---

* [5:24] Enoch is in the important seventh position in the ten-member genealogy. In place of the usual formula "then he died," the change to "Enoch walked with God" implies that he did not die, but like Elijah (2 Kgs 2:11–12) was taken alive to God's abode. This mysterious narrative spurred much speculation and writing (beginning as early as the third century B.C.) about Enoch the sage who knew the secrets of heaven and who could communicate them to human beings (see Sir 44:16; 49:14; Heb 11:5; Jude 14–15 and the apocryphal work 1 Enoch).
† [5:29] The sound of the Hebrew word *noah*, "Noah," is echoed in the word *yenahamenu*, "he will bring us relief"; the latter refers both to the curse put on the soil because of human disobedience (3:17–19) and to Noah's success in agriculture, especially in raising grapes for wine (9:20–21).
‡ [5:32] **Shem, Ham, and Japheth:** like the genealogies in 4:17–24 and 11:10–26, the genealogy ends in three individuals who engage in important activity. Their descendants will be detailed in chap. 10, where it will be seen that the lineage is political-geographical as well as "ethnic."

d. [5:24] Wis 4:10–11; Sir 44:16; 49:14; Heb 11:5.
e. [5:29] Gn 3:17–19.
f. [5:32] Gn 6:10; 10:1.

c. [5:3] Gn 4:25.

CHAPTER 6

Origin of the Nephilim.[*] ¹When human beings began to grow numerous on the earth and daughters were born to them, ²the sons of God[†] saw how beautiful the daughters of human beings were, and so they took for their wives whomever they pleased.[a] ³Then the LORD said: My spirit shall not remain in human beings forever, because they are only flesh. Their days shall comprise one hundred and twenty years.

⁴The Nephilim appeared on earth in those days, as well as later,[‡] after the sons of God had intercourse with the daughters of human beings, who bore them sons. They were the heroes of old, the men of renown.[b]

Warning of the Flood. ⁵[§]When the LORD saw how great the wickedness of human beings was on earth, and how every desire that their heart conceived was always nothing but evil,[c] ⁶the LORD regretted making human beings on the earth, and his heart was grieved.[¶]

⁷So the LORD said: I will wipe out from the earth the human beings I have created, and not only the human beings, but also the animals and the crawling things and the birds of the air, for I regret that I made them.[**] ⁸But Noah found favor with the LORD.

⁹These are the descendants of Noah. Noah was a righteous man and blameless in his generation;[d] Noah walked with God. ¹⁰Noah begot three sons: Shem, Ham, and Japheth.

¹¹But the earth was corrupt[††] in the view of God and full of lawlessness.[e] ¹²When God saw how corrupt the earth had become, since all mortals had corrupted their ways on earth,[f] ¹³God said to Noah: I see that the end of all mortals has come, for the earth is full of lawlessness because of them. So I am going to destroy them with the earth.[g]

Preparation for the Flood. ¹⁴Make yourself an ark of gopherwood,[‡‡] equip the ark with various compartments, and cover it inside and out with pitch. ¹⁵This is how you shall build it: the length of the ark will be three hundred

---

* [6:1–4] These enigmatic verses are a transition between the expansion of the human race illustrated in the genealogy of chap. 5 and the flood depicted in chaps. 6–9. The text, apparently alluding to an old legend, shares a common ancient view that the heavenly world was populated by a multitude of beings, some of whom were wicked and rebellious. It is incorporated here, not only in order to account for the prehistoric giants, whom the Israelites called the Nephilim, but also to introduce the story of the flood with a moral orientation—the constantly increasing wickedness of humanity. This increasing wickedness leads God to reduce the human life span imposed on the first couple. As the ages in the preceding genealogy show, life spans had been exceptionally long in the early period, but God further reduces them to something near the ordinary life span.

† [6:2] **The sons of God**: other heavenly beings. See note on 1:26.

‡ [6:4] **As well as later**: the belief was common that human beings of gigantic stature once lived on earth. In some cultures, such heroes could make positive contributions, but the Bible generally regards them in a negative light (cf. Nm 13:33; Ez 32:27). The point here is that even these heroes, filled with vitality from their semi-divine origin, come under God's decree in v. 3.

§ [6:5–8:22] The story of the great flood is commonly regarded as a composite narrative based on separate sources woven together. To the Yahwist source, with some later editorial additions, are usually assigned 6:5–8; 7:1–5, 7–10, 12, 16b, 17b, 22–23; 8:2b–3a, 6–12, 13b, 20–22. The other sections are usually attributed to the Priestly writer. There are differences between the two sources: the Priestly source has two pairs of every animal, whereas the Yahwist source has seven pairs of clean animals and two pairs of unclean; the floodwater in the Priestly source is the waters under and over the earth that burst forth, whereas in the Yahwist source the floodwater is the rain lasting forty days and nights. In spite of many obvious discrepancies in these two sources, one should read the story as a coherent narrative. The biblical story ultimately draws upon an ancient Mesopotamian tradition of a great flood, preserved in the Sumerian flood story, the eleventh tablet of the Gilgamesh Epic, and (embedded in a longer creation story) the Atrahasis Epic.

a. [6:2] Mt 24:38; Lk 17:26–27.
b. [6:4] Wis 14:6; Bar 3:26.

¶ [6:6] **His heart was grieved**: the expression can be misleading in English, for "heart" in Hebrew is the seat of memory and judgment rather than emotion. The phrase is actually parallel to the first half of the sentence ("the LORD regretted . . .").

** [6:7] Human beings are an essential part of their environment, which includes all living things. In the new beginning after the flood, God makes a covenant with human beings and every living creature (9:9–10). The same close link between human beings and nature is found elsewhere in the Bible; e.g., in Is 35, God's healing transforms human beings along with their physical environment, and in Rom 8:19–23, all creation, not merely human beings, groans in labor pains awaiting the salvation of God.

†† [6:11] **Corrupt**: God does not punish arbitrarily but simply brings to its completion the corruption initiated by human beings.

‡‡ [6:14] **Gopherwood**: an unidentified wood mentioned only in connection with the ark. It may be the wood of the cypress, which in Hebrew sounds like "gopher" and was widely used in antiquity for shipbuilding.

c. [6:5] Ps 14:2–3.
d. [6:9] Wis 10:4; Sir 44:17.
e. [6:11] Jb 22:15–17.
f. [6:12] Ps 14:2.
g. [6:13] Sir 40:9–10; 44:17; Mt 24:37–39.

cubits, its width fifty cubits, and its height thirty cubits.* [16]Make an opening for daylight[†] and finish the ark a cubit above it. Put the ark's entrance on its side; you will make it with bottom, second and third decks. [17]I, on my part, am about to bring the flood waters on the earth, to destroy all creatures under the sky in which there is the breath of life; everything on earth shall perish.[h] [18]I will establish my covenant with you. You shall go into the ark, you and your sons, your wife and your sons' wives with you.[i] [19]Of all living creatures you shall bring two of every kind into the ark, one male and one female[‡], to keep them alive along with you. [20]Of every kind of bird, of every kind of animal, and of every kind of thing that crawls on the ground, two of each will come to you, that you may keep them alive. [21]Moreover, you are to provide yourself with all the food that is to be eaten, and store it away, that it may serve as provisions for you and for them. [22]Noah complied; he did just as God had commanded him.[§]

CHAPTER 7

[1]Then the LORD said to Noah: Go into the ark, you and all your household, for you alone in this generation have I found to be righteous before me.[a] [2]Of every clean animal, take with you seven pairs, a male and its mate; and of the unclean animals, one pair, a male and its mate; [3]likewise, of every bird of the air, seven pairs, a male and a female, to keep their progeny alive over all the earth. [4]For seven days from now I will bring rain down on the earth for forty days and forty nights, and so I will wipe out from the face of the earth every being that I have made.[b] [5]Noah complied, just as the LORD had commanded.

The Great Flood. [6]Noah was six hundred years old when the flood came upon the earth. [7]Together with his sons, his wife, and his sons' wives, Noah went into the ark because of the waters of the flood.[c] [8]Of the clean animals and the unclean, of the birds, and of everything that crawls on the ground, [9]two by two, male and female came to Noah into the ark, just as God had commanded him.[d] [10]When the seven days were over, the waters of the flood came upon the earth.

[11]In the six hundredth year of Noah's life, in the second month, on the seventeenth day of the month: on that day

All the fountains of the great abyss[¶]
　　burst forth,
　　and the floodgates of the sky were
　　　　opened.

[12]For forty days and forty nights heavy rain poured down on the earth. [13]On the very same day, Noah and his sons Shem, Ham, and Japheth, and Noah's wife, and the three wives of Noah's sons had entered the ark,

---

* [6:15] Hebrew "cubit," lit., "forearm," is the distance from the elbow to the tip of the middle finger, about eighteen inches (a foot and a half). The dimensions of Noah's ark were approximately 440 × 73 × 44 feet. The ark of the Babylonian flood story was an exact cube, 120 cubits (180 feet) in length, width, and height.

† [6:16] **Opening for daylight**: a conjectural rendering of the Hebrew word *sohar*, occurring only here. The reference is probably to an open space on all sides near the top of the ark to admit light and air. The ark also had a window or hatch, which could be opened and closed (8:6).

‡ [6:19–21] **You shall bring two of every kind . . . one male and one female**: For the Priestly source (P), there is no distinction between clean and unclean animals until Sinai (Lv 11), no altars or sacrifice until Sinai, and all diet is vegetarian (Gn 1:29–30); even after the flood P has no distinction between clean and unclean, since "any living creature that moves about" may be eaten (9:3). Thus P has Noah take the minimum to preserve all species, one pair of each, without distinction between clean and unclean, but he must also take on provisions for food (6:21). The Yahwist source (J), which assumes the clean-unclean distinction always existed but knows no other restriction on eating meat (Abel was a shepherd and offered meat as a sacrifice), requires additional clean animals ("seven pairs") for food and sacrifice (7:2–3; 8:20).

§ [6:22] **Just as God had commanded him**: as in the creation of the world in chap. 1 and in the building of the tabernacle in Ex 25–31, 35–40 (all from the Priestly source), everything takes place by the command of God. In this passage and in Exodus, the commands of God are carried out to the letter by human agents, Noah and Moses. Divine speech is important. God speaks to Noah seven times in the flood story.

¶ [7:11] **Abyss**: the subterranean ocean; see note on 1:2.

a. [7:1] Wis 10:4; Sir 44:17; 2 Pt 2:5.
b. [7:4] Gn 6:17; 2 Pt 2:5.
c. [7:7] Wis 14:6; 1 Pt 3:20; 2 Pt 2:5.
d. [7:9] Gn 6:19.

h. [6:17] Gn 7:4, 21; 2 Pt 2:5.
i. [6:18] Gn 9:9; Wis 14:6; Heb 11:7; 1 Pt 3:20.

GN

¹⁴together with every kind of wild animal, every kind of tame animal, every kind of crawling thing that crawls on the earth, and every kind of bird. ¹⁵Pairs of all creatures in which there was the breath of life came to Noah into the ark. ¹⁶Those that entered were male and female; of all creatures they came, as God had commanded Noah. Then the LORD shut him in.

¹⁷The flood continued upon the earth for forty days. As the waters increased, they lifted the ark, so that it rose above the earth. ¹⁸The waters swelled and increased greatly on the earth, but the ark floated on the surface of the waters. ¹⁹Higher and higher on the earth the waters swelled, until all the highest mountains under the heavens were submerged. ²⁰The waters swelled fifteen cubits higher than the submerged mountains. ²¹All creatures that moved on earth perished: birds, tame animals, wild animals, and all that teemed on the earth, as well as all humankind.ᵉ ²²Everything on dry land with the breath of life in its nostrils died. ²³The LORD wiped out every being on earth: human beings and animals, the crawling things and the birds of the air; all were wiped out from the earth. Only Noah and those with him in the ark were left.

²⁴And when the waters had swelled on the earth for one hundred and fifty days,

CHAPTER 8

¹God remembered Noah and all the animals, wild and tame, that were with him in the ark. So God made a wind sweep over the earth, and the waters began to subside. ²The fountains of the abyss and the floodgates of the sky were closed, and the downpour from the sky was held back. ³Gradually the waters receded from the earth. At the end of one hundred and fifty days, the waters had so diminished ⁴that, in the seventh month, on the seventeenth day of the month,

the ark came to rest on the mountains of Ararat.* ⁵The waters continued to diminish until the tenth month, and on the first day of the tenth month the tops of the mountains appeared.

⁶At the end of forty days Noah opened the hatch of the ark that he had made, ⁷†and he released a raven. It flew back and forth until the waters dried off from the earth. ⁸Then he released a dove, to see if the waters had lessened on the earth. ⁹But the dove could find no place to perch, and it returned to him in the ark, for there was water over all the earth. Putting out his hand, he caught the dove and drew it back to him inside the ark. ¹⁰He waited yet seven days more and again released the dove from the ark. ¹¹In the evening the dove came back to him, and there in its bill was a plucked-off olive leaf! So Noah knew that the waters had diminished on the earth. ¹²He waited yet another seven days and then released the dove; but this time it did not come back.

¹³‡In the six hundred and first year, in the first month, on the first day of the month, the water began to dry up on the earth. Noah then removed the covering of the ark and saw that the surface of the ground had dried. ¹⁴In the second month, on the twenty-seventh day of the month, the earth was dry.

¹⁵Then God said to Noah: ¹⁶Go out of the ark, together with your wife and your sons and your sons' wives. ¹⁷Bring out with you every living thing that is with you—all creatures, be they birds or animals or crawling things that crawl on the earth—and let them abound on the earth, and be fertile and

---

* [8:4] **The mountains of Ararat**: the mountain country of ancient Arartu in northwest Iraq, which was the highest part of the world to the biblical writer. There is no Mount Ararat in the Bible.

† [8:7–12] In the eleventh tablet of the Gilgamesh Epic, Utnapishtim (the equivalent of Noah) released in succession a dove, a swallow, and a raven. When the raven did not return, Utnapishtim knew it was safe to leave the ark. The first century A.D. Roman author Pliny tells of Indian sailors who release birds in order to follow them toward land.

‡ [8:13–14] On the first day of the first month, the world was in the state it had been on the day of creation in chap. 1. Noah had to wait another month until the earth was properly dry as in 1:9.

e. [7:21–23] Jb 22:16; Mt 24:39; Lk 17:27; 2 Pt 3:6.

GN

multiply on it.*a* *18*So Noah came out, together with his sons and his wife and his sons' wives; *19*and all the animals, all the birds, and all the crawling creatures that crawl on the earth went out of the ark by families.

*20*Then Noah built an altar to the LORD, and choosing from every clean animal and every clean bird, he offered burnt offerings on the altar. *21*When the LORD smelled the sweet odor, the LORD said to himself: Never again will I curse the ground because of human beings, since the desires of the human heart are evil from youth; nor will I ever again strike down every living being, as I have done.*b*

*22*All the days of the earth,
    seedtime and harvest,
    cold and heat,
Summer and winter,
    and day and night
    shall not cease.*c*

CHAPTER 9

Covenant with Noah. *1**God blessed Noah and his sons and said to them: Be fertile and multiply and fill the earth.*a* *2†*Fear and dread of you shall come upon all the animals of the earth and all the birds of the air, upon all the creatures that move about on the ground and all the fishes of the sea; into your power they are delivered. *3b*Any living creature that moves about shall be yours to eat; I give them all to you as I did the green plants. *4c*Only meat with its lifeblood still

in it you shall not eat.*‡* *5*Indeed for your own lifeblood I will demand an accounting: from every animal I will demand it, and from a human being, each one for the blood of another, I will demand an accounting for human life.*d*

*6§*Anyone who sheds the blood of a
    human being,
    by a human being shall that one's
    blood be shed;
For in the image of God
    have human beings been made.*e*

*7*Be fertile, then, and multiply; abound on earth and subdue it.*f*

*8¶*God said to Noah and to his sons with him: *9*See, I am now establishing my covenant with you and your descendants after you*g* *10*and with every living creature that was with you: the birds, the tame animals, and all the wild animals that were with you—all that came out of the ark. *11*I will establish my covenant with you, that never again shall all creatures be destroyed by the waters of a flood; there shall not be another flood to devastate the earth.*h* *12*God said: This is the sign of the covenant that I am making between me and you and every living creature with you for all ages to come: *13i*I set my bow in the clouds to serve as a sign of the covenant between me and the earth. *14*When I bring clouds over the earth, and the bow appears in

---

‡ [9:4] Because a living being dies when it loses most of its blood, the ancients regarded blood as the seat of life, and therefore sacred. Jewish tradition considered the prohibition against eating meat with blood to be binding on all, because it was given by God to Noah, the new ancestor of all humankind; therefore the early Christian Church retained it for a time (Acts 15:20, 29).

§ [9:6] The image of God, given to the first man and woman and transmitted to every human being, is the reason that no violent attacks can be made upon human beings. That image is the basis of the dignity of every individual who, in some sense, "represents" God in the world.

¶ [9:8–17] God makes a covenant with Noah and his descendants and, remarkably, with all the animals who come out of the ark: never again shall the world be destroyed by flood. The sign of this solemn promise is the appearance of a rainbow.

---

* [9:1] God reaffirms without change the original blessing and mandate of 1:28. In the Mesopotamian epic Atrahasis, on which the Genesis story is partly modeled, the gods changed their original plan by restricting human population through such means as childhood diseases, birth demons, and mandating celibacy among certain groups of women.

† [9:2–3] Pre-flood creatures, including human beings, are depicted as vegetarians (1:29–30). In view of the human propensity to violence, God changes the original prohibition against eating meat.

---

a. [8:17] Gn 1:22, 28.
b. [8:21] Sir 44:18; Is 54:9; Rom 7:18.
c. [8:22] Jer 33:20, 25.

a. [9:1] Gn 1:22, 28; 8:17.
b. [9:3] Gn 1:29–30; Dt 12:15.
c. [9:4] Lv 7:26–27; 17:4; Dt 12:16, 23; 1 Sm 14:33; Acts 15:20.

d. [9:5] Gn 4:10–11; Ex 21:12.
e. [9:6] Gn 1:26–27; Lv 24:17; Nm 35:33; Jas 3:9.
f. [9:7] Gn 1:28; 8:17; 9:2; Jas 3:7.
g. [9:9] Gn 6:18.
h. [9:11] Sir 44:18; Is 54:9.
i. [9:13] Sir 43:12.

GN

the clouds, **¹⁵**I will remember my covenant between me and you and every living creature—every mortal being—so that the waters will never again become a flood to destroy every mortal being.*ʲ* **¹⁶**When the bow appears in the clouds, I will see it and remember the everlasting covenant between God and every living creature—every mortal being that is on earth. **¹⁷**God told Noah: This is the sign of the covenant I have established between me and every mortal being that is on earth.

Noah and His Sons. **¹⁸***The sons of Noah who came out of the ark were Shem, Ham and Japheth. Ham was the father of Canaan.*ᵏ* **¹⁹**These three were the sons of Noah, and from them the whole earth was populated.

²⁰Noah, a man of the soil, was the first to plant a vineyard. **²¹**He drank some of the wine, became drunk, and lay naked inside his tent.*ˡ* **²²**Ham, the father of Canaan, saw his father's nakedness, and he told his two brothers outside. **²³**Shem and Japheth, however, took a robe, and holding it on their shoulders, they walked backward and covered their father's nakedness; since their faces were turned the other way, they did not see their father's nakedness. **²⁴**When Noah woke up from his wine and learned what his youngest son had done to him, **²⁵**he said:

"Cursed be Canaan!
   The lowest of slaves
      shall he be to his brothers."*ᵐ*

²⁶He also said:

"Blessed be the Lᴏʀᴅ, the God of
   Shem!

Let Canaan be his slave.
²⁷May God expand Japheth,†
   and may he dwell among the
      tents of Shem;
   and let Canaan be his slave."

²⁸Noah lived three hundred and fifty years after the flood. **²⁹**The whole lifetime of Noah was nine hundred and fifty years; then he died.

CHAPTER 10

Table of the Nations.‡ **¹**These are the descendants of Noah's sons, Shem, Ham and Japheth, to whom children were born after the flood.

²ᵃThe descendants of Japheth: Gomer,§ Magog, Madai, Javan, Tubal, Meshech and Tiras.*ᵇ* **³**The descendants of Gomer: Ashkenaz,¶ Diphath and

---

* [9:18–27] The character of the three sons is sketched here. The fault is not Noah's (for he could not be expected to know about the intoxicating effect of wine) but Ham's, who shames his father by looking on his nakedness, and then tells the other sons. Ham's conduct is meant to prefigure the later shameful sexual practices of the Canaanites, which are alleged in numerous biblical passages. The point of the story is revealed in Noah's curse of Ham's son Canaan and his blessing of Shem and Japheth.

j. [9:15] Is 54:9.
k. [9:18] Gn 5:32; 10:1.
l. [9:21] Lam 4:21; Hb 2:15.
m. [9:25] Dt 27:16; Wis 12:11.

† [9:27] In the Hebrew text there is a play on the words *yapt* ("expand") and *yepet* ("Japheth").

‡ [10:1–32] Verse 1 is the fourth of the Priestly formulas (2:4; 5:1; 6:9; 11:10) that structure Part I of Genesis; it introduces 10:2–11:9, the populating of the world and the building of the city. In a sense, chaps. 4–9 are concerned with the first of the two great commands given to the human race in 1:28, "Be fertile and multiply," whereas chaps. 10–11 are concerned with the second command, "Fill the earth and subdue it." ("Subdue it" refers to each nation's taking the land assigned to it by God.) Gn 9:19 already noted that all nations are descended from the three sons of Noah; the same sentiment is repeated in 10:5, 18, 25, 32; 11:8. The presupposition of the chapter is that every nation has a land assigned to it by God (cf. Dt 32:8–9). The number of the nations is seventy (if one does not count Noah and his sons, and counts Sidon [vv. 15, 19] only once), which is a traditional biblical number (Jgs 8:30; Lk 10:1, 17). According to Gn 46:27 and Ex 1:5, Israel also numbered seventy persons, which shows that it in some sense represents the nations of the earth.

This chapter classifies the various peoples known to the ancient Israelites; it is theologically important as stressing the basic family unity of all peoples on earth. It is sometimes called the Table of the Nations. The relationship between the various peoples is based on linguistic, geographic, or political grounds (v. 31). In general, the descendants of Japheth (vv. 2–5) are the peoples of the Indo-European languages to the north and west of Mesopotamia and Syria; the descendants of Ham (vv. 6–20) are the Hamitic-speaking peoples of northern Africa; and the descendants of Shem (vv. 21–31) are the Semitic-speaking peoples of Mesopotamia, Syria and Arabia. But there are many exceptions to this rule; the Semitic-speaking peoples of Canaan are considered descendants of Ham, because at one time they were subject to Hamitic Egypt (vv. 6, 15–19). This chapter is generally considered to be a composite from the Yahwist source (vv. 8–19, 21, 24–30) and the Priestly source (vv. 1–7, 20, 22–23, 31–32). Presumably that is why certain tribes of Arabia are listed under both Ham (v. 7) and Shem (vv. 26–28).

§ [10:2] **Gomer**: the Cimmerians; **Madai**: the Medes; **Javan**: the Greeks.

¶ [10:3] **Ashkenaz**: an Indo-European people, which later became the medieval rabbinic name for Germany. It now designates one of the great divisions of Judaism, Eastern European Yiddish-speaking Jews.

a. [10:2–8] 1 Chr 1:5–10.
b. [10:2] Ez 38:2.

Togarmah. [4]The descendants of Javan: Elishah,[*] Tarshish, the Kittim and the Rodanim. [5]From these branched out the maritime nations.

These are the descendants of Japheth by their lands, each with its own language, according to their clans, by their nations.

[6]The descendants of Ham: Cush,[†] Mizraim, Put and Canaan. [7]The descendants of Cush: Seba, Havilah, Sabtah, Raamah and Sabteca. The descendants of Raamah: Sheba and Dedan.

[8]Cush[‡] became the father of Nimrod, who was the first to become a mighty warrior on earth. [9]He was a mighty hunter in the eyes of the LORD; hence the saying, "Like Nimrod, a mighty hunter in the eyes of the LORD." [10]His kingdom originated in Babylon, Erech and Accad, all of them in the land of Shinar.[§] [11]From that land he went forth to Assyria, where he built Nineveh, Rehoboth-Ir[¶] and Calah, [12]as well as Resen, between Nineveh and Calah,[**] the latter being the principal city.

[13c]Mizraim became the father of the Ludim, the Anamim, the Lehabim, the Naphtuhim, [14]the Pathrusim,[††] the Casluhim, and the Caphtorim from whom the Philistines came.

[15]Canaan became the father of Sidon, his firstborn, and of Heth;[‡‡] [16]also of the Jebusites, the Amorites, the Girgashites, [17]the Hivites, the Arkites, the Sinites, [18]the Arvadites, the Zemarites, and the Hamathites. Afterward, the clans of the Canaanites spread out, [19]so that the Canaanite borders extended from Sidon all the way to Gerar, near Gaza, and all the way to Sodom, Gomorrah, Admah and Zeboiim, near Lasha.

[20]These are the descendants of Ham, according to their clans, according to their languages, by their lands, by their nations.

[21]To Shem also, Japheth's oldest brother and the ancestor of all the children of Eber,[§§] children were born. [22d]The descendants of Shem: Elam, Asshur, Arpachshad, Lud and Aram. [23]The descendants of Aram: Uz, Hul, Gether and Mash.

[24]Arpachshad became the father of Shelah, and Shelah became the father of Eber. [25]To Eber two sons were born: the name of the first was Peleg, for in his time the world was divided;[¶¶] and the name of his brother was Joktan.

[26]Joktan became the father of Almodad, Sheleph, Hazarmaveth, Jerah, [27]Hadoram, Uzal, Diklah, [28]Obal, Abimael, Sheba, [29]Ophir, Havilah and Jobab. All these were descendants of Joktan. [30]Their settlements extended all the way from Mesha to Sephar, the eastern hill country.

[31]These are the descendants of Shem, according to their clans, according to their languages, by their lands, by their nations.

[32]These are the clans of Noah's sons, according to their origins and by their nations. From these the nations of the earth branched out after the flood.

CHAPTER 11

Tower of Babel.[***] [1]The whole world had the same language and the same

* [10:4] Elishah: Cyprus; the Kittim: certain inhabitants of Cyprus; the Rodanim: the inhabitants of Rhodes.
† [10:6] Cush: biblical Ethiopia, modern Nubia. Mizraim: Lower (i.e., northern) Egypt; Put: either Punt in East Africa or Libya.
‡ [10:8] Cush: here seems to be Cossea, the country of the Kassites; see note on 2:10–14. Nimrod: possibly Tukulti-Ninurta I (thirteenth century B.C.), the first Assyrian conqueror of Babylonia and a famous city-builder at home.
§ [10:10] Shinar: the land of ancient Babylonia, embracing Sumer and Akkad, present-day southern Iraq, mentioned also in 11:2; 14:1.
¶ [10:11] Rehoboth-Ir: lit., "wide-streets city," was probably not the name of another city, but an epithet of Nineveh; cf. Jon 3:3.
** [10:12] Calah: Assyrian Kalhu, the capital of Assyria in the ninth century B.C.
†† [10:14] The Pathrusim: the people of Upper (southern) Egypt; cf. Is 11:11; Jer 44:1; Ez 29:14; 30:13. Caphtorim: Crete; for Caphtor as the place of origin of the Philistines, cf. Dt 2:23; Am 9:7; Jer 47:4.
‡‡ [10:15] Heth: the biblical Hittites; see note on 23:3.

c. [10:13–18] 1 Chr 1:11–16.

§§ [10:21] Eber: the eponymous ancestor of the Hebrews, that is, the one to whom they traced their name.
¶¶ [10:25] In the Hebrew text there is a play on the name Peleg and the word niplega, "was divided."
*** [11:1–9] This story illustrates increasing human wickedness, shown here in the sinful pride that human beings take in their own achievements apart from God. Secondarily, the story explains the diversity of languages among the peoples of the earth.

d. [10:22–29] 1 Chr 1:17–23.

words. ²When they were migrating from the east, they came to a valley in the land of Shinar* and settled there. ³They said to one another, "Come, let us mold bricks and harden them with fire." They used bricks for stone, and bitumen for mortar. ⁴Then they said, "Come, let us build ourselves a city and a tower with its top in the sky,† and so make a name for ourselves; otherwise we shall be scattered all over the earth."

⁵The LORD came down to see the city and the tower that the people had built. ⁶Then the LORD said: If now, while they are one people and all have the same language, they have started to do this, nothing they presume to do will be out of their reach. ⁷Come, let us go down and there confuse their language, so that no one will understand the speech of another. ⁸So the LORD scattered them from there over all the earth, and they stopped building the city. ⁹That is why it was called Babel,‡ because there the LORD confused the speech of all the world. From there the LORD scattered them over all the earth.

Descendants from Shem to Abraham.§ ¹⁰ᵃThese are the descendants of Shem. When Shem was one hundred years old, he begot Arpachshad, two years after the flood. ¹¹Shem lived five hundred years after he begot Arpachshad, and he had other sons and daughters. ¹²When Arpachshad was thirty-five years old, he begot Shelah.¶ ¹³Arpachshad lived four hundred and three years after he begot Shelah, and he had other sons and daughters.

¹⁴When Shelah was thirty years old, he begot Eber. ¹⁵Shelah lived four hundred and three years after he begot Eber, and he had other sons and daughters. ¹⁶When Eber** was thirty-four years old, he begot Peleg. ¹⁷Eber lived four hundred and thirty years after he begot Peleg, and he had other sons and daughters.

¹⁸When Peleg was thirty years old, he begot Reu. ¹⁹Peleg lived two hundred and nine years after he begot Reu, and he had other sons and daughters. ²⁰When Reu was thirty-two years old, he begot Serug. ²¹Reu lived two hundred and seven years after he begot Serug, and he had other sons and daughters. ²²When Serug was thirty years old, he begot Nahor. ²³Serug lived two hundred years after he begot Nahor, and he had other sons and daughters. ²⁴When Nahor was twenty-nine years old, he begot Terah. ²⁵Nahor lived one hundred and nineteen years after he begot Terah, and he had other sons and daughters. ²⁶When Terah was seventy years old, he begot Abram,†† Nahor and Haran.ᵇ

II. THE STORY OF THE ANCESTORS OF ISRAEL

Terah. ²⁷These are the descendants of Terah.‡‡ Terah begot Abram, Nahor, and

---

* [11:2] **Shinar**: see note on 10:10.

† [11:4] **Tower with its top in the sky**: possibly a reference to the chief ziggurat of Babylon, *E-sag-ila*, lit., "the house that raises high its head."

‡ [11:9] **Babel**: the Hebrew form of the name "Babylon"; the Babylonians interpreted their name for the city, *Bab-ili*, as "gate of god." The Hebrew word *balal*, "he confused," has a similar sound.

§ [11:10–26] The second Priestly genealogy goes from Shem to Terah and his three sons Abram, Nahor, and Haran, just as the genealogy in 5:3–32 went from Adam to Noah and his three sons Shem, Ham, and Japheth. This genealogy marks the important transition in Genesis between the story of the nations in 1:1–11:26 and the story of Israel in the person of its ancestors (11:27–50:26). As chaps. 1–11 showed the increase and spread of the nations, so chaps. 12–50 will show the increase and spread of Israel. The contrast between Israel and the nations is a persistent biblical theme. The ages given here are from the Hebrew text; the Samaritan and Greek texts have divergent sets of numbers in most cases. In comparable accounts of the pre-flood period, enormous life spans are attributed to human beings. It may be an attempt to show that the pre-flood generations were extraordinary and more vital than post-flood human beings.

¶ [11:12] The Greek text adds Kenan (cf. 5:9–10) between Arpachshad and Shelah. The Greek listing is followed in Lk 3:36.

** [11:16] **Eber**: the eponymous ancestor of the Hebrews, "descendants of Eber" (10:21, 24–30); see note on 14:13.

†† [11:26] Abram is a dialectal variant of Abraham. God will change his name in view of his new task in 17:4.

‡‡ [11:27] **Descendants of Terah**: elsewhere in Genesis the story of the son is introduced by the name of the father (25:12, 19; 36:1; 37:2). The Abraham-Sarah stories begin (11:27–32) and end with genealogical notices (25:1–18), which concern, respectively, the families of Terah and of Abraham. Most of the traditions in the cycle are from the Yahwist source. The so-called Elohist source (E) is somewhat shadowy, denied by some scholars but recognized by others in passages that duplicate other narratives (20:1–18 and 21:22–34). The Priestly source consists mostly of brief editorial notices, except for chaps. 17 and 23.

a. [11:10–26] 1 Chr 1:24–27; Lk 3:34–36.

b. [11:26] Jos 24:2; 1 Chr 1:26–27.

Haran, and Haran begot Lot. ²⁸Haran died before Terah his father, in his native land, in Ur of the Chaldeans.[*] ²⁹Abram and Nahor took wives; the name of Abram's wife was Sarai,[†] and the name of Nahor's wife was Milcah, daughter of Haran, the father of Milcah and Iscah.^c ³⁰Sarai was barren; she had no child.

³¹Terah took his son Abram, his grandson Lot, son of Haran, and his daughter-in-law Sarai, the wife of his son Abram, and brought them out of Ur of the Chaldeans, to go to the land of Canaan. But when they reached Haran, they settled there.^d ³²The lifetime of Terah was two hundred and five years; then Terah died in Haran.[‡]

CHAPTER 12

Abram's Call and Migration. ¹The LORD said to Abram: Go forth[§] from your land, your relatives, and from your father's house to a land that I will show you.^a ^{2¶}I will make of you a great nation, and I will bless you; I will make your name great, so that you will be a blessing.^b ^{3c}I will bless those who bless you and curse those who curse you. All the families of the earth will find blessing in you.^{**}

^{4d}Abram went as the LORD directed him, and Lot went with him. Abram was seventy-five years old when he left Haran. ^{5††}Abram took his wife Sarai, his brother's son Lot, all the possessions that they had accumulated, and the persons they had acquired in Haran, and they set out for the land of Canaan. When they came to the land of Canaan, ^{6‡‡}Abram passed through the land as far as the sacred place at Shechem, by the oak of Moreh. The Canaanites were then in the land.

⁷The LORD appeared to Abram and said: To your descendants I will give this land. So Abram built an altar there to the LORD who had appeared to him.^e ⁸From there he moved on to the hill country east of Bethel, pitching his tent with Bethel to the west and Ai to

---

* [11:28] **Ur of the Chaldeans**: Ur was an extremely ancient city of the Sumerians (later, of the Babylonians) in southern Mesopotamia. The Greek text has "the land of the Chaldeans." After a millennium of relative unimportance, Ur underwent a revival during the Neo-Babylonian/Chaldean empire (625–539 B.C.). The sixth-century author here identified the place by its contemporary name. As chap. 24 shows, Haran in northern Mesopotamia is in fact the native place of Abraham. In the Genesis perspective, the human race originated in the East (3:24; 4:16) and migrated from there to their homelands (11:2). Terah's family moved from the East (Ur) and Abraham will complete the journey to the family's true homeland in the following chapters.

† [11:29] **Sarai**: like Abram, a dialectal variant of the more usual form of the name Sarah. In 17:15, God will change it to Sarah in view of her new task.

‡ [11:32] Since Terah was seventy years old when his son Abraham was born (v. 26), and Abraham was seventy-five when he left Haran (12:4), Terah lived in Haran for sixty years after Abraham's departure. According to the tradition in the Samaritan text, Terah died when he was one hundred and forty-five years old, therefore, in the same year in which Abraham left Haran. This is the tradition followed in Stephen's speech: Abraham left Haran "after his father died" (Acts 7:4).

§ [12:1–3] **Go forth . . . find blessing in you**: the syntax of the Hebrew suggests that the blessings promised to Abraham are contingent on his going to Canaan.

¶ [12:2] The call of Abraham begins a new history of blessing (18:18; 22:15–18), which is passed on in each instance to the chosen successor (26:2–4; 28:14). This call evokes the last story in the primeval history (11:1–9) by reversing its themes: Abraham goes forth rather than settle down; it is God rather than Abraham who will make a name for him; the families of the earth will find blessing in him.

** [12:3] **Will find blessing in you**: the Hebrew conjugation of the verb here and in 18:18 and 28:14 can be either reflexive ("shall bless themselves by you" = people will invoke Abraham as an example of someone blessed by God) or passive ("by you all the families of earth will be blessed" = the religious privileges of Abraham and his descendants ultimately will be extended to the nations). In 22:18 and 26:4, another conjugation of the same verb is used in a similar context that is undoubtedly reflexive ("bless themselves"). Many scholars suggest that the two passages in which the sense is clear should determine the interpretation of the three ambiguous passages: the privileged blessing enjoyed by Abraham and his descendants will awaken in all peoples the desire to enjoy those same blessings. Since the term is understood in a passive sense in the New Testament (Acts 3:25; Gal 3:8), it is rendered here by a neutral expression that admits of both meanings.

†† [12:5] The ancestors appear in Genesis as pastoral nomads living at the edge of settled society, and having occasional dealings with the inhabitants, sometimes even moving into towns for brief periods. Unlike modern nomads such as the Bedouin, however, ancient pastoralists fluctuated between following the herds and sedentary life, depending on circumstances. Pastoralists could settle down and farm and later resume a pastoral way of life. Indeed, there was a symbiotic relationship between pastoralists and villagers, each providing goods to the other. **Persons**: servants and others who formed the larger household under the leadership of Abraham; cf. 14:14.

‡‡ [12:6] Abraham's journey to the center of the land, Shechem, then to Bethel, and then to the Negeb, is duplicated in Jacob's journeys (33:18; 35:1, 6, 27; 46:1) and in the general route of the conquest under Joshua (Jos 7:2; 8:9, 30). Abraham's journey is a symbolic "conquest" of the land he has been promised. In building altars here (vv. 7, 8) and elsewhere, Abraham acknowledges his God as Lord of the land.

---

c. [11:29] Gn 17:15.
d. [11:31] Jos 24:3; Neh 9:7; Jdt 5:6–9; Acts 7:4.

a. [12:1] Acts 7:3; Heb 11:8.

b. [12:2] Gn 17:6; Sir 44:20–21; Rom 4:17–22.
c. [12:3] Gn 18:18; 22:18; Acts 3:25; Gal 3:8.
d. [12:4–5] Gn 11:31; Jos 24:3; Acts 7:4.
e. [12:7] Ex 33:1; Dt 34:4; Acts 7:5.

the east. He built an altar there to the LORD and invoked the LORD by name. [9]Then Abram journeyed on by stages to the Negeb.*

Abram and Sarai in Egypt.† [10]There

was famine in the land; so Abram went down to Egypt to sojourn there, since the famine in the land was severe.[f] [11]When he was about to enter Egypt, he said to his wife Sarai: "I know that you are a beautiful woman. [12]When the Egyptians see you, they will say, 'She is his wife'; then they will kill me, but let you live. [13]Please say, therefore, that you are my sister,‡ so that I may fare well on your account and my life may be spared for your sake."[g] [14]When Abram arrived in Egypt, the Egyptians saw that the woman was very beautiful. [15]When Pharaoh's officials saw her they praised her to Pharaoh, and the woman was taken into Pharaoh's house. [16]Abram fared well on her account, and he acquired sheep, oxen, male and female servants, male and female donkeys, and camels.§

[17]But the LORD struck Pharaoh and his household with severe plagues because of Sarai, Abram's wife.[h] [18]Then Pharaoh summoned Abram and said to him: "How could you do this to me! Why did you not tell me she was your wife? [19]Why did you say, 'She is my sister,' so that I took her for my wife? Now, here is your wife. Take her and leave!"

[20]Then Pharaoh gave his men orders concerning Abram, and they sent

him away, with his wife and all that belonged to him.

CHAPTER 13

Abram and Lot Part. [1]From Egypt Abram went up to the Negeb with his wife and all that belonged to him, and Lot went with him.[a] [2]¶Now Abram was very rich in livestock, silver, and gold.[b] [3]From the Negeb he traveled by stages toward Bethel, to the place between Bethel and Ai where his tent had formerly stood, [4]the site where he had first built the altar; and there Abram invoked the LORD by name.[c]

[5]Lot, who went with Abram, also had flocks and herds and tents, [6]so that the land could not support them if they stayed together; their possessions were so great that they could not live together. [7]There were quarrels between the herders of Abram's livestock and the herders of Lot's livestock. At this time the Canaanites and the Perizzites were living in the land.

[8]So Abram said to Lot: "Let there be no strife between you and me, or between your herders and my herders, for we are kindred. [9]Is not the whole land available? Please separate from me. If you prefer the left, I will go to the right; if you prefer the right, I will go to the left." [10]Lot looked about and saw how abundantly watered the whole Jordan Plain was as far as Zoar, like the LORD's own garden, or like Egypt. This was before the LORD had destroyed Sodom and Gomorrah. [11]Lot, therefore, chose for himself the whole Jordan Plain and set out eastward. Thus they separated from each

---

* [12:9] **The Negeb:** the semidesert land south of Judah.

† [12:10–13:1] Abraham and Sarah's sojourn in Egypt and encounter with Pharaoh foreshadow their descendants' experience, suggesting a divine design in which they must learn to trust. The story of Sarah, the ancestor in danger, is told again in chap. 20, and also in 26:1–11 with Rebekah instead of Sarah. Repetition of similar events is not unusual in literature that has been orally shaped.

‡ [12:13] **You are my sister:** the text does not try to excuse Abraham's deception, though in 20:12 a similar deception is somewhat excused.

§ [12:16] **Camels:** domesticated camels did not come into common use in the ancient Near East until the end of the second millennium B.C. Thus the mention of camels here (24:11–64; 30:43; 31:17, 34; 32:8, 16; 37:25) is seemingly an anachronism.

f. [12:10] Gn 26:1.
g. [12:13] Gn 20:12–13; 26:7.
h. [12:17] Ps 105:14.

¶ [13:2–18] In this story of Abraham and Lot going their separate ways, Abraham resolves a family dispute by an act that shows both trust in God and generosity toward his nephew. The story suggests Lot rather than Abraham is the natural choice to be the ancestor of a great family; he is young and he takes the most fertile land (outside the land of Canaan). In contrast to Lot, who lifts his eyes to choose for himself (vv. 10–11), Abraham waits for God to tell him to lift his eyes and see the land he will receive (v. 14). Chaps. 18–19 continue the story of Abraham and Lot. Abraham's visionary possession of the land foreshadows that of Moses (Dt 3:27; 34:4).

a. [13:1] Gn 12:9.
b. [13:2] Ps 112:1–3; Prv 10:22.
c. [13:4] Gn 12:8.

other. [12]Abram settled in the land of Canaan, while Lot settled among the cities of the Plain, pitching his tents near Sodom. [13]Now the inhabitants of Sodom were wicked, great sinners against the LORD.[d]

[14]After Lot had parted from him, the LORD said to Abram: Look about you, and from where you are, gaze to the north and south, east and west;[e] [15]all the land that you see I will give to you and your descendants forever.[f] [16]I will make your descendants like the dust of the earth; if anyone could count the dust of the earth, your descendants too might be counted.[g] [17]Get up and walk through the land, across its length and breadth, for I give it to you. [18]Abram moved his tents and went on to settle near the oak of Mamre, which is at Hebron. There he built an altar to the LORD.[h]

CHAPTER 14

The Four Kings. [1*]When Amraphel king of Shinar, Arioch king of Ellasar, Chedorlaomer king of Elam, and Tidal king of Goiim [2]made war on Bera king of Sodom, Birsha king of Gomorrah, Shinab king of Admah, Shemeber king of Zeboiim, and the king of Bela (that is, Zoar), [3]all the latter kings joined forces in the Valley of Siddim (that is, the Salt Sea[†]). [4]For twelve years they had served Chedorlaomer, but in the thirteenth year they rebelled. [5]In the fourteenth year Chedorlaomer and the kings allied with him came and defeated the Rephaim in Ashteroth-karnaim, the

Zuzim in Ham, the Emim in Shaveh-kiriathaim, [6]and the Horites in the hill country of Seir, as far as El-paran, close by the wilderness.[a] [7]They then turned back and came to En-mishpat (that is, Kadesh), and they subdued the whole country of both the Amalekites and the Amorites who lived in Hazazon-tamar. [8]Thereupon the king of Sodom, the king of Gomorrah, the king of Admah, the king of Zeboiim, and the king of Bela (that is, Zoar) marched out, and in the Valley of Siddim they went into battle against them: [9]against Chedorlaomer king of Elam, Tidal king of Goiim, Amraphel king of Shinar, and Arioch king of Ellasar—four kings against five. [10]Now the Valley of Siddim was full of bitumen pits; and as the king of Sodom and the king of Gomorrah fled, they fell into these, while the rest fled to the mountains. [11]The victors seized all the possessions and food supplies of Sodom and Gomorrah and then went their way. [12]They took with them Abram's nephew Lot, who had been living in Sodom, as well as his possessions, and departed.[b]

[13]A survivor came and brought the news to Abram the Hebrew,[‡] who was camping at the oak of Mamre the Amorite, a kinsman of Eshcol and Aner; these were allies of Abram. [14]When Abram heard that his kinsman had been captured, he mustered three hundred and eighteen of his retainers,[§] born in his house, and went in pursuit as far as Dan. [15]He and his servants deployed against them at night, defeated them, and pursued them as far as Hobah, which is north of

---

* [14:1] Abraham plays a role with other world leaders. He defeats a coalition of five kings from the east (where, later, Israel's enemies lived) and is recognized by a Canaanite king as blessed by God Most High. The historicity of the events is controverted; apart from Shinar (Babylon), Tidal (Hittite Tudhaliya), and Elam, the names and places cannot be identified with certainty. The five cities were apparently at the southern end of the Dead Sea, and all but Bela (i.e., Zoar) were destined for destruction (19:20–24; Hos 11:8). The passage belongs to none of the traditional Genesis sources; it has some resemblance to reports of military campaigns in Babylonian and Assyrian royal annals.
† [14:3] **The Salt Sea:** the Dead Sea.

d. [13:13] Gn 18:20; Ez 16:49; 2 Pt 2:6–8; Jude 7.
e. [13:14] Gn 28:14.
f. [13:15] Gn 12:7; Mt 5:5; Lk 1:55, 73; Acts 7:5; Rom 4:13; Gal 3:16.
g. [13:16] Gn 22:17; Nm 23:10.
h. [13:18] Gn 14:13.

‡ [14:13] **Abram the Hebrew:** "Hebrew" was used by biblical writers for the pre-Israelite ancestors. Linguistically, it is an ethnic term; it may be built on the root Eber, who is the eponymous ancestor of the Israelites, that is, the one to whom they traced their name (10:21, 24–25; 11:14–17), or it may reflect the tradition that the ancestors came from beyond (*eber*) the Euphrates. It is used only by non-Israelites, or by Israelites speaking to foreigners.
§ [14:14] **Retainers:** the Hebrew word *hanik* is used only here in the Old Testament. Cognate words appear in Egyptian and Akkadian texts, signifying armed soldiers belonging to the household of a local leader.

a. [14:6] Dt 2:12.
b. [14:12] Gn 13:10–12.

Damascus. ¹⁶He recovered all the possessions. He also recovered his kinsman Lot and his possessions, along with the women and the other people. ¹⁷When Abram returned from his defeat of Chedorlaomer and the kings who were allied with him, the king of Sodom went out to greet him in the Valley of Shaveh (that is, the King's Valley).

¹⁸Melchizedek, king of Salem,* brought out bread and wine. He was a priest of God Most High. ¹⁹He blessed Abram with these words:^c

"Blessed be Abram by God Most
    High,
    the creator of heaven and earth;
²⁰And blessed be God Most High,
    who delivered your foes into your
        hand."

Then Abram gave him a tenth of everything.

²¹The king of Sodom said to Abram, "Give me the captives; the goods you may keep." ²²But Abram replied to the king of Sodom: "I have sworn to the LORD, God Most High,[†] the creator of heaven and earth, ²³that I would not take so much as a thread or a sandal strap from anything that is yours, so that you cannot say, 'I made Abram rich.' ²⁴Nothing for me except what my servants have consumed and the share that is due to the men who went with me—Aner, Eshcol and Mamre; let them take their share."

CHAPTER 15

The Covenant with Abram.[‡] ¹Some time afterward, the word of the LORD came to Abram in a vision: Do not fear, Abram! I am your shield; I will make your reward very great.

²But Abram said, "Lord GOD, what can you give me, if I die childless and have only a servant of my household, Eliezer of Damascus?" ³Abram continued, "Look, you have given me no offspring, so a servant of my household will be my heir." ⁴Then the word of the LORD came to him: No, that one will not be your heir; your own offspring will be your heir.^a ⁵He took him outside and said: Look up at the sky and count the stars, if you can. Just so, he added, will your descendants be.^b ^{6c}Abram put his faith in the LORD, who attributed it to him as an act of righteousness.[§]

⁷He then said to him: I am the LORD who brought you from Ur of the Chaldeans to give you this land as a possession.^d ⁸"Lord GOD," he asked, "how will I know that I will possess it?" ⁹He answered him: Bring me a three-year-old heifer, a three-year-old

---

* [14:18] Melchizedek, king of Salem (Jerusalem, cf. Ps 76:3), appears with majestic suddenness to recognize Abraham's great victory, which the five local kings were unable to achieve. He prepares a feast in his honor and declares him blessed or made powerful by God Most High, evidently the highest God in the Canaanite pantheon. Abraham acknowledges the blessing by giving a tenth of the recaptured spoils as a tithe to Melchizedek. The episode is one of several allusions to David, king at Jerusalem, who also exercised priestly functions (2 Sm 6:17). Heb 7 interprets Melchizedek as a prefiguration of Christ. **God Most High:** in Heb. *El Elyon*, one of several "El names" for God in Genesis, others being *El Olam* (21:33), *El* the God of Israel (33:20), *El Roi* (16:13), *El Bethel* (35:7), and *El Shaddai* (the usual P designation for God in Genesis). All the sources except the Yahwist use El as the proper name for God used by the ancestors. The god El was well-known across the ancient Near East and in comparable religious literature. The ancestors recognized this God as their own when they encountered him in their journeys and in the shrines they found in Canaan.

† [14:22] In vv. 22–24, Abraham refuses to let anyone but God enrich him. Portrayed with the traits of a later Israelite judge or tribal hero, Abraham acknowledges that his victory is from God alone.

c. [14:19] Ps 110:4; Heb 5:6, 10; 7:1.

‡ [15:1–21] In the first section (vv. 1–6), Abraham is promised a son and heir, and in the second (vv. 7–21), he is promised a land. The structure is similar in both: each of the two promises is not immediately accepted; the first is met with a complaint (vv. 2–3) and the second with a request for a sign (v. 8). God's answer differs in each section—a sign in v. 5 and an oath in vv. 9–21. Some scholars believe that the Genesis promises of progeny and land were originally separate and only later combined, but progeny and land are persistent concerns especially of ancient peoples and it is hard to imagine one without the other.

§ [15:6] Abraham's act of faith in God's promises was regarded as an act of righteousness, i.e., as fully expressive of his relationship with God. St. Paul (Rom 4:1–25; Gal 3:6–9) makes Abraham's faith a model for Christians.

¶ [15:9–17] Cutting up animals was a well-attested way of making a treaty in antiquity. Jer 34:17–20 shows the rite is a form of self-imprecation in which violators invoke the fate of the animals upon themselves. The eighth-century B.C. Sefire treaty from Syria reads, "As this calf is cut up, thus Matti'el shall be cut up." The smoking fire pot and the flaming torch (v. 17), which represent God, pass between the pieces, making God a signatory to the covenant.

a. [15:4] Gn 17:16.

b. [15:5] Gn 22:17; 28:14; Ex 32:13; Dt 1:10; Sir 44:21; Rom 4:18; Heb 11:12.

c. [15:6] 1 Mc 2:52; Rom 4:3, 9, 22; Gal 3:6–7; Jas 2:23.

d. [15:7] Gn 11:31; 12:1; Ex 32:13; Neh 9:7–8; Acts 7:2–3.

female goat, a three-year-old ram, a turtledove, and a young pigeon.*e* **10**He brought him all these, split them in two, and placed each half opposite the other; but the birds he did not cut up. **11**Birds of prey swooped down on the carcasses, but Abram scared them away. **12**As the sun was about to set, a deep sleep fell upon Abram, and a great, dark dread descended upon him. **13***Then the Lord said to Abram: Know for certain that your descendants will reside as aliens in a land not their own, where they shall be enslaved and oppressed for four hundred years.*f* **14**But I will bring judgment on the nation they must serve, and after this they will go out with great wealth.*g* **15**You, however, will go to your ancestors in peace; you will be buried at a ripe old age. **16**In the fourth generation† your descendants will return here, for the wickedness of the Amorites is not yet complete.*h*

17When the sun had set and it was dark, there appeared a smoking fire pot and a flaming torch, which passed between those pieces. **18‡**On that day the Lord made a covenant with Abram, saying: To your descendants I give this land, from the Wadi of Egypt to the Great River, the Euphrates,*i*

19*j*the land of the Kenites, the Kenizzites, the Kadmonites, **20**the Hittites, the Perizzites, the Rephaim, **21**the Amorites, the Canaanites, the Girgashites, and the Jebusites.

CHAPTER 16

Birth of Ishmael.§ **1**Abram's wife Sarai had borne him no children. Now she had an Egyptian maidservant named Hagar.*a* **2**Sarai said to Abram: "The Lord has kept me from bearing children. Have intercourse with my maid; perhaps I will have sons through her." Abram obeyed Sarai.¶*b* **3**Thus, after Abram had lived ten years in the land of Canaan, his wife Sarai took her maid, Hagar the Egyptian, and gave her to her husband Abram to be his wife. **4**He had intercourse with her, and she became pregnant. As soon as Hagar knew she was pregnant, her mistress lost stature in her eyes.*******c* **5***d*So Sarai said to Abram: "This outrage against me is your fault. I myself gave my maid to your embrace; but ever since she knew she was pregnant, I have lost stature in her eyes. May the Lord decide between you and me!" **6**Abram told Sarai: "Your maid is in your power. Do to her what you regard

---

* [15:13–16] The verses clarify the promise of the land by providing a timetable of its possession: after four hundred years of servitude, your descendants will actually possess the land in the fourth generation (a patriarchal generation seems to be one hundred years). The iniquity of the current inhabitants (called here the Amorites) has not yet reached the point where God must intervene in punishment. Another table is given in Ex 12:40, which is not compatible with this one.

† [15:16] **Generation:** the Hebrew term *dor* is commonly rendered as "generation," but it may signify a period of varying length. A "generation" is the period between the birth of children and the birth of their parents, normally about twenty to twenty-five years. The actual length of a generation can vary, however; in Jb 42:16 it is thirty-five and in Nm 32:13 it is forty. The meaning may be life spans, which in Gn 6:3 is one hundred twenty years and in Is 65:20 is one hundred years.

‡ [15:18–21] The **Wadi,** i.e., a gully or ravine, **of Egypt** is the Wadi-el-'Arish, which is the boundary between the settled land and the Sinai desert. Some scholars suggest that the boundaries are those of a Davidic empire at its greatest extent; others that they are idealized boundaries. Most lists of the ancient inhabitants of the promised land give three, six, or seven peoples, but vv. 19–21 give a grand total of ten.

§ [16:1–16] In the previous chapter Abraham was given a timetable of possession of the land, but nothing was said about when the child was to be born. In this chapter, Sarah takes matters into her own hands, for she has been childless ten years since the promise (cf. 12:4 with 16:16). The story is about the two women, Sarah the infertile mistress and Hagar the fertile slave; Abraham has only a single sentence. In the course of the story, God intervenes directly on the side of Hagar, for she is otherwise without resources.

¶ [16:2] The custom of an infertile wife providing her husband with a concubine to produce children is widely attested in ancient Near Eastern law; e.g., an Old Assyrian marriage contract states that the wife must provide her husband with a concubine if she does not bear children within two years.

** [16:4] Because barrenness was at that time normally blamed on the woman and regarded as a disgrace, it is not surprising that Hagar looks down on Sarah. Ancient Near Eastern legal practice addresses such cases of insolent slaves and allows disciplining of them. Prv 30:23 uses as an example of intolerable behavior "a maidservant when she ousts her mistress."

---

e. [15:9] Lv 1:14.
f. [15:13] Ex 12:40; Nm 20:15; Jdt 5:9–10; Is 52:4; Acts 13:20; Gal 3:17.
g. [15:14] Ex 3:8, 21–22.
h. [15:16] 1 Kgs 21:26.
i. [15:18] Ex 32:13; Neh 9:8; Ps 105:11; Sir 44:21.

j. [15:19–20] Dt 7:1.

a. [16:1] Gn 11:30.
b. [16:2] Gn 21:8–9; Gal 4:22.
c. [16:4] 1 Sm 1:6; Prv 30:23.
d. [16:5–16] Gn 21:10–19.

GN

as right." Sarai then mistreated her so much that Hagar ran away from her.

⁷The LORD's angel* found her by a spring in the wilderness, the spring on the road to Shur,ᵉ ⁸and he asked, "Hagar, maid of Sarai, where have you come from and where are you going?" She answered, "I am running away from my mistress, Sarai." ⁹But the LORD's angel told her: "Go back to your mistress and submit to her authority. ¹⁰I will make your descendants so numerous," added the LORD's angel, "that they will be too many to count."ᶠ ¹¹Then the LORD's angel said to her:

"You are now pregnant and shall
    bear a son;
  you shall name him Ishmael,†
For the LORD has heeded your
    affliction.
¹²He shall be a wild ass of a man,
  his hand against everyone,
    and everyone's hand against him;
Alongside‡ all his kindred
    shall he encamp."ᵍ

¹³To the LORD who spoke to her she gave a name, saying, "You are God who sees me";§ she meant, "Have I really seen God and remained alive after he saw me?"ʰ ¹⁴That is why the well

is called Beer-lahai-roi.¶ It is between Kadesh and Bered.

¹⁵Hagar bore Abram a son, and Abram named the son whom Hagar bore him Ishmael.ⁱ ¹⁶Abram was eighty-six years old when Hagar bore him Ishmael.

CHAPTER 17

Covenant of Circumcision.** ¹When Abram was ninety-nine years old, the LORD appeared to Abram and said: I am God the Almighty. Walk in my presence and be blameless.ᵃ ²Between you and me I will establish my covenant, and I will multiply you exceedingly.ᵇ

³Abram fell face down and God said to him: ⁴For my part, here is my covenant with you: you are to become the father of a multitude of nations.ᶜ ⁵No longer will you be called Abram; your name will be Abraham,†† for I am making you the father of a multitude of nations.ᵈ ⁶I will make you exceedingly fertile; I will make nations of you; kings will stem from you. ⁷I will maintain my covenant between me and you and your descendants after you throughout the ages as an everlasting covenant, to be your God and the God of your descendants after you.ᵉ ⁸I will

---

¶ [16:14] **Beer-lahai-roi**: possible translations of the name of the well include: "spring of the living one who sees me"; "the well of the living sight"; or "the one who sees me lives." See note on v. 13.

** [17:1–27] The Priestly source gathers the major motifs of the story so far and sets them firmly within a covenant context; the word "covenant" occurs thirteen times. There are links to the covenant with Noah (v. 1 = 6:9; v. 7 = 9:9; v. 11 = 9:12–17). In this chapter, vv. 1–8 promise progeny and land; vv. 9–14 are instructions about circumcision; vv. 15–21 repeat the promise of a son to Sarah and distinguish this promise from that to Hagar; vv. 22–27 describe Abraham's carrying out the commands. **The Almighty**: traditional rendering of Hebrew *El Shaddai*, which is P's favorite designation of God in the period of the ancestors. Its etymology is uncertain, but its root meaning is probably "God, the One of the Mountains."

†† [17:5] Abram and Abraham are merely two forms of the same name, both meaning, "the father is exalted"; another variant form is Abiram (Nm 16:1; 1 Kgs 16:34). The additional *-ha-* in the form Abraham is explained by popular etymology as coming from *ab-hamon goyim*, "father of a multitude of nations."

---

* [16:7] **The LORD's angel**: a manifestation of God in human form; in v. 13 the messenger is identified with God. See note on Ex 3:2.

† [16:11] **Ishmael**: in Hebrew the name means "God has heard." It is the same Hebrew verb that is translated "heeded" in the next clause. In other ancient Near Eastern texts, the name commemorated the divine answer to the parents' prayer to have a child, but here it is broadened to mean that God has "heard" Hagar's plight. In vv. 13–14, the verb "to see" is similarly broadened to describe God's special care for those in need.

‡ [16:12] **Alongside**: lit., "against the face of"; the same phrase is used of the lands of Ishmael's descendants in 25:18. It can be translated "in opposition to" (Dt 21:16; Jb 1:11; 6:28; 21:31), but here more likely means that Ishmael's settlement was near but not in the promised land.

§ [16:13] **God who sees me**: Hebrew *el-ro'i* is multivalent, meaning either "God of seeing," i.e., extends his protection to me, or "God sees," which can imply seeing human suffering (29:32; Ex 2:25; Is 57:18; 58:3). It is probable that Hagar means to express both of these aspects. **Remained alive**: for the ancient notion that a person died on seeing God, see Gn 32:31; Ex 20:19; Dt 4:33; Jgs 13:22.

---

e. [16:7] Ex 15:22.
f. [16:10] Gn 17:20; 21:13, 18; 25:12–18.
g. [16:12] Gn 21:20; 25:18.
h. [16:13] Gn 24:62.

i. [16:15] Gn 16:2; Gal 4:22.

a. [17:1] Gn 35:11; Ex 6:3.
b. [17:2] Gn 12:2; 13:16; Ex 32:13.
c. [17:4] Sir 44:21; Rom 4:17.
d. [17:5] Neh 9:7.
e. [17:7] Ps 105:42; Lk 1:72–73; Gal 3:16.

GN

give to you and to your descendants after you the land in which you are now residing as aliens, the whole land of Canaan, as a permanent possession; and I will be their God.*f* 9God said to Abraham: For your part, you and your descendants after you must keep my covenant throughout the ages. 10This is the covenant between me and you and your descendants after you that you must keep: every male among you shall be circumcised.*g* 11Circumcise the flesh of your foreskin. That will be the sign of the covenant between me and you.*h* 12Throughout the ages, every male among you, when he is eight days old, shall be circumcised, including houseborn slaves and those acquired with money from any foreigner who is not of your descendants.*i* 13Yes, both the houseborn slaves and those acquired with money must be circumcised. Thus my covenant will be in your flesh as an everlasting covenant. 14If a male is uncircumcised, that is, if the flesh of his foreskin has not been cut away, such a one will be cut off from his people; he has broken my covenant.

15God further said to Abraham: As for Sarai your wife, do not call her Sarai; her name will be Sarah.† 16I will bless her, and I will give you a son by her. Her also will I bless; she will give rise to nations, and rulers of peoples will issue from her.*j* 17Abraham fell face down and laughed‡ as he said to himself, "Can a child be born to a man who is a hundred years old? Can Sarah give birth at ninety?"*k* 18So Abraham

said to God, "If only Ishmael could live in your favor!" 19God replied: Even so, your wife Sarah is to bear you a son, and you shall call him Isaac. It is with him that I will maintain my covenant as an everlasting covenant and with his descendants after him.*l* 20Now as for Ishmael, I will heed you: I hereby bless him. I will make him fertile and will multiply him exceedingly. He will become the father of twelve chieftains, and I will make of him a great nation.*m* 21But my covenant I will maintain with Isaac, whom Sarah shall bear to you by this time next year.*n* 22When he had finished speaking with Abraham, God departed from him.

23Then Abraham took his son Ishmael and all his slaves, whether born in his house or acquired with his money—every male among the members of Abraham's household—and he circumcised the flesh of their foreskins on that same day, as God had told him to do. 24Abraham was ninety-nine years old when the flesh of his foreskin was circumcised,*o* 25and his son Ishmael was thirteen years old when the flesh of his foreskin was circumcised. 26Thus, on that same day Abraham and his son Ishmael were circumcised; 27and all the males of his household, including the slaves born in his house or acquired with his money from foreigners, were circumcised with him.

CHAPTER 18

Abraham's Visitors. 1§The Lord appeared to Abraham by the oak of Mamre, as he sat in the entrance of his tent, while the day was growing hot. 2Looking up, he saw three men

---

* [17:10] **Circumcised**: circumcision was widely practiced in the ancient world, usually as an initiation rite for males at puberty. By shifting the time of circumcision to the eighth day after birth, biblical religion made it no longer a "rite of passage" but the sign of the eternal covenant between God and the community descending from Abraham.

† [17:15] Sarai and Sarah are variant forms of the same name, both meaning "princess."

‡ [17:17] **Laughed**: *yishaq*, which is also the Hebrew form of the name "Isaac"; similar explanations of the name are given in Gn 18:12 and 21:6.

f. [17:8] Ex 32:13; Dt 1:8; 14:2; Lk 1:55; Acts 7:5.
g. [17:10] Jn 7:22; Acts 7:8; Rom 4:11.
h. [17:11] Sir 44:20.
i. [17:12] Lv 12:3; Lk 1:59; 2:21.
j. [17:16] Gn 18:10; Gal 4:23.
k. [17:17] Rom 4:19; Heb 11:11–12.

§ [18:1] Chapters 18 and 19 combined form a continuous narrative, concluding the story of Abraham and his nephew Lot that began in 13:2–18. The mysterious men visit Abraham in Mamre to promise him and Sarah a child the following year (18:1–15) and then visit Lot in Sodom to investigate and then to punish the corrupt city (19:1–29). Between the two visits, Abraham questions God about the justice of punishing Sodom (18:16–33). At the end of the destruction of Sodom, there is a short narrative about Lot as the ancestor of Moab and the Ammonites (19:30–38).

l. [17:19] Gn 11:30; 21:2; Ex 32:13; Sir 44:22.
m. [17:20] Gn 16:10; 21:13, 18; 25:12–16.
n. [17:21] Gn 18:14; 21:2; 26:2–5; Rom 9:7.
o. [17:24] Gn 17:10; Rom 4:11.

standing near him. When he saw them, he ran from the entrance of the tent to greet them; and bowing to the ground,[a] [3]he said: "Sir,* if it please you, do not go on past your servant. [4]Let some water be brought, that you may bathe your feet, and then rest under the tree. [5]Now that you have come to your servant, let me bring you a little food, that you may refresh yourselves; and afterward you may go on your way." "Very well," they replied, "do as you have said."

[6]Abraham hurried into the tent to Sarah and said, "Quick, three measures[†] of bran flour! Knead it and make bread." [7]He ran to the herd, picked out a tender, choice calf, and gave it to a servant, who quickly prepared it. [8]Then he got some curds[‡] and milk, as well as the calf that had been prepared, and set these before them, waiting on them under the tree while they ate.

[9]"Where is your wife Sarah?" they asked him. "There in the tent," he replied. [10]One of them[§] said, "I will return to you about this time next year, and Sarah will then have a son." Sarah was listening at the entrance of the tent, just behind him.[b] [11]Now Abraham and Sarah were old, advanced in years, and Sarah had stopped having her menstrual periods.[c] [12]So Sarah laughed[¶] to herself and said, "Now that I am worn out and my husband is old, am I still to have sexual pleasure?" [13]But the LORD said to Abraham: "Why did Sarah laugh and say, 'Will I really bear a child, old as I am?' [14]Is anything too marvelous for the LORD to do? At the appointed time, about this time next year, I will return to you, and

Sarah will have a son."[d] [15]Sarah lied, saying, "I did not laugh," because she was afraid. But he said, "Yes, you did."

Abraham Intercedes for Sodom. [16]With Abraham walking with them to see them on their way, the men set out from there and looked down toward Sodom. [17]The LORD considered: Shall I hide from Abraham what I am about to do, [18]now that he is to become a great and mighty nation, and all the nations of the earth are to find blessing in him?[e] [19]Indeed, I have singled him out that he may direct his children and his household in the future to keep the way of the LORD by doing what is right and just, so that the LORD may put into effect for Abraham the promises he made about him. [20][f]So the LORD said: The outcry against Sodom and Gomorrah is so great, and their sin so grave,** [21]that I must go down to see whether or not their actions are as bad as the cry against them that comes to me. I mean to find out.

[22]As the men turned and walked on toward Sodom, Abraham remained standing before the LORD. [23]Then Abraham drew near and said: "Will you really sweep away the righteous with the wicked? [24]Suppose there were fifty righteous people in the city; would you really sweep away and not spare the place for the sake of the fifty righteous people within it? [25]Far be it from you to do such a thing, to kill the righteous with the wicked, so that the righteous and the wicked are treated alike! Far be it from you! Should not the judge of all the world do what is just?"[g] [26]The LORD

---

* [18:3] Abraham addresses the leader of the group, whom he does not yet recognize as the Lord; in the next two verses he speaks to all three men. The other two are later (Gn 19:1) identified as angels. The shifting numbers and identification of the visitors are a narrative way of expressing the mysterious presence of God.
† [18:6] **Three measures:** Hebrew *seah*; three seahs equal one ephah, about half a bushel.
‡ [18:8] **Curds:** a type of soft cheese or yogurt.
§ [18:10] **One of them:** i.e., the Lord.
¶ [18:12] **Sarah laughed:** a play on the verb "laugh," which prefigures the name of Isaac; see note on 17:17.

a. [18:2] Heb 13:1–2.
b. [18:10] Gn 17:19; 21:1; 2 Kgs 4:16; Rom 9:9.
c. [18:11] Gn 17:17; Rom 4:19; Heb 11:11–12.

** [18:20] The immorality of the cities was already hinted at in 13:13, when Lot made his choice to live there. The "outcry" comes from the victims of the injustice and violence rampant in the city, which will shortly be illustrated in the treatment of the visitors. The outcry of the Hebrews under the harsh treatment of Pharaoh (Ex 3:7) came up to God who reacts in anger at mistreatment of the poor (cf. Ex 22:21–23; Is 5:7). Sodom and Gomorrah became types of sinful cities in biblical literature. Is 1:9–10; 3:9 sees their sin as lack of social justice, Ez 16:46–51, as disregard for the poor, and Jer 23:14, as general immorality. In the Genesis story, the sin is violation of the sacred duty of hospitality by the threatened rape of Lot's guests.

d. [18:14] Mt 19:26; Mk 10:27; Lk 1:37; 18:27; Rom 4:21.
e. [18:18] Lk 1:55.
f. [18:20] Gn 19:13; Is 3:9; Lk 17:28; Jude 7.
g. [18:25] Dt 32:4; Jb 8:3, 20; Wis 12:15.

replied: If I find fifty righteous people in the city of Sodom, I will spare the whole place for their sake. **27**Abraham spoke up again: "See how I am presuming to speak to my Lord, though I am only dust and ashes!*h* **28**What if there are five less than fifty righteous people? Will you destroy the whole city because of those five?" I will not destroy it, he answered, if I find forty-five there. **29**But Abraham persisted, saying, "What if only forty are found there?" He replied: I will refrain from doing it for the sake of the forty. **30**Then he said, "Do not let my Lord be angry if I go on. What if only thirty are found there?" He replied: I will refrain from doing it if I can find thirty there. **31**Abraham went on, "Since I have thus presumed to speak to my Lord, what if there are no more than twenty?" I will not destroy it, he answered, for the sake of the twenty. **32**But he persisted: "Please, do not let my Lord be angry if I speak up this last time. What if ten are found there?" For the sake of the ten, he replied, I will not destroy it.*i*

33The LORD departed as soon as he had finished speaking with Abraham, and Abraham returned home.

CHAPTER 19

Destruction of Sodom and Gomorrah.*** **1**The two angels reached Sodom in the evening, as Lot was sitting at the gate of Sodom. When Lot saw them, he got up to greet them; and bowing down with his face to the ground, **2**he said, "Please, my lords,*†* come aside into your servant's house for the night, and bathe your feet; you can get up early to continue your journey." But they replied, "No, we will pass the night in the town square."*a* **3**He urged

them so strongly, however, that they turned aside to his place and entered his house. He prepared a banquet for them, baking unleavened bread, and they dined.

4*b*Before they went to bed, the townsmen of Sodom, both young and old—all the people to the last man—surrounded the house. **5**They called to Lot and said to him, "Where are the men who came to your house tonight? Bring them out to us that we may have sexual relations with them." **6**Lot went out to meet them at the entrance. When he had shut the door behind him, **7**he said, "I beg you, my brothers, do not do this wicked thing! **8**I have two daughters who have never had sexual relations with men. Let me bring them out to you,*‡* and you may do to them as you please. But do not do anything to these men, for they have come under the shelter of my roof." **9**They replied, "Stand back! This man," they said, "came here as a resident alien, and now he dares to give orders! We will treat you worse than them!" With that, they pressed hard against Lot, moving in closer to break down the door.*c* **10**But his guests put out their hands, pulled Lot inside with them, and closed the door; **11**they struck the men at the entrance of the house, small and great, with such a blinding light*§* that they were utterly unable to find the doorway.

12Then the guests said to Lot: "Who else belongs to you here? Sons-in-law, your sons, your daughters, all who belong to you in the city—take them away from this place!*d* **13**We are about to destroy this place, for the outcry reaching the LORD against those here is so great that the LORD has sent us to destroy it."*e* **14**So Lot went out and spoke to his sons-in-law, who had

***** [19:1–29] The story takes place in one day (counting a day from the previous evening): evening (v. 1), dawn (v. 15), and sunrise (v. 23). The passage resembles Jgs 19:15–25, which suggests dependence of one story on the other.

† [19:2] **My lords**: Lot does not yet know that the men are God's messengers; cf. 18:3.

h. [18:27] Sir 10:9; 17:27.
i. [18:32] Jer 5:1; Ez 22:30.

a. [19:2] Heb 13:1–2.

‡ [19:8] **Let me bring them out to you**: the authority of a patriarch within his house was virtually absolute. Lot's extreme response of offering his daughters to a violent mob seems to be motivated by the obligation of hospitality.

§ [19:11] **Blinding light**: an extraordinary flash that temporarily dazed the wicked men and revealed to Lot the true nature of his guests.

b. [19:4–9] Jgs 19:22–25; Jude 7.
c. [19:9] Gn 13:12; 2 Pt 2:7–8.
d. [19:12] 2 Pt 2:7–9.
e. [19:13] Is 1:7, 9; Ez 16:49–50; Zep 2:9.

contracted marriage with his daughters.* "Come on, leave this place," he told them; "the LORD is about to destroy the city." But his sons-in-law thought he was joking.

¹⁵As dawn was breaking, the angels urged Lot on, saying, "Come on! Take your wife with you and your two daughters who are here, or you will be swept away in the punishment of the city." ¹⁶When he hesitated, the men, because of the LORD's compassion for him, seized his hand and the hands of his wife and his two daughters and led them to safety outside the city. ¹⁷As soon as they had brought them outside, they said: "Flee for your life! Do not look back or stop anywhere on the Plain. Flee to the hills at once, or you will be swept away."ᶠ ¹⁸"Oh, no, my lords!" Lot replied to them. ¹⁹"You have already shown favor to your servant, doing me the great kindness of saving my life. But I cannot flee to the hills, or the disaster will overtake and kill me. ²⁰Look, this town ahead is near enough to escape to. It is only a small place.† Let me flee there—is it not a small place?—to save my life." ²¹"Well, then," he replied, "I grant you this favor too. I will not overthrow the town you have mentioned. ²²Hurry, escape there! I cannot do anything until you arrive there." That is why the town is called Zoar.ᵍ

²³The sun had risen over the earth when Lot arrived in Zoar, ²⁴and the LORD rained down sulfur upon Sodom and Gomorrah, fire from the LORD out of heaven.ʰ ²⁵He overthrew‡ those cities and the whole Plain, together with the inhabitants of the cities and the produce of the soil.ⁱ ²⁶But Lot's wife looked back, and she was turned into a pillar of salt.ʲ

²⁷The next morning Abraham hurried to the place where he had stood before the LORD. ²⁸As he looked down toward Sodom and Gomorrah and the whole region of the Plain,§ he saw smoke over the land rising like the smoke from a kiln.ᵏ

²⁹When God destroyed the cities of the Plain, he remembered Abraham and sent Lot away from the upheaval that occurred when God overthrew the cities where Lot had been living.

Moabites and Ammonites.¶ ³⁰Since Lot was afraid to stay in Zoar, he and his two daughters went up from Zoar and settled in the hill country, where he lived with his two daughters in a cave. ³¹The firstborn said to the younger: "Our father is getting old, and there is not a man in the land to have intercourse with us as is the custom everywhere. ³²Come, let us ply our father with wine and then lie with him, that we may ensure posterity by our father." ³³So that night they plied their father with wine, and the firstborn went in and lay with her father; but he was not aware of her lying down or getting up. ³⁴The next day the firstborn said to the younger: "Last night I lay with my father. Let us ply him with wine again tonight, and then you go in and lie with him, that we may ensure posterity by our father." ³⁵So that night, too, they plied their father with wine, and then the younger one went in and lay

---

* [19:14] It is uncertain whether Lot's sons-in-law were fully married to his daughters or only "engaged" to them (Israelite "engagement" was the first part of the marriage ceremony), or even whether the daughters involved were the same as, or different from, the two daughters who were still in their father's house.

† [19:20] **A small place**: the Hebrew word *misar*, lit., "a little thing," has the same root consonants as the name of the town Zoar in v. 22.

‡ [19:25] **Overthrew**: this term, lit., "turned upside down," is used consistently to describe the destruction of the cities of the Plain. The imagery of earthquake and subsequent fire fits the geology of this region.

f. [19:17] Wis 10:6.
g. [19:22] Wis 10:6.
h. [19:24] Ps 9:6; 11:6; 107:34; Wis 10:7; Sir 16:8; Is 1:9; Lk 17:29; 2 Pt 2:6.

---

§ [19:28–29] In a deft narrative detail, Abraham looks down from the height east of Hebron, from which he could easily see the region at the southern end of the Dead Sea, where the cities of the Plain were probably located.

¶ [19:30–38] This Israelite tale about the origin of Israel's neighbors east of the Jordan and the Dead Sea was told partly to ridicule these ethnically related but rival nations and partly to give popular etymologies for their names. The stylized nature of the story is seen in the names of the daughters ("the firstborn" and "the younger"), the ease with which they fool their father, and the identical descriptions of the encounters.

i. [19:25] Dt 29:22; Is 13:19; Jer 50:40; Lam 4:6; Am 4:11.
j. [19:26] Wis 10:7; Lk 17:32.
k. [19:28] Rev 9:2; 14:10–11.

with him; but he was not aware of her lying down or getting up.

³⁶Thus the two daughters of Lot became pregnant by their father. ³⁷The firstborn gave birth to a son whom she named Moab, saying, "From my father."* He is the ancestor of the Moabites of today.ˡ ³⁸The younger one, too, gave birth to a son, and she named him Ammon, saying, "The son of my kin."† He is the ancestor of the Ammonites of today.ᵐ

CHAPTER 20

Abraham at Gerar.‡ ¹From there Abraham journeyed on to the region of the Negeb, where he settled between Kadesh and Shur.§ While he resided in Gerar as an alien, ²Abraham said of his wife Sarah, "She is my sister." So Abimelech, king of Gerar, sent and took Sarah. ³But God came to Abimelech in a dream one night and said to him: You are about to die because of the woman you have taken, for she has a husband. ⁴Abimelech, who had not approached her, said: "O Lord, would you kill an innocent man? ⁵Was he not the one who told me, 'She is my sister'? She herself also stated, 'He is my brother.' I acted with pure heart and with clean hands." ⁶¶God answered him in the dream: Yes, I know you did it with a pure heart. In fact, it was I who kept you from sinning against me; that is why I did not let you touch her. ⁷So now, return the man's wife so

that he may intercede for you, since he is a prophet,** that you may live. If you do not return her, you can be sure that you and all who are yours will die.

⁸Early the next morning Abimelech called all his servants and informed them of everything that had happened, and the men were filled with fear. ⁹Then Abimelech summoned Abraham and said to him: "What have you done to us! What wrong did I do to you that you would have brought such great guilt on me and my kingdom? You have treated me in an intolerable way. ¹⁰What did you have in mind," Abimelech asked him, "that you would do such a thing?" ¹¹Abraham answered, "I thought there would be no fear of God†† in this place, and so they would kill me on account of my wife. ¹²Besides, she really is my sister,‡‡ but only my father's daughter, not my mother's; and so she became my wife. ¹³When God sent me wandering from my father's house, I asked her: 'Would you do me this favor? In whatever place we come to, say: He is my brother.'ᵃ

¹⁴Then Abimelech took flocks and herds and male and female slaves and gave them to Abraham; and he restored his wife Sarah to him. ¹⁵Then Abimelech said, "Here, my land is at your disposal; settle wherever you please." ¹⁶To Sarah he said: "I hereby give your brother a thousand shekels of silver. This will preserve your honor before all who are with you and will exonerate you before everyone." ¹⁷Abraham then interceded with God, and God restored health to Abimelech, to his wife, and his maidservants, so that they bore children; ¹⁸for the LORD had closed

---

* [19:37] **From my father**: in Hebrew, *me'abi*, similar in sound to the name "Moab."

† [19:38] **The son of my kin**: in Hebrew, *ben-ammi*, similar in sound to the name "Ammonites."

‡ [20:1–18] Abraham again passes off his wife Sarah as his sister to escape trouble in a foreign land (cf. 12:10–13:1, the J source). The story appears to draw on a different source (according to some, E) and deals with the ethical questions of the incident. Gn 26:6–11 is yet another retelling of the story, but with Isaac and Rebekah as characters instead of Abraham and Sarah.

§ [20:1] **Kadesh and Shur**: Kadesh-barnea was a major oasis on the southernmost border of Canaan, and Shur was probably the "way to Shur," the road to Egypt. Gerar was a royal city in the area, but has not been identified with certainty.

¶ [20:6] Abimelech is exonerated of blame, but by that fact not cleared of the consequences of his act. He is still under the sentence of death for abducting another man's wife; the consequences result from the deed not the intention.

** [20:7] **Prophet**: only here is Abraham explicitly called "prophet," Hebrew *nabi* (cf. Ps 105:15).

†† [20:11] **Fear of God** is the traditional though unsatisfactory rendering of Hebrew *yir'at YHWH*, literally, "revering Yahweh." The phrase refers neither to the emotion of fear nor to religious reverence of a general kind. Rather it refers to adherence to a single deity (in a polytheistic culture), honoring that deity with prayers, rituals, and obedience. The phrase occurs again in 26:24; 43:23; and 50:19. It is very common in the wisdom literature of the Bible.

‡‡ [20:12] **My sister**: Marrying one's half sister was prohibited later in Israel's history.

l. [19:37] Dt 2:9.
m. [19:38] Dt 2:19.

a. [20:13] Gn 12:13.

every womb in Abimelech's household on account of Abraham's wife Sarah.

CHAPTER 21

Birth of Isaac.[*] [1]The LORD took note of Sarah as he had said he would; the LORD did for her as he had promised.[a] [2]Sarah became pregnant and bore Abraham a son in his old age, at the set time that God had stated.[b] [3]Abraham gave the name Isaac to this son of his whom Sarah bore him.[c] [4]When his son Isaac was eight days old, Abraham circumcised him, as God had commanded.[d] [5]Abraham was a hundred years old when his son Isaac was born to him. [6]Sarah then said, "God has given me cause to laugh,[†] and all who hear of it will laugh with me.[e] [7]Who would ever have told Abraham," she added, "that Sarah would nurse children! Yet I have borne him a son in his old age." [8]The child grew and was weaned, and Abraham held a great banquet on the day of the child's weaning.

[9]Sarah noticed the son whom Hagar the Egyptian had borne to Abraham playing with her son Isaac; [10]so she demanded of Abraham: "Drive out that slave and her son! No son of that slave is going to share the inheritance with my son Isaac!"[f] [11]Abraham was greatly distressed because it concerned a son of his.[‡]

[12]But God said to Abraham: Do not be distressed about the boy or about your slave woman. Obey Sarah, no matter what she asks of you; for it is through Isaac that descendants will bear your name.[g] [13]As for the son of the slave woman, I will make a nation of him also,[§] since he too is your offspring.

[14]Early the next morning Abraham got some bread and a skin of water and gave them to Hagar. Then, placing the child on her back,[¶] he sent her away. As she roamed aimlessly in the wilderness of Beer-sheba, [15]the water in the skin was used up. So she put the child down under one of the bushes, [16]and then went and sat down opposite him, about a bowshot away; for she said to herself, "I cannot watch the child die." As she sat opposite him, she wept aloud. [17]God heard the boy's voice, and God's angel called to Hagar from heaven: "What is the matter, Hagar? Do not fear; God has heard the boy's voice in this plight of his.[h] [18]Get up, lift up the boy and hold him by the hand; for I will make of him a great nation." [19]Then God opened her eyes, and she saw a well of water. She went and filled the skin with water, and then let the boy drink.

[20]God was with the boy as he grew up. He lived in the wilderness and became an expert bowman. [21]He lived in the wilderness of Paran. His mother got a wife for him from the land of Egypt.

---

* [21:1–21] The long-awaited birth of Isaac parallels the birth of Ishmael in chap. 16, precipitating a rivalry and expulsion as in that chapter. Though this chapter is unified, the focus of vv. 1–7 is exclusively on Sarah and Isaac, and the focus of vv. 8–21 is exclusively on Hagar and Ishmael. The promise of a son to the barren Sarah and elderly Abraham has been central to the previous chapters and now that promise comes true with the birth of Isaac. The other great promise, that of land, will be resolved, at least in an anticipatory way, in Abraham's purchase of the cave at Machpelah in chap. 23. The parallel births of the two boys has influenced the Lucan birth narratives of John the Baptist and Jesus (Lk 1–2).

† [21:6] **Laugh:** for the third time (cf. 17:17 and 18:12) there is laughter, playing on the similarity in Hebrew between the pronunciation of the name Isaac and words associated with laughter.

‡ [21:11] **A son of his:** Abraham is the father of both boys, but Sarah is the mother only of Isaac. Abraham is very concerned that Ishmael have a sufficient inheritance.

a. [21:1] Gn 17:19; 18:10.
b. [21:2] Gal 4:23; Heb 11:11.
c. [21:3] Mt 1:2; Lk 3:34.
d. [21:4] Gn 17:10–14; Acts 7:8.
e. [21:6] Gn 17:17.
f. [21:10] Jgs 11:2; Gal 4:30.

§ [21:13] **I will make a nation of him also:** Ishmael's descendants are named in 25:12–18.

¶ [21:14] **Placing the child on her back:** a reading based on an emendation of the traditional Hebrew text. In the traditional Hebrew text, Abraham put the bread and the waterskin on Hagar's back, while her son apparently walked beside her. In this way the traditional Hebrew text harmonizes the data of the Priestly source, in which Ishmael would have been at least fourteen years old when Isaac was born; compare 16:16 with 21:5; cf. 17:25. But in the present Elohist (?) story, Ishmael is obviously a little boy, not much older than Isaac; cf. vv. 15, 18.

g. [21:12] Rom 9:7; Heb 11:18.
h. [21:17] Gn 16:7.

GN

The Covenant at Beer-sheba. 22*At that time Abimelech, accompanied by Phicol, the commander of his army, said to Abraham: "God is with you in everything you do. ²³So now, swear to me by God at this place† that you will not deal falsely with me or with my progeny and posterity, but will act as loyally toward me and the land in which you reside as I have acted toward you." ²⁴Abraham replied, "I so swear." ²⁵Abraham, however, reproached Abimelech about a well that Abimelech's servants had seized by force. ²⁶"I have no idea who did that," Abimelech replied. "In fact, you never told me about it, nor did I ever hear of it until now."

²⁷Then Abraham took sheep and cattle and gave them to Abimelech and the two made a covenant. ²⁸Abraham also set apart seven ewe lambs of the flock, ²⁹and Abimelech asked him, "What is the purpose of these seven ewe lambs that you have set apart?" ³⁰Abraham answered, "The seven ewe lambs you shall accept from me that you may be my witness that I dug this well." ³¹This is why the place is called Beer-sheba; the two of them took an oath there. ³²When they had thus made the covenant in Beer-sheba, Abimelech, along with Phicol, the commander of his army, left to return to the land of the Philistines.‡

³³Abraham planted a tamarisk at Beer-sheba, and there he invoked by name the LORD, God the Eternal.§

³⁴Abraham resided in the land of the Philistines for a long time.

CHAPTER 22

The Testing of Abraham.¶ ¹Some time afterward, God put Abraham to the test and said to him: Abraham! "Here I am!" he replied.ᵃ ²Then God said: Take your son Isaac, your only one, whom you love, and go to the land of Moriah. There offer him up as a burnt offering on one of the heights that I will point out to you.ᵇ ³Early the next morning Abraham saddled his donkey, took with him two of his servants and his son Isaac, and after cutting the wood for the burnt offering, set out for the place of which God had told him.

⁴On the third day Abraham caught sight of the place from a distance. ⁵Abraham said to his servants: "Stay here with the donkey, while the boy and I go on over there. We will worship and then come back to you." ⁶So Abraham took the wood for the burnt offering and laid it on his son Isaac, while he himself carried the fire and the knife. As the two walked on together, ⁷Isaac spoke to his father Abraham. "Father!" he said. "Here I am," he replied. Isaac continued, "Here are the fire and the wood, but where is the sheep for the burnt offering?" ⁸"My son," Abraham answered, "God will provide the sheep for the burnt offering." Then the two walked on together.

---

* [21:22] Of the two related promises of progeny and land, that of progeny has been fulfilled in the previous chapter. Now the claim on the land begins to be solidified by Abimelech's recognition of Abraham's claim on the well at Beer-sheba; it will be furthered by Abraham's purchase of the cave at Machpelah in chap. 23. Two levels of editing are visible in the story: (1) vv. 22–24, 27, 32, the general covenant with Abimelech; (2) vv. 25–26, 28–30, 31, Abraham's claim on the well. Both versions play on the root of the Hebrew word *sheba'*, which means "seven" and "swear," and the place name Beer-sheba.

† [21:23] **This place**: Beer-sheba (v. 31). Abimelech had come from Gerar (20:2), about thirty miles west of Beer-sheba.

‡ [21:32] **Philistines**: one of the Sea Peoples, who migrated from Mycenaean Greece around 1200 B.C. and settled on the coastland of Canaan, becoming a principal rival of Israel. Non-biblical texts do not use the term "Philistine" before ca. 1200 B.C.; it is probable that this usage and those in chap. 26 are anachronistic, perhaps applying a later ethnic term for an earlier, less-known one.

§ [21:33] **God the Eternal**: in Hebrew, *'el 'olam*, perhaps the name of the deity of the pre-Israelite sanctuary at Beer-sheba, but used by Abraham as a title of God; cf. Is 40:28.

¶ [22:1–19] The divine demand that Abraham sacrifice to God the son of promise is the greatest of his trials; after the successful completion of the test, he has only to buy a burial site for Sarah and find a wife for Isaac. The story is widely recognized as a literary masterpiece, depicting in a few lines God as the absolute Lord, inscrutable yet ultimately gracious, and Abraham, acting in moral grandeur as the great ancestor of Israel. Abraham speaks simply, with none of the wordy evasions of chaps. 13 and 21. The style is laconic; motivations and thoughts are not explained, and the reader cannot but wonder at the scene. In vv. 15–18, the angel repeats the seventh and climactic promise. **Moriah**: the mountain is not given a precise geographical location here, though 2 Chr 3:1 identifies Moriah as the mountain of Jerusalem where Solomon built the Temple; Abraham is thus the first to worship there. The word "Moriah" is a play on the verb "to see" (Heb. *ra'ah*); the wordplay is continued in v. 8, "God will provide (lit., "see")" and in v. 14, Yahweh-yireh, meaning "the Lord will see/provide."

a. [22:1] Sir 44:20.
b. [22:2] 2 Chr 3:1; 1 Mc 2:52; Heb 11:17.

[9] When they came to the place of which God had told him, Abraham built an altar there and arranged the wood on it. Next he bound* his son Isaac, and put him on top of the wood on the altar.[c] [10] Then Abraham reached out and took the knife to slaughter his son.[d] [11] But the angel of the LORD called to him from heaven, "Abraham, Abraham!" "Here I am," he answered. [12] "Do not lay your hand on the boy," said the angel. "Do not do the least thing to him. For now I know that you fear God, since you did not withhold from me your son, your only one."[e] [13] Abraham looked up and saw a single ram caught by its horns in the thicket. So Abraham went and took the ram and offered it up as a burnt offering in place of his son.† [14] Abraham named that place Yahweh-yireh;‡ hence people today say, "On the mountain the LORD will provide."

[15] §A second time the angel of the LORD called to Abraham from heaven [16] f and said: "I swear by my very self— oracle of the LORD—that because you acted as you did in not withholding from me your son, your only one, [17] I will bless you and make your descendants as countless as the stars of the sky and the sands of the seashore; your descendants will take possession of the gates of their enemies,[g] [18] and in your descendants all the nations of the earth will find blessing, because you obeyed my command."[h]

[19] Abraham then returned to his servants, and they set out together for Beer-sheba, where Abraham lived.

Nahor's Descendants.¶ [20] Some time afterward, the news came to Abraham: "Milcah too has borne sons to your brother Nahor: [21] Uz, his firstborn, his brother Buz, Kemuel the father of Aram, [22] Chesed, Hazo, Pildash, Jidlaph, and Bethuel." [23] Bethuel became the father of Rebekah. These eight Milcah bore to Nahor, Abraham's brother. [24] His concubine, whose name was Reumah, also bore children: Tebah, Gaham, Tahash, and Maacah.

CHAPTER 23

Purchase of a Burial Plot.** [1] The span of Sarah's life was one hundred and twenty-seven years. [2] She died in Kiriath-arba—now Hebron—in the land of Canaan, and Abraham proceeded to mourn and weep for her. [3] Then he left the side of his deceased wife and addressed the Hittites:†† [4] "Although I am a resident alien‡‡

¶ [22:20–24] The descendants to the second generation of Nahor, Abraham's brother, who married Milcah. Of Terah's three sons (11:27), the oldest, Abraham, fathered Isaac (21:1–7), and the youngest, Haran (who died in Ur), fathered Lot. Abraham is now told that Nahor had eight children by Milcah and four by his concubine Reumah. Apart from the notice about the children born to Abraham by his second wife, Keturah (25:1–6), all the information about Terah's family to the second generation is now complete. It is noteworthy that Jacob will, like Nahor, have eight children by his wives and four by his concubines.

** [23:1–20] The occasion for purchasing the land is the need for a burial site for Sarah, for it would be unthinkable to bury Sarah outside of the promised land. One of the two great promises to Abraham, that of progeny, has been fulfilled (21:1–7). And now the promise of land is to be fulfilled, through a kind of down payment on the full possession that will take place only with the conquest under Joshua and during the reign of David. This purchase has been prepared for by Abimelech's recognition of Abraham's claim to the well at Beer-sheba (21:22–34). Among the ancestral stories this narrative is one of two that are entirely from the P source (chap. 17 being the other). The Priestly writers may have intended to encourage the generation of the exile by a renewed hope of repossessing their land.

†† [23:3] The Hittites: in the Bible the term is applied to several different groups—inhabitants of the second-millennium Hittite empire in Asia Minor and northern Syria, residents of the Neo-Hittite kingdoms in northern Syria in the first part of the first millennium, and (following Assyrian terminology) the inhabitants of Syria and Palestine. The third group is meant here.

‡‡ [23:4] A resident alien: such a one would normally not have the right to own property. The importance of Abraham's purchase of the field in Machpelah, which is worded in technical legal terms, lies in the fact that it gave his descendants their first, though small, land rights in the country that God had promised the patriarch they would one day inherit as their own. Abraham therefore insists on purchasing the field and not receiving it as a gift.

---

* [22:9] **Bound**: the Hebrew verb is 'aqad, from which is derived the noun Akedah, "the binding (of Isaac)," the traditional Jewish name for this incident.

† [22:13] While the Bible recognizes that firstborn males belong to God (Ex 13:11–16; 34:19–20), and provides an alternate sacrifice to redeem firstborn sons, the focus here is on Abraham's being tested by God (v. 1). But the widely attested practice of child sacrifice underscores, for all its horror today, the realism of the test.

‡ [22:14] **Yahweh-yireh**: a Hebrew expression meaning "the Lord will see/provide." See note on vv. 1–19.

§ [22:15–19] The seventh and climactic statement of the blessings to Abraham. Unlike the other statements, which were purely promissory, this one is presented as a reward for Abraham's extraordinary trust.

---

c. [22:9] Jas 2:21.

d. [22:10] Wis 10:5.

e. [22:12] Rom 8:32; 1 Jn 4:9.

f. [22:16–17] Gn 15:5; Ex 32:13; Lk 1:73; Rom 4:13; Heb 6:13–14; 11:12.

g. [22:17] Gn 24:60.

h. [22:18] Gn 12:3; 18:18; 26:4; Sir 44:21; Acts 3:25; Gal 3:16.

among you, sell me from your holdings a burial place, that I may bury my deceased wife."ᵃ ⁵The Hittites answered Abraham: "Please, ⁶sir, listen to us! You are a mighty leader among us. Bury your dead in the choicest of our burial sites. None of us would deny you his burial ground for the burial of your dead." ⁷Abraham, however, proceeded to bow low before the people of the land, the Hittites, ⁸and said to them: "If you will allow me room for burial of my dead, listen to me! Intercede for me with Ephron, son of Zohar, ⁹so that he will sell me the cave of Machpelah that he owns; it is at the edge of his field. Let him sell it to me in your presence at its full price for a burial place."

¹⁰Now Ephron was sitting with the Hittites. So Ephron the Hittite replied to Abraham in the hearing of the Hittites, all who entered the gate of his city: ¹¹"Please, sir, listen to me! I give you both the field and the cave in it; in the presence of my people I give it to you. Bury your dead!" ¹²But Abraham, after bowing low before the people of the land, ¹³addressed Ephron in the hearing of these men: "If only you would please listen to me! I will pay you the price of the field. Accept it from me, that I may bury my dead there." ¹⁴Ephron replied to Abraham, "Please, ¹⁵sir, listen to me! A piece of land worth four hundred shekels* of silver—what is that between you and me? Bury your dead!" ¹⁶ᵇAbraham accepted Ephron's terms; he weighed out to him the silver that Ephron had stipulated in the hearing of the Hittites, four hundred shekels of silver at the current market value.†

¹⁷ᶜThus Ephron's field in Machpelah, facing Mamre, together with its cave and all the trees anywhere within its limits, was conveyed ¹⁸to Abraham by purchase in the presence of the Hittites, all who entered the gate of Ephron's city. ¹⁹After this, Abraham buried his wife Sarah in the cave of the field of Machpelah, facing Mamre—now Hebron—in the land of Canaan. ²⁰Thus the field with its cave was transferred from the Hittites to Abraham as a burial place.

CHAPTER 24

Isaac and Rebekah.‡ ¹Abraham was old, having seen many days, and the LORD had blessed him in every way. ²ᵃAbraham said to the senior servant of his household, who had charge of all his possessions: "Put your hand under my thigh,§ ³and I will make you swear by the LORD, the God of heaven and the God of earth, that you will not take a wife for my son from the daughters of the Canaanites among whom I live,ᵇ ⁴but that you will go to my own land and to my relatives to get a wife for my son Isaac." ⁵The servant asked him: "What if the woman is unwilling to follow me to this land? Should I then take your son back to the land from which you came?" ⁶Abraham told him, "Never take my son back there for any reason! ⁷The LORD, the God of heaven, who took me from my father's house and the land of my relatives, and who confirmed by oath

‡ [24:1–67] The story of Abraham and Sarah is drawing to a close. The promises of progeny (21:1–7) and land (chap. 23) have been fulfilled and Sarah has died (23:1–2). Abraham's last duty is to ensure that his son Isaac shares in the promises. Isaac must take a wife from his own people (vv. 3–7), so the promises may be fulfilled. The extraordinary length of this story and its development of a single theme contrast strikingly with the spare style of the preceding Abraham and Sarah stories. It points ahead to the Jacob and Joseph stories.
    The length of the story is partly caused by its meticulous attention to the sign (vv. 12–14), its fulfillment (vv. 15–20), and the servant's retelling of sign and fulfillment to Rebekah's family to win their consent (vv. 34–49).
§ [24:2] **Put your hand under my thigh**: the symbolism of this act was apparently connected with the Hebrew concept of children issuing from their father's "thigh" (the literal meaning of "direct descendants" in 46:26; Ex 1:5). Perhaps the man who took such an oath was thought to bring the curse of sterility on himself if he did not fulfill his sworn promise. Jacob made Joseph swear in the same way (Gn 47:29). In both these instances, the oath was taken to carry out the last request of a man upon his death.

* [23:15] **Four hundred shekels**: probably an exorbitant sum; Jeremiah (32:9) paid only seventeen shekels for his field in Anathoth, though the Babylonian invasion no doubt helped to reduce the price.
† [23:16] **The current market value**: the standard weight called a shekel varied according to time and place.

a. [23:4] Gn 33:19; Acts 7:16; Heb 11:9.
b. [23:16] Acts 7:16.
c. [23:17–18] Gn 49:29–30.

a. [24:2–3] Gn 47:29.
b. [24:3] Gn 24:37; 28:1–2; Jgs 14:3; Tb 4:12.

the promise he made to me, 'I will give this land to your descendants'—he will send his angel before you, and you will get a wife for my son there.[c] [8]If the woman is unwilling to follow you, you will be released from this oath to me. But never take my son back there!" [9]So the servant put his hand under the thigh of his master Abraham and swore to him concerning this matter.

[10]The servant then took ten of his master's camels, and bearing all kinds of gifts from his master, he made his way to the city of Nahor* in Aram Naharaim. [11]Near evening, at the time when women go out to draw water, he made the camels kneel by the well outside the city. [12]Then he said: "LORD, God of my master Abraham, let it turn out favorably for me[†] today and thus deal graciously with my master Abraham. [13]While I stand here at the spring and the daughters of the townspeople are coming out to draw water, [14]if I say to a young woman, 'Please lower your jug, that I may drink,' and she answers, 'Drink, and I will water your camels, too,' then she is the one whom you have decided upon for your servant Isaac. In this way I will know that you have dealt graciously with my master."

[15d]He had scarcely finished speaking when Rebekah—who was born to Bethuel, son of Milcah, the wife of Abraham's brother Nahor—came out with a jug on her shoulder. [16]The young woman was very beautiful, a virgin, untouched by man. She went down to the spring and filled her jug. As she came up, [17]the servant ran toward her and said, "Please give me a sip of water from your jug." [18]"Drink,

sir," she replied, and quickly lowering the jug into her hand, she gave him a drink. [19]When she had finished giving him a drink, she said, "I will draw water for your camels, too, until they have finished drinking." [20]With that, she quickly emptied her jug into the drinking trough and ran back to the well to draw more water, until she had drawn enough for all the camels. [21]The man watched her the whole time, silently waiting to learn whether or not the LORD had made his journey successful. [22]When the camels had finished drinking, the man took out a gold nose-ring weighing half a shekel, and two gold bracelets weighing ten shekels for her wrists. [23]Then he asked her: "Whose daughter are you? Tell me, please. And is there a place in your father's house for us to spend the night?" [24]She answered: "I am the daughter of Bethuel the son of Milcah, whom she bore to Nahor. [25]We have plenty of straw and fodder," she added, "and also a place to spend the night." [26]The man then knelt and bowed down to the LORD, [27]saying: "Blessed be the LORD, the God of my master Abraham, who has not let his kindness and fidelity toward my master fail. As for me, the LORD has led me straight to the house of my master's brother."

[28]Then the young woman ran off and told her mother's household what had happened. [29e]Now Rebekah had a brother named Laban. Laban rushed outside to the man at the spring. [30‡]When he saw the nose-ring and the bracelets on his sister's arms and when he heard Rebekah repeating what the man had said to her, he went to him while he was standing by the camels at the spring. [31]He said: "Come, blessed of the LORD! Why are you standing outside when I have made the house

---

* [24:10] **Nahor**: it is uncertain whether this is the place where Abraham's brother Nahor (11:27) had lived or whether it is the city Nahur, named in the Mari documents (nineteenth and eighteenth centuries B.C.), near the confluence of the Balikh and Middle Euphrates rivers. **Aram Naharaim**: lit., "Aram between the two rivers," is the Yahwist designation for Terah's homeland. The two rivers are the Habur and the Euphrates. The Priestly designation for the area is Paddan-aram, which is from the Assyrian *padana*, "road or garden," and Aram, which refers to the people or land of the Arameans.

† [24:12] **Let it turn out favorably for me**: let me have a favorable sign; cf. end of v. 14.

c. [24:7] Gn 12:7; Ex 6:8; Tb 5:17; Gal 3:16.
d. [24:15] Gn 22:23.

‡ [24:30] Laban becomes hospitable only when he sees the servant's rich gifts, which is in humorous contrast to his sister's spontaneous generosity toward the servant. Laban's opportunism points forward to his behavior in the Jacob stories (31:14–16).

e. [24:29] Gn 27:43.

GN

ready, as well as a place for the camels?" ³²The man then went inside; and while the camels were being unloaded and provided with straw and fodder, water was brought to bathe his feet and the feet of the men who were with him. ³³But when food was set before him, he said, "I will not eat until I have told my story." "Go ahead," they replied.

³⁴"I am Abraham's servant," he began. ³⁵"The Lord has blessed my master so abundantly that he has become wealthy; he has given him flocks and herds, silver and gold, male and female slaves, and camels and donkeys. ³⁶My master's wife Sarah bore a son to my master in her old age, and he has given him everything he owns. ³⁷My master put me under oath, saying: 'You shall not take a wife for my son from the daughters of the Canaanites in whose land I live; ³⁸instead, you must go to my father's house, to my own family, to get a wife for my son.' ³⁹When I asked my master, 'What if the woman will not follow me?' ⁴⁰he replied: 'The Lord, in whose presence I have always walked, will send his angel with you and make your journey successful, and so you will get a wife for my son from my own family and my father's house.ᶠ ⁴¹Then you will be freed from my curse. If you go to my family and they refuse you, then, too, you will be free from my curse.'*

⁴²"When I came to the spring today, I said: 'Lord, God of my master Abraham, please make successful the journey I am on. ⁴³While I stand here at the spring, if I say to a young woman who comes out to draw water, 'Please give me a little water from your jug,' ⁴⁴and she answers, 'Drink, and I will draw water for your camels, too—then she is the woman whom the Lord has decided upon for my master's son.'

⁴⁵"I had scarcely finished saying this to myself when Rebekah came out with a jug on her shoulder. After she went down to the spring and drew water, I said to her, 'Please let me have a drink.' ⁴⁶She quickly lowered the jug she was carrying and said, 'Drink, and I will water your camels, too.' So I drank, and she watered the camels also. ⁴⁷When I asked her, 'Whose daughter are you?' she answered, 'The daughter of Bethuel, son of Nahor, borne to Nahor by Milcah.' So I put the ring on her nose and the bracelets on her wrists. ⁴⁸Then I knelt and bowed down to the Lord, blessing the Lord, the God of my master Abraham, who had led me on the right road to obtain the daughter of my master's kinsman for his son. ⁴⁹Now, if you will act with kindness and fidelity toward my master, let me know; but if not, let me know that too. I can then proceed accordingly."

⁵⁰ᵍLaban and Bethuel said in reply: "This thing comes from the Lord; we can say nothing to you either for or against it. ⁵¹Here is Rebekah, right in front of you; take her and go, that she may become the wife of your master's son, as the Lord has said." ⁵²When Abraham's servant heard their answer, he bowed to the ground before the Lord. ⁵³Then he brought out objects of silver and gold and clothing and presented them to Rebekah; he also gave costly presents to her brother and mother. ⁵⁴After he and the men with him had eaten and drunk, they spent the night there.

When they got up the next morning, he said, "Allow me to return to my master."ʰ ⁵⁵Her brother and mother replied, "Let the young woman stay with us a short while, say ten days; after that she may go." ⁵⁶But he said to them, "Do not detain me, now that the Lord has made my journey successful; let me go back to my master." ⁵⁷They answered, "Let us call the young woman and see what she herself has to say about it." ⁵⁸So they called Rebekah and asked her, "Will you go with this

---

* [24:41] **Curse**: this would be the consequence of failing to carry out the oath referred to in v. 3.

f. [24:40] Tb 5:17; 10:13.

g. [24:50–51] Tb 7:11–12.
h. [24:54] Tb 7:14; 8:20.

man?" She answered, "I will."* ⁵⁹At this they sent off their sister Rebekah and her nurse with Abraham's servant and his men. ⁶⁰They blessed Rebekah and said:

"Sister, may you grow
 into thousands of myriads;
And may your descendants gain
   possession
 of the gates of their enemies!"ⁱ

⁶¹Then Rebekah and her attendants started out; they mounted the camels and followed the man. So the servant took Rebekah and went on his way.

⁶²Meanwhile Isaac had gone from Beer-lahai-roi and was living in the region of the Negeb.ʲ ⁶³One day toward evening he went out to walk in the field, and caught sight of camels approaching. ⁶⁴Rebekah, too, caught sight of Isaac, and got down from her camel. ⁶⁵She asked the servant, "Who is the man over there, walking through the fields toward us?" "That is my master," replied the servant. Then she took her veil and covered herself.

⁶⁶The servant recounted to Isaac all the things he had done. ⁶⁷Then Isaac brought Rebekah into the tent of his mother Sarah. He took Rebekah as his wife. Isaac loved her and found solace after the death of his mother.

CHAPTER 25

Abraham's Sons by Keturah. ¹†ᵃAbraham took another wife, whose name was Keturah. ²She bore him Zimran, Jokshan, Medan, Midian, Ish-

bak, and Shuah.‡ ³Jokshan became the father of Sheba and Dedan. The descendants of Dedan were the Asshurim, the Letushim, and the Leummim.ᵇ ⁴The descendants of Midian were Ephah, Epher, Hanoch, Abida, and Eldaah. All of these were descendants of Keturah. ⁵Abraham gave everything that he owned to his son Isaac.§ ⁶To the sons of his concubines, however, he gave gifts while he was still living, as he sent them away eastward, to the land of Kedem,¶ away from his son Isaac.

Death of Abraham. ⁷The whole span of Abraham's life was one hundred and seventy-five years. ⁸Then he breathed his last, dying at a ripe old age, grown old after a full life; and he was gathered to his people. ⁹His sons Isaac and Ishmael buried him in the cave of Machpelah, in the field of Ephron, son of Zohar the Hittite, which faces Mamre,ᶜ ¹⁰the field that Abraham had bought from the Hittites; there he was buried next to his wife Sarah. ¹¹After the death of Abraham, God blessed his son Isaac, who lived near Beer-lahai-roi.

Descendants of Ishmael. ¹²**These are the descendants of Abraham's son Ishmael, whom Hagar the Egyptian, Sarah's slave, bore to Abraham. ¹³ᵈThese are the names of Ishmael's sons, listed in the order of their birth: Ishmael's firstborn Nebaioth, Kedar, Adbeel, Mibsam,ᵉ ¹⁴Mishma, Dumah, Massa, ¹⁵Hadad, Tema, Jetur, Naphish,

---

* [24:58] Marriages arranged by the woman's father did not require the woman's consent, but marriages arranged by the woman's brother did. Laban is the brother and Rebekah is therefore free to give her consent or not.

† [25:1–11] As with the story of Terah in 11:27–32, this section lists all the descendants of Abraham as a means of concluding the story. The Jacob story ends similarly with the listing of the twelve sons (35:22–26), the death of Isaac (35:27–29), and the descendants of Esau (chap. 36). **Abraham took another wife:** though mentioned here, Abraham's marriage to a "concubine," or wife of secondary rank, is not to be understood as happening chronologically after the events narrated in the preceding chapter.

‡ [25:2] Three of the six names can be identified: the Midianites are a trading people, mentioned in the Bible as dwelling east of the Gulf of Aqaba in northwest Arabia; Ishbak a north Syrian tribe; Shuah is a city on the right bank of the Middle Euphrates. The other names are probably towns or peoples on the international trade routes.

§ [25:5] Amid so many descendants, Abraham takes steps that Isaac will be his favored heir.

¶ [25:6] **The land of Kedem:** or "the country of the East," the region inhabited by the Kedemites or Easterners (29:1; Jgs 6:3, 33; Jb 1:3; Is 11:14). The names mentioned in vv. 2–4, as far as they can be identified, are those of tribes in the Arabian desert.

** [25:12] Like the conclusion of the Jacob story (chap. 36), where the numerous descendants of the rejected Esau are listed, the descendants of the rejected Ishmael conclude the story.

---

i. [24:60] Gn 22:17.
j. [24:62] Gn 16:13–14; 25:11.

a. [25:1–4] 1 Chr 1:32–33.

b. [25:3] Is 21:13.
c. [25:9–10] Gn 23:3–20.
d. [25:13–16] 1 Chr 1:29–31.
e. [25:13] Is 60:7.

and Kedemah. **¹⁶**These are the sons of Ishmael, their names by their villages and encampments; twelve chieftains of as many tribal groups.**ᶠ**

¹⁷The span of Ishmael's life was one hundred and thirty-seven years. After he had breathed his last and died, he was gathered to his people. **¹⁸**The Ishmaelites ranged from Havilah, by Shur, which is on the border of Egypt, all the way to Asshur; and they pitched camp* alongside their various kindred.**ᵍ**

Birth of Esau and Jacob. ¹⁹†These are the descendants of Isaac, son of Abraham; Abraham begot Isaac. **²⁰**Isaac was forty years old when he married Rebekah, the daughter of Bethuel the Aramean of Paddan-aram‡ and the sister of Laban the Aramean.**ʰ** **²¹**Isaac entreated the Lord on behalf of his wife, since she was sterile. The Lord heard his entreaty, and his wife Rebekah became pregnant. **²²**But the children jostled each other in the womb so much that she exclaimed, "If it is like this,§ why go on living!" She went to consult the Lord, **²³**and the Lord answered her:

Two nations are in your womb,
two peoples are separating while
still within you;
But one will be stronger than the
other,
and the older will serve the
younger.**¶ⁱ**

²⁴When the time of her delivery came, there were twins in her womb.**ʲ** **²⁵**The first to emerge was reddish,** and his whole body was like a hairy mantle; so they named him Esau. **²⁶**Next his brother came out, gripping Esau's heel;†† so he was named Jacob. Isaac was sixty years old when they were born.**ᵏ**

²⁷When the boys grew up, Esau became a skillful hunter, a man of the open country; whereas Jacob was a simple‡‡ man, who stayed among the tents.**ˡ** **²⁸**Isaac preferred Esau, because he was fond of game; but Rebekah preferred Jacob. **²⁹**Once, when Jacob was cooking a stew, Esau came in from the open country, famished. **³⁰**He said to Jacob, "Let me gulp down some of that red stuff;§§ I am famished." That is why he was called Edom. **³¹**But Jacob replied, "First sell me your right as

---

* [25:18] **Pitched camp:** lit., "fell"; the same Hebrew verb is used in Jgs 7:12 in regard to the hostile encampment of desert tribes. The present passage shows the fulfillment of the prediction contained in Gn 16:12.

† [25:19–36:43] The Jacob cycle is introduced as the family history of Isaac (Jacob's father), just as the Abraham stories were introduced as the record of the descendants of Terah (Abraham's father, 11:27). The cycle, made up of varied stories, is given unity by several recurring themes: birth, blessing and inheritance, which are developed through the basic contrasts of barrenness/fertility, non-blessing/blessing, and inheritance/exile/homeland. The large story has an envelope structure in which Jacob's youth is spent in Canaan striving with his older brother Esau (25:19–28:22), his early adulthood in Paddan-aram building a family and striving with his brother-in-law Laban (chaps. 29–31), and his later years back in Canaan (chaps. 32–36).

‡ [25:20] **Paddan-aram:** the name used by the Priestly tradition for the northwest region of Mesopotamia, between the Habur and the Euphrates rivers. In Assyrian, *padana* is a road or a garden, and Aram refers to the people or the land of the Arameans. The equivalent geographical term in the Yahwist source is Aram Naharaim, "Aram between two rivers."

§ [25:22] **If it is like this:** in Hebrew, the phrase *lamah zeh* is capable of several meanings; it occurs again in v. 32 ("What good . . . ?"), 32:30 ("Why do you want . . . ?"), and 33:15 ("For what reason?"). It is one of several words and motifs that run through the story, suggesting that a divine pattern (unknown to the actors) is at work.

¶ [25:23] **The older will serve the younger:** Rebekah now knows something that no one else knows, that God favors Jacob over Esau. The text does not say if she shared this knowledge with anyone or kept it to herself, but, from their actions, it seems unlikely that either Isaac or Esau knew. That fact must be borne in mind in assessing Rebekah's role in chap. 27, the theft of Esau's blessing.

** [25:25] **Reddish:** in Hebrew, *'admoni*, a reference to Edom, another name for Esau (v. 30; 36:1). Edom was also the name of the country south of Moab (southeast of the Dead Sea) where the descendants of Esau lived. It was called the "red" country because of its reddish sandstone. Moreover, "red" points ahead to the red stew in the next scene. **Hairy:** in Hebrew, *se'ar*, a reference to Seir, another name for Edom (36:8).

†† [25:26] **Heel:** in Hebrew *'aqeb*, a wordplay on the name Jacob; cf. 27:36. The first of three scenes of striving with Esau. The second is vv. 27–34, and the third, chap. 27. In all the scenes, Jacob values the blessing more than his ardent but unreflective brother Esau does.

‡‡ [25:27] **Simple:** the Hebrew word denotes soundness, integrity, health, none of which fit here. Whatever its precise meaning, it must be opposite to the qualities of Esau.

§§ [25:30] **Red stuff:** in Hebrew, *'adom*; another play on the word Edom, the "red" land.

i. [25:23] Gn 27:29; Nm 24:18; Mal 1:2–5; Rom 9:10–13.
j. [25:24] Hos 12:4.
k. [25:26] Mt 1:2.
l. [25:27] Gn 27:6–7.

f. [25:16] Gn 17:20.
g. [25:18] Gn 16:12.
h. [25:20] Gn 24:67.

firstborn."*m 32"Look," said Esau, "I am on the point of dying. What good is the right as firstborn to me?" 33But Jacob said, "Swear to me first!" So he sold Jacob his right as firstborn under oath.n 34Jacob then gave him some bread and the lentil stew; and Esau ate, drank, got up, and went his way. So Esau treated his right as firstborn with disdain.

CHAPTER 26

Isaac and Abimelech. 1†aThere was a famine in the land, distinct from the earlier one that had occurred in the days of Abraham, and Isaac went down to Abimelech, king of the Philistines in Gerar.b 2The LORD appeared to him and said: Do not go down to Egypt, but camp in this land wherever I tell you. 3Sojourn in this land, and I will be with you and bless you; for to you and your descendants I will give all these lands, in fulfillment of the oath that I swore to your father Abraham.c 4I will make your descendants as numerous as the stars in the sky, and I will give them all these lands, and in your descendants all the nations of the earth will find blessing—d 5this because Abraham obeyed me, keeping my mandate, my commandments, my ordinances, and my instructions.

6‡So Isaac settled in Gerar. 7When the men of the place asked questions about his wife, he answered, "She is my sister." He was afraid that, if he called her his wife, the men of the place would kill him on account of Rebekah, since she was beautiful. 8But when they had been there for a long time, Abimelech, king of the Philistines, looked out of a window and saw Isaac fondling his wife Rebekah. 9He called for Isaac and said: "She must certainly be your wife! How could you have said, 'She is my sister'?" Isaac replied, "I thought I might lose my life on her account." 10"How could you have done this to us!" exclaimed Abimelech. "It would have taken very little for one of the people to lie with your wife, and so you would have brought guilt upon us!" 11Abimelech then commanded all the people: "Anyone who maltreats this man or his wife shall be put to death."

12§Isaac sowed a crop in that region and reaped a hundredfold the same year. Since the LORD blessed him, 13ehe became richer and richer all the time, until he was very wealthy. 14He acquired flocks and herds, and a great work force, and so the Philistines became envious of him. 15fThe Philistines had stopped up and filled with dirt all the wells that his father's servants had dug back in the days of his father Abraham. 16So Abimelech said to Isaac, "Go away from us; you have become far too numerous for us." 17Isaac left there and camped in the Wadi Gerar where he stayed. 18Isaac reopened the wells which his father's servants had dug back in the days of his father Abraham and which the Philistines had stopped up after Abraham's death; he gave them names like

---

* [25:31] **Right as firstborn**: the privilege that entitled the firstborn son to a position of honor in the family and to a double share in the possessions inherited from the father. There is a persistent wordplay between *bekorah*, "right of the firstborn," and *berakah*, "the blessing." Contrary to custom, the preference here is for the younger son, as it was in the choice of Isaac over Ishmael.
† [26:1] The promise of land and numerous descendants given to Abraham (12:1–3; 15; 17; 22:17–18) is renewed for his son Isaac. The divine blessing to Isaac is mentioned also in vv. 12, 24, and 29.
‡ [26:6–11] This scene is the third version of the wife-in-danger story (cf. chaps. 12 and 20). The mention of the famine in 26:1 recalls the famine in 12:10; the name Abimelech, king of the Philistines in Gerar, recalls 20:2. The deception, according to all the stories, is the claim that the wife is a sister. This story (from the Yahwist source) departs from the two previous accounts in that the wife is not taken into the harem of the foreign king.

m. [25:31] Dt 21:17.
n. [25:33] Heb 12:16.

a. [26:1–14] Gn 12:10–20.
b. [26:1] Gn 12:10.
c. [26:3] Gn 12:7; 15:18; Ex 32:13; Ps 105:9; Sir 44:22; Heb 11:9.
d. [26:4] Gn 12:3; 22:17–18; 28:14; Ex 32:13.

§ [26:12–33] The dispute is over water rights. In a sparsely watered land, wells were precious and claims on water could function as a kind of claim on the land. Scholars generally judge the account of the dispute over water rights and its settlement by a legal agreement between Isaac and Abimelech to be a Yahwist version of the similar story about Abraham in 21:22–34. Here, Abimelech realizes that Isaac has brought blessing to his people and thus desires a covenant with him. The feast in v. 30 is part of the covenant ceremony.

e. [26:13–14] Jb 1:3.
f. [26:15–24] Gn 21:25–31.

those that his father had given them. ¹⁹But when Isaac's servants dug in the wadi and reached spring water in their well, ²⁰the shepherds of Gerar argued with Isaac's shepherds, saying, "The water belongs to us!" So he named the well Esek,* because they had quarreled there. ²¹Then they dug another well, and they argued over that one too; so he named it Sitnah.† ²²So he moved on from there and dug still another well, but over this one they did not argue. He named it Rehoboth,‡ and said, "Because the LORD has now given us ample room, we shall flourish in the land."

²³From there Isaac went up to Beer-sheba. ²⁴The same night the LORD appeared to him and said: I am the God of Abraham, your father. Do not fear, for I am with you. I will bless you and multiply your descendants for the sake of Abraham, my servant.ᵍ ²⁵So Isaac built an altar there and invoked the LORD by name. After he had pitched his tent there, Isaac's servants began to dig a well nearby.

²⁶ʰThen Abimelech came to him from Gerar, with Ahuzzath, his councilor, and Phicol, the general of his army. ²⁷Isaac asked them, "Why have you come to me, since you hate me and have driven me away from you?" ²⁸They answered: "We clearly see that the LORD has been with you, so we thought: let there be a sworn agreement between our two sides—between you and us. Let us make a covenant with you: ²⁹you shall do no harm to us, just as we have not maltreated you, but have always acted kindly toward you and have let you depart in peace. So now, may you be blessed by the LORD!" ³⁰Isaac then made a feast for them, and they ate and drank. ³¹Early the next morning they exchanged oaths. Then Isaac sent them on their

way, and they departed from him in peace.

³²That same day Isaac's servants came and informed him about the well they had been digging; they told him, "We have reached water!" ³³He called it Shibah;§ hence the name of the city is Beer-sheba to this day. ³⁴¶When Esau was forty years old, he married Judith, daughter of Beeri the Hittite, and Basemath, daughter of Elon the Hivite.ⁱ ³⁵But they became a source of bitterness to Isaac and Rebekah.

CHAPTER 27

Jacob's Deception.** ¹When Isaac was so old that his eyesight had failed him, he called his older son Esau and said to him, "My son!" "Here I am!" he replied. ²Isaac then said, "Now I have grown old. I do not know when I might die. ³So now take your hunting gear—your quiver and bow—and go out into the open country to hunt some game for me. ⁴Then prepare for me a dish in the way I like, and bring it to me to eat, so that I may bless you†† before I die."

⁵Rebekah had been listening while Isaac was speaking to his son Esau. So when Esau went out into the open

---

* [26:20] **Esek**: "quarrel."
† [26:21] **Sitnah**: "opposition."
‡ [26:22] **Rehoboth**: "wide spaces," i.e., ample room to live; site is probably SW of modern day Beer-sheba.

g. [26:24] Gn 46:3.
h. [26:26–33] Gn 21:22–31; Prv 16:7.

§ [26:33] **Shibah**: the place name Shibah is a play on two Hebrew words, *shebu'ah*, "oath," and *shwebaa'*, "seven." In v. 31, they exchanged oaths.
¶ [26:34–35] These verses from the Priestly source introduce the next section on Esau's loss of his right as firstborn by suggesting a motivation for this in Isaac's and Rebekah's dislike for Esau's Canaanite wives.
** [27:1–45] The chapter, a literary masterpiece, is the third and climactic wresting away of the blessing of Esau. Rebekah manages the entire affair, using perhaps her privileged information about Jacob's status (25:23); Jacob's only qualm is that if his father discovers the ruse, he will receive a curse instead of a blessing (vv. 11–12). Isaac is passive as he was in chaps. 22 and 24. The deception is effected through clothing (Jacob wears Esau's clothing), which points ahead to a similar deception of a patriarch by means of clothing in the Joseph story (37:21–33). Such recurrent acts and scenes let the reader know a divine purpose is moving the story forward even though the human characters are unaware of it.
†† [27:4] **I may bless you**: Isaac's blessing confers fertility (vv. 27–28) and dominion (v. 29). The "dew of heaven" is rain that produces grain and wine, two of the principal foodstuffs of the ancient Near East. The "fertility of the earth" may allude to oil, the third basic foodstuff. The full agricultural year may be implied here: the fall rains are followed by the grain harvests of the spring and the grape harvest of late summer, and then the olive harvest of the fall (cf. Dt 11:14; Ps 104:13–15).

i. [26:34–35] Gn 27:46.

GN

country to hunt some game for his father,[a] [6] Rebekah said to her son Jacob, "Listen! I heard your father tell your brother Esau, [7] 'Bring me some game and prepare a dish for me to eat, that I may bless you with the LORD's approval before I die.' [8] Now, my son, obey me in what I am about to order you. [9] Go to the flock and get me two choice young goats so that with these I might prepare a dish for your father in the way he likes. [10] Then bring it to your father to eat, that he may bless you before he dies." [11] But Jacob said to his mother Rebekah, "But my brother Esau is a hairy man and I am smooth-skinned![b] [12] Suppose my father feels me? He will think I am making fun of him, and I will bring on myself a curse instead of a blessing." [13] His mother, however, replied: "Let any curse against you, my son, fall on me! Just obey me. Go and get me the young goats."

[14] So Jacob went and got them and brought them to his mother, and she prepared a dish in the way his father liked. [15] Rebekah then took the best clothes of her older son Esau that she had in the house, and gave them to her younger son Jacob to wear; [16] and with the goatskins she covered up his hands and the hairless part of his neck. [17] Then she gave her son Jacob the dish and the bread she had prepared.

[18] Going to his father, Jacob said, "Father!" "Yes?" replied Isaac. "Which of my sons are you?" [19] Jacob answered his father: "I am Esau, your firstborn. I did as you told me. Please sit up and eat some of my game, so that you may bless me." [20] But Isaac said to his son, "How did you get it so quickly, my son?" He answered, "The LORD, your God, directed me." [21] Isaac then said to Jacob, "Come closer, my son, that I may feel you, to learn whether you really are my son Esau or not." [22] So Jacob moved up closer to his father. When Isaac felt him, he said, "Although the voice is Jacob's, the hands are Esau's." [23] (He failed to identify him because his hands were hairy, like those of his brother Esau; so he blessed him.) [24] Again Isaac said, "Are you really my son Esau?" And Jacob said, "I am." [25] Then Isaac said, "Serve me, my son, and let me eat of the game so that I may bless you." Jacob served it to him, and Isaac ate; he brought him wine, and he drank. [26] Finally his father Isaac said to him, "Come closer, my son, and kiss me." [27] As Jacob went up to kiss him, Isaac smelled the fragrance of his clothes. With that, he blessed him, saying,

"Ah, the fragrance of my son
  is like the fragrance of a field
  that the LORD has blessed![c]
[28] May God give to you
  of the dew of the heavens
And of the fertility of the earth
  abundance of grain and wine.
[29][d] May peoples serve you,
  and nations bow down to you;
Be master of your brothers,
  and may your mother's sons bow
    down to you.
Cursed be those who curse you,
  and blessed be those who bless
    you."

[30] Jacob had scarcely left his father after Isaac had finished blessing him, when his brother Esau came back from his hunt. [31] Then he too prepared a dish, and bringing it to his father, he said, "Let my father sit up and eat some of his son's game, that you may then give me your blessing." [32] His father Isaac asked him, "Who are you?" He said, "I am your son, your firstborn son, Esau." [33] Isaac trembled greatly. "Who was it, then," he asked, "that hunted game and brought it to me? I ate it all just before you came, and I blessed him. Now he is blessed!" [34] As he heard his father's words, Esau burst into loud, bitter sobbing and said, "Father, bless me too!" [35] When Isaac said, "Your brother came here

a. [27:5] Gn 25:28.
b. [27:11] Gn 25:25.

c. [27:27] Gn 22:17–18; Heb 11:20.
d. [27:29] Gn 25:23; 49:8; Nm 24:9.

by a ruse and carried off your blessing," ³⁶Esau exclaimed, "He is well named Jacob, is he not! He has supplanted me* twice! First he took away my right as firstborn, and now he has taken away my blessing." Then he said, "Have you not saved a blessing for me?"ᵉ ³⁷Isaac replied to Esau: "I have already appointed him your master, and I have assigned to him all his kindred as his servants; besides, I have sustained him with grain and wine. What then can I do for you, my son?" ³⁸But Esau said to his father, "Have you only one blessing, father? Bless me too, father!" and Esau wept aloud.ᶠ ³⁹His father Isaac said in response:

"See, far from the fertile earth
   will be your dwelling;
   far from the dew of the heavens
      above!ᵍ
⁴⁰By your sword you will live,
   and your brother you will serve;
But when you become restless,
   you will throw off his yoke from
      your neck."ʰ

⁴¹Esau bore a grudge against Jacob because of the blessing his father had given him. Esau said to himself, "Let the time of mourning for my father come, so that I may kill my brother Jacob."ⁱ ⁴²When Rebekah got news of what her older son Esau had in mind, she summoned her younger son Jacob and said to him: "Listen! Your brother Esau intends to get his revenge by killing you. ⁴³So now, my son, obey me: flee at once to my brother Laban in Haran, ⁴⁴and stay with him a while until your brother's fury subsides— ⁴⁵until your brother's anger against you subsides and he forgets what you did to him. Then I will send for you

and bring you back. Why should I lose both of you in a single day?"

Jacob Sent to Laban. ⁴⁶Rebekah said to Isaac: "I am disgusted with life because of the Hittite women. If Jacob also should marry a Hittite woman, a native of the land, like these women, why should I live?"ʲ

CHAPTER 28

¹†Isaac therefore summoned Jacob and blessed him, charging him: "You shall not marry a Canaanite woman!ᵃ ²Go now to Paddan-aram, to the home of your mother's father Bethuel, and there choose a wife for yourself from among the daughters of Laban, your mother's brother.ᵇ ³May God Almighty bless you and make you fertile, multiply you that you may become an assembly of peoples. ⁴May God extend to you and your descendants the blessing of Abraham, so that you may gain possession of the land where you are residing, which he assigned to Abraham."ᶜ ⁵Then Isaac sent Jacob on his way; he went to Paddan-aram, to Laban, son of Bethuel the Aramean, and brother of Rebekah, the mother of Jacob and Esau.ᵈ

⁶Esau noted that Isaac had blessed Jacob when he sent him to Paddan-aram to get himself a wife there, and that, as he gave him his blessing, he charged him, "You shall not marry a

---

† [28:1–9] A glimpse of Rebekah's shrewdness is provided by 27:42–28:2. She is aware of Esau's murderous plot against Jacob (27:42–45) but realizes the episode of the stolen blessing is still painful to Isaac; she therefore uses another motive to persuade Isaac to send Jacob away—he must marry within the family (endogamy), unlike Esau. Esau, unreflective as usual, realizes too late he also should marry within the family but, significantly, marries from Abraham's rejected line. At this point in the story, Jacob (and his mother) have taken the blessing for themselves. Their actions have put Jacob in a precarious position: he must flee the land because of his brother's murderous intent and find a wife in a far country. One might ask how God's blessing can be given to such an unworthy schemer. There is a biblical pattern of preferring the younger brother or sister over the older—Isaac over Ishmael, Jacob over Esau, Rachel over Leah, Joseph over his older brothers, Ephraim over Manasseh (Gn 48:14), David over his older brothers.

---

* [27:36] **He has supplanted me:** in Hebrew, *wayyaqebeni*, a wordplay on the name Jacob, *ya'aqob*; see Jer 9:3 and Gn 25:26. There is also a play between the Hebrew words *bekorah* ("right of the firstborn") and *berakah* ("blessing").

e. [27:36] Gn 25:26, 29–34; Hos 12:4.
f. [27:38] Heb 12:17.
g. [27:39] Heb 11:20.
h. [27:40] 2 Kgs 8:20, 22; 2 Chr 21:8.
i. [27:41] Wis 10:10; Ob 10.

j. [27:46] Gn 26:34–35.

a. [28:1] Gn 24:3–4; 26:35.
b. [28:2] Gn 22:22.
c. [28:4] Ex 32:13.
d. [28:5] Jdt 8:26.

Canaanite woman," [7] and that Jacob had obeyed his father and mother and gone to Paddan-aram. [8] Esau realized how displeasing the Canaanite women were to his father Isaac, [9] so Esau went to Ishmael, and in addition to the wives he had, married Mahalath, the daughter of Abraham's son Ishmael and sister of Nebaioth.[e]

Jacob's Dream at Bethel.[*] [10] Jacob departed from Beer-sheba and proceeded toward Haran. [11] When he came upon a certain place,[†] he stopped there for the night, since the sun had already set. Taking one of the stones at the place, he put it under his head and lay down in that place. [12] Then he had a dream: a stairway[‡] rested on the ground, with its top reaching to the heavens; and God's angels were going up and down on it.[f] [13] And there was the LORD standing beside him and saying: I am the LORD, the God of Abraham your father and the God of Isaac; the land on which you are lying I will give to you and your descendants.[g] [14] Your descendants will be like the dust of the earth, and through them you will spread to the west and the east, to the north and the south. In you and your descendants all the families of the earth will find blessing.[h] [15] I am with you and will protect you wherever you go, and bring you back to this land. I will never leave you until I have done what I promised you.[i]

[16] When Jacob awoke from his sleep, he said, "Truly, the LORD is in this place and I did not know it!" [17] He was afraid and said: "How awesome this place is! This is nothing else but the house of God, the gateway to heaven!" [18] Early the next morning Jacob took the stone that he had put under his head, set it up as a sacred pillar,[§] and poured oil on top of it.[j] [19] He named that place Bethel,[¶] whereas the former name of the town had been Luz.[k]

[20] Jacob then made this vow:[**] "If God will be with me and protect me on this journey I am making and give me food to eat and clothes to wear, [21] and I come back safely to my father's house, the LORD will be my God. [22] This stone that I have set up as a sacred pillar will be the house of God. Of everything you give me, I will return a tenth part to you without fail."

CHAPTER 29

Arrival in Haran.[††] [1a] After Jacob resumed his journey, he came to the

§ [28:18] **Sacred pillar**: in Hebrew, *masseba*, a stone which might vary in shape and size, set upright and usually intended for some religious purpose. The custom of erecting such sacred pillars in Palestine went back to its pre-Israelite period; but since their polytheistic associations were often retained, later Israelite religion forbade their erection (Lv 26:1; Dt 16:22) and ordered the destruction of those that were associated with other religions (Ex 34:13; Dt 12:3).

¶ [28:19] **Bethel**: i.e., "house of God"; the reference is to the house of God in v. 17.

** [28:20] **This vow**: knowing well that Esau's murderous wrath stands between him and the possession of the land promised him, Jacob makes his vow very precise. He vows to make the God who appeared to him his own if the God guides him safely to Paddan-aram and back to this land.

†† [29:1–14] Jacob's arrival in Haran. The sight of Rachel inspires Jacob to the superhuman feat of rolling back the enormous stone by himself. The scene evokes the meeting of Abraham's steward and Jacob's mother Rebekah at a well (24:11–27).

The verse begins the story of Jacob's time in Mesopotamia (29:1–31:54), which is framed on either side by Jacob's time in Canaan, 25:19–28:22 and 32:1–36:43. In these chapters, Jacob suffers Laban's duplicity as Esau had to suffer his, though eventually Jacob outwits Laban and leaves Mesopotamia a wealthy man. An elaborate chiastic (or envelope) structure shapes the diverse material: (A) Jacob's arrival in Haran in 29:1–4; (B) contract with Laban in 29:15–20; (C) Laban's deception of Jacob in 29:21–30; (D) the center, the birth of Jacob's children in 29:31–30:24; (C') Jacob's deception of Laban in 30:25–43; (B') dispute with Laban in 31:17–42; (A') departure from Laban in 31:43–54. As the chiasm reverses, so do the fortunes of Laban and Jacob. **Kedemites**: see note on 25:6.

---

* [28:10–22] As Jacob is leaving the land on his way to an uncertain future in Paddan-aram, God appears to him at a sacred place that Jacob had visited only to take a night's rest. Jacob's unawareness of the holiness of the place underscores the graciousness of the gift. On his return to Canaan, he will again encounter a divine visitor in the form of the mysterious attacker (32:23–33) and, after his return and reconciliation with Esau, he will again go to Bethel (35:1–15).

† [28:11] **Place**: the Hebrew word is often used specifically of a sacred site. The ambiguous word "place" is used here, for the text emphasizes that Jacob has no idea the place he has come upon is sacred; only when he wakes up does he realize it is sacred. The place was Bethel (v. 19), a sacred site as early as the time of Abraham (12:8).

‡ [28:12] **Stairway**: in Hebrew, *sullam*, traditionally but inaccurately translated as "ladder." The corresponding verb, *salal*, means "to heap up" something, such as dirt for a highway or a ramp. The imagery in Jacob's dream may be derived from the Babylonian ziggurat or temple tower, "with its top in the sky" (11:4), and with brick steps leading up to a small temple at the top.

---

e. [28:9] Gn 36:2–3.
f. [28:12] Jn 1:51.
g. [28:13] Dt 1:8; Mi 7:20.
h. [28:14] Gn 12:3; 13:14–15; 15:5–6; 18:18; 22:17–18; 26:4; Dt 19:8; Sir 44:21.

i. [28:15] Gn 31:3.
j. [28:18] Gn 31:13; 35:14–15.
k. [28:19] Gn 35:6; 48:3; Jos 18:13; Jgs 1:23; Hos 12:5.

a. [29:1] Wis 10:10.

land of the Kedemites. ²Looking about, he saw a well in the open country, with three flocks of sheep huddled near it, for flocks were watered from that well. A large stone covered the mouth of the well.*b* ³When all the shepherds were assembled there they would roll the stone away from the mouth of the well and water the sheep. Then they would put the stone back again in its place over the mouth of the well.

⁴Jacob said to them, "My brothers, where are you from?" "We are from Haran," they replied. ⁵Then he asked them, "Do you know Laban, son of Nahor?" "We do," they answered.*c* ⁶He inquired further, "Is he well?" "He is," they answered; "and here comes his daughter Rachel with the sheep." ⁷Then he said: "There is still much daylight left; it is hardly the time to bring the animals home. Water the sheep, and then continue pasturing them." ⁸They replied, "We cannot until all the shepherds are here to roll the stone away from the mouth of the well; then can we water the flocks."

⁹While he was still talking with them, Rachel arrived with her father's sheep, for she was the one who tended them. ¹⁰As soon as Jacob saw Rachel, the daughter of his mother's brother Laban, and the sheep of Laban, he went up, rolled the stone away from the mouth of the well, and watered Laban's sheep. ¹¹Then Jacob kissed Rachel and wept aloud. ¹²Jacob told Rachel that he was her father's relative, Rebekah's son. So she ran to tell her father. ¹³When Laban heard the news about Jacob, his sister's son, he ran to meet him. After embracing and kissing him, he brought him to his house. Jacob then repeated to Laban all these things, ¹⁴and Laban said to him, "You are indeed my bone and my flesh."*ᵃ*

Marriage to Leah and Rachel.

After Jacob had stayed with him a full month, ¹⁵†Laban said to him: "Should you serve me for nothing just because you are a relative of mine? Tell me what your wages should be." ¹⁶Now Laban had two daughters; the older was called Leah, the younger Rachel. ¹⁷Leah had dull eyes,‡ but Rachel was shapely and beautiful. ¹⁸Because Jacob loved Rachel, he answered, "I will serve you seven years for your younger daughter Rachel."§ ¹⁹Laban replied, "It is better to give her to you than to another man. Stay with me." ²⁰So Jacob served seven years for Rachel, yet they seemed to him like a few days because of his love for her.*d*

²¹Then Jacob said to Laban, "Give me my wife, that I may consummate my marriage with her, for my term is now completed." ²²So Laban invited all the local inhabitants and gave a banquet. ²³At nightfall he took his daughter Leah and brought her to Jacob, and he consummated the marriage with her. ²⁴Laban assigned his maidservant Zilpah to his daughter Leah as her maidservant. ²⁵In the morning, there was Leah! So Jacob said to Laban: "How could you do this to me! Was it not for Rachel that I served you? Why did you deceive me?" ²⁶Laban replied, "It is not the custom in our country to give the younger daughter before the firstborn. ²⁷Finish the bridal week¶ for this one, and then the other will also be given to you in return for another seven years of service with me."*e*

²⁸Jacob did so. He finished the bridal week for the one, and then Laban gave him his daughter Rachel as a wife.

---

* [29:14] **Bone and . . . flesh**: the Hebrew idiom for English "flesh and blood" (cf. 2:23; Jgs 9:2; 2 Sm 5:1 = 1 Chr 11:1).

b. [29:2] Gn 24:11–12.
c. [29:5] Tb 7:4.

† [29:15–30] Laban's deception and Jacob's marriages. There are many ironies in the passage. Jacob's protest to Laban, "How could you do this to me?" echoes the question put to Abraham (20:9) and Isaac (26:10) when their deceptions about their wives were discovered. The major irony is that Jacob, the deceiver of his father and brother about the blessing (chap. 27), is deceived by his uncle (standing in for the father) about his wife.

‡ [29:17] **Dull eyes**: in the language of beauty used here, "dull" probably means lacking in the luster that was the sign of beautiful eyes, as in 1 Sm 16:12 and Sg 4:1.

§ [29:18] Jacob offers to render service (Jos 15:16–17; 1 Sm 17:25; 18:17) to pay off the customary bridal price (Ex 22:15–16; Dt 22:29).

¶ [29:27] **The bridal week**: an ancient wedding lasted for seven days; cf. Jgs 14:12, 17.

d. [29:20] Hos 12:13.
e. [29:27] Hos 12:13.

²⁹Laban assigned his maidservant Bilhah to his daughter Rachel as her maidservant. ³⁰Jacob then consummated his marriage with Rachel also, and he loved her more than Leah. Thus he served Laban another seven years.ᶠ

Jacob's Children.˙ ³¹When the LORD saw that Leah was unloved, he made her fruitful, while Rachel was barren. ³²Leah conceived and bore a son, and she named him Reuben;† for she said, "It means, 'The LORD saw my misery; surely now my husband will love me.'"ᵍ ³³She conceived again and bore a son, and said, "It means, 'The LORD heard that I was unloved,' and therefore he has given me this one also"; so she named him Simeon.‡ ³⁴Again she conceived and bore a son, and she said, "Now at last my husband will become attached to me, since I have now borne him three sons"; that is why she named him Levi.§ ³⁵Once more she conceived and bore a son, and she said, "This time I will give thanks to the LORD"; therefore she named him Judah.¶ Then she stopped bearing children.ʰ

CHAPTER 30

¹When Rachel saw that she had not borne children to Jacob, she became envious of her sister. She said to Jacob, "Give me children or I shall die!"ᵃ ²Jacob became angry with Rachel and said, "Can I take the place of God, who has denied you the fruit of the womb?"ᵇ ³She replied, "Here is my maidservant Bilhah. Have intercourse with her, and let her give birth on my knees,** so that I too may have children through her."ᶜ ⁴So she gave him her maidservant Bilhah as wife,†† and Jacob had intercourse with her. ⁵When Bilhah conceived and bore a son for Jacob, ⁶Rachel said, "God has vindicated me; indeed he has heeded my plea and given me a son." Therefore she named him Dan.‡‡ ⁷Rachel's maidservant Bilhah conceived again and bore a second son for Jacob, ⁸and Rachel said, "I have wrestled strenuously with my sister, and I have prevailed." So she named him Naphtali.§§

⁹When Leah saw that she had ceased to bear children, she took her maidservant Zilpah and gave her to Jacob as wife. ¹⁰So Leah's maidservant Zilpah bore a son for Jacob. ¹¹Leah then said, "What good luck!" So she named him Gad.¶¶ ¹²Then Leah's maidservant Zilpah bore a second son to Jacob; ¹³and Leah said, "What good fortune, because women will call me fortunate!" So she named him Asher.***

¹⁴One day, during the wheat harvest, Reuben went out and came upon some mandrakes††† in the field which

---

* [29:31–30:24] The note of strife, first sounded between Jacob and Esau in chaps. 25–27, continues between the two wives, since Jacob loved Rachel more than Leah (29:30). Jacob's neglect of Leah moves God to make her fruitful (29:31). Leah's fertility provokes Rachel. Leah bears Jacob four sons (Reuben, Levi, Simeon, and Judah) and her maidservant Zilpah, two (Gad and Asher). Rachel's maidservant Bilhah bears two (Dan and Naphtali). After the mandrakes (30:14–17), Leah bears Issachar and Zebulun and a daughter Dinah. Rachel then bears Joseph and, later in the land of Canaan, Benjamin (35:18).

† [29:32] **Reuben**: the literal meaning of the Hebrew name is disputed. One interpretation is *re'u ben*, "look, a son!", but here in Genesis (as also with the names of all the other sons of Jacob), it is given a symbolic rather than an etymological interpretation. Name and person were regarded as closely interrelated. The symbolic interpretation of Reuben's name, according to the Yahwist source, is based on the similar-sounding *ra'a be'onyi*, "he saw my misery." In the Elohist source, the name is explained by the similar-sounding *ye'ehabani*, "he will love me."

‡ [29:33] **Simeon**: in popular etymology, related to *shama'*, "he heard."

§ [29:34] **Levi**: related to *yillaweh*, "he will become attached."

¶ [29:35] **Judah**: related to *'odeh*, "I will give thanks, praise."

f. [29:30] Dt 21:15–17.
g. [29:32] Gn 49:3.
h. [29:35] Mt 1:2; Lk 3:33.

** [30:3] **On my knees**: in the ancient Near East, a father would take a newborn child in his lap to signify that he acknowledged it as his own; Rachel uses the ceremony in order to adopt the child and establish her legal rights to it.

†† [30:4] **As wife**: in 35:22 Bilhah is called a "concubine" (Heb. *pilegesh*). In v. 9, Zilpah is called "wife," and in 37:2 both women are called wives. The basic difference between a wife and a concubine was that no bride price was paid for the latter. The interchange of terminology shows that there was some blurring in social status between the wife and the concubine.

‡‡ [30:6] **Dan**: explained by the term *dannanni*, "he has vindicated me."

§§ [30:8] **Naphtali**: explained by the Hebrew term *naftulim*, lit., "contest" or "struggle."

¶¶ [30:11] **Gad**: explained by the Hebrew term *begad*, lit., "in luck," i.e., "what good luck!"

*** [30:13] **Asher**: explained by the term *be'oshri*, lit., "in my good fortune," i.e., "what good fortune," and by the term *ye'ashsheruni*, "they call me fortunate."

††† [30:14] **Mandrakes**: an herb whose root was thought to promote conception. The Hebrew word for mandrakes, *duda'im*, has erotic connotations, since it sounds like the words *daddayim* ("breasts") and *dodim* ("sexual pleasure").

a. [30:1] Prv 30:16.
b. [30:2] 2 Kgs 5:7.
c. [30:3] Gn 16:2–4.

he brought home to his mother Leah. Rachel said to Leah, "Please give me some of your son's mandrakes." **15**Leah replied, "Was it not enough for you to take away my husband, that you must now take my son's mandrakes too?" Rachel answered, "In that case Jacob may lie with you tonight in exchange for your son's mandrakes." **16**That evening, when Jacob came in from the field, Leah went out to meet him. She said, "You must have intercourse with me, because I have hired you with my son's mandrakes." So that night he lay with her, **17**and God listened to Leah; she conceived and bore a fifth son to Jacob. **18**Leah then said, "God has given me my wages for giving my maidservant to my husband"; so she named him Issachar.* **19**Leah conceived again and bore a sixth son to Jacob; **20**and Leah said, "God has brought me a precious gift. This time my husband will honor me, because I have borne him six sons"; so she named him Zebulun.† **21**Afterwards she gave birth to a daughter, and she named her Dinah.

22Then God remembered Rachel. God listened to her and made her fruitful. **23**She conceived and bore a son, and she said, "God has removed my disgrace."ᵈ **24**She named him Joseph,‡ saying, "May the LORD add another son for me!"

Jacob Outwits Laban.§ **25**After Rachel gave birth to Joseph, Jacob said to Laban: "Allow me to go to my own region and land. **26**Give me my wives and my children for whom I served you and let me go, for you know the service that I rendered you." **27**Laban

answered him: "If you will please! I have learned through divination that the LORD has blessed me because of you." **28**He continued, "State the wages I owe you, and I will pay them." **29**Jacob replied: "You know what work I did for you and how well your livestock fared under my care; **30**the little you had before I came has grown into an abundance, since the LORD has blessed you in my company. Now, when can I do something for my own household as well?" **31**Laban asked, "What should I give you?" Jacob answered: "You do not have to give me anything. If you do this thing for me, I will again pasture and tend your sheep. **32**Let me go through your whole flock today and remove from it every dark animal among the lambs and every spotted or speckled one among the goats.¶ These will be my wages. **33**In the future, whenever you check on my wages, my honesty will testify for me: any animal that is not speckled or spotted among the goats, or dark among the lambs, got into my possession by theft!" **34**Laban said, "Very well. Let it be as you say."

35That same day Laban removed the streaked and spotted he-goats and all the speckled and spotted she-goats, all those with some white on them, as well as every dark lamb, and he put them in the care of his sons.** **36**Then he put a three days' journey between himself and Jacob, while Jacob was pasturing the rest of Laban's flock.

37Jacob, however, got some fresh shoots of poplar, almond and plane††

---

* [30:18] **Issachar**: explained by the terms, *sekari*, "my reward," and in v. 16, *sakor sekartika*, "I have hired you."

† [30:20] **Zebulun**: explained by the terms, *zebadani...zebed tob*, "he has brought me a precious gift," and *yizbeleni*, "he will honor me."

‡ [30:24] **Joseph**: explained by the words *yosep*, "may he add," and in v. 23, *'asap*, "he has removed."

§ [30:25–43] Jacob's deception of Laban. Jacob has been living in Laban's household as an indentured worker paying off the bride price. Having paid off all his obligations, he wants to settle his accounts with Laban. His many children attest to the fulfillment of the Lord's promise of numerous progeny; the birth of Joseph to his beloved Rachel signals the fulfillment in a special way. To enter into the Lord's second promise, the land, he must now return to Canaan.

d. [30:23] Lk 1:25.

¶ [30:32] **Dark...lambs...spotted or speckled...goats**: in the Near East the normal color of sheep is light gray, whereas that of goats is dark brown or black. A minority of sheep in that part of the world have dark patches, and a minority of goats, white markings. Laban is quick to agree to the offer, for Jacob would have received only a few animals. But Jacob gets the better of him, using two different means: (1) he separates out the weaker animals and then provides visual impressions to the stronger animals at mating time (a folkloric belief); (2) in 31:8–12, he transmits the preferred characteristics through controlled propagation. It should be noted that Jacob has been told what to do in a dream (31:10) and that God is behind the increase in his flocks.

** [30:35] By giving the abnormally colored animals to his sons, Laban not only deprived Jacob of his first small wages, but he also schemed to prevent the future breeding of such animals in the flock entrusted to Jacob.

†† [30:37] **Plane**: also called the Oriental Plane, a deciduous tree found in riverine forests and marshes.

trees, and he peeled white stripes in them by laying bare the white core of the shoots. **38**The shoots that he had peeled he then set upright in the watering troughs where the animals came to drink, so that they would be in front of them. When the animals were in heat as they came to drink, **39**the goats mated by the shoots, and so they gave birth to streaked, speckled and spotted young. **40**The sheep, on the other hand, Jacob kept apart, and he made these animals face the streaked or completely dark animals of Laban. Thus he produced flocks of his own, which he did not put with Laban's flock. **41**Whenever the hardier animals were in heat, Jacob would set the shoots in the troughs in full view of these animals, so that they mated by the shoots; **42**but with the weaker animals he would not put the shoots there. So the feeble animals would go to Laban, but the hardy ones to Jacob. **43**So the man grew exceedingly prosperous, and he owned large flocks, male and female servants, camels, and donkeys.

CHAPTER 31

Flight from Laban. **1***Jacob heard that Laban's sons were saying, "Jacob has taken everything that belonged to our father, and he has produced all this wealth from our father's property." **2**Jacob perceived, too, that Laban's attitude toward him was not what it had previously been. **3**Then the LORD said to Jacob: Return to the land of your ancestors, where you were born, and I will be with you.ᵃ

4So Jacob sent for Rachel and Leah to meet him in the field where his flock was. **5**There he said to them: "I have noticed that your father's attitude toward me is not as it was in the past;

but the God of my father has been with me. **6**You know well that with all my strength I served your father; **7**yet your father cheated me and changed my wages ten times. God, however, did not let him do me any harm.ᵇ **8**Whenever your father said, 'The speckled animals will be your wages,' the entire flock would bear speckled young; whenever he said, 'The streaked animals will be your wages,' the entire flock would bear streaked young. **9**So God took away your father's livestock and gave it to me. **10**Once, during the flock's mating season, I had a dream in which I saw he-goats mating that were streaked, speckled and mottled. **11**In the dream God's angel said to me, 'Jacob!' and I replied, 'Here I am!' **12**Then he said: 'Look up and see. All the he-goats that are mating are streaked, speckled and mottled, for I have seen all the things that Laban has been doing to you. **13**I am the God of Bethel, where you anointed a sacred pillar and made a vow to me. Get up now! Leave this land and return to the land of your birth.'"ᶜ

14Rachel and Leah answered him: "Do we still have an heir's portion in our father's house? **15**Are we not regarded by him as outsiders?† He not only sold us; he has even used up the money that he got for us! **16**All the wealth that God took away from our father really belongs to us and our children. So do whatever God has told you."ᵈ **17**Jacob proceeded to put his children and wives on camels, **18**and he drove off all his livestock and all the property he had acquired in Paddan-aram, to go to his father Isaac in the land of Canaan.

19Now Laban was away shearing his sheep, and Rachel had stolen her

---

* [31:1–54] Jacob flees with his family from Laban. The strife that has always accompanied Jacob continues as Laban's sons complain, "he has taken everything that belonged to our father"; the brothers' complaint echoes Esau's in 27:36. Rachel and Leah overcome their mutual hostility and are able to leave together, a harbinger of the reconciliation with Esau in chap. 33.

a. [31:3] Gn 26:3; 28:15; 32:10.

† [31:15] **Outsiders**: lit., "foreign women"; they lacked the favored legal status of native women. **Used up**: lit., "eaten, consumed"; the bridal price that a man received for giving his daughter in marriage was legally reserved as her inalienable dowry. Perhaps this is the reason that Rachel took the household images belonging to Laban.

b. [31:7] Jdt 8:26.
c. [31:13] Gn 28:18.
d. [31:16] Wis 10:10–11.

GN

father's household images.*e 20Jacob had hoodwinked† Laban the Aramean by not telling him that he was going to flee. 21Thus he fled with all that he had. Once he was across the Euphrates, he headed for the hill country of Gilead.

22On the third day, word came to Laban that Jacob had fled. 23Taking his kinsmen with him, he pursued him for seven days‡ until he caught up with him in the hill country of Gilead. 24But that night God appeared to Laban the Aramean in a dream and said to him: Take care not to say anything to Jacob.f

Jacob and Laban in Gilead. 25When Laban overtook Jacob, Jacob's tents were pitched in the hill country; Laban also pitched his tents in the hill country of Gilead. 26Laban said to Jacob, "How could you hoodwink me and carry off my daughters like prisoners of war?§ 27Why did you dupe me by stealing away secretly? You did not tell me! I would have sent you off with joyful singing to the sound of tambourines and harps. 28You did not even allow me a parting kiss to my daughters and grandchildren! Now what you have done makes no sense. 29I have it in my power to harm all of you; but last night the God of your father said to me, 'Take care not to say anything to Jacob!' 30Granted that you had to

leave because you were longing for your father's house, why did you steal my gods?" 31Jacob replied to Laban, "I was frightened at the thought that you might take your daughters away from me by force. 32As for your gods, the one you find them with shall not remain alive! If, with our kinsmen looking on, you identify anything here as belonging to you, take it." Jacob had no idea that Rachel had stolen the household images.

33Laban then went in and searched Jacob's tent and Leah's tent, as well as the tents of the two maidservants; but he did not find them. Leaving Leah's tent, he went into Rachel's. 34¶Meanwhile Rachel had taken the household images, put them inside the camel's saddlebag, and seated herself upon them. When Laban had rummaged through her whole tent without finding them,g 35she said to her father, "Do not let my lord be angry that I cannot rise in your presence; I am having my period." So, despite his search, he did not find the household images.

36Jacob, now angered, confronted Laban and demanded, "What crime or offense have I committed that you should hound me? 37Now that you have rummaged through all my things, what have you found from your household belongings? Produce it here before your kinsmen and mine, and let them decide between the two of us.

38"In the twenty years that I was under you, no ewe or she-goat of yours ever miscarried, and I have never eaten rams of your flock. 39hI never brought you an animal torn by wild beasts; I made good the loss myself. You held me responsible for anything stolen by day or night.** 40Often the scorching

---

* [31:19] **Household images:** in Hebrew, *teraphim,* figurines used in divination (Ez 21:26; Zec 10:2). Laban calls them his "gods" (v. 30). The traditional translation "idols" is avoided because it suggests false gods, whereas Genesis seems to accept the fact that the ancestors did not always live according to later biblical religious standards and laws.

† [31:20] **Hoodwinked:** lit., "stolen the heart of," i.e., lulled the mind of. **Aramean:** the earliest extra-biblical references to the Arameans date later than the time of Jacob, if Jacob is dated to the mid-second millennium; to call Laban an Aramean and to have him speak Aramaic (Jegar-sahadutha, v. 47) is an apparent anachronism. The word may have been chosen to underscore the growing estrangement between the two men and the fact that their descendants will be two different peoples.

‡ [31:23] **For seven days:** lit., "a way of seven days," a general term to designate a long distance; it would actually have taken a camel caravan many more days to travel from Haran to Gilead, the region east of the northern half of the Jordan. The mention of camels in this passage is apparently anachronistic since camels were not domesticated until the late second millennium.

§ [31:26] **Prisoners of war:** lit., "women captured by the sword"; the women of a conquered people were treated as part of the victor's spoil; cf. 1 Sm 30:2; 2 Kgs 5:2.

¶ [31:34] As in chap. 27, a younger child (Rachel) deceives her father to gain what belongs to him.

** [31:39] Jacob's actions are more generous than the customs suggested in the Code of Hammurabi: "If in a sheepfold an act of god has occurred, or a lion has made a kill, the shepherd shall clear himself before the deity, and the owner of the fold must accept the loss" (par. 266); cf. Ex 22:12.

e. [31:19] Gn 31:34; 1 Sm 19:13.
f. [31:24] Wis 10:12.
g. [31:34] Gn 31:19.
h. [31:39] Ex 22:12.

heat devoured me by day, and the frost by night, while sleep fled from my eyes! ⁴¹Of the twenty years that I have now spent in your household, I served you fourteen years for your two daughters and six years for your flock, while you changed my wages ten times. ⁴²If the God of my father, the God of Abraham and the Fear of Isaac, had not been on my side, you would now have sent me away empty-handed. But God saw my plight and the fruits of my toil, and last night he reproached you."*i*

⁴³*Laban replied to Jacob: "The daughters are mine, their children are mine, and the flocks are mine; everything you see belongs to me. What can I do now for my own daughters and for the children they have borne? ⁴⁴†Come, now, let us make a covenant, you and I; and it will be a treaty between you and me."

⁴⁵Then Jacob took a stone and set it up as a sacred pillar.*j* ⁴⁶Jacob said to his kinsmen, "Gather stones." So they got stones and made a mound; and they ate there at the mound. ⁴⁷Laban called it Jegar-sahadutha,‡ but Jacob called it Galeed. ⁴⁸Laban said, "This mound will be a witness from now on between you and me." That is why it was named Galeed—⁴⁹and also Mizpah,§ for he said: "May the LORD keep watch between you and me when we are out of each other's sight. ⁵⁰If you mistreat my daughters, or take other wives besides my daughters, know that even though no one else is there, God will be a witness between you and me."

⁵¹Laban said further to Jacob: "Here is this mound, and here is the sacred pillar that I have set up between you and me. ⁵²This mound will be a witness, and this sacred pillar will be a witness, that, with hostile intent, I may not pass beyond this mound into your territory, nor may you pass beyond it into mine. ⁵³May the God of Abraham and the God of Nahor, the God of their father, judge between us!" Jacob took the oath by the Fear of his father Isaac.¶ ⁵⁴He then offered a sacrifice on the mountain and invited his kinsmen to share in the meal. When they had eaten, they passed the night on the mountain.

CHAPTER 32

¹**Early the next morning, Laban kissed his grandchildren and his daughters and blessed them; then he set out on his journey back home. ²Meanwhile Jacob continued on his own way, and God's angels encountered him. ³When Jacob saw them he said, "This is God's encampment." So he named that place Mahanaim.††

Envoys to Esau. ⁴Jacob sent messengers ahead to his brother Esau in the land of Seir, the country of Edom,ª ⁵ordering them: "Thus you shall say to my lord Esau: 'Thus says your servant Jacob: I have been residing with Laban and have been delayed until now. ⁶I own oxen, donkeys and sheep, as well as male and female servants. I have sent my lord this message in the hope of gaining your favor.'" ⁷When the messengers returned to Jacob, they

---

* [31:43–54] In this account of the non-aggression treaty between Laban and Jacob, the different objects that serve as witness (sacred pillar in v. 45, cairn of stones in v. 46), their different names (Jegar-sahadutha in v. 47, Mizpah in v. 49), and the two references to the covenant meal (vv. 46, 54) suggest that two versions have been fused. One version is the Yahwist source, and another source has been used to supplement it.

† [31:44–54] The treaty is a typical covenant between two parties: Jacob was bound to treat his wives (Laban's daughters) well, and Laban was bound not to cross Jacob's boundaries with hostile intent.

‡ [31:47–48] **Jegar-sahadutha:** an Aramaic term meaning "mound of witness." **Galeed:** in Hebrew, "the mound of witness."

§ [31:49] **Mizpah:** a town in Gilead; cf. Jgs 10:17; 11:11, 34; Hos 5:1. The Hebrew name *mispa* ("lookout") is allied to *yisep yhwh* ("may the Lord keep watch"), and also echoes the word *masseba* ("sacred pillar").

¶ [31:53] **Fear of . . . Isaac:** an archaic title for Jacob's God of the Father.

** [32:1–22] Jacob's negotiations with Esau. Laban kisses his daughters and grandchildren good-bye but not Jacob. On leaving Mesopotamia, Jacob has an encounter with angels of God (vv. 2–3), which provokes him to exclaim, "This is God's encampment," just as he exclaimed upon leaving Canaan, "This is the house of God, the gateway to heaven" (28:11–17).

†† [32:3] **Mahanaim:** a town in Gilead (Jos 13:26, 30; 21:38; 2 Sm 2:8; etc.). The Hebrew name means "two camps." There are other allusions to the name in vv. 8, 11.

i. [31:42] Gn 31:24, 29.
j. [31:45] Gn 28:18; 35:14.

a. [32:4] Gn 36:6.

said, "We found your brother Esau. He is now coming to meet you, and four hundred men are with him."

8 Jacob was very much frightened. In his anxiety, he divided the people who were with him, as well as his flocks, herds and camels, into two camps. **9** "If Esau should come and attack one camp," he reasoned, "the remaining camp may still escape." **10** Then Jacob prayed: "God of my father Abraham and God of my father Isaac! You, LORD, who said to me, 'Go back to your land and your relatives, and I will be good to you.'*b* **11** I am unworthy of all the acts of kindness and faithfulness that you have performed for your servant: although I crossed the Jordan here with nothing but my staff, I have now grown into two camps. **12** Save me from the hand of my brother, from the hand of Esau! Otherwise I fear that he will come and strike me down and the mothers with the children. **13** You yourself said, 'I will be very good to you, and I will make your descendants like the sands of the sea, which are too numerous to count.'"*c*

14 After passing the night there, Jacob selected from what he had with him a present for his brother Esau: **15** two hundred she-goats and twenty he-goats; two hundred ewes and twenty rams; **16** thirty female camels and their young; forty cows and ten bulls; twenty female donkeys and ten male donkeys. **17** He put these animals in the care of his servants, in separate herds, and he told the servants, "Go on ahead of me, but keep some space between the herds." **18** He ordered the servant in the lead, "When my brother Esau meets you and asks, 'To whom do you belong? Where are you going? To whom do these animals ahead of you belong?' **19** tell him, 'To your servant Jacob, but they have been sent as a gift to my lord Esau. Jacob himself is right behind us.'" **20** He also ordered the second servant and the third and

all the others who followed behind the herds: "Thus and so you shall say to Esau, when you reach him; **21** and also tell him, 'Your servant Jacob is right behind us.'" For Jacob reasoned, "If I first appease him with a gift that precedes me, then later, when I face him, perhaps he will forgive me." **22** So the gifts went on ahead of him, while he stayed that night in the camp.

Jacob's New Name.* **23** That night, however, Jacob arose, took his two wives, with the two maidservants and his eleven children, and crossed the ford of the Jabbok. **24** After he got them and brought them across the wadi and brought over what belonged to him, **25** Jacob was left there alone. Then a man† wrestled with him until the break of dawn. **26** When the man saw that he could not prevail over him, he struck Jacob's hip at its socket, so that Jacob's socket was dislocated as he wrestled with him.*d* **27** The man then said, "Let me go, for it is daybreak." But Jacob said, "I will not let you go until you bless me." **28** "What is your name?" the man asked. He answered, "Jacob."*e* **29** Then the man said, "You shall no longer be named Jacob, but Israel,‡ because you have contended with divine and human beings and have prevailed." **30** Jacob

---

* [32:23–33] As Jacob crosses over to the land promised him, worried about the impending meeting with Esau, he encounters a mysterious adversary in the night with whom he wrestles until morning. The cunning Jacob manages to wrest a blessing from the night stranger before he departs. There are folkloric elements in the tale—e.g., the trial of the hero before he can return home, the nocturnal demon's loss of strength at sunrise, the demon protecting its river, the power gained by knowledge of an opponent's name—but these have been worked into a coherent though elliptical narrative. The point of the tale seems to be that the ever-striving, ever-grasping Jacob must eventually strive with God to attain full possession of the blessing.

† [32:25] **A man**: as with Abraham's three visitors in chap. 18, who appear sometimes as three, two, and one (the latter being God), this figure is fluid; he loses the match but changes Jacob's name (v. 29), an act elsewhere done only by God (17:5, 15). A few deft narrative touches manage to express intimate contact with Jacob while preserving the transcendence proper to divinity.

‡ [32:29] **Israel**: the first part of the Hebrew name *Yisrael* is given a popular explanation in the word *saritha*, "you contended"; the second part is the first syllable of *'elohim,* "divine beings." The present incident, with a similar allusion to the name Israel, is referred to in Hos 12:5, where the mysterious wrestler is explicitly called an angel.

---

b. [32:10] Gn 31:3.
c. [32:13] Gn 28:14; 48:16; Ex 32:13; Heb 11:12.
d. [32:26] Hos 12:5.
e. [32:28] Gn 35:10; 1 Kgs 18:31; 2 Kgs 17:34.

GN

then asked him, "Please tell me your name." He answered, "Why do you ask for my name?" With that, he blessed him. ³¹Jacob named the place Peniel,* "because I have seen God face to face," he said, "yet my life has been spared."^f

³²At sunrise, as he left Penuel, Jacob limped along because of his hip. ³³That is why, to this day, the Israelites do not eat the sciatic muscle that is on the hip socket, because he had struck Jacob's hip socket at the sciatic muscle.

CHAPTER 33

Jacob and Esau Meet.[†] ¹Jacob looked up and saw Esau coming, and with him four hundred men. So he divided his children among Leah, Rachel, and the two maidservants, ²putting the maidservants and their children first, Leah and her children next, and Rachel and Joseph last. ³He himself went on ahead of them, bowing to the ground seven times, until he reached his brother. ⁴Esau ran to meet him, embraced him, and flinging himself on his neck, kissed him as he wept.

⁵Then Esau looked up and saw the women and children and asked, "Who are these with you?" Jacob answered, "They are the children with whom God has graciously favored your servant." ⁶Then the maidservants and their children came forward and bowed low; ⁷next, Leah and her children came forward and bowed low; lastly, Joseph and Rachel came forward and bowed low. ⁸Then Esau asked, "What did you intend with all those herds that I encountered?" Jacob answered, "It was

to gain my lord's favor." ⁹Esau replied, "I have plenty; my brother, you should keep what is yours." ¹⁰"No, I beg you!" said Jacob. "If you will do me the favor, accept this gift from me, since to see your face is for me like seeing the face of God—and you have received me so kindly. ¹¹Accept the gift I have brought you. For God has been generous toward me, and I have an abundance." Since he urged him strongly, Esau accepted.

¹²Then Esau said, "Let us break camp and be on our way; I will travel in front of you." ¹³But Jacob replied: "As my lord knows, the children are too young. And the flocks and herds that are nursing are a concern to me; if overdriven for even a single day, the whole flock will die. ¹⁴Let my lord, then, go before his servant, while I proceed more slowly at the pace of the livestock before me and at the pace of my children, until I join my lord in Seir." ¹⁵Esau replied, "Let me at least put at your disposal some of the people who are with me." But Jacob said, "Why is this that I am treated so kindly, my lord?" ¹⁶So on that day Esau went on his way back to Seir, ¹⁷and Jacob broke camp for Succoth.[‡] There Jacob built a home for himself and made booths for his livestock. That is why the place was named Succoth.

¹⁸Jacob arrived safely at the city of Shechem, which is in the land of Canaan, when he came from Paddan-aram. He encamped in sight of the city.^a ¹⁹The plot of ground on which he had pitched his tent he bought for a hundred pieces of money[§] from the descendants of Hamor, the father of Shechem.^b ²⁰He set up an altar there and invoked "El, the God of Israel."^c

---

* [32:31] **Peniel**: a variant of the word Penuel (v. 32), the name of a town on the north bank of the Jabbok in Gilead (Jgs 8:8–9, 17; 1 Kgs 12:25). The name is explained as meaning "the face of God," *peni-'el.* **Yet my life has been spared**: see note on 16:13.

† [33:1–20] The truly frightening confrontation seems to have already occurred in Jacob's meeting the divine stranger in the previous chapter. In contrast, this meeting brings reconciliation. Esau, impulsive but largehearted, kisses the cunning Jacob and calls him brother (v. 9). Jacob in return asks Esau to accept his blessing (*berakah*, translated "gift," v. 11), giving back at least symbolically what he had taken many years before and responding to Esau's erstwhile complaint ("he has taken away my blessing," 27:36). Verses 12–17 show that the reconciliation is not total and, further, that Jacob does not intend to share the ancestral land with his brother.

f. [32:31] Jgs 13:22.

‡ [33:17] **Succoth**: an important town near the confluence of the Jabbok and the Jordan (Jos 13:27; Jgs 8:5–16; 1 Kgs 7:46). **Booths**: in Hebrew, *sukkot*, of the same sound as the name of the town.

§ [33:19] **Pieces of money**: in Hebrew, *qesita*, a monetary unit of which the value is unknown. **Descendants of Hamor**: Hamorites, "the people of Hamor"; cf. Jgs 9:28. Hamor was regarded as the eponymous ancestor of the pre-Israelite inhabitants of Shechem.

a. [33:18] Gn 12:6; Jn 4:5.
b. [33:19] Jos 24:32; Jn 4:5; Acts 7:16.
c. [33:20] Jgs 6:24.

CHAPTER 34

The Rape of Dinah. ¹*Dinah, the daughter whom Leah had borne to Jacob, went out to visit some of the women of the land. ²When Shechem, son of Hamor the Hivite,† the leader of the region, saw her, he seized her and lay with her by force. ³He was strongly attracted to Dinah, daughter of Jacob, and was in love with the young woman. So he spoke affectionately to her. ⁴Shechem said to his father Hamor, "Get me this young woman for a wife."

⁵Meanwhile, Jacob heard that Shechem had defiled his daughter Dinah; but since his sons were out in the field with his livestock, Jacob kept quiet until they came home. ⁶Now Hamor, the father of Shechem, went out to discuss the matter with Jacob, ⁷just as Jacob's sons were coming in from the field. When they heard the news, the men were indignant and extremely angry. Shechem had committed an outrage in Israel by lying with Jacob's daughter; such a thing is not done.ᵃ ⁸Hamor appealed to them, saying: "My son Shechem has his heart set on your daughter. Please give her to him as a wife. ⁹Intermarry with us; give your daughters to us, and take our daughters for yourselves. ¹⁰Thus you can live among us. The land is open before you. Settle and move about freely in it and acquire holdings here."‡ ¹¹Then Shechem appealed to Dinah's father and brothers: "Do me this favor, and whatever you ask from me, I will give. ¹²No matter how high you set the bridal price and gift, I will give you whatever you ask from me; only give me the young woman as a wife."

Revenge of Jacob's Sons. ¹³Jacob's sons replied to Shechem and his father Hamor with guile, speaking as they did because he had defiled their sister Dinah. ¹⁴They said to them, "We are not able to do this thing: to give our sister to an uncircumcised man. For that would be a disgrace for us. ¹⁵Only on this condition will we agree to that: that you become like us by having every male among you circumcised. ¹⁶Then we will give you our daughters and take your daughters in marriage; we will settle among you and become one people. ¹⁷But if you do not listen to us and be circumcised, we will take our daughter and go."

¹⁸Their proposal pleased Hamor and his son Shechem. ¹⁹The young man lost no time in acting on the proposal, since he wanted Jacob's daughter. Now he was more highly regarded than anyone else in his father's house. ²⁰So Hamor and his son Shechem went to the gate of their city and said to the men of their city: ²¹"These men are friendly toward us. Let them settle in the land and move about in it freely; there is ample room in the land for them. We can take their daughters in marriage and give our daughters to them. ²²But only on this condition will the men agree to live with us and form one people with us: that every male among us be circumcised as they themselves are. ²³Would not their livestock, their property, and all their animals then be ours? Let us just agree with them, so that they will settle among us."

²⁴All who went out of the gate of the city listened to Hamor and his son Shechem, and all the males, all those who went out of the gate of the city,§

* [34:1–31] The story of the rape of Dinah and the revenge of Jacob's sons on the men of the city of Shechem may reflect the relations of the tribes of Simeon and Levi to their Canaanite neighbors around Shechem; the tribes are represented by their eponymous ancestors. Jacob's farewell testament (49:5–7) cites this incident as the reason for the decline of the tribes of Simeon and Levi. Ominously, vv. 30–31 leave the situation unresolved, with Jacob concerned about the welfare of the whole family, and Simeon and Levi concerned only about the honor of their full sister. The danger to the family from narrow self-interest will continue in the Joseph story.

† [34:2] **Hivite**: the Greek text has "Horite"; the terms were apparently used indiscriminately to designate the Hurrian or other non-Semitic elements in Palestine.

‡ [34:10] Hamor seems to be making concessions to Jacob's family in the hope of avoiding warfare between the two families.

a. [34:7] 2 Sm 13:12.

§ [34:24] **All those who went out of the gate of the city**: apparently meaning all the residents. By temporarily crippling the men through circumcision, Jacob's sons deprived the city of its defenders.

were circumcised. ²⁵On the third day, while they were still in pain, two of Jacob's sons, Simeon and Levi, brothers of Dinah, each took his sword, advanced against the unsuspecting city and massacred all the males.ᵇ ²⁶After they had killed Hamor and his son Shechem with the sword, they took Dinah from Shechem's house and left.ᶜ ²⁷Then the other sons of Jacob followed up the slaughter and sacked the city because their sister had been defiled. ²⁸They took their sheep, cattle and donkeys, whatever was in the city and in the surrounding country. ²⁹They carried off all their wealth, their children, and their women, and looted whatever was in the houses.ᵈ

³⁰Jacob said to Simeon and Levi: "You have brought trouble upon me by making me repugnant to the inhabitants of the land, the Canaanites and the Perizzites. I have so few men that, if these people unite against me and attack me, I and my household will be wiped out." ³¹But they retorted, "Should our sister be treated like a prostitute?"

CHAPTER 35

Bethel Revisited. ¹*God said to Jacob: Go up now to Bethel. Settle there and build an altar there to the God who appeared to you when you were fleeing from your brother Esau.ᵃ ²So Jacob told his household and all who were with him: "Get rid of the foreign gods† among you; then purify yourselves and change your clothes. ³Let us now go up to Bethel so that I might build an altar there to the God who answered me in the day of my distress and who has been with me wherever I have gone." ⁴They gave Jacob all the foreign gods in their possession and also the rings they had in their ears‡ and Jacob buried them under the oak that is near Shechem. ⁵Then, as they set out, a great terror fell upon the surrounding towns, so that no one pursued the sons of Jacob.

⁶Thus Jacob and all the people who were with him arrived in Luz (now Bethel) in the land of Canaan.ᵇ ⁷There he built an altar and called the place El-Bethel,§ for it was there that God had revealed himself to him when he was fleeing from his brother.ᶜ

⁸Deborah, Rebekah's nurse, died. She was buried under the oak below Bethel, and so it was named Allon-bacuth.¶

⁹On Jacob's arrival from Paddan-aram, God appeared to him again and blessed him. ¹⁰God said to him:

Your name is Jacob.
You will no longer be named Jacob,
but Israel will be your name.ᵈ

So he was named Israel. ¹¹Then God said to him: I am God Almighty; be fruitful and multiply. A nation, indeed an assembly of nations, will stem from you, and kings will issue from your loins. ¹²The land I gave to Abraham and Isaac I will give to you; and to your descendants after you I will give the land.ᵉ

¹³Then God departed from him. ¹⁴In the place where God had spoken with him, Jacob set up a sacred pillar, a stone pillar, and upon it he made a libation and poured out oil.ᶠ ¹⁵Jacob

---

* [35:1–7] Jacob returns to Bethel and founds the sanctuary, an event that forms a "bookend" to the first visit to Bethel in 28:10–22. To enter the Lord's sanctuary, one must purify oneself and get rid of all signs of allegiance to other gods (Jos 24:23; Jgs 10:16). Jacob also seems to initiate the custom of making a pilgrimage to Bethel (see Ps 122:1 and Is 2:3, 5).

† [35:2] **Foreign gods**: divine images, including those of household deities (see note on 31:19), that Jacob's people brought with them from Paddan-aram.

b. [34:25] Gn 49:6.
c. [34:26] Jdt 9:2.
d. [34:29] Jdt 9:3–4.

a. [35:1] Gn 28:12–13.

‡ [35:4] **Rings . . . their ears**: the earrings may have belonged to the gods because earrings were often placed on statues.

§ [35:7] **El-Bethel**: probably to be translated "the god of Bethel." This is one of several titles of God in Genesis that begin with *El* (= God), e.g., *El Olam* (21:33), *El Elyon* (14:18), *El* the God of Israel (33:20), *El Roi* (16:13), and *El Shaddai*. Most of these (except *El Shaddai*) are tied to specific Israelite shrines.

¶ [35:8] **Allon-bacuth**: the Hebrew name means "oak of weeping."

b. [35:6] Gn 28:19; Jos 18:13; Jgs 1:22–23.
c. [35:7] Gn 28:12–13.
d. [35:10] 1 Kgs 18:31; 2 Kgs 17:34.
e. [35:12] Ex 32:13; Heb 11:9.
f. [35:14] Gn 28:18; 31:45.

GN

named the place where God spoke to him Bethel.

Jacob's Family. ¹⁶Then they departed from Bethel; but while they still had some distance to go to Ephrath, Rachel went into labor and suffered great distress. ¹⁷When her labor was most intense, the midwife said to her, "Do not fear, for now you have another son." ¹⁸With her last breath—for she was at the point of death—she named him Ben-oni;[*] but his father named him Benjamin. ¹⁹Thus Rachel died; and she was buried on the road to Ephrath (now Bethlehem).^{†g} ²⁰Jacob set up a sacred pillar on her grave, and the same pillar marks Rachel's grave to this day.

²¹Israel moved on and pitched his tent beyond Migdal-eder. ²²While Israel was encamped in that region, Reuben went and lay with Bilhah, his father's concubine. When Israel heard of it, he was greatly offended.^{‡h}

The sons of Jacob were now twelve. ²³The sons of Leah: Reuben, Jacob's firstborn, Simeon, Levi, Judah, Issachar, and Zebulun; ^{24§}the sons of Rachel: Joseph and Benjamin; ²⁵the sons of Rachel's maidservant Bilhah: Dan and Naphtali; ²⁶the sons of Leah's maidservant Zilpah: Gad and Asher. These are the sons of Jacob who were born to him in Paddan-aram.

²⁷Jacob went home to his father Isaac at Mamre, in Kiriath-arba (now Hebron), where Abraham and Isaac had resided. ²⁸The length of Isaac's life was one hundred and eighty years; ²⁹then he breathed his last. He died as an old man and was gathered to his people. After a full life, his sons Esau and Jacob buried him.

CHAPTER 36

Edomite Lists.¶ ¹These are the descendants of Esau (that is, Edom). ²"Esau took his wives from among the Canaanite women: Adah, daughter of Elon the Hittite; Oholibamah, the daughter of Anah the son of Zibeon the Hivite;^a ³and Basemath, daughter of Ishmael and sister of Nebaioth. ⁴Adah bore Eliphaz to Esau; Basemath bore Reuel;^b ⁵and Oholibamah bore Jeush, Jalam and Korah. These are the sons of Esau who were born to him in the land of Canaan.^c

⁶Esau took his wives, his sons, his daughters, and all the members of his household, as well as his livestock, all his cattle, and all the property he had acquired in the land of Canaan, and went to the land of Seir, away from his brother Jacob.^d ⁷Their possessions had become too great for them to dwell together, and the land in which they were residing could not support them because of their livestock. ⁸So Esau settled in the highlands of Seir. (Esau is Edom.)^e ⁹These are the descendants

---

* [35:18] **Ben-oni:** means either "son of my vigor" or, more likely in the context, "son of affliction." **Benjamin:** "son of the right hand," meaning a son who is his father's help and support.

† [35:19] **Bethlehem:** the gloss comes from a later tradition that identified the site with Bethlehem, also called Ephrath or Ephratha (Jos 15:59; Ru 4:11; Mi 5:1). But Rachel's grave was actually near Ramah (Jer 31:15), a few miles north of Jerusalem, in the territory of Benjamin (1 Sm 10:2).

‡ [35:22] The genealogy in vv. 23–29 is prefaced by a notice about Reuben's sleeping with Bilhah, his father's concubine. Such an act is a serious challenge to the authority of the father (cf. 2 Sm 3:7 and 16:21). In his final testament in chap. 49, Jacob cites this act of Reuben as the reason for Reuben's loss of the authority he had as firstborn son (49:4). Reuben's act is one more instance of strife in the family and of discord between father and son.

§ [35:24–26] Benjamin is here said to have been born in Paddan-aram, apparently because all twelve sons of Jacob are considered as a unit.

¶ [36:1–43] The line of Esau. In the preceding chapter (35:22–26), the list of Jacob's children completes the narrative of Jacob; in this chapter, the narrative of Esau is complete when his descendants are listed. The notice of Abraham's death and burial in 25:7–10 was followed by a list of the line of his elder son Ishmael (25:12–18) and here Jacob's death and burial are followed by the line of Esau. The lines of both Ishmael and Esau are introduced by the same double formula, "These are the descendants of . . . " (25:12; 36:9) and "These are the names of the sons of . . . " (25:13; 36:10). The chapter consists of diverse material: vv. 1–3, Esau's wives; vv. 9–14, Esau's descendants; vv. 15–19, the clans of Esau; vv. 20–30, the Horites of Seir; vv. 31–39, the Edomite kings; vv. 40–43, the Edomites.

** [36:2–14] The names of Esau's wives and of their fathers given here differ considerably from their names cited from other old sources in 26:34 and 28:9. **Zibeon the Hivite:** in v. 20 he is called a "Horite"; see note on 34:2.

---

a. [36:2] Gn 26:34.
b. [36:4] 1 Chr 1:35.
c. [36:5] 1 Chr 1:35.
d. [36:6] Gn 32:4.
e. [36:8] Dt 2:4–5; Jos 24:4.

---

g. [35:19] Gn 48:7; 1 Sm 10:2; Mi 5:1.
h. [35:22] Gn 49:4; 1 Chr 5:1.

of Esau,* ancestor of the Edomites, in the highlands of Seir.

10These are the names of the sons of Esau: Eliphaz, son of Adah, wife of Esau, and Reuel, son of Basemath, wife of Esau. **11f**The sons of Eliphaz were Teman, Omar, Zepho, Gatam, and Kenaz. **12**Timna was a concubine of Eliphaz, the son of Esau, and she bore Amalek to Eliphaz. Those were the sons of Adah, the wife of Esau. **13**These were the sons of Reuel: Nahath, Zerah, Shammah, and Mizzah. Those were the sons of Basemath, the wife of Esau.*g* **14**These were the sons of Esau's wife Oholibamah—the daughter of Anah, son of Zibeon—whom she bore to Esau: Jeush, Jalam, and Korah.*h*

15These are the clans of the sons of Esau. The sons of Eliphaz, Esau's firstborn: the clans of Teman, Omar, Zepho, Kenaz, **16**Korah, Gatam, and Amalek. These are the clans of Eliphaz in the land of Edom; they are the sons of Adah. **17**These are the sons of Reuel, son of Esau: the clans of Nahath, Zerah, Shammah, and Mizzah. These are the clans of Reuel in the land of Edom; they are the sons of Basemath, wife of Esau. **18**These were the sons of Oholibamah, wife of Esau: the clans of Jeush, Jalam, and Korah. These are the clans of Esau's wife Oholibamah, daughter of Anah. **19**These are the sons of Esau—that is, Edom—according to their clans.

20These are the sons of Seir the Horite,† the inhabitants of the land: Lotan, Shobal, Zibeon, Anah,*i* **21**Dishon, Ezer, and Dishan; those are the clans of the Horites, sons of Seir in the land of Edom. **22j**The sons of Lotan were Hori and Hemam, and Lotan's sister was Timna. **23**These are the sons of Shobal: Alvan, Mahanath, Ebal, Shepho, and Onam. **24**These are the sons of Zibeon: Aiah and Anah. He is the Anah who found water in the desert while he was pasturing the donkeys of his father Zibeon. **25**These are the children of Anah: Dishon and Oholibamah, daughter of Anah. **26**These are the sons of Dishon: Hemdan, Eshban, Ithran, and Cheran. **27**These are the sons of Ezer: Bilhan, Zaavan, and Akan. **28**These are the sons of Dishan: Uz and Aran. **29**These are the clans of the Horites: the clans of Lotan, Shobal, Zibeon, Anah, **30**Dishon, Ezer, and Dishan; those are the clans of the Horites, clan by clan, in the land of Seir.

31k These are the kings who reigned in the land of Edom before any king reigned over the Israelites.‡ **32**Bela, son of Beor, became king in Edom; the name of his city was Dinhabah. **33**When Bela died, Jobab, son of Zerah, from Bozrah, succeeded him as king. **34**When Jobab died, Husham, from the land of the Temanites, succeeded him as king. **35**When Husham died, Hadad, son of Bedad, succeeded him as king. He is the one who defeated Midian in the country of Moab; the name of his city was Avith. **36**When Hadad died, Samlah, from Masrekah, succeeded him as king. **37**When Samlah died, Shaul, from Rehoboth-on-the-River, succeeded him as king. **38**When Shaul died, Baal-hanan, son of Achbor, succeeded him as king. **39**When Baal-hanan, son of Achbor, died, Hadad succeeded him as king; the name of his city was Pau. His wife's name was Mehetabel, the daughter of Matred, son of Mezahab.

40These are the names of the clans of Esau identified according to their

---

* [36:9] **These are the descendants of Esau**: the original heading of the genealogy is preserved in v. 10 ("These are the names of the sons of Esau"). This use of the Priestly formula is secondary and should not be counted in the list of ten such formulas in Genesis.

† [36:20] **Seir the Horite**: according to Dt 2:12, the highlands of Seir were inhabited by Horites before they were occupied by the Edomites.

f. [36:11–12] 1 Chr 1:36.
g. [36:13] 1 Chr 1:37.
h. [36:14] 1 Chr 1:35.
i. [36:20–21] 1 Chr 1:38.
j. [36:22–28] 1 Chr 1:39–42.

‡ [36:31] **Before any king reigned over the Israelites**: obviously this statement was written after the time of Saul, Israel's first king. According to 1 Sm 14:47, Saul waged war against the Edomites; according to 2 Sm 8:2, 13–14 and 1 Kgs 11:14–17, David made Edom a vassal state and nearly wiped out the royal line. These events reflect the words of the Lord to Rebekah at the birth of the boys, "the older shall serve the younger" (25:23).

k. [36:31–43] 1 Chr 1:43–54.

families and localities: the clans of Timna, Alvah, Jetheth, **41**Oholibamah, Elah, Pinon, **42**Kenaz, Teman, Mibzar, **43**Magdiel, and Iram. Those are the clans of the Edomites, according to their settlements in their territorial holdings—that is, of Esau, the ancestor of the Edomites.

CHAPTER 37

Joseph Sold into Egypt. 1 Jacob settled in the land where his father had sojourned, the land of Canaan.* **2**This is the story of the family of Jacob.† When Joseph was seventeen years old, he was tending the flocks with his brothers; he was an assistant to the sons of his father's wives Bilhah and Zilpah, and Joseph brought their father bad reports about them. **3**Israel loved Joseph best of all his sons, for he was the child of his old age; and he had made him a long ornamented tunic.‡ **4**When his brothers saw that their father loved him best of all his brothers, they hated him so much that they could not say a kind word to him.

5 §Once Joseph had a dream, and when he told his brothers, they hated him even more.**a 6**He said to them, "Listen to this dream I had. **7**There we were, binding sheaves in the field, when suddenly my sheaf rose to an upright position, and your sheaves formed a ring around my sheaf and bowed down to it." **8**His brothers said to him, "Are you really going to make yourself king over us? Will you rule over us?" So they hated him all the more because of his dreams and his reports.**b**

9Then he had another dream, and told it to his brothers. "Look, I had another dream," he said; "this time, the sun and the moon and eleven stars were bowing down to me." **10**When he told it to his father and his brothers, his father reproved him and asked, "What is the meaning of this dream of yours? Can it be that I and your mother and your brothers are to come and bow to the ground before you?" **11**So his brothers were furious at him but his father kept the matter in mind.

12One day, when his brothers had gone to pasture their father's flocks at Shechem, **13**Israel said to Joseph, "Are your brothers not tending our flocks at Shechem? Come and I will send you to them." "I am ready," Joseph answered. **14**"Go then," he replied; "see if all is well with your brothers and the flocks, and bring back word." So he sent him off from the valley of Hebron. When Joseph reached Shechem, **15**a man came upon him as he was wandering about in the fields. "What are you looking for?" the man asked him. **16**"I am looking for my brothers," he answered. "Please tell me where they are tending the flocks." **17**The man told him, "They have moved on from here; in fact, I heard them say, 'Let us go on to Dothan.'" So Joseph went after his

---

* [37:1] The statement points ahead to 47:27, "Thus Israel settled in the land of Egypt, in the region of Goshen." These two statements frame the Joseph narrative; the later material (47:28–49:33) is about Jacob; chap. 50 brings to a conclusion themes remaining from the earlier story. One aim of the Joseph story is to explain how Israel came to Egypt after sojourning so long in Canaan.

† [37:2] The Joseph story is great literature not only in its themes but in its art. The stories show an interest in the psychology of the characters; everyone acts "in character" yet there is never a doubt that a divine purpose is bringing events to their conclusion. According to a literary analysis, vv. 1–4 set the scene; vv. 5–36 introduce the dramatic tension in the form of a conflict within the family; chaps. 38–41 describe the journeys away from their family of the eponymous ancestors of the two great tribes of later times, Judah (chap. 38) and Joseph (chaps. 39–41) and their preliminary conclusions; chaps. 42–44 detail the famine and journeys for food (chaps. 42, 43) that bring the brothers and (indirectly) the father into fresh contact with a mature Joseph who now has the power of life and death over them; 45:1–47:27 is the resolution (reconciliation of Joseph to his brothers) and the salvation of the family.

‡ [37:3] Jacob's favoring Joseph over his other sons is a cause of the brothers' attempt on his life. Throughout the story, Jacob is unaware of the impact of his favoritism on his other sons (cf. vv. 33–35; 42:36). **Long ornamented tunic:** the meaning of the Hebrew phrase is unclear. In 2 Sm 13:18–19, it is the distinctive dress of unmarried royal daughters. The "coat of many colors" in the Septuagint became the traditional translation. Ancient depictions of Semites in formal dress show them with long, ornamented robes and that is the most likely meaning here. Possibly, the young Joseph is given a coat that symbolizes honor beyond his years. Later, Pharaoh will clothe Joseph in a robe that symbolizes honor (41:42).

§ [37:5–10] Joseph's dreams of ruling his brothers appear at first glance to be merely adolescent grandiosity, and they bring him only trouble. His later successes make it clear, however, that they were from God. Another confirmation of their divine source is the doubling of dreams (cf. 41:32).

a. [37:5] Gn 42:9.
b. [37:8] Gn 50:17–18.

brothers and found them in Dothan. [18]They saw him from a distance, and before he reached them, they plotted to kill him. [19]They said to one another: "Here comes that dreamer! [20]Come now, let us kill him and throw him into one of the cisterns here; we could say that a wild beast devoured him. We will see then what comes of his dreams."[c]

[21]*But when Reuben heard this, he tried to save him from their hands, saying: "We must not take his life." [22]Then Reuben said, "Do not shed blood! Throw him into this cistern in the wilderness; but do not lay a hand on him." His purpose was to save him from their hands and restore him to his father.[d]

[23]So when Joseph came up to his brothers, they stripped him of his tunic, the long ornamented tunic he had on; [24]then they took him and threw him into the cistern. The cistern was empty; there was no water in it.

[25]Then they sat down to eat. Looking up, they saw a caravan of Ishmaelites coming from Gilead, their camels laden with gum, balm, and resin to be taken down to Egypt.[e] [26]Judah said to his brothers: "What is to be gained by killing our brother and concealing his blood?[f] [27]Come, let us sell him to these Ishmaelites, instead of doing away with him ourselves. After all, he is our brother, our own flesh." His brothers agreed.

[28]Midianite traders passed by, and they pulled Joseph up out of the cistern. They sold Joseph for twenty pieces of silver[†] to the Ishmaelites, who took him to Egypt.[g] [29]When Reuben went back to the cistern and saw that Joseph was not in it, he tore his garments,[‡] [30]and returning to his brothers, he exclaimed: "The boy is gone! And I—where can I turn?" [31]They took Joseph's tunic, and after slaughtering a goat, dipped the tunic in its blood. [32]Then they sent someone to bring the long ornamented tunic to their father, with the message: "We found this. See whether it is your son's tunic or not." [33]He recognized it and exclaimed: "My son's tunic! A wild beast has devoured him! Joseph has been torn to pieces!"[h] [34]Then Jacob tore his garments, put sackcloth on his loins, and mourned his son many days. [35]Though his sons and daughters tried to console him, he refused all consolation, saying, "No, I will go down mourning to my son in Sheol."[§] Thus did his father weep for him.[i]

[36]The Midianites, meanwhile, sold Joseph in Egypt to Potiphar, an official of Pharaoh and his chief steward.[j]

CHAPTER 38

Judah and Tamar.[¶] [1]About that time Judah went down, away from

---

† [37:28] **They sold Joseph...silver:** editors tried to solve the confusion, created by different sources, by supposing that it was the Midianite traders who pulled Joseph out of the pit and sold him to Ishmaelites. In all probability, one source had the brothers selling Joseph to Ishmaelites, whereas the other had them cast him into the pit whence he was taken by Midianite traders.

‡ [37:29] **Tore his garments:** the traditional sign of mourning in the ancient Near East.

§ [37:35] **Sheol:** see note on Ps 6:6.

¶ [38:1–30] This chapter has subtle connections to the main Joseph story. It tells of the eponymous founder of the other great tribe of later times, Judah. Having already been introduced as one of the two good brothers in 37:26–27, he appears here as the father-in-law of the twice-widowed Tamar; he has reneged on his promise to provide his son Shelah to her in a levirate marriage. Unjustly treated, Tamar takes matters into her own hands and tricks Judah into becoming the father of her children, Perez and Zerah. Judah ultimately acknowledges that his daughter-in-law was right ("She is in the right rather than I," v. 26). In contrast to Judah's expectations, the family line does not continue through his son Shelah, but through the children of Tamar. Similarities relate this little story to the main narrative: the deception involving an article of clothing (the widow's garments of Tamar, Judah's seal, cord, and staff) point back to the bloody tunic that deceives Jacob in 37:31–33; a woman attempts the seduction of a man separated from his family, for righteous purposes in chap. 38, for unrighteous purposes in chap. 39.

---

* [37:21–36] The chapter thus far is from the Yahwist source, as are also vv. 25–28a. But vv. 21–24 and 28b–36 are from another source (sometimes designated the Elohist source). In the latter, Reuben tries to rescue Joseph, who is taken in Reuben's absence by certain Midianites; in the Yahwist source, it is Judah who saves Joseph's life by having him sold to certain Ishmaelites. Although the two variant forms in which the story was handed down in early oral tradition differ in these minor points, they agree on the essential fact that Joseph was brought as a slave into Egypt because of the jealousy of his brothers.

c. [37:20] Gn 44:28.
d. [37:22] Gn 42:22.
e. [37:25] Gn 43:11.
f. [37:26] Jb 16:18.

g. [37:28] Ps 105:17; Wis 10:13; Acts 7:9.
h. [37:33] Gn 44:28.
i. [37:35] Gn 42:38.
j. [37:36] Ps 105:17.

GN

his brothers, and pitched his tent near a certain Adullamite named Hirah. ²There Judah saw the daughter of a Canaanite named Shua; he married her, and had intercourse with her.ᵃ ³She conceived and bore a son, whom she named Er. ⁴Again she conceived and bore a son, whom she named Onan. ⁵Then she bore still another son, whom she named Shelah. She was in Chezib* when she bore him.ᵇ

⁶Judah got a wife named Tamar for his firstborn, Er. ⁷But Er, Judah's firstborn, greatly offended the LORD; so the LORD took his life.ᶜ ⁸ᵈThen Judah said to Onan, "Have intercourse with your brother's wife, in fulfillment of your duty as brother-in-law, and thus preserve your brother's line."† ⁹Onan, however, knew that the offspring would not be his; so whenever he had intercourse with his brother's wife, he wasted his seed on the ground, to avoid giving offspring to his brother. ¹⁰What he did greatly offended the LORD, and the LORD took his life too. ¹¹Then Judah said to his daughter-in-law Tamar, "Remain a widow in your father's house until my son Shelah grows up"—for he feared that Shelah also might die like his brothers. So Tamar went to live in her father's house.

¹²Time passed, and the daughter of Shua, Judah's wife, died. After Judah completed the period of mourning, he went up to Timnah, to those who were shearing his sheep, in company with his friend Hirah the Adullamite. ¹³Then Tamar was told, "Your father-in-law is on his way up to Timnah to shear his sheep." ¹⁴So she took off her widow's garments, covered herself with a shawl, and having wrapped

herself sat down at the entrance to Enaim, which is on the way to Timnah; for she was aware that, although Shelah was now grown up, she had not been given to him in marriage.ᵉ ¹⁵When Judah saw her, he thought she was a harlot, since she had covered her face. ¹⁶So he went over to her at the roadside and said, "Come, let me have intercourse with you," for he did not realize that she was his daughter-in-law. She replied, "What will you pay me for letting you have intercourse with me?" ¹⁷He answered, "I will send you a young goat from the flock." "Very well," she said, "provided you leave me a pledge until you send it." ¹⁸Judah asked, "What pledge should I leave you?" She answered, "Your seal and cord,‡ and the staff in your hand." So he gave them to her and had intercourse with her, and she conceived by him. ¹⁹After she got up and went away, she took off her shawl and put on her widow's garments again.

²⁰Judah sent the young goat by his friend the Adullamite to recover the pledge from the woman; but he did not find her. ²¹So he asked the men of that place, "Where is the prostitute,§ the one by the roadside in Enaim?" But they answered, "No prostitute has been here." ²²He went back to Judah and told him, "I did not find her; and besides, the men of the place said, 'No prostitute has been here.'" ²³"Let her keep the things," Judah replied; "otherwise we will become a laughingstock. After all, I did send her this young goat, but you did not find her."

²⁴About three months later, Judah was told, "Your daughter-in-law Tamar has acted like a harlot and now she

* [38:5] **Chezib**: a variant form of Achzib (Jos 15:44; Mi 1:14), a town in the Judean Shephelah.
† [38:8] **Preserve your brother's line**: lit., "raise up seed for your brother": an allusion to the law of levirate, or "brother-in-law," marriage; see notes on Dt 25:5; Ru 2:20. Onan's violation of this law brought on him God's punishment (vv. 9–10).

a. [38:2] 1 Chr 2:3.
b. [38:5] 1 Chr 4:21.
c. [38:7] 1 Chr 2:3.
d. [38:8] Dt 25:5; Mt 22:24; Mk 12:19; Lk 20:28.

‡ [38:18] **Seal and cord**: the cylinder seal, through which a hole was bored lengthwise so that it could be worn from the neck by a cord, was a distinctive means of identification. Apparently one's staff could also be marked with some sign of identification (cf. Nm 17:17–18).
§ [38:21] **Prostitute**: the Hebrew term *qedesha*, lit., "consecrated woman," designates a woman associated with a sanctuary whose activities could include prostitution; cf. Dt 23:18; Hos 4:14, where the same Hebrew word is used. In 38:15 and 24 the common word for prostitute, *zona*, is used.

e. [38:14] Prv 7:10.

is pregnant from her harlotry." Judah said, "Bring her out; let her be burned." ²⁵But as she was being brought out, she sent word to her father-in-law, "It is by the man to whom these things belong that I am pregnant." Then she said, "See whose seal and cord and staff these are." ²⁶Judah recognized them and said, "She is in the right rather than I, since I did not give her to my son Shelah." He had no further sexual relations with her.

²⁷When the time of her delivery came, there were twins in her womb.^f ²⁸While she was giving birth, one put out his hand; and the midwife took and tied a crimson thread on his hand, noting, "This one came out first." ^{29g}But as he withdrew his hand, his brother came out; and she said, "What a breach you have made for yourself!" So he was called Perez.[*] ³⁰Afterward his brother, who had the crimson thread on his hand, came out; he was called Zerah.^{†h}

CHAPTER 39

Joseph's Temptation. ¹When Joseph was taken down to Egypt, an Egyptian, Potiphar, an official of Pharaoh and his chief steward, bought him from the Ishmaelites who had brought him there. ^{2a}The LORD was with Joseph and he enjoyed great success and was assigned to the household of his Egyptian master. ³When his master saw that the LORD was with him and brought him success in whatever he did, ⁴he favored Joseph and made him his personal attendant; he put him in charge of his household and entrusted to him all his possessions.^b ⁵From the moment that he put him in charge of his household and all his possessions, the LORD blessed the Egyptian's house for Joseph's sake; the LORD's blessing was on everything he owned, both inside the house and out. ⁶Having left everything he owned in Joseph's charge, he gave no thought, with Joseph there, to anything but the food he ate.

Now Joseph was well-built and handsome. ⁷After a time, his master's wife looked at him with longing and said, "Lie with me." ⁸But he refused and said to his master's wife, "Look, as long as I am here, my master does not give a thought to anything in the house, but has entrusted to me all he owns. ⁹He has no more authority in this house than I do. He has withheld from me nothing but you, since you are his wife. How, then, could I do this great wrong and sin against God?" ¹⁰Although she spoke to him day after day, he would not agree to lie with her, or even be near her.^c

¹¹One such day, when Joseph came into the house to do his work, and none of the household servants were then in the house, ¹²she laid hold of him by his cloak, saying, "Lie with me!" But leaving the cloak in her hand, he escaped and ran outside. ¹³When she saw that he had left his cloak in her hand as he escaped outside, ¹⁴she cried out to her household servants and told them, "Look! My husband has brought us a Hebrew man to mock us! He came in here to lie with me, but I cried out loudly. ¹⁵When he heard me scream, he left his cloak beside me and escaped and ran outside."

¹⁶She kept the cloak with her until his master came home. ¹⁷Then she told him the same story: "The Hebrew slave whom you brought us came to me to amuse himself at my expense. ¹⁸But when I screamed, he left his cloak beside me and escaped outside." ¹⁹When the master heard his wife's story in which she reported, "Thus and

---

* [38:29] **He was called Perez:** the Hebrew word means "breach."
† [38:30] **He was called Zerah:** a name connected here by popular etymology with a Hebrew word for the red light of dawn, alluding apparently to the crimson thread.

f. [38:27] 1 Chr 2:4.
g. [38:29] Ru 4:12; Mt 1:3; Lk 3:33.
h. [38:30] Nm 26:20; 1 Chr 2:4; Mt 1:3.

a. [39:2] 1 Sm 3:19; 10:7; 18:14; 2 Sm 5:10; 2 Kgs 18:7; Acts 7:9.
b. [39:4] Dn 1:9.

c. [39:10] 1 Mc 2:53.

so your servant did to me," he became enraged. ²⁰Joseph's master seized him and put him into the jail where the king's prisoners were confined.^d And there he sat, in jail.

²¹But the LORD was with Joseph, and showed him kindness by making the chief jailer well-disposed toward him.^e ²²The chief jailer put Joseph in charge of all the prisoners in the jail. Everything that had to be done there, he was the one to do it. ²³The chief jailer did not have to look after anything that was in Joseph's charge, since the LORD was with him and was bringing success to whatever he was doing.

CHAPTER 40

The Dreams Interpreted. ¹*Some time afterward, the royal cupbearer and baker offended their lord, the king of Egypt. ²Pharaoh was angry with his two officials, the chief cupbearer and the chief baker, ³and he put them in custody in the house of the chief steward, the same jail where Joseph was confined. ⁴The chief steward assigned Joseph to them, and he became their attendant.

After they had been in custody for some time, ⁵the cupbearer and the baker of the king of Egypt who were confined in the jail both had dreams on the same night, each his own dream and each dream with its own meaning. ⁶When Joseph came to them in the morning, he saw that they looked disturbed. ⁷So he asked Pharaoh's officials who were with him in custody in his master's house, "Why do you look so troubled today?" ⁸They answered him, "We have had dreams, but there is no one to interpret them." Joseph said to them, "Do interpretations not come from God? Please tell me the dreams."^a

⁹Then the chief cupbearer told Joseph his dream. "In my dream," he said, "I saw a vine in front of me, ¹⁰and on the vine were three branches. It had barely budded when its blossoms came out, and its clusters ripened into grapes. ¹¹Pharaoh's cup was in my hand; so I took the grapes, pressed them out into his cup, and put it in Pharaoh's hand." ¹²Joseph said to him: "This is its interpretation. The three branches are three days; ¹³within three days Pharaoh will single you out[†] and restore you to your post. You will be handing Pharaoh his cup as you formerly did when you were his cupbearer. ¹⁴Only think of me when all is well with you, and please do me the great favor of mentioning me to Pharaoh, to get me out of this place. ¹⁵The truth is that I was kidnapped from the land of the Hebrews, and I have not done anything here that they should have put me into a dungeon."

¹⁶When the chief baker saw that Joseph had given a favorable interpretation, he said to him: "I too had a dream. In it I had three bread baskets on my head; ¹⁷in the top one were all kinds of bakery products for Pharaoh, but the birds were eating them out of the basket on my head." ¹⁸Joseph said to him in reply: "This is its interpretation. The three baskets are three days; ¹⁹within three days Pharaoh will single you out and will impale you on a stake, and the birds will be eating your flesh."

²⁰And so on the third day, which was Pharaoh's birthday, when he gave a banquet to all his servants, he singled out the chief cupbearer and chief baker in the midst of his servants. ²¹He restored the chief cupbearer to his office, so that he again handed the cup to Pharaoh; ²²but the chief baker he impaled—just as Joseph had told them in his interpretation. ²³Yet the chief cupbearer did not think of Joseph; he forgot him.

---

* [40:1] Joseph interprets the dreams of the Pharaoh's two officials. His ability to interpret the dreams shows that God is still with him and points forward to his role of dream interpreter for Pharaoh in chap. 41.

d. [39:20] Ps 105:18.
e. [39:21] Acts 7:9–10.

a. [40:8] Gn 41:16.

† [40:13] **Single you out:** lit., "lift up your head" (see also vv. 19, 20).

CHAPTER 41

Pharaoh's Dream. ¹*After a lapse of two years, Pharaoh had a dream. He was standing by the Nile, ²when up out of the Nile came seven cows, fine-looking and fat; they grazed in the reed grass. ³Behind them seven other cows, poor-looking and gaunt, came up out of the Nile; and standing on the bank of the Nile beside the others, ⁴the poor-looking, gaunt cows devoured the seven fine-looking, fat cows. Then Pharaoh woke up.

⁵He fell asleep again and had another dream. He saw seven ears of grain, fat and healthy, growing on a single stalk. ⁶Behind them sprouted seven ears of grain, thin and scorched by the east wind; ⁷and the thin ears swallowed up the seven fat, healthy ears. Then Pharaoh woke up—it was a dream!

⁸Next morning his mind was agitated. So Pharaoh had all the magicians† and sages of Egypt summoned and recounted his dream to them; but there was no one to interpret it for him. ⁹Then the chief cupbearer said to Pharaoh: "Now I remember my negligence! ¹⁰Once, when Pharaoh was angry with his servants, he put me and the chief baker in custody in the house of the chief steward. ¹¹Later, we both had dreams on the same night, and each of our dreams had its own meaning. ¹²There was a Hebrew youth with us, a slave of the chief steward; and when we told him our dreams, he interpreted them for us and explained for each of us the meaning of his dream.ᵃ ¹³Things turned out just as he

had told us: I was restored to my post, but the other man was impaled."

¹⁴Pharaoh therefore had Joseph summoned, and they hurriedly brought him from the dungeon. After he shaved and changed his clothes, he came to Pharaoh.ᵇ ¹⁵Pharaoh then said to Joseph: "I had a dream but there was no one to interpret it. But I hear it said of you, 'If he hears a dream he can interpret it.'" ¹⁶"It is not I," Joseph replied to Pharaoh, "but God who will respond for the well-being of Pharaoh."ᶜ

¹⁷Then Pharaoh said to Joseph: "In my dream, I was standing on the bank of the Nile, ¹⁸when up from the Nile came seven cows, fat and well-formed; they grazed in the reed grass. ¹⁹Behind them came seven other cows, scrawny, most ill-formed and gaunt. Never have I seen such bad specimens as these in all the land of Egypt! ²⁰The gaunt, bad cows devoured the first seven fat cows. ²¹But when they had consumed them, no one could tell that they had done so, because they looked as bad as before. Then I woke up. ²²In another dream I saw seven ears of grain, full and healthy, growing on a single stalk. ²³Behind them sprouted seven ears of grain, shriveled and thin and scorched by the east wind; ²⁴and the seven thin ears swallowed up the seven healthy ears. I have spoken to the magicians, but there is no one to explain it to me."

²⁵Joseph said to Pharaoh: "Pharaoh's dreams have the same meaning. God has made known to Pharaoh what he is about to do. ²⁶The seven healthy cows are seven years, and the seven healthy ears are seven years—the same in each dream. ²⁷The seven thin, bad cows that came up after them are seven years, as are the seven thin ears scorched by the east wind; they are seven years of famine. ²⁸Things are just as I told Pharaoh: God has revealed to Pharaoh what he is about to do. ²⁹Seven years of great abundance are

---

* [41:1–57] Joseph correctly interprets Pharaoh's dream and becomes second in command over all Egypt.

† [41:8] **Magicians:** one of the tasks of the "magicians" was interpreting dreams. The interpretation of dreams was a long-standing practice in Egypt. A manual of dream interpretation has been found, written in the early second millennium and re-published later in which typical dreams are given ("If a man sees himself in a dream . . .") followed by a judgment of "good" or "bad." Interpreters were still needed for dreams, however, and Pharaoh complains that none of his dream interpreters can interpret his unprecedented dream. The same term will be used of Pharaoh's magicians in Exodus.

a. [41:12] Dn 1:17.

b. [41:14] Ps 105:20.
c. [41:16] Gn 40:8.

now coming throughout the land of Egypt; [30]but seven years of famine will rise up after them, when all the abundance will be forgotten in the land of Egypt. When the famine has exhausted the land, [31]no trace of the abundance will be found in the land because of the famine that follows it, for it will be very severe. [32]That Pharaoh had the same dream twice means that the matter has been confirmed by God and that God will soon bring it about.

[33]"Therefore, let Pharaoh seek out a discerning and wise man and put him in charge of the land of Egypt. [34]Let Pharaoh act and appoint overseers for the land to organize it during the seven years of abundance. [35]They should collect all the food of these coming good years, gathering the grain under Pharaoh's authority, for food in the cities, and they should guard it. [36]This food will serve as a reserve for the country against the seven years of famine that will occur in the land of Egypt, so that the land may not perish in the famine."

[37]This advice pleased Pharaoh and all his servants.[d] [38]"Could we find another like him," Pharaoh asked his servants, "a man so endowed with the spirit of God?" [39]So Pharaoh said to Joseph: "Since God has made all this known to you, there is no one as discerning and wise as you are. [40]You shall be in charge of my household, and all my people will obey your command. Only in respect to the throne will I outrank you."[e] [41]Then Pharaoh said to Joseph, "Look, I put you in charge of the whole land of Egypt." [42]With that, Pharaoh took off his signet ring* and put it on Joseph's finger. He dressed him in robes of fine linen and put a gold chain around his neck. [43]He then had him ride in his second chariot, and they shouted "Abrek!"[†] before him.

Thus was Joseph installed over the whole land of Egypt. [44]"I am Pharaoh," he told Joseph, "but without your approval no one shall lift hand or foot in all the land of Egypt." [45]Pharaoh also bestowed the name of Zaphenath-paneah[‡] on Joseph, and he gave him in marriage Asenath, the daughter of Potiphera, priest of Heliopolis. And Joseph went out over the land of Egypt. [46]Joseph was thirty years old when he entered the service of Pharaoh, king of Egypt.

After Joseph left Pharaoh, he went throughout the land of Egypt. [47]During the seven years of plenty, when the land produced abundant crops, [48]he collected all the food of these years of plenty that the land of Egypt was enjoying and stored it in the cities, placing in each city the crops of the fields around it. [49]Joseph collected grain like the sands of the sea, so much that at last he stopped measuring it, for it was beyond measure.

[50]Before the famine years set in, Joseph became the father of two sons, borne to him by Asenath, daughter of Potiphera, priest of Heliopolis.[f] [51]Joseph named his firstborn Manasseh,[§] meaning, "God has made me forget entirely my troubles and my father's house"; [52]and the second he named Ephraim,[¶] meaning, "God has made me fruitful in the land of my affliction."

[53]When the seven years of abundance enjoyed by the land of Egypt came to an end, [54]the seven years of

---

† [41:43] **Abrek:** apparently a cry of homage, though the word's derivation and actual meaning are uncertain.

‡ [41:45] **Zaphenath-paneah:** a Hebrew transcription of an Egyptian name meaning "the god speaks and he (the newborn child) lives." **Asenath:** means "belonging to (the Egyptian goddess) Neith." **Potiphera:** means "he whom Ra (the Egyptian god) gave"; a shorter form of the same name was borne by Joseph's master (37:36). **Heliopolis:** in Hebrew, *On,* a city seven miles northeast of modern Cairo, site of the chief temple of the sun god; it is mentioned also in v. 50; 46:20; Ez 30:17.

§ [41:51] **Manasseh:** an allusion to this name is in the Hebrew expression, *nishshani,* "he made me forget."

¶ [41:52] **Ephraim:** related to the Hebrew expression *hiphrani,* "(God) has made me fruitful." The name originally meant something like "fertile land."

* [41:42] **Signet ring:** a finger ring in which was set a stamp seal, different from the cylinder seal such as Judah wore; see note on 38:18. By receiving Pharaoh's signet ring, Joseph was made vizier of Egypt (v. 43); the vizier was known as "seal-bearer of the king of Lower Egypt." The gold chain was a symbol of high office in ancient Egypt.

d. [41:37] Acts 7:10.
e. [41:40] 1 Mc 2:53; Ps 105:21; Wis 10:14; Acts 7:10.
f. [41:50] Gn 46:20; 48:5.

GN

famine set in, just as Joseph had said. Although there was famine in all the other countries, food was available throughout the land of Egypt.*g* 55When all the land of Egypt became hungry and the people cried to Pharaoh for food, Pharaoh said to all the Egyptians: "Go to Joseph and do whatever he tells you." 56When the famine had spread throughout the land, Joseph opened all the cities that had grain and rationed it to the Egyptians, since the famine had gripped the land of Egypt. 57Indeed, the whole world came to Egypt to Joseph to buy grain, for famine had gripped the whole world.

CHAPTER 42

The Brothers' First Journey to Egypt.* 1When Jacob learned that grain rations were for sale in Egypt, he said to his sons: "Why do you keep looking at one another?" 2He went on, "I hear that grain is for sale in Egypt. Go down there and buy some for us, that we may stay alive and not die."*a* 3So ten of Joseph's brothers went down to buy grain from Egypt. 4But Jacob did not send Joseph's brother Benjamin with his brothers, for he thought some disaster might befall him. 5And so the sons of Israel were among those who came to buy grain, since there was famine in the land of Canaan.*b*

6Joseph, as governor of the country, was the one who sold grain to all the people of the land. When Joseph's brothers came, they bowed down to him with their faces to the ground.*c* 7He recognized them as soon as he

saw them. But he concealed his own identity from them and spoke harshly to them. "Where do you come from?" he asked them. They answered, "From the land of Canaan, to buy food."

8When Joseph recognized his brothers, although they did not recognize him, 9he was reminded of the dreams he had about them. He said to them: "You are spies.*d* You have come to see the weak points† of the land." 10"No, my lord," they replied. "On the contrary, your servants have come to buy food. 11All of us are sons of the same man. We are honest men; your servants have never been spies." 12But he answered them: "Not so! It is the weak points of the land that you have come to see." 13"We your servants," they said, "are twelve brothers, sons of a certain man in Canaan; but the youngest one is at present with our father, and the other one is no more."*e* 14"It is just as I said," Joseph persisted; "you are spies. 15This is how you shall be tested: I swear by the life of Pharaoh that you shall not leave here unless your youngest brother comes here. 16So send one of your number to get your brother, while the rest of you stay here under arrest. Thus will your words be tested for their truth; if they are untrue, as Pharaoh lives, you are spies!" 17With that, he locked them up in the guardhouse for three days.

18On the third day Joseph said to them: "Do this, and you shall live; for I am a God-fearing man. 19If you are honest men, let one of your brothers be confined in this prison, while the rest of you go and take home grain for your starving families. 20But you must bring me your youngest brother. Your words will thus be verified, and you will not die." To this they agreed.*f* 21To one another, however, they said: "Truly we are being punished because

---

* [42:1–38] The first journey of the brothers to Egypt. Its cause is famine, which was also the reason Abraham and Sarah undertook their dangerous journey to Egypt. The brothers bow to Joseph in v. 6, which fulfills Joseph's dream in 37:5–11. Endowed with wisdom, Joseph begins a process of instruction or "discipline" for his brothers that eventually forces them to recognize the enormity of their sin against him and the family. He controls their experience of the first journey with the result that the second journey in chaps. 43–44 leads to full acknowledgment and reconciliation.

g. [41:54] Ps 105:16; Acts 7:11.

a. [42:2] Acts 7:12.
b. [42:5] Jdt 5:10; Acts 7:11.
c. [42:6] Ps 105:21.

† [42:9, 12] **Weak points:** lit., "the nakedness of the land"; the military weakness of the land, like human nakedness, should not be seen by strangers.

d. [42:9] Gn 37:5.
e. [42:13] Gn 44:20.
f. [42:20] Gn 43:5.

of our brother. We saw the anguish of his heart when he pleaded with us, yet we would not listen. That is why this anguish has now come upon us."[g] [22]Then Reuben responded, "Did I not tell you, 'Do no wrong to the boy'? But you would not listen! Now comes the reckoning for his blood."[h] [23]They did not know, of course, that Joseph understood what they said, since he spoke with them through an interpreter. [24]But turning away from them, he wept. When he was able to speak to them again, he took Simeon from among them and bound him before their eyes. [25]Then Joseph gave orders to have their containers filled with grain, their money replaced in each one's sack, and provisions given them for their journey. After this had been done for them, [26]they loaded their donkeys with the grain and departed.

[27]At the night encampment, when one of them opened his bag to give his donkey some fodder, he saw his money there in the mouth of his bag. [28]He cried out to his brothers, "My money has been returned! Here it is in my bag!" At that their hearts sank. Trembling, they asked one another, "What is this that God has done to us?"

[29]When they got back to their father Jacob in the land of Canaan, they told him all that had happened to them. [30]"The man who is lord of the land," they said, "spoke to us harshly and put us in custody on the grounds that we were spying on the land. [31]But we said to him: 'We are honest men; we have never been spies. [32]We are twelve brothers, sons of the same father; but one is no more, and the youngest one is now with our father in the land of Canaan.' [33]Then the man who is lord of the land said to us: 'This is how I will know if you are honest men: leave one of your brothers with me, then take grain for your starving families and go. [34]When you bring me your youngest brother, and I know that you

are not spies but honest men, I will restore your brother to you, and you may move about freely in the land.'"

[35]When they were emptying their sacks, there in each one's sack was his moneybag! At the sight of their moneybags, they and their father were afraid. [36]Their father Jacob said to them: "Must you make me childless? Joseph is no more, Simeon is no more, and now you would take Benjamin away! All these things have happened to me!" [37]Then Reuben told his father: "You may kill my own two sons if I do not return him to you! Put him in my care, and I will bring him back to you." [38]But Jacob replied: "My son shall not go down with you. Now that his brother is dead, he is the only one left. If some disaster should befall him on the journey you must make, you would send my white head down to Sheol in grief."[i]

CHAPTER 43

The Second Journey to Egypt.[*] [1]Now the famine in the land grew severe. [2]So when they had used up all the grain they had brought from Egypt, their father said to them, "Go back and buy us a little more food." [3]But Judah replied: "The man strictly warned us, 'You shall not see me unless your brother is with you.'[a] [4]If you are willing to let our brother go with us, we will go down to buy food for you. [5]But if you are not willing, we will not go down, because the man told us, 'You shall not see me unless your brother is with you.'"[b] [6]Israel demanded, "Why did you bring this trouble on me by telling the man that you had another brother?" [7]They answered: "The man kept asking about us and our family:

---

* [43:1–34] The second journey to Egypt. Joseph the sage has carefully prepared the brothers for a possible reconciliation. In this chapter and the following one Judah steps forward as the hero, in contrast to chaps. 37 and 42 where Reuben was the hero. Here Judah serves as guarantee for Benjamin.

i. [42:38] Gn 37:35.

---

g. [42:21] Gn 37:18–27.
h. [42:22] Gn 37:22.

a. [43:3] Gn 44:23.
b. [43:5] Gn 42:20.

'Is your father still living? Do you have another brother?' We answered him accordingly. How could we know that he would say, 'Bring your brother down here'?"

⁸Then Judah urged his father Israel: "Let the boy go with me, that we may be off and on our way if you and we and our children are to keep from starving to death.ᶜ ⁹I myself will serve as a guarantee for him. You can hold me responsible for him. If I fail to bring him back and set him before you, I will bear the blame before you forever.ᵈ ¹⁰Had we not delayed, we could have been there and back twice by now!"

¹¹Israel their father then told them: "If it must be so, then do this: Put some of the land's best products in your baggage and take them down to the man as gifts: some balm and honey, gum and resin, and pistachios and almonds.ᵉ ¹²Also take double the money along, for you must return the amount that was put back in the mouths of your bags; it may have been a mistake. ¹³Take your brother, too, and be off on your way back to the man. ¹⁴May God Almighty grant you mercy in the presence of the man, so that he may let your other brother go, as well as Benjamin. As for me, if I am to suffer bereavement, I shall suffer it."

¹⁵So the men took those gifts and double the money and Benjamin. They made their way down to Egypt and presented themselves before Joseph. ¹⁶When Joseph saw them and Benjamin, he told his steward, "Take the men into the house, and have an animal slaughtered and prepared, for they are to dine with me at noon." ¹⁷Doing as Joseph had ordered, the steward conducted the men to Joseph's house. ¹⁸But they became apprehensive when they were led to his house. "It must be," they thought, "on account of the money put back in our bags the first time, that we are taken inside—in order to attack us and take our donkeys and seize us as slaves."

¹⁹So they went up to Joseph's steward and talked to him at the entrance of the house. ²⁰"If you please, sir," they said, "we came down here once before to buy food.ᶠ ²¹But when we arrived at a night's encampment and opened our bags, there was each man's money in the mouth of his bag—our money in the full amount! We have now brought it back.ᵍ ²²We have brought other money to buy food. We do not know who put our money in our bags." ²³He replied, "Calm down! Do not fear! Your God and the God of your father must have put treasure in your bags for you. As for your money, I received it." With that, he led Simeon out to them.

²⁴The steward then brought the men inside Joseph's house. He gave them water to wash their feet, and gave fodder to their donkeys. ²⁵Then they set out their gifts to await Joseph's arrival at noon, for they had heard that they were to dine there. ²⁶When Joseph came home, they presented him with the gifts they had brought inside, while they bowed down before him to the ground. ²⁷After inquiring how they were, he asked them, "And how is your aged father, of whom you spoke? Is he still alive?"ʰ ²⁸"Your servant our father is still alive and doing well," they said, as they knelt and bowed down. ²⁹Then Joseph looked up and saw Benjamin, his brother, the son of his mother. He asked, "Is this your youngest brother, of whom you told me?" Then he said to him, "May God be gracious to you, my son!"ⁱ ³⁰With that, Joseph hurried out, for he was so overcome with affection for his brother that he was on the verge of tears. So he went into a private room and wept there.

³¹After washing his face, he reappeared and, now having collected himself, gave the order, "Serve the meal." ³²It was served separately to him,* to the

---

* [43:32] **Separately to him**: that Joseph did not eat with the other Egyptians was apparently a matter of rank.

c. [43:8] Gn 42:37.
d. [43:9] Gn 44:32.
e. [43:11] Gn 45:23.
f. [43:20] Gn 42:3.
g. [43:21] Gn 42:27–28.
h. [43:27] Tb 7:4.
i. [43:29] Gn 42:13.

brothers, and to the Egyptians who partook of his board. Egyptians may not eat with Hebrews; that is abhorrent to them. [33]When they were seated before him according to their age, from the oldest to the youngest, they looked at one another in amazement; [34]and as portions were brought to them from Joseph's table, Benjamin's portion was five times as large as* anyone else's. So they drank freely and made merry with him.

CHAPTER 44

Final Test.[†] [1]Then Joseph commanded his steward: "Fill the men's bags with as much food as they can carry, and put each man's money in the mouth of his bag. [2]In the mouth of the youngest one's bag put also my silver goblet, together with the money for his grain." The steward did as Joseph said. [3]At daybreak the men and their donkeys were sent off. [4]They had not gone far out of the city when Joseph said to his steward: "Go at once after the men! When you overtake them, say to them, 'Why did you repay good with evil? Why did you steal my silver goblet? [5]Is it not the very one from which my master drinks and which he uses for divination?[‡] What you have done is wrong.'"

[6]When the steward overtook them and repeated these words to them, [7]they said to him: "Why does my lord say such things? Far be it from your servants

to do such a thing! [8]We even brought back to you from the land of Canaan the money that we found in the mouths of our bags. How could we steal silver or gold from your master's house? [9]If any of your servants is found to have the goblet, he shall die, and as for the rest of us, we shall become my lord's slaves." [10]But he replied, "Now what you propose is fair enough, but only the one who is found to have it shall become my slave, and the rest of you can go free." [11]Then each of them quickly lowered his bag to the ground and opened it; [12]and when a search was made, starting with the oldest and ending with the youngest, the goblet turned up in Benjamin's bag. [13]At this, they tore their garments. Then, when each man had loaded his donkey again, they returned to the city.

[14]When Judah and his brothers entered Joseph's house, he was still there; so they flung themselves on the ground before him. [15]"How could you do such a thing?" Joseph asked them. "Did you not know that such a man as I could discern by divination what happened?" [16]Judah replied: "What can we say to my lord? How can we plead or how try to prove our innocence? God has uncovered your servants' guilt.[§] Here we are, then, the slaves of my lord—the rest of us no less than the one in whose possession the goblet was found." [17]Joseph said, "Far be it from me to act thus! Only the one in whose possession the goblet was found shall become my slave; the rest of you may go back unharmed to your father."

[18]Judah then stepped up to him and said: "I beg you, my lord, let your servant appeal to my lord, and do not become angry with your servant, for you are the equal of Pharaoh. [19]My lord asked his servants,[¶] 'Have you a father, or another brother?' [20]So we said to my lord, 'We have an aged father, and a younger brother, the child

---

* [43:34] **Five times as large as**: probably an idiomatic expression for "much larger than." Cf. 45:22.

† [44:1–34] Joseph's pressure on his brothers and Judah's great speech. Judah has the longest speech in the Book of Genesis; it summarizes the recent past (vv. 18–29), shows the pain Joseph's actions have imposed on their aged father (vv. 30–32), and ends with the offer to take the place of Benjamin as servant of Joseph (vv. 33–34). The role of Judah in the entire story is exceedingly important and is easily underrated: he tries to rescue Joseph (37:26–27), his "going down away from the brothers" is parallel to Joseph's (chap. 38) and prepares him (as it prepares Joseph) for the reconciliation, his speech in chap. 44 persuades Joseph to reveal himself and be reconciled to his brothers. Here, Judah effectively replaces Reuben as a spokesman for the brothers. Jacob in his testament (chap. 49) devotes the most attention to Judah and Joseph. In one sense, the story can be called the story of Joseph and Judah.

‡ [44:5] **Divination**: seeking omens through liquids poured into a cup or bowl was a common practice in the ancient Near East; cf. v. 15. Even though divination was frowned on in later Israel (Lv 19:31), it is in this place an authentic touch which is ascribed to Joseph, the wisest man in Egypt.

§ [44:16] **Guilt**: in trying to do away with Joseph when he was young.

¶ [44:19] **My lord asked his servants**: such frequently repeated expressions in Judah's speech show the formal court style used by a subject in speaking to a high official.

GN

of his old age. This one's full brother is dead, and since he is the only one by his mother who is left, his father is devoted to him.'[a] [21]Then you told your servants, 'Bring him down to me that I might see him.' [22]We replied to my lord, 'The boy cannot leave his father; his father would die if he left him.' [23]But you told your servants, 'Unless your youngest brother comes down with you, you shall not see me again.'[b] [24]When we returned to your servant my father, we reported to him the words of my lord.

[25]"Later, our father said, 'Go back and buy some food for us.' [26]So we reminded him, 'We cannot go down there; only if our youngest brother is with us can we go, for we may not see the man if our youngest brother is not with us.' [27]Then your servant my father said to us, 'As you know, my wife bore me two sons. [28]One of them, however, has gone away from me, and I said, "He must have been torn to pieces by wild beasts!" I have not seen him since.[c] [29]If you take this one away from me too, and a disaster befalls him, you will send my white head down to Sheol in grief.'

[30]"So now, if the boy is not with us when I go back to your servant my father, whose very life is bound up with his, he will die as soon as he sees that the boy is missing; [31]and your servants will thus send the white head of your servant our father down to Sheol in grief. [32]Besides, I, your servant, have guaranteed the boy's safety for my father by saying, 'If I fail to bring him back to you, father, I will bear the blame before you forever.'[d] [33]So now let me, your servant, remain in place of the boy as the slave of my lord, and let the boy go back with his brothers. [34]How could I go back to my father if the boy were not with me? I could not bear to see the anguish that would overcome my father."

---

a. [44:20] Gn 42:13.
b. [44:23] Gn 43:3.
c. [44:28] Gn 37:20, 33.
d. [44:32] Gn 43:9.

CHAPTER 45

The Truth Revealed.[*] [1]Joseph could no longer restrain himself in the presence of all his attendants, so he cried out, "Have everyone withdraw from me!" So no one attended him when he made himself known to his brothers. [2]But his sobs were so loud that the Egyptians heard him, and so the news reached Pharaoh's house. [3a]"I am Joseph," he said to his brothers. "Is my father still alive?" But his brothers could give him no answer, so dumbfounded were they at him.

[4]"Come closer to me," Joseph told his brothers. When they had done so, he said: "I am your brother Joseph, whom you sold into Egypt. [5]But now do not be distressed, and do not be angry with yourselves for having sold me here. It was really for the sake of saving lives that God sent me here ahead of you.[b] [6]The famine has been in the land for two years now, and for five more years cultivation will yield no harvest. [7]God, therefore, sent me on ahead of you to ensure for you a remnant on earth and to save your lives in an extraordinary deliverance. [8]So it was not really you but God who had me come here; and he has made me a father to Pharaoh,[†] lord of all his household, and ruler over the whole land of Egypt.

[9‡]"Hurry back, then, to my father and tell him: 'Thus says your son Joseph: God has made me lord of all Egypt; come down to me without delay.[c] [10]You can settle in the region of Goshen,[§] where you will be near me—

---

* [45:1–28] Joseph reveals his identity and the family is reconciled.
† [45:8] **Father to Pharaoh**: a term applied to a vizier in ancient Egypt.
‡ [45:9–15] In these verses, as in 46:31–47:5a, all from the Yahwist source, Joseph in his own name invites his father and brothers to come to Egypt. Only after their arrival is Pharaoh informed of the fact. On the other hand, in 45:16–20, which scholars have traditionally attributed to the Elohist source, it is Pharaoh himself who invites Joseph's family to migrate to his domain.
§ [45:10] **The region of Goshen**: the meaning of the term is unknown. It is found in no Egyptian source. It is generally thought to be in the modern Wadi Tumilat in the eastern part of the Nile Delta.

---

a. [45:3–4] Acts 7:13.
b. [45:5] Gn 50:20.
c. [45:9] Acts 7:14.

you and your children and children's children, your flocks and herds, and everything that you own. ¹¹I will provide for you there in the five years of famine that lie ahead, so that you and your household and all that are yours will not suffer want.' ¹²Surely, you can see for yourselves, and Benjamin can see for himself, that it is I who am speaking to you. ¹³Tell my father all about my high position in Egypt and all that you have seen. But hurry and bring my father down here." ¹⁴Then he threw his arms around his brother Benjamin and wept on his shoulder. ¹⁵Joseph then kissed all his brothers and wept over them; and only then were his brothers able to talk with him.

¹⁶The news reached Pharaoh's house: "Joseph's brothers have come." Pharaoh and his officials were pleased. ¹⁷So Pharaoh told Joseph: "Say to your brothers: 'This is what you shall do: Load up your animals and go without delay to the land of Canaan. ¹⁸There get your father and your households, and then come to me; I will assign you the best land in Egypt, where you will live off the fat of the land.'ᵈ ¹⁹Instruct them further: 'Do this. Take wagons from the land of Egypt for your children and your wives and bring your father back here. ²⁰Do not be concerned about your belongings, for the best in the whole land of Egypt shall be yours.'"

²¹The sons of Israel acted accordingly. Joseph gave them the wagons, as Pharaoh had ordered, and he supplied them with provisions for the journey. ²²He also gave to each of them a set of clothes, but to Benjamin he gave three hundred shekels of silver and five sets of clothes. ²³Moreover, what he sent to his father was ten donkeys loaded with the finest products of Egypt and another ten loaded with grain and bread and provisions for his father's journey. ²⁴As he sent his brothers on their way, he told them, "Do not quarrel on the way."

²⁵So they went up from Egypt and came to the land of Canaan, to their father Jacob. ²⁶When they told him, "Joseph is still alive—in fact, it is he who is governing all the land of Egypt," he was unmoved, for he did not believe them. ²⁷But when they recounted to him all that Joseph had told them, and when he saw the wagons that Joseph had sent to transport him, the spirit of their father Jacob came to life. ²⁸"Enough," said Israel. "My son Joseph is still alive! I must go and see him before I die."

CHAPTER 46

Migration to Egypt. ¹*Israel set out with all that was his. When he arrived at Beer-sheba, he offered sacrifices to the God of his father Isaac. ²There God, speaking to Israel in a vision by night, called: Jacob! Jacob! He answered, "Here I am." ³Then he said: I am God,† the God of your father. Do not be afraid to go down to Egypt, for there I will make you a great nation. ⁴I will go down to Egypt with you and I will also bring you back here, after Joseph has closed your eyes.

⁵So Jacob departed from Beer-sheba, and the sons of Israel put their father and their wives and children on the wagons that Pharaoh had sent to transport him. ⁶They took with them their livestock and the possessions they had acquired in the land of Canaan. So Jacob and all his descendants came to Egypt.ᵃ ⁷His sons and his grandsons, his daughters and his granddaughters—all his descendants—he took with him to Egypt.

⁸These are the names of the Israelites, Jacob and his children, who came to Egypt.

Reuben, Jacob's firstborn,ᵇ ⁹‡and the sons of Reuben: Hanoch, Pallu,

* [46:1–47:26] Jacob and his family settle in Egypt. Joseph's economic policies.
† [46:3] **I am God**: more precisely according to the Hebrew text, "I am El." "El" is here a divine name, not the common noun "god."
‡ [46:9–27] This genealogical list is based on the clan lists (Nm 26:5–50) from the Mosaic period.

a. [46:6] Ex 1:1; Jos 24:4; Jdt 5:10; Acts 7:15.
b. [46:8] Ex 1:2.

d. [45:18] Acts 7:14.

Hezron, and Carmi.*c* *10*The sons of Simeon: Jemuel, Jamin, Ohad, Jachin, Zohar, and Shaul, son of a Canaanite woman.*d* *11*The sons of Levi: Gershon, Kohath, and Merari.*e* *12*The sons of Judah: Er, Onan, Shelah, Perez, and Zerah—but Er and Onan had died in the land of Canaan; and the sons of Perez were Hezron and Hamul.*f* *13*The sons of Issachar: Tola, Puah, Jashub, and Shimron.*g* *14*The sons of Zebulun: Sered, Elon, and Jahleel.*h* *15*These were the sons whom Leah bore to Jacob in Paddan-aram, along with his daughter Dinah—thirty-three persons in all, sons and daughters.

*16*The sons of Gad: Zephon, Haggi, Shuni, Ezbon, Eri, Arod, and Areli.*i* *17*The sons of Asher: Imnah, Ishvah, Ishvi, and Beriah, with their sister Serah; and the sons of Beriah: Heber and Malchiel.*j* *18*These are the children of Zilpah, whom Laban had given to his daughter Leah; these she bore to Jacob—sixteen persons in all.

*19*The sons of Jacob's wife Rachel: Joseph and Benjamin. *20*In the land of Egypt Joseph became the father of Manasseh and Ephraim, whom Asenath, daughter of Potiphera, priest of Heliopolis, bore to him.*k* *21*The sons of Benjamin: Bela, Becher, Ashbel, Gera, Naaman, Ahiram, Shupham, Hupham, and Ard.*l* *22*These are the sons whom Rachel bore to Jacob—fourteen persons in all.

*23*The sons of Dan: Hushim.*m* *24*The sons of Naphtali: Jahzeel, Guni, Jezer, and Shillem.*n* *25*These are the sons of Bilhah, whom Laban had given to his daughter Rachel; these she bore to Jacob—seven persons in all.

*26*Jacob's people who came to Egypt—his direct descendants, not counting the wives of Jacob's sons—numbered sixty-six persons in all.*o* *27*Together with Joseph's sons who were born to him in Egypt—two persons—all the people comprising the household of Jacob who had come to Egypt amounted to seventy persons* in all.*p*

*28*Israel had sent Judah ahead to Joseph, so that he might meet him in Goshen. On his arrival in the region of Goshen, *29*Joseph prepared his chariot and went up to meet his father Israel in Goshen. As soon as Israel made his appearance, Joseph threw his arms around him and wept a long time on his shoulder. *30*And Israel said to Joseph, "At last I can die, now that I have seen for myself that you are still alive."

*31*Joseph then said to his brothers and his father's household: "I will go up and inform Pharaoh, telling him: 'My brothers and my father's household, whose home is in the land of Canaan, have come to me. *32*The men are shepherds, having been owners of livestock;† and they have brought with them their flocks and herds, as well as everything else they own.' *33*So when Pharaoh summons you and asks what your occupation is, *34*you must answer, 'We your servants, like our ancestors, have been owners of livestock from our youth until now,' in order that you may stay in the region of Goshen, since all shepherds are abhorrent to the Egyptians."

CHAPTER 47

Settlement in Goshen. *1*Joseph went and told Pharaoh, "My father and my brothers have come from the land of Canaan, with their flocks and

---

* [46:27] **Seventy persons:** it is difficult to get this exact number by adding up the persons mentioned in the preceding genealogies. One might assume it refers to Jacob and sixty-nine descendants, excluding Er and Onan but including Dinah. Ex 1:5 repeats the number but excludes Jacob. Dt 10:22 refers to seventy persons descending to Egypt. The best solution is to take the number as expressing totality. Since there are seventy nations in chap. 10, it is likely that the text is drawing a parallel between the two entities and suggesting that Israel "represents" the nations before God.

† [46:32] **Owners of livestock:** the phrase occurs only here and in v. 34. The difference between this term and "shepherds" is not clear, for the brothers do not mention it to Pharaoh in 47:3.

o. [46:26] Ex 1:5.
p. [46:27] Ex 1:5; Dt 10:22; Acts 7:14.

c. [46:9] Ex 6:14; Nm 26:5; 1 Chr 5:3.
d. [46:10] Ex 6:15; Nm 26:12; 1 Chr 4:24.
e. [46:11] Ex 6:16; Nm 3:17; 26:57; 1 Chr 6:1.
f. [46:12] Gn 38:3–10, 29–30; Nm 26:19; Ru 4:12; 1 Chr 2:5.
g. [46:13] Nm 26:23–24; 1 Chr 7:1.
h. [46:14] Nm 26:26.
i. [46:16] Nm 26:15–16.
j. [46:17] Nm 26:44; 1 Chr 7:30–31.
k. [46:20] Gn 41:50; Nm 26:28, 35.
l. [46:21] Nm 26:38; 1 Chr 7:6; 8:1–4.
m. [46:23] Nm 26:42.
n. [46:24] Nm 26:48–49; 1 Chr 7:13.

herds and everything else they own; and they are now in the region of Goshen." ²He then presented to Pharaoh five of his brothers whom he had selected from their full number. ³When Pharaoh asked them, "What is your occupation?" they answered, "We, your servants, like our ancestors, are shepherds. ⁴We have come," they continued, "in order to sojourn in this land, for there is no pasture for your servants' flocks, because the famine has been severe in the land of Canaan. So now please let your servants settle in the region of Goshen."ᵃ ⁵Pharaoh said to Joseph, "Now that your father and your brothers have come to you, ⁶the land of Egypt is at your disposal; settle your father and brothers in the pick of the land. Let them settle in the region of Goshen. And if you know of capable men among them, put them in charge of my livestock." ⁷Then Joseph brought his father Jacob and presented him to Pharaoh. And Jacob blessed Pharaoh. ⁸Then Pharaoh asked Jacob, "How many years have you lived?" ⁹Jacob replied: "The years I have lived as a wayfarer amount to a hundred and thirty. Few and hard have been these years of my life, and they do not compare with the years that my ancestors lived as wayfarers."* ¹⁰Then Jacob blessed Pharaoh and withdrew from his presence.

¹¹Joseph settled his father and brothers and gave them a holding in Egypt on the pick of the land, in the region of Rameses,† as Pharaoh had ordered. ¹²And Joseph provided food for his father and brothers and his father's whole household, down to the youngest.

Joseph's Land Policy. ¹³Since there was no food in all the land because of the extreme severity of the famine, and the lands of Egypt and Canaan were languishing from hunger, ¹⁴Joseph gathered in, as payment for the grain that they were buying, all the money that was to be found in Egypt and Canaan, and he put it in Pharaoh's house. ¹⁵When all the money in Egypt and Canaan was spent, all the Egyptians came to Joseph, pleading, "Give us food! Why should we perish in front of you? For our money is gone." ¹⁶"Give me your livestock if your money is gone," replied Joseph. "I will give you food in return for your livestock." ¹⁷So they brought their livestock to Joseph, and he gave them food in exchange for their horses, their flocks of sheep and herds of cattle, and their donkeys. Thus he supplied them with food in exchange for all their livestock in that year. ¹⁸That year ended, and they came to him in the next one and said: "We cannot hide from my lord that, with our money spent and our livestock made over to my lord, there is nothing left to put at my lord's disposal except our bodies and our land. ¹⁹Why should we and our land perish before your very eyes? Take us and our land in exchange for food, and we will become Pharaoh's slaves and our land his property; only give us seed, that we may survive and not perish, and that our land may not turn into a waste."

²⁰So Joseph acquired all the land of Egypt for Pharaoh. Each of the Egyptians sold his field, since the famine weighed heavily upon them. Thus the land passed over to Pharaoh, ²¹and the people were reduced to slavery, from one end of Egypt's territory to the other. ²²Only the priests' lands Joseph did not acquire. Since the priests had a fixed allowance from Pharaoh and lived off the allowance Pharaoh had granted them, they did not have to sell their land.

²³Joseph told the people: "Now that I have acquired you and your land for Pharaoh, here is your seed for sowing the land. ²⁴But when the harvest is in, you must give a fifth of it to Pharaoh, while you keep four-fifths as seed for your fields and as food for yourselves and your households and as food for

---

* [47:9] **Wayfarer . . . wayfarers**: human beings are merely sojourners on earth; cf. Ps 39:13.
† [47:11] **The region of Rameses**: same as the region of Goshen; see note on 45:10.

a. [47:4] Ex 23:9; Dt 23:8.

your children." **25** "You have saved our lives!" they answered. "We have found favor with my lord; now we will be Pharaoh's slaves." **26** Thus Joseph made it a statute for the land of Egypt, which is still in force, that a fifth of its produce should go to Pharaoh. Only the land of the priests did not pass over to Pharaoh.

Israel Blesses Ephraim and Manasseh.
27 Thus Israel settled in the land of Egypt, in the region of Goshen. There they acquired holdings, were fertile, and multiplied greatly.[b] **28***Jacob lived in the land of Egypt for seventeen years; the span of his life came to a hundred and forty-seven years. **29** When the time approached for Israel to die, he called his son Joseph and said to him: "If it pleases you, put your hand under my thigh as a sign of your enduring fidelity to me; do not bury me in Egypt. **30** When I lie down with my ancestors, take me out of Egypt and bury me in their burial place."[c] "I will do as you say," he replied. **31** But his father demanded, "Swear it to me!" So Joseph swore to him. Then Israel bowed at the head of the bed.[†]

CHAPTER 48

1‡ Some time afterward, Joseph was informed, "Your father is failing." So he took along with him his two sons, Manasseh and Ephraim. **2** When Jacob was told, "Your son Joseph has come to you," Israel rallied his strength and sat up in bed.

3a Jacob then said to Joseph: "God Almighty appeared to me at Luz[§] in the land of Canaan, and blessing me, **4** he said, 'I will make you fertile and multiply you and make you into an assembly of peoples, and I will give this land to your descendants after you as a permanent possession.' **5** So now your two sons who were born to you in the land of Egypt before I joined you here, shall be mine; Ephraim and Manasseh shall be mine as much as Reuben and Simeon are mine. **6** Progeny born to you after them shall remain yours; but their heritage shall be recorded in the names of their brothers. **7b** I do this because, when I was returning from Paddan, your mother Rachel died, to my sorrow, during the journey in Canaan, while we were still a short distance from Ephrath; and I buried her there on the way to Ephrath [now Bethlehem]."[¶]

8 When Israel saw Joseph's sons, he asked, "Who are these?" **9** "They are my sons," Joseph answered his father, "whom God has given me here." "Bring them to me," said his father, "that I may bless them." **10** Now Israel's eyes were dim from age; he could not see well. When Joseph brought his sons close to him, he kissed and embraced them. **11** Then Israel said to Joseph, "I never expected to see your face again, and now God has allowed me to see your descendants as well!"

12 Joseph removed them from his father's knees and bowed down before him with his face to the ground. **13** Then Joseph took the two, Ephraim with his right hand, to Israel's left, and Manasseh with his left hand, to Israel's right, and brought them up to

---

* [47:28–50:26] Supplements to the Joseph story. Most of the material in this section centers on Jacob—his blessing of Joseph's sons, his farewell testament, and his death and burial in Canaan. Only the last verses (50:15–26) redirect attention to Jacob's sons, the twelve brothers; they are assured that the reconciliation will not collapse after the death of the patriarch.

† [47:31] **Israel bowed at the head of the bed:** meaning perhaps that he gave a nod of assent and appreciation as he lay on his bed. The oath and gesture are the same as Abraham's in 24:2. Israel's bowing here suggests the fulfillment of Joseph's dreams in 37:9–10, when parents and brothers bowed down to Joseph (cf. 42:6; 43:26). By using different vowels for the Hebrew word for "bed," the Greek version translated it as "staff," and understood the phrase to mean that he bowed in worship, leaning on the top of his staff; it is thus quoted in Heb 11:21.

‡ [48:1–22] Jacob continues his preparations for death. In a scene that evokes the nearly blind Isaac blessing Jacob and Esau (chap. 27), Jacob blesses Joseph's two sons. He adopts them, elevating them to a status equal to that of Jacob's first sons Reuben and Simeon (cf. 1 Chr 5:1). The adoption is one more instance of Jacob's favoring Rachel and those born of her. The mention of Jacob's failing eyesight and his selection of the younger son over the older evokes the great deathbed scene in chap. 27. He reaffirms to Joseph the ancient divine promise of progeny and land.

§ [48:3] **Luz:** an older name of Bethel (28:19).
¶ [48:7] Since her early death prevented Rachel from bearing more than two sons, Jacob feels justified in treating her two grandsons as if they were her own offspring.

b. [47:27] Ex 1:7.
c. [47:30] Gn 50:5.

a. [48:3–4] Gn 28:12–15; 35:6.
b. [48:7] Gn 35:19.

GN

him. **14**But Israel, crossing his hands, put out his right hand and laid it on the head of Ephraim, although he was the younger, and his left hand on the head of Manasseh, although he was the firstborn. **15**Then he blessed them with these words:

"May the God in whose presence
    my fathers Abraham and Isaac
    walked,
The God who has been my
    shepherd
    from my birth to this day,*c*
16The angel who has delivered me
    from all harm,
    bless these boys
That in them my name be recalled,
    and the names of my fathers,
    Abraham and Isaac,
And they may become teeming
    multitudes
    upon the earth!"

17When Joseph saw that his father had laid his right hand on Ephraim's head, this seemed wrong to him; so he took hold of his father's hand, to remove it from Ephraim's head to Manasseh's, **18**saying, "That is not right, father; the other one is the firstborn; lay your right hand on his head!" **19**But his father refused. "I know it, son," he said, "I know. That one too shall become a people, and he too shall be great. Nevertheless, his younger brother shall surpass him, and his descendants shall become a multitude of nations." **20**So he blessed them that day and said, "By you shall the people of Israel pronounce blessings, saying, 'God make you like Ephraim and Manasseh.'" Thus he placed Ephraim before Manasseh.*d*
21Then Israel said to Joseph: "I am about to die. But God will be with you and will restore you to the land of your ancestors. **22**eAs for me, I give to you, as to the one above his brothers,

Shechem, which I captured from the Amorites with my sword and bow."*

CHAPTER 49

Jacob's Testament.† **1**Jacob called his sons and said: "Gather around, that I may tell you what is to happen to you in days to come.

2"Assemble and listen, sons of
    Jacob,
    listen to Israel, your father.

3"You, Reuben, my firstborn,
    my strength and the first fruit of
    my vigor,
    excelling in rank and excelling in
    power!
4Turbulent as water, you shall no
    longer excel,
    for you climbed into your father's
    bed
    and defiled my couch to my
    sorrow.*a*

5‡"Simeon and Levi, brothers
    indeed,
    weapons of violence are their
    knives.§

---

* [48:22] Both the meaning of the Hebrew and the historical reference in this verse are obscure. By taking the Hebrew word for Shechem as a common noun meaning shoulder or mountain slope, some translators render the verse, "I give you one portion more than your brothers, which I captured . . . " The reference may be to the capture of Shechem by the sons of Jacob (34:24–29). Shechem lay near the border separating the tribal territory of Manasseh from that of Ephraim (Jos 16:4–9; 17:1–2, 7).

† [49:1–27] The testament, or farewell discourse, of Jacob, which has its closest parallel in Moses' farewell in Dt 33:6–25. From his privileged position as a patriarch, he sees the future of his children (the eponymous ancestors of the tribes) and is able to describe how they will fare and so gives his blessing. The dense and archaic poetry is obscure in several places. The sayings often involve wordplays (explained in the notes). The poem begins with the six sons of Leah (vv. 2–15), then deals with the sons of the two secondary wives, and ends with Rachel's two sons, Joseph and Benjamin. Reuben, the oldest son, loses his position of leadership as a result of his intercourse with Bilhah (35:22), and the words about Simeon and Levi allude to their taking revenge for the rape of Dinah (chap. 34). The preeminence of Judah reflects his rise in the course of the narrative (mirroring the rise of Joseph). See note on 44:1–34.

‡ [49:5–7] This passage probably refers to their attack on the city of Shechem (Gn 34). Because there is no indication that the warlike tribe of Levi will be commissioned as a priestly tribe (Ex 32:26–29; Dt 33:11), this passage reflects an early, independent tradition.

§ [49:5] **Knives:** if this is the meaning of the obscure Hebrew word here, the reference may be to the knives used in circumcising the men of Shechem (34:24; cf. Jos 5:2).

---

c. [48:15] Heb 11:21.
d. [48:20] Heb 11:21.
e. [48:22] Jos 17:14, 17–18; Jn 4:5.

a. [49:4] Gn 35:22; 1 Chr 5:1–2.

GN

⁶Let not my person enter their
    council,
  or my honor be joined with their
    company;
For in their fury they killed men,
  at their whim they maimed
    oxen.^b
⁷Cursed be their fury so fierce,
  and their rage so cruel!
I will scatter them in Jacob,
  disperse them throughout Israel.

⁸"You, Judah, shall your brothers
    praise
  —your hand on the neck of your
    enemies;
  the sons of your father shall bow
    down to you.
⁹Judah is a lion's cub,
  you have grown up on prey, my
    son.
He crouches, lies down like a lion,
  like a lioness—who would dare
    rouse him?^c
¹⁰The scepter shall never depart
    from Judah,
  or the mace from between his
    feet,
Until tribute comes to him,[*]
  and he receives the people's
    obedience.
¹¹He tethers his donkey to the vine,
  his donkey's foal to the choicest
    stem.
In wine he washes his garments,
  his robe in the blood of grapes.[†]
¹²His eyes are darker than wine,
  and his teeth are whiter than
    milk.

¹³"Zebulun shall dwell by the
    seashore;
  he will be a haven for ships,
  and his flank shall rest on Sidon.

¹⁴"Issachar is a rawboned donkey,
  crouching between the
    saddlebags.
¹⁵When he saw how good a settled
    life was,
  and how pleasant the land,
He bent his shoulder to the burden
  and became a toiling serf.

¹⁶"Dan shall achieve justice[‡] for his
    people
  as one of the tribes of Israel.
¹⁷Let Dan be a serpent by the
    roadside,
  a horned viper by the path,
That bites the horse's heel,
  so that the rider tumbles
    backward.

¹⁸"I long for your deliverance, O
    LORD![§]

¹⁹"Gad shall be raided by raiders,
  but he shall raid at their heels.[¶]

²⁰"Asher's produce is rich,
  and he shall furnish delicacies for
    kings.

²¹"Naphtali is a hind let loose,
  which brings forth lovely fawns.

²²"Joseph is a wild colt,
  a wild colt by a spring,
  wild colts on a hillside.
²³Harrying him and shooting,
  the archers opposed him;
²⁴But his bow remained taut,
  and his arms were nimble,
By the power of the Mighty One of
    Jacob,
  because of the Shepherd, the
    Rock of Israel,
²⁵The God of your father, who
    helps you,^{**}
  God Almighty, who blesses you,
With the blessings of the heavens
    above,

---

*   [49:10] **Until tribute comes to him**: this translation is based on
    a slight change in the Hebrew text, which, as it stands, would
    seem to mean, "until he comes to Shiloh." A somewhat differ-
    ent reading of the Hebrew text would be, "until he comes to
    whom it belongs." This last has been traditionally understood
    in a messianic sense. In any case, the passage aims at the
    supremacy of the tribe of Judah and of the Davidic dynasty.
†   [49:11] **In wine . . . the blood of grapes**: Judah's clothes are
    poetically pictured as soaked with grape juice from tram-
    pling in the wine press, the rich vintage of his land; cf. Is 63:2.

b. [49:6] Gn 34:25.
c. [49:9] 1 Chr 5:2.

‡   [49:16] In Hebrew the verb for "achieve justice" is from the
    same root as the name Dan.
§   [49:18] This short plea for divine mercy has been inserted
    into the middle of Jacob's testament.
¶   [49:19] In Hebrew there is assonance between the name
    Gad and the words for "raided," "raiders," and "raid."
** [49:25–26] A very similar description of the agricultural
    riches of the tribal land of Joseph is given in Dt 33:13–16.

the blessings of the abyss that
crouches below,
The blessings of breasts and womb,
²⁶the blessings of fresh grain and
blossoms,
the blessings of the everlasting
mountains,
the delights of the eternal hills.
May they rest on the head of
Joseph,
on the brow of the prince among
his brothers.

²⁷"Benjamin is a ravenous wolf;
mornings he devours the prey,
and evenings he distributes the
spoils."

Farewell and Death. ²⁸All these are
the twelve tribes of Israel, and this is
what their father said about them, as
he blessed them. To each he gave a
suitable blessing. ²⁹Then he gave them
this charge: "Since I am about to be
gathered to my people, bury me with
my ancestors in the cave that lies in
the field of Ephron the Hittite, ³⁰the
cave in the field of Machpelah, facing
on Mamre, in the land of Canaan, the
field that Abraham bought from Ephron the Hittite for a burial ground.ᵈ
³¹There Abraham and his wife Sarah
are buried, and so are Isaac and his
wife Rebekah, and there, too, I buried Leah— ³²the field and the cave
in it that had been purchased from
the Hittites."

³³When Jacob had finished giving
these instructions to his sons, he drew
his feet into the bed, breathed his last,
and was gathered to his people.

CHAPTER 50

Jacob's Funeral. ¹Joseph flung himself upon his father and wept over
him as he kissed him. ²Then Joseph
ordered the physicians in his service to embalm his father. When the
physicians embalmed Israel, ³they
spent forty days at it, for that is the
full period of embalming; and the
Egyptians mourned him for seventy
days. ⁴When the period of mourning
was over, Joseph spoke to Pharaoh's
household. "If you please, appeal to
Pharaoh, saying: ⁵My father made
me swear: 'I am dying. Bury me in my
grave that I have prepared for myself
in the land of Canaan.' So now let me
go up to bury my father. Then I will
come back."ᵃ ⁶Pharaoh replied, "Go
and bury your father, as he made you
promise on oath."

⁷So Joseph went up to bury his
father; and with him went all of Pharaoh's officials who were senior members of his household and all the other
elders of the land of Egypt, ⁸as well as
Joseph's whole household, his brothers, and his father's household; only
their children and their flocks and
herds were left in the region of Goshen. ⁹Chariots, too, and horsemen
went up with him; it was a very impos-
ing retinue.

¹⁰When they arrived at Goren-ha-
atad,* which is beyond the Jordan, they
held there a very great and solemn
memorial service; and Joseph observed
seven days of mourning for his father.
¹¹When the Canaanites who inhabited
the land saw the mourning at Goren-
ha-atad, they said, "This is a solemn
funeral on the part of the Egyptians!"
That is why the place was named Abel-
mizraim. It is beyond the Jordan.

¹²Thus Jacob's sons did for him as
he had instructed them. ¹³They carried him to the land of Canaan and
buried him in the cave in the field of
Machpelah, facing on Mamre, the field
that Abraham had bought for a burial
ground from Ephron the Hittite.ᵇ

---

* [50:10–11] **Goren-ha-atad**: "Threshing Floor of the Bram-
bles." **Abel-mizraim**: although the name really means
"watercourse of the Egyptians," it is understood here, by
a play on the first part of the term, to mean "mourning of
the Egyptians." The site has not been identified through
either reading of the name. But it is difficult to see why the
mourning rites should have been held in the land beyond
the Jordan when the burial was at Hebron. Perhaps an
earlier form of the story placed the mourning rites beyond
the Wadi of Egypt, the traditional boundary between
Canaan and Egypt (Nm 34:5; Jos 15:4, 47).

a. [50:5] Gn 47:30.
b. [50:13] Gn 23:16; Jos 24:32; Acts 7:16.

d. [49:30] Gn 23:17.

14 After Joseph had buried his father he returned to Egypt, together with his brothers and all who had gone up with him for the burial of his father.

Plea for Forgiveness. 15*Now that their father was dead, Joseph's brothers became fearful and thought, "Suppose Joseph has been nursing a grudge against us and now most certainly will pay us back in full for all the wrong we did him!" **16** So they sent to Joseph and said: "Before your father died, he gave us these instructions: **17***Thus you shall say to Joseph: Please forgive the criminal wrongdoing of your brothers, who treated you harmfully.' So now please forgive the crime that we, the servants of the God of your father, committed." When they said this to him, Joseph broke into tears. **18** Then his brothers also proceeded to fling themselves down before him and said, "We are your slaves!" **19** But Joseph replied to them: "Do not fear. Can I take the place of God? **20** Even though you meant harm to me, God meant it for good, to achieve this present end, the survival of many people.*c* **21** So now, do not fear. I will provide for you and for your children." By thus speaking kindly to them, he reassured them.*d*

22 Joseph remained in Egypt, together with his father's household. He lived a hundred and ten years. **23** He saw Ephraim's children to the third generation, and the children of Manasseh's son Machir were also born on Joseph's knees.*e*

Death of Joseph. 24 Joseph said to his brothers: "I am about to die. God will surely take care of you and lead you up from this land to the land that he promised on oath to Abraham, Isaac and Jacob."*f* **25** Then, putting the sons of Israel under oath, he continued, "When God thus takes care of you, you must bring my bones up from this place."*g* **26** Joseph died at the age of a hundred and ten. He was embalmed and laid to rest in a coffin in Egypt.*h*

---

* [50:15–26] The final reconciliation of the brothers. Fearful of what may happen after the death of their father, the brothers engage in a final deception, inventing the dying wish of Jacob. Again, Joseph weeps, and, again, his brothers fall down before him, offering to be his slaves (44:16, 33). Joseph's assurance is also a summation of the story: "Even though you meant harm to me, God meant it for good, to achieve this present end, the survival of many people" (v. 20). Joseph's adoption of the children of Manasseh's son Machir recalls Jacob's adoption of his grandchildren (48:5, 13–20); the adoptions reflect tribal history (cf. Jgs 5:14).

c. [50:20] Gn 45:5.
d. [50:21] Gn 47:12.
e. [50:23] Nm 32:39; Jos 17:1.
f. [50:24] Ex 3:8; Heb 11:22.
g. [50:25] Ex 13:19; Heb 11:22.
h. [50:26] Sir 49:15.

THE BOOK OF EXODUS

Introduction

The second book of the Pentateuch is called Exodus, from the Greek word for "departure," because its central event was understood by the Septuagint's translators to be the departure of the Israelites from Egypt. Its Hebrew title, *Shemoth* ("Names"), is from the book's opening phrase, "These are the names...." Continuing the history of Israel from the point where the Book of Genesis leaves off, Exodus recounts the Egyptian oppression of Jacob's ever-increasing descendants and their miraculous deliverance by God through Moses, who led them across the Red Sea to Mount Sinai where they entered into a covenant with the Lord. Covenantal laws and detailed prescriptions for the tabernacle (a portable sanctuary foreshadowing the Jerusalem Temple) and its service are followed by a dramatic episode of rebellion, repentance, and divine mercy. After the broken covenant is renewed, the tabernacle is constructed, and the cloud signifying God's glorious presence descends to cover it.

These events made Israel a nation and confirmed their unique relationship with God. The "law" (Hebrew *torah*) given by God through Moses to the Israelites at Mount Sinai constitutes the moral, civil, and ritual legislation by which they were to become a holy people. Many elements of it were fundamental to the teaching of Jesus (Mt 5:21–30; 15:4) as well as to New Testament and Christian moral teaching (Rom 13:8–10; 1 Cor 10:1–5; 1 Pt 2:9).

The principal divisions of Exodus are:

I. Introduction: The Oppression of the Israelites in Egypt (1:1–2:22)
II. The Call and Commission of Moses (2:23–7:7)
III. The Contest with Pharaoh (7:8–13:16)
IV. The Deliverance of the Israelites from Pharaoh and Victory at the Sea (13:17–15:21)
V. The Journey in the Wilderness to Sinai (15:22–18:27)
VI. Covenant and Legislation at Mount Sinai (19:1–31:18)
VII. Israel's Apostasy and God's Renewal of the Covenant (32:1–34:35)
VIII. The Building of the Tabernacle and the Descent of God's Glory upon It (35:1–40:38) ✠

EX

I. INTRODUCTION: THE OPPRESSION OF THE ISRAELITES IN EGYPT

CHAPTER 1

Jacob's Descendants in Egypt. ¹These are the names of the sons of Israel* who, accompanied by their households, entered into Egypt with Jacob: ²†Reuben, Simeon, Levi and Judah; ³Issachar, Zebulun and Benjamin; ⁴Dan and Naphtali; Gad and Asher. ⁵The total number of Jacob's direct descendants‡ was seventy.ᵃ Joseph was already in Egypt.

⁶Now Joseph and all his brothers and that whole generation died.ᵇ ⁷But the Israelites were fruitful and prolific. They multiplied and became so very numerous that the land was filled with them.§

The Oppression. ⁸ᶜThen a new king, who knew nothing of Joseph,¶ rose to power in Egypt. ⁹He said to his people, "See! The Israelite people have multiplied and become more numerous than we are! ¹⁰Come, let us deal shrewdly with them to stop their increase;** otherwise, in time of war they too may join our enemies to fight against us, and so leave the land."

¹¹Accordingly, they set supervisors over the Israelites to oppress them with forced labor.ᵈ Thus they had to build for Pharaoh†† the garrison cities of Pithom and Raamses. ¹²Yet the more they were oppressed, the more they multiplied and spread, so that the Egyptians began to loathe the Israelites. ¹³So the Egyptians reduced the Israelites to cruel slavery, ¹⁴making life bitter for them with hard labor, at mortar‡‡ and brick and all kinds of field work—cruelly oppressed in all their labor.

Command to the Midwives. ¹⁵The king of Egypt told the Hebrew midwives, one of whom was called Shiphrah and the other Puah, ¹⁶"When you act as midwives for the Hebrew women, look on the birthstool:§§ if it is a boy, kill him; but if it is a girl, she may live." ¹⁷The midwives, however, feared God; they did not do as the king of Egypt had ordered them, but let the boys live. ¹⁸So the king of Egypt summoned the midwives and asked them, "Why have you done this, allowing the boys to live?" ¹⁹The midwives answered Pharaoh, "The Hebrew women are not like the Egyptian women. They are robust and give birth before the midwife arrives." ²⁰Therefore God dealt well with the midwives; and the people multiplied and grew very numerous. ²¹And because the midwives feared God, God built up families for them. ²²Pharaoh then commanded all his people, "Throw into the Nile every boy that is born,ᵉ but you may let all the girls live."

---

* [1:1] **Sons of Israel**: here literally the first-generation sons of Jacob/Israel. Cf. v. 5. However, beginning with v. 7 the same Hebrew phrase refers to Jacob's more remote descendants; hence, from there on, it is ordinarily rendered "the Israelites." **Households**: the family in its fullest sense, including wives, children and servants.

† [1:2] Jacob's sons are listed here according to their respective mothers. Cf. Gn 29:31; 30:20; 35:16–26.

‡ [1:5] **Direct descendants**: lit., "persons coming from Jacob's loins"; hence, wives of Jacob's sons and servants are not included. Cf. Gn 46:26. **Seventy**: Gn 46:26, along with the Septuagint for the verse, agrees on a total of sixty-six coming down to Egypt with Jacob, but in v. 27 the Hebrew text adds the two sons born to Joseph in Egypt and presupposes Jacob himself and Joseph for a total of seventy; the Septuagint adds "nine sons" born to Joseph to get a total of seventy-five. This is the figure the Septuagint and 4QExᵇ have here in Ex 1:5.

§ [1:7] **Fruitful . . . multiplied . . . the land was filled with them**: the language used here to indicate the fecundity of the Israelite population echoes the divine blessing bestowed upon humanity at creation (Gn 1:28) and after the flood (Gn 9:1) as well as suggesting fulfillment of the promises to the ancestors Abraham, Isaac, and Jacob (Gn 12:2; 13:16; 15:5; 28:14; passim).

¶ [1:8] **Who knew nothing of Joseph**: the nuance intended by the Hebrew verb "know" here goes beyond precise determination. The idea may be not simply that a new king came to power who had not heard of Joseph but that this king ignored the services that Joseph had rendered to Egypt, repudiating the special relationship that existed between Joseph and his predecessor on the throne.

** [1:10] **Increase**: Pharaoh's actions thereby immediately pit him against God's will for the Israelites to multiply; see note on v. 7 above.

†† [1:11] **Pharaoh**: not a personal name, but a title common to all the kings of Egypt.

‡‡ [1:14] **Mortar**: either the wet clay with which the bricks were made, as in Na 3:14, or the cement used between the bricks in building, as in Gn 11:3.

§§ [1:16] **Birthstool**: apparently a pair of stones on which the mother is seated for childbirth opposite the midwife. The Hebrew word elsewhere is used to refer to the stones of a potter's wheel.

a. [1:5] Gn 46:26–27; Dt 10:22; Acts 7:14.
b. [1:6] Gn 50:26.
c. [1:8–10] Acts 7:18–19.
d. [1:11] Dt 26:6.
e. [1:22] Acts 7:19.

CHAPTER 2

Birth and Adoption of Moses.
¹Now a man* of the house of Levi married a Levite woman,ᵃ ²and the woman conceived and bore a son. Seeing what a fine child he was, she hid him for three months.ᵇ ³But when she could no longer hide him, she took a papyrus basket,† daubed it with bitumen and pitch, and putting the child in it, placed it among the reeds on the bank of the Nile. ⁴His sister stationed herself at a distance to find out what would happen to him.

⁵Then Pharaoh's daughter came down to bathe at the Nile, while her attendants walked along the bank of the Nile. Noticing the basket among the reeds, she sent her handmaid to fetch it. ⁶On opening it, she looked, and there was a baby boy crying! She was moved with pity for him and said, "It is one of the Hebrews' children." ⁷Then his sister asked Pharaoh's daughter, "Shall I go and summon a Hebrew woman to nurse the child for you?" ⁸Pharaoh's daughter answered her, "Go." So the young woman went and called the child's own mother. ⁹Pharaoh's daughter said to her, "Take this child and nurse him for me, and I will pay your wages."‡ So the woman took the child and nursed him. ¹⁰When the

child grew,§ she brought him to Pharaoh's daughter, and he became her son.ᶜ She named him Moses; for she said, "I drew him out of the water."

Moses' Flight to Midian. ¹¹ᵈOn one occasion, after Moses had grown up,¶ when he had gone out to his kinsmen and witnessed their forced labor, he saw an Egyptian striking a Hebrew, one of his own kinsmen. ¹²Looking about and seeing no one, he struck down the Egyptian and hid him in the sand. ¹³The next day he went out again, and now two Hebrews were fighting! So he asked the culprit, "Why are you striking your companion?" ¹⁴But he replied, "Who has appointed you ruler and judge over us? Are you thinking of killing me as you killed the Egyptian?" Then Moses became afraid and thought, "The affair must certainly be known." ¹⁵When Pharaoh heard of the affair, he sought to kill Moses. But Moses fled from Pharaoh and went to the land of Midian.**ᵉ There he sat down by a well.

---

§ [2:10] **When the child grew:** while v. 9 implies that the boy's mother cared for him as long as he needed to be nursed (presumably, between two and four years), the same verb appears in v. 11 to describe the attainment of adulthood. **And he became her son:** Pharaoh's daughter adopts Moses, thus adding to the irony of the account. The king of Egypt had ordered the killing of all the sons of the Hebrews, and one now becomes the son of his own daughter! **Moses:** in Hebrew, *mosheh*. There is a play on words here: Hebrew *mosheh* echoes *meshithihu* ("I drew him out"). However, the name Moses actually has nothing to do with that Hebrew verb, but is probably derived from Egyptian "beloved" or "has been born," preserved in such Pharaonic names as Thutmoses (meaning approximately "Beloved of the god Thoth" or "The god Thoth is born, has given birth to [the child]"). The original meaning of Moses' name was no longer remembered (if it was Egyptian, it may have contained an Egyptian divine element as well, perhaps the name of the Nile god Hapi), and a secondary explanation was derived from this story (or gave rise to it, if the drawing from the water of the Nile was intended to foreshadow the Israelites' escape from Egypt through the Red Sea).

* [2:1] **Now a man:** the chapter begins abruptly, without names for the man or woman (in contrast to the midwives of 1:15), who in 6:20 are identified as Amram and Jochebed.

† [2:3] **Basket:** the same Hebrew word is used in Gn 6:14 and throughout the flood narrative for Noah's ark, but nowhere else in the Bible. Here, however, the "ark" or "chest" was made of papyrus stalks. Presumably the allusion to Genesis is intentional. Just as Noah and his family were preserved safe from the threatening waters of the flood in the ark he built, so now Moses is preserved from the threatening waters of the Nile in the ark prepared by his mother. **Among the reeds:** the Hebrew noun for "reed" is overwhelmingly used in the phrase "Reed Sea," traditionally translated "Red Sea."

‡ [2:9] **And I will pay your wages:** the idea that the child's mother will be paid for nursing her child—and by Pharaoh's own daughter—heightens the narrative's irony.

¶ [2:11] **After Moses had grown up:** cf. 7:7, where Moses is said to be eighty years old at the time of his mission to Pharaoh. **Striking:** probably in the sense of "flogging"; in v. 12, however, the same verb is used in the sense of "killing."

** [2:15] **Land of Midian:** the territory under the control of a confederation made up, according to Nm 31:8, of five Midianite tribes. According to Gn 25:1–2, Midian was a son of Abraham by Keturah. In view of the extreme hostility in later periods between Israel and Midian (cf. Nm 31; Jgs 6–8), the relationship is striking, as is the account here in Exodus of good relations between Moses and no less than a Midianite priest.

---

a. [2:1] Ex 6:20; Nm 26:59.
b. [2:2] Acts 7:20; Heb 11:23.
c. [2:10] Acts 7:21; Heb 11:24.
d. [2:11–14] Acts 7:23–28.
e. [2:15] Acts 7:29; Heb 11:27.

EX

16Now the priest of Midian had seven daughters, and they came to draw water and fill the troughs to water their father's flock. 17But shepherds came and drove them away. So Moses rose up in their defense and watered their flock. 18When they returned to their father Reuel,* he said to them, "How is it you have returned so soon today?" 19They answered, "An Egyptian† delivered us from the shepherds. He even drew water for us and watered the flock!" 20"Where is he?" he asked his daughters. "Why did you leave the man there? Invite him to have something to eat." 21Moses agreed to stay with him, and the man gave Moses his daughter Zipporah in marriage. 22She conceived and bore a son, whom he named Gershom;‡ for he said, "I am a stranger residing in a foreign land."f

II. THE CALL AND COMMISSION OF MOSES

The Burning Bush. 23A long time passed, during which the king of Egypt died. The Israelites groaned under their bondage and cried out, and from their bondage their cry for help went up to God.g 24God heard their moaning and God was mindful of his covenant h with Abraham, Isaac and Jacob. 25God saw the Israelites, and God knew....§

* [2:18] **Reuel:** also called Jethro. Cf. 3:1; 4:18; 18:1.
† [2:19] **An Egyptian:** Moses was probably wearing Egyptian dress, or spoke Egyptian to Reuel's daughters.
‡ [2:22] **Gershom:** the name is explained unscientifically as if it came from the Hebrew word *ger,* "sojourner, resident alien," and the Hebrew word *sham,* "there." **Stranger residing:** Hebrew *ger,* one who seeks and finds shelter and a home away from his or her own people or land.
§ [2:25] **God knew:** in response to the people's cry, God, mindful of the covenant, looks on their plight and acknowledges firsthand the depth of their suffering (see 3:7). In vv. 23–25, traditionally attributed to the Priestly writer, God is mentioned five times, in contrast to the rest of chaps. 1–2, where God is rarely mentioned. These verses serve as a fitting transition to Moses' call in chap. 3.

f. [2:22] Ex 18:3.
g. [2:23] Ex 3:7, 9; Dt 26:7.
h. [2:24] Ex 6:5; Ps 105:8–9; 106:44–45.

CHAPTER 3

1¶Meanwhile Moses was tending the flock of his father-in-law Jethro, the priest of Midian. Leading the flock beyond the wilderness, he came to the mountain of God, Horeb.** 2There the angel of the LORD†† appeared to him as fire flaming out of a bush.a When he looked, although the bush was on fire, it was not being consumed. 3So Moses decided, "I must turn aside to look at this remarkable sight. Why does the bush not burn up?" 4When the LORD saw that he had turned aside to look, God called out to him from the bush: Moses! Moses! He answered, "Here I am." 5God said: Do not come near! Remove your sandals from your feet, for the place where you stand is holy ground.b 6I am the God of your

¶ [3:1–4:17] After the introduction to the narrative in 2:23–25, the commissioning itself falls into three sections: God's appearance under the aspect of a burning bush (3:1–6); the explicit commission (3:7–10); and an extended dialogue between Moses and God, in the course of which Moses receives the revelation of God's personal name. Although in the J source of the Pentateuch people have known and invoked God's personal name in worship since the time of Seth (Gn 4:26), for the E and P sources (see 6:2–4) God first makes this name publicly available here through Moses.

** [3:1] **The mountain of God, Horeb:** traditionally, "Horeb" is taken to be an alternate name in E source material and Deuteronomy (e.g., Dt 1:2) for what in J and P is known as Mount Sinai, the goal of the Israelites' journey after leaving Egypt and the site of the covenant God makes with Israel. However, it is not clear that originally the two names reflect the same mountain, nor even that "Horeb" refers originally to a mountain and not simply the dry, ruined region (from Hebrew *horeb,* "dryness, devastation") around the mountain. Additionally, the position of "Horeb" at the end of the verse may indicate that the identification of the "mountain of God" with Horeb (= Sinai?) represents a later stage in the evolution of the tradition about God's meeting with Moses. The phrase "mountain of God" simply anticipates the divine apparitions which would take place there, both on this occasion and after the Israelites' departure from Egypt; alternatively, it means that the place was already sacred or a place of pilgrimage in pre-Israelite times. In any case, the narrative offers no indications of its exact location.

†† [3:2] **The angel of the LORD:** Hebrew *mal'ak* or "messenger" is regularly translated *angelos* by the Septuagint, from which the English word "angel" is derived, but the Hebrew term lacks connotations now popularly associated with "angel" (such as wings). Although angels frequently assume human form (cf. Gn 18–19), the term is also used to indicate the visual form under which God occasionally appeared and spoke to people, referred to indifferently in some Old Testament texts either as God's "angel," *mal'ak,* or as God. Cf. Gn 16:7, 13; Ex 14:19, 24–25; Nm 22:22–35; Jgs 6:11–18. **The bush:** Hebrew *seneh,* perhaps "thorny bush," occurring only here in vv. 2–4 and in Dt 33:16. Its use here is most likely a wordplay on Sinai (Hebrew *sinay*), implying a popular etymology for the name of the sacred mountain.

a. [3:2–10] Acts 7:30–35.
b. [3:5] Jos 5:15.

father,[*] he continued, the God of Abraham, the God of Isaac, and the God of Jacob.[c] Moses hid his face, for he was afraid to look at God.

The Call and Commission of Moses. [7]But the LORD said: I have witnessed the affliction of my people in Egypt and have heard their cry against their taskmasters, so I know well what they are suffering. [8]Therefore I have come down[†] to rescue them from the power of the Egyptians and lead them up from that land into a good and spacious land, a land flowing with milk and honey, the country of the Canaanites, the Hittites, the Amorites, the Perizzites, the Girgashites, the Hivites and the Jebusites.[d] [9]Now indeed the outcry of the Israelites has reached me, and I have seen how the Egyptians are oppressing them. [10]Now, go! I am sending you to Pharaoh to bring my people, the Israelites, out of Egypt. [11]But Moses said to God, "Who am I[‡] that I should go to Pharaoh and bring the Israelites out of Egypt?" [12]God answered: I will be with you; and this will be your sign[§] that I have sent you. When you have brought the people out of Egypt, you will serve God at this mountain. [13]"But," said Moses to God, "if I go to the Israelites and say to them, 'The God of your ancestors has sent me to you,' and they ask me, 'What is his name?' what do I tell them?" [14]God replied to Moses: I am who I am.[¶] Then he added: This is what you will tell the Israelites: I AM has sent me to you.

[15]God spoke further to Moses: This is what you will say to the Israelites: The LORD, the God of your ancestors, the God of Abraham, the God of Isaac, and the God of Jacob, has sent me to you.

---

* [3:6] **God of your father**: a frequently used epithet in Genesis (along with the variants "my father" and "your father") for God as worshiped by the ancestors. As is known from its usage outside of the Bible in the ancient Near East, it suggests a close, personal relationship between the individual and the particular god in question, who is both a patron and a protector, a god traditionally revered by the individual's family and whose worship is passed down from father to son. **The God of Abraham . . . Jacob**: this precise phrase (only here and in v. 15; 4:5) stresses the continuity between the new revelation to Moses and the earlier religious experience of Israel's ancestors, identifying the God who is now addressing Moses with the God who promised land and numerous posterity to the ancestors. Cf. Mt 22:32; Mk 12:26; Lk 20:37. **Afraid to look at God**: the traditions about Moses are not uniform in regard to his beholding or not being able to look at God (cf. 24:11; 33:11, 18–23; 34:29–35). Here Moses' reaction is the natural and spontaneous gesture of a person suddenly confronted with a direct experience of God. Aware of his human frailty and the gulf that separates him from the God who is holy, he hides his face. To encounter the divine was to come before an awesome and mysterious power unlike any other a human being might experience and, as such, potentially threatening to one's very identity or existence (see Gn 32:30).

† [3:8] **I have come down**: cf. Gn 11:5, 7; 18:21. **Flowing with milk and honey**: an expression denoting agricultural prosperity, which seems to have been proverbial in its application to the land of Canaan. Cf. Ex 13:5; Nm 13:27; Jos 5:6; Jer 11:5; 32:22; Ez 20:6, 15.

‡ [3:11] **Who am I**: this question is always addressed by an inferior to a superior (to the ruler in 1 Sm 18:18; to God in 2 Sm 7:18 and its parallel, 1 Chr 17:16; 1 Chr 29:14; 2 Chr 2:5). In response to some special opportunity or invitation, the question expresses in a style typical of the ancient Near East the speaker's humility or gratitude or need of further assistance, but never unwillingness or an outright refusal to respond. Instead the question sets the stage for further support from the superior should that be needed (as here).

§ [3:12] **Sign**: a visible display of the power of God. The ancient notion of a sign from God does not coincide with the modern understanding of "miracle," which suggests some disruption in the laws governing nature. While most any phenomenon can become a vehicle for displaying the purposes and providence of God, here the sign intended to confirm Moses' commission by God seems to be the burning bush itself. Since normally the giving of such a sign would follow the commission rather than precede it (see Jgs 6:11–24), some see Israel's service of God at Sinai after the exodus from Egypt as the confirmatory sign, albeit retroactively. It is more likely, however, that its mention here is intended to establish the present episode with Moses alone as a prefigurement of God's fiery theophany to all Israel on Mount Sinai. **Serve God**: Hebrew '-b-d, "serve," includes among its meanings both the notion of "serving or working for another" and the notion of "worship." The implication here is that the Israelites' service/worship of God is incompatible with their service to Pharaoh.

¶ [3:14] **I am who I am**: Moses asks in v. 13 for the name of the One speaking to him, but God responds with a wordplay which preserves the utterly mysterious character of the divine being even as it appears to suggest something of the inner meaning of God's name: 'ehyeh "I am" or "I will be(come)" for "Yhwh," the personal name of the God of Israel. While the phrase "I am who I am" resists unraveling, it nevertheless suggests an etymological linking between the name "Yhwh" and an earlier form of the Hebrew verbal root h-y-h "to be." On that basis many have interpreted the name "Yhwh" as a third-person form of the verb meaning "He causes to be, creates," itself perhaps a shortened form of a longer liturgical name such as "(God who) creates (the heavenly armies)." Note in this connection the invocation of Israel's God as "LORD (Yhwh) of Hosts" (e.g., 1 Sm 17:45). In any case, out of reverence for God's proper name, the term Adonai, "my Lord," was later used as a substitute. The word LORD (in small capital letters) indicates that the Hebrew text has the sacred name (Yhwh), the tetragrammaton. The word "Jehovah" arose from a false reading of this name as it is written in the current Hebrew text. The Septuagint has egō eimi ho ōn, "I am the One who is" (ōn being the participle of the verb "to be"). This can be taken as an assertion of God's aseity or self-existence, and has been understood as such by the Church, since the time of the Fathers, as a true expression of God's being, even though it is not precisely the meaning of the Hebrew.

c. [3:6] Ex 4:5; Mt 22:32; Mk 12:26; Lk 20:37.

d. [3:8] Gn 15:19–21.

This is my name forever;^e
  this is my title for all generations.

¹⁶Go and gather the elders of the Israelites, and tell them, The Lord, the God of your ancestors, the God of Abraham, Isaac, and Jacob, has appeared to me and said: I have observed you and what is being done to you in Egypt; ¹⁷so I have decided to lead you up out of your affliction in Egypt into the land of the Canaanites, the Hittites, the Amorites, the Perizzites, the Girgashites, the Hivites and the Jebusites, a land flowing with milk and honey. ¹⁸They will listen to you. Then you and the elders of Israel will go to the king of Egypt and say to him:^f The Lord, the God of the Hebrews, has come to meet us. So now, let us go a three days' journey in the wilderness to offer sacrifice to the Lord, our God. ¹⁹Yet I know that the king of Egypt will not allow you to go unless his hand is forced. ²⁰So I will stretch out my hand and strike Egypt with all the wondrous deeds I will do in its midst. After that he will let you go. ^{21g}I will even make the Egyptians so well-disposed toward this people that, when you go, you will not go empty-handed. ²²Every woman will ask her neighbor and the resident alien in her house for silver and gold articles* and for clothing, and you will put them on your sons and daughters. So you will plunder the Egyptians.

CHAPTER 4

¹"But," objected Moses, "suppose they do not believe me or listen to me? For they may say, 'The Lord did not appear to you.'" ²The Lord said to him: What is in your hand? "A staff," he answered. ³God said: Throw it on the ground. So he threw it on the ground and it became a snake,^a and Moses backed away from it. ⁴Then the Lord said to Moses: Now stretch out your hand and take hold of its tail. So he stretched out his hand and took hold of it, and it became a staff in his hand. ⁵That is so they will believe that the Lord, the God of their ancestors, the God of Abraham, the God of Isaac, and the God of Jacob, did appear to you.

⁶Again the Lord said to him: Put your hand into the fold of your garment. So he put his hand into the fold of his garment, and when he drew it out, there was his hand covered with scales, like snowflakes. ⁷Then God said: Put your hand back into the fold of your garment. So he put his hand back into the fold of his garment, and when he drew it out, there it was again like his own flesh. ⁸If they do not believe you or pay attention to the message of the first sign, they should believe the message of the second sign. ⁹And if they do not believe even these two signs and do not listen to you, take some water from the Nile and pour it on the dry land. The water you take from the Nile will become blood on the dry land.^b

Aaron's Office as Assistant. ¹⁰Moses, however, said to the Lord, "If you please, my Lord, I have never been eloquent, neither in the past nor now that you have spoken to your servant; but I am slow of speech and tongue."^c ¹¹The Lord said to him: Who gives one person speech? Who makes another mute or deaf, seeing or blind? Is it not I, the Lord? ¹²Now go, I will assist you in speaking[†] and teach you what you are to say. ¹³But he said, "If you please, my Lord, send someone else!"[‡] ¹⁴Then the Lord became angry with Moses and said: I know there is your brother, Aaron the Levite, who is a good speaker; even now he is on his way to meet you. When he sees you, he

---

* [3:22] **Articles**: probably jewelry.

e. [3:15] Ps 135:13.
f. [3:18] Ex 5:3.
g. [3:21–22] Ex 11:2–3; 12:35–36.

a. [4:3] Ex 7:10.

† [4:12] **Assist you in speaking**: lit., "be with your mouth"; cf. v. 15, lit., "be with your mouth and with his mouth."
‡ [4:13] **Send someone else**: lit., "send by means of him whom you will send," that is, "send whom you will."

b. [4:9] Ex 7:17, 19–20.
c. [4:10] Ex 6:12.

will truly be glad. [15]You will speak to him and put the words in his mouth. I will assist both you and him in speaking and teach you both what you are to do. [16]He will speak to the people for you: he will be your spokesman,* and you will be as God to him.[d] [17]Take this staff[†] in your hand; with it you are to perform the signs.

Moses' Return to Egypt. [18]After this Moses returned to Jethro[‡] his father-in-law and said to him, "Let me return to my kindred in Egypt, to see whether they are still living." Jethro replied to Moses, "Go in peace." [19]Then the LORD said to Moses in Midian: Return to Egypt, for all those who sought your life are dead. [20]So Moses took his wife and his sons, mounted them on the donkey, and started back to the land of Egypt. Moses took the staff of God with him. [21]The LORD said to Moses: On your return to Egypt, see that you perform before Pharaoh all the wonders I have put in your power. But I will harden his heart[§] and he will not let the people go. [22][e]So you will say to Pharaoh, Thus says the LORD: Israel is my son, my firstborn. [23]I said to you: Let my son go, that he may serve me. Since you refused to let him go, I will kill your son, your firstborn.[f]

[24]¶On the journey, at a place where they spent the night, the LORD came upon Moses and sought to put him to death. [25][g]But Zipporah took a piece of flint and cut off her son's foreskin and, touching his feet,** she said, "Surely you are a spouse of blood to me." [26]So God let Moses alone. At that time she said, "A spouse of blood," in regard to the circumcision.

[27]The LORD said to Aaron: Go into the wilderness to meet Moses. So he went; when meeting him at the mountain of God, he kissed him. [28]Moses told Aaron everything the LORD had sent him to say, and all the signs he had commanded him to do. [29]Then Moses and Aaron went and gathered all the elders of the Israelites. [30]Aaron told them everything the LORD had said to Moses, and he performed the signs before the people. [31]The people believed, and when they heard that the LORD had observed the Israelites and had seen their affliction,[††] they knelt and bowed down.

CHAPTER 5

Pharaoh's Hardness of Heart. [1]Afterwards, Moses and Aaron went to Pharaoh and said, "Thus says the

---

* [4:16] **Spokesman**: lit., "mouth"; Aaron was to serve as a mouthpiece for Moses, as a prophet does for God; hence the relation between Moses and Aaron is compared to that between God and his prophet: Moses "will be as God to," i.e., lit., "will become God for him." Cf. 7:1.

† [4:17] **This staff**: probably the same as that of vv. 2–4; but some understand that a new staff is now given by God to Moses.

‡ [4:18] **Jethro**: the Hebrew text has "Jether," apparently a variant form of "Jethro" found in the same verse. **To see whether they are still living**: Moses did not tell his father-in-law his main reason for returning to Egypt.

§ [4:21] **Harden his heart**: in the biblical view, the heart, whose actual function in the circulation of blood was unknown, typically performs functions associated today more with the brain than with the emotions. Therefore, while it may be used in connection with various emotional states ranging from joy to sadness, it very commonly designates the seat of intellectual and volitional activities. For God to harden Pharaoh's heart is to harden his resolve against the Israelites' desire to leave. In the ancient world, actions which are out of character are routinely attributed not to the person but to some "outside" superhuman power acting upon the person (Jgs 14:16; 1 Sm 16:10). Uncharacteristically negative actions or states are explained in the same way (1 Sm 16:14). In this instance, the opposition of Pharaoh, in the face of God's displays of power, would be unintelligible to the ancient Israelites unless he is seen as under some divine constraint. But this does not diminish Pharaoh's own responsibility. In the anthropology of the ancient Israelites there is no opposition between individual responsibility and God's sovereignty over all of creation. Cf. Rom 9:17–18.

¶ [4:24–26] This story continues to perplex commentators and may have circulated in various forms before finding its place here in Exodus. Particularly troublesome is the unique phrase "spouse of blood." Nevertheless, v. 26, which apparently comes from the hand of a later commentator on the original story, is intended to offer some clarification. It asserts that when Zipporah used the problematic expression (addressing it either to Moses or her son), she did so with reference to the circumcision performed on her son—the only place in the Bible where this rite is performed by a woman. Whatever the precise meaning of the phrase "spouse of blood," circumcision is the key to understanding it as well as the entire incident. One may conclude, therefore, that God was angry with Moses for having failed to keep the divine command given to Abraham in Gn 17:10–12 and circumcise his son. Moses' life is spared when his wife circumcises their son.

** [4:25] **Touching his feet**: a euphemism most probably for the male sexual organ (see 2 Kgs 18:27; Is 7:20); whether the genitals of the child (after Zipporah circumcised him) or of Moses (after the circumcision of his son) is not clear.

†† [4:31] **Observed . . . their affliction**: the same phrases used in God's dialogue with Moses in 3:16–17.

---

d. [4:16] Ex 7:1.
e. [4:22] Sir 36:11.

f. [4:23] Ex 11:5; 12:29.
g. [4:25] Is 6:2; 7:20.

LORD, the God of Israel: Let my people go, that they may hold a feast* for me in the wilderness." **2**Pharaoh answered, "Who is the LORD, that I should obey him and let Israel go? I do not know the LORD,† and I will not let Israel go." **3**They replied, "The God of the Hebrews has come to meet us. Let us go a three days' journey in the wilderness, that we may offer sacrifice to the LORD, our God,ᵃ so that he does not strike us with the plague or the sword." **4**The king of Egypt answered them, "Why, Moses and Aaron, do you make the people neglect their work? Off to your labors!" **5**Pharaoh continued, "Look how they are already more numerous‡ than the people of the land, and yet you would give them rest from their labors!"

6That very day Pharaoh gave the taskmasters of the people and their foremen§ this order: **7**"You shall no longer supply the people with straw for their brickmaking¶ as before. Let them go and gather their own straw! **8**Yet you shall levy upon them the same quota of bricks as they made previously. Do not reduce it. They are lazy; that is why they are crying, 'Let us go to offer sacrifice to our God.' **9**Increase the work for the men, so that they attend to it and not to deceitful words."

10So the taskmasters of the people and their foremen went out and told the people, "Thus says Pharaoh,** 'I will not provide you with straw. **11**Go and get your own straw from wherever you can find it. But there will not be the slightest reduction in your work.'" **12**The people, then, scattered throughout the land of Egypt to gather stubble for straw, **13**while the taskmasters kept driving them on, saying, "Finish your work, the same daily amount as when the straw was supplied to you." **14**The Israelite foremen, whom the taskmasters of Pharaoh had placed over them, were beaten, and were asked, "Why have you not completed your prescribed amount of bricks yesterday and today, as before?"

Complaint of the Foremen. 15 Then the Israelite foremen came and cried out to Pharaoh:†† "Why do you treat your servants in this manner? **16**No straw is supplied to your servants, and still we are told, 'Make bricks!' Look how your servants are beaten! It is you who are at fault." **17**He answered, "Lazy! You are lazy! That is why you keep saying, 'Let us go and offer sacrifice to the LORD.' **18**Now off to work! No straw will be supplied to you, but you must supply your quota of bricks."

19The Israelite foremen realized they were in trouble, having been told, "Do not reduce your daily amount of bricks!" **20**So when they left Pharaoh they assailed Moses and Aaron, who were waiting to meet them, **21**and said to them, "The LORD look upon you and judge! You have made us offensive to Pharaoh and his servants, putting a sword into their hands to kill us."

Renewal of God's Promise. 22 Then Moses again had recourse to the LORD and said, "LORD, why have you treated this people badly? And why did you

---

* [5:1] **Hold a feast**: the Hebrew verb used here, *hagag* ("to celebrate a feast or a festival"; see 12:14; 23:14), refers to a community celebration marked above all by a procession to the sanctuary. It is used especially of three major feasts: Unleavened Bread, Pentecost (in 23:16, "the Feast of Harvest," but customarily "the Feast of Weeks" [*Shavuot*]), and Succoth/Sukkoth (in 34:16, "the Feast of Ingathering," but more frequently "of Booths, or Tabernacles," as in Dt 16:13, 16; 31:10; Lv 23:34; Zec 14:16; passim) and—along with the related noun *hag*—the Passover in 12:14. See 23:14–18; 34:18–25.

† [5:2] **I do not know the LORD**: whether or not he had heard of the Lord, the God of Israel, Pharaoh here refuses to acknowledge the Lord's authority. See note on 1:8.

‡ [5:5] **They are already more numerous**: a recollection of Pharaoh's earlier words to his subjects in 1:9.

§ [5:6] **The taskmasters of the people and their foremen**: the former were higher officials and probably Egyptians; the latter were lower officials (perhaps recordkeepers or clerks), chosen from the Israelites themselves. Cf. v. 14.

¶ [5:7] Straw was mixed with clay to give sun-dried bricks greater cohesion and durability.

** [5:10] **Thus says Pharaoh**: the standard formula for prophetic oracles, but with Pharaoh rather than the Lord as the subject. This heightens the sense of personal conflict between Pharaoh, who acts as if he were God, and the Lord, whose claims are spurned by Pharaoh.

†† [5:15] **Cried out to Pharaoh**: the Hebrew verb translated "cry out" and its related noun are normally used of appeals to God by Moses (8:8; 14:15; 15:25; 17:4), the people (3:7, 9; 14:10), or an oppressed individual (22:22, 26). Here, by implication, these minor Israelite officials appeal to Pharaoh as if he were their God. See v. 10.

a. [5:3] Ex 3:18.

send me? ²³From the time I went to Pharaoh to speak in your name, he has treated this people badly, and you have done nothing to rescue your people."

CHAPTER 6

¹The Lord answered Moses: Now you will see what I will do to Pharaoh. For by a strong hand, he will let them go; by a strong hand,* he will drive them from his land.

Confirmation of the Promise to the Ancestors. ^{2†}Then God spoke to Moses, and said to him: I am the Lord. ³As God the Almighty[‡] I appeared^a to Abraham, Isaac, and Jacob, but by my name, Lord, I did not make myself known to them. ⁴I also established my covenant with them, to give them the land of Canaan, the land in which they were residing as aliens.^b ⁵Now that I have heard the groaning of the Israelites, whom the Egyptians have reduced to slavery, I am mindful of my covenant.^c ⁶Therefore, say to the Israelites: I am the Lord. I will free you from the burdens of the Egyptians and will deliver you from their slavery. I will redeem you by my outstretched arm and with mighty acts of judgment. ⁷I will take you as my own people, and I will be your God;^d and you will know that I, the Lord, am your God who has freed you from the burdens of the Egyptians ⁸and I will bring you into the land which I swore to give to Abraham, Isaac, and Jacob. I will give it to you as your own possession—I, the Lord! ⁹But when Moses told this to the Israelites, they would not listen to him because of their dejection and hard slavery.

¹⁰Then the Lord spoke to Moses: ¹¹Go, tell Pharaoh, king of Egypt, to let the Israelites leave his land. ¹²However, Moses protested to the Lord, "If the Israelites did not listen to me, how is it possible that Pharaoh will listen to me, poor speaker^{§e} that I am!" ¹³But the Lord spoke to Moses and Aaron regarding the Israelites and Pharaoh, king of Egypt, and charged them to bring the Israelites out of the land of Egypt.

Genealogy of Moses and Aaron. ¹⁴These are the heads of their ancestral houses.[¶] The sons of Reuben,^f the firstborn of Israel: Hanoch, Pallu, Hezron and Carmi; these are the clans of Reuben. ¹⁵The sons of Simeon:^g Jemuel, Jamin, Ohad, Jachin, Zohar and Shaul, the son of a Canaanite woman; these are the clans of Simeon. ¹⁶These are the names of the sons of Levi,^h in their genealogical order: Gershon, Kohath and Merari. Levi lived one hundred and thirty-seven years.

¹⁷The sons of Gershon,ⁱ by their clans: Libni and Shimei. ¹⁸The sons of Kohath:^j Amram, Izhar, Hebron and Uzziel. Kohath lived one hundred and thirty-three years. ¹⁹The sons of Merari:^k Mahli and Mushi. These are the clans of Levi in their genealogical order.

²⁰Amram married his aunt** Jochebed,^l who bore him Aaron,

---

* [6:1] **By a strong hand:** By God's hand or Pharaoh's hand? The Hebrew is ambiguous; although it may be an allusion to God's hand of 3:19–20, both interpretations are possible.

† [6:2–7:7] According to the standard source criticism of the Pentateuch, 6:2–7:7 represents a Priestly version of the JE call narrative in 3:1–4:17. But in context the present account does more than simply repeat the earlier passage. See note below.

‡ [6:3] **God the Almighty:** in Hebrew, *El Shaddai*. This traditional translation does not have a firm philological basis. **But by my name . . . I did not make myself known to them:** although the text implies that the name Lord was unknown previously, in context the emphasis in the passage falls on the understanding of God that comes with knowledge of the name. In this way God responds to the worsening plight of the Israelites and Moses' complaint in 5:23 that God has done nothing at all to rescue them.

§ [6:12] **Poor speaker:** lit., "uncircumcised of lips": a metaphor expressing the hindrance of good communication expressed as "slow of speech and tongue" (4:10). Also used as a metaphor for impeded "heart" (Lv 26:41; Dt 10:16).

¶ [6:14] The purpose of the genealogy here is to give the line from which Moses and Aaron sprang, with special emphasis placed on the line of Aaron. Reuben and Simeon are mentioned first because, as older brothers of Levi, their names occur before his in the genealogy.

** [6:20] **His aunt:** more exactly, "his father's sister." Later on such a marriage was forbidden. Cf. Lv 18:12. Hence, the Greek and Latin versions render here, "his cousin."

---

a. [6:3] Gn 17:1; 35:11.
b. [6:4] Gn 15:18; 17:4–8.
c. [6:5] Ex 2:24.
d. [6:7] Lv 26:12.

e. [6:12] Ex 4:10.
f. [6:14] Nm 26:5–6; 1 Chr 5:3.
g. [6:15] Nm 26:12; 1 Chr 4:24.
h. [6:16] Nm 3:17; 1 Chr 6:1; 23:6.
i. [6:17] Nm 3:21; 1 Chr 6:2; 23:7.
j. [6:18] Nm 3:27; 1 Chr 6:3, 18.
k. [6:19] Nm 3:20; 1 Chr 6:4, 14; 23:21.
l. [6:20] Nm 26:59.

Moses, and Miriam. Amram lived one hundred and thirty-seven years. ²¹The sons of Izhar: Korah, Nepheg and Zichri. ²²The sons of Uzziel: Mishael, Elzaphan and Sithri. ²³Aaron married Elisheba, Amminadab's^m daughter, the sister of Nahshon; she bore him Nadab, Abihu, Eleazar and Ithamar. ²⁴The sons of Korah: Assir, Elkanah and Abiasaph. These are the clans of the Korahites. ²⁵Eleazar, Aaron's son, married one of Putiel's daughters, who bore him Phinehas.* These are the heads of the ancestral houses of the Levites by their clans. ²⁶These are the Aaron and the Moses to whom the LORD said, "Bring the Israelites out from the land of Egypt, company by company." ²⁷They are the ones who spoke to Pharaoh, king of Egypt, to bring the Israelites out of Egypt—the same Moses and Aaron.

²⁸When the LORD spoke to Moses in the land of Egypt ²⁹the LORD said to Moses: I am the LORD. Say to Pharaoh, king of Egypt, all that I tell you. ³⁰But Moses protested to the LORD, "Since I am a poor speaker, how is it possible that Pharaoh will listen to me?"

CHAPTER 7

¹The LORD answered Moses: See! I have made you a god to Pharaoh,^a and Aaron your brother will be your prophet.^† ²You will speak all that I command you. In turn, your brother Aaron will tell Pharaoh to let the Israelites go out of his land. ³Yet I will make Pharaoh so headstrong that, despite the many signs and wonders that I work in the land of Egypt, ⁴Pharaoh will not listen to you. Therefore I will lay my hand on Egypt and with mighty acts of judgment I will bring my armies, my people the Israelites, out of the land of Egypt. ⁵All Egyptians will know that I am the LORD, when I stretch out my hand against Egypt and bring the Israelites out of their midst.

⁶This, then, is what Moses and Aaron did. They did exactly as the LORD had commanded them. ⁷Moses was eighty years old, and Aaron eighty-three, when they spoke to Pharaoh.

III. THE CONTEST WITH PHARAOH

The Staff Turned into a Serpent.
⁸The LORD spoke to Moses and Aaron: ⁹When Pharaoh demands of you, "Produce a sign or wonder," you will say to Aaron: "Take your staff and throw it down before Pharaoh, and it will turn into a serpent."^b ¹⁰Then Moses and Aaron went to Pharaoh and did just as the LORD had commanded. Aaron threw his staff down before Pharaoh and his servants, and it turned into a serpent. ¹¹Pharaoh, in turn, summoned the wise men and the sorcerers, and they also, the magicians^c of Egypt, did the same thing by their magic arts. ¹²Each one threw down his staff, and they turned into serpents. But Aaron's staff swallowed their staffs. ¹³Pharaoh, however, hardened his heart and would not listen to them, just as the LORD had foretold.

First Plague: Water Turned into Blood.^‡ ¹⁴Then the LORD said to Moses: Pharaoh is obstinate^§ in refusing to

---

* [6:25] **Phinehas:** according to Nm 25:13, Phinehas was given by God "the covenant of an everlasting priesthood" because of his zeal for God when the Israelites committed apostasy by worshiping the Baal of Peor in the plains of Moab (see Nm 25:1–18).

† [7:1] **Prophet:** Hebrew *nabi*, one who can legitimately speak for God and in God's name to another or others. Just as God spoke to Moses, so Moses will speak to Aaron, who will be a "prophet" to Pharaoh. Cf. 4:16.

m. [6:23] Ru 4:19–20; 1 Chr 2:10.

a. [7:1] Ex 4:15–16.

‡ [7:14–12:30] After a brief preface (vv. 8–13) drawn from the Priestly source, a narrative depicting the series of ten disasters that God brings upon Pharaoh because of his stubbornness ensues. Although most of these disasters, known traditionally as the "ten plagues of Egypt," could be interpreted as naturally occurring phenomena, they are clearly represented by the biblical authors as extraordinary events indicative of God's intervention on behalf of Israel and as occurring exactly according to Moses' commands. See Ps 78:43–51 and 105:27–36 for poetic versions of these plagues, which also differ significantly from the account here.

§ [7:14] **Pharaoh is obstinate:** lit., "Pharaoh's heart is heavy" (*kabed*); thus not precisely the same Hebrew idiom as found in vv. 13 and 22, "stubborn," lit., "Pharaoh's heart was hard(ened)" (*hazaq*) (cf. the related idiom with Pharaoh as the object, e.g., 4:21).

b. [7:9] Ex 4:3.

c. [7:11] 2 Tm 3:8.

let the people go. ¹⁵In the morning, just when he sets out for the water, go to Pharaoh and present yourself by the bank of the Nile, holding in your hand the staff that turned into a snake.* ¹⁶Say to him: The LORD, the God of the Hebrews, sent me to you with the message: Let my people go to serve me in the wilderness. But as yet you have not listened. ¹⁷Thus says the LORD: This is how you will know that I am the LORD. With the staff here in my hand, I will strike the water in the Nile and it will be changed into blood.ᵈ ¹⁸The fish in the Nile will die, and the Nile itself will stink so that the Egyptians will be unable to drink water from the Nile.

¹⁹The LORD then spoke to Moses: Speak to Aaron: Take your staff and stretch out your hand over the waters of Egypt—its streams, its canals, its ponds, and all its supplies of water—that they may become blood. There will be blood throughout the land of Egypt, even in the wooden pails and stone jars.

²⁰This, then, is what Moses and Aaron did, exactly as the LORD had commanded. Aaron raised his staff and struck the waters in the Nile in full view of Pharaoh and his servants, and all the water in the Nile was changed into blood. ²¹The fish in the Nile died, and the Nile itself stank so that the Egyptians could not drink water from it. There was blood throughout the land of Egypt. ²²But the Egyptian magicians did the same† by their magic arts. So Pharaoh hardened his heart and would not listen to them, just as the LORD had said. ²³Pharaoh turned away and went into his house, with no concern even for this. ²⁴All the Egyptians had to dig round about the Nile for drinking water, since they could not drink any water from the Nile.

Second Plague: the Frogs. ²⁵Seven days passed after the LORD had struck the Nile. ²⁶Then the LORD said to Moses: Go to Pharaoh and tell him:ᵉ Thus says the LORD: Let my people go to serve me. ²⁷If you refuse to let them go, then I will send a plague of frogs over all your territory. ²⁸The Nile will teem with frogs. They will come up and enter into your palace and into your bedroom and onto your bed, into the houses of your servants, too, and among your people, even into your ovens and your kneading bowls. ²⁹The frogs will come up over you and your people and all your servants.

CHAPTER 8

¹The LORD then spoke to Moses: Speak to Aaron: Stretch out your hand with your staff over the streams, the canals, and the ponds, and make frogs overrun the land of Egypt. ²So Aaron stretched out his hand over the waters of Egypt, and the frogs came up and covered the land of Egypt. ³But the magicians did the same by their magic arts and made frogs overrun the land of Egypt.

⁴Then Pharaoh summoned Moses and Aaron and said, "Pray to the LORD to remove the frogs from me and my people, and I will let the people go to sacrifice to the LORD." ⁵Moses answered Pharaoh, "Please designate for me the time when I am to pray for you and your servants and your people, to get rid of the frogs from you and your houses. They will be left only in the Nile." ⁶"Tomorrow," he said. Then Moses replied, "It will be as you have said, so that you may know that there is none like the LORD, our God. ⁷The frogs will leave you and your houses, your servants and your people; they will be left only in the Nile."

---

* [7:15] **The staff that turned into a snake**: the allusion is to 4:2–4 rather than 7:9–12. The latter comes from the hand of the Priestly writer and features Aaron—with his staff—as the principal actor.

† [7:22] **The Egyptian magicians did the same**: this is an exaggeration, presumably influenced by the similar statement in v. 11; whereas the magicians could turn their staffs into snakes after Aaron had done so, after Aaron's sign there should not have been any water in Egypt still unchanged to blood for the magicians "to do the same" with it (cf. v. 24).

---

d. [7:17–21] Ex 4:9; Ps 78:44; 105:29; Wis 11:5–7.

e. [7:26–29] Ps 78:45; 105:30.

⁸After Moses and Aaron left Pharaoh's presence, Moses cried out to the LORD on account of the frogs that he had inflicted on Pharaoh; ⁹and the LORD did as Moses had asked. The frogs died off in the houses, the courtyards, and the fields. ¹⁰Heaps of them were piled up, and the land stank. ¹¹But when Pharaoh saw there was a respite, he became obstinate and would not listen to them, just as the LORD had said.

Third Plague: the Gnats. ¹²Thereupon the LORD spoke to Moses: Speak to Aaron: Stretch out your staff and strike the dust of the earth, and it will turn into gnats^{*a} throughout the land of Egypt. ¹³They did so. Aaron stretched out his hand with his staff and struck the dust of the earth, and gnats came upon human being and beast alike. All the dust of the earth turned into gnats throughout the land of Egypt. ¹⁴Though the magicians did the same thing to produce gnats by their magic arts, they could not do so.^b The gnats were on human being and beast alike, ¹⁵and the magicians said to Pharaoh, "This is the finger of God."[†] Yet Pharaoh hardened his heart and would not listen to them, just as the LORD had said.

Fourth Plague: the Flies. ¹⁶Then the LORD spoke to Moses: Early tomorrow morning present yourself to Pharaoh when he sets out toward the water, and say to him: Thus says the LORD: Let my people go to serve me.

¹⁷For if you do not let my people go, I will send swarms of flies upon you and your servants and your people and your houses. The houses of the Egyptians and the very ground on which they stand will be filled with swarms of flies. ¹⁸But on that day I will make an exception of the land of Goshen, where my people are, and no swarms of flies will be there, so that you may know that I the LORD am in the midst of the land. ¹⁹I will make a distinction[‡] between my people and your people. This sign will take place tomorrow. ²⁰This the LORD did. Thick swarms of flies entered the house of Pharaoh and the houses of his servants; throughout Egypt the land was devastated on account of the swarms of flies.^c

²¹Then Pharaoh summoned Moses and Aaron and said, "Go sacrifice to your God within the land." ²²But Moses replied, "It is not right to do so, for what we sacrifice to the LORD, our God, is abhorrent to the Egyptians.[§] If we sacrifice what is abhorrent to the Egyptians before their very eyes, will they not stone us? ²³We must go a three days' journey in the wilderness and sacrifice to the LORD, our God, as he commands us." ²⁴Pharaoh said, "I will let you go to sacrifice to the LORD, your God, in the wilderness, provided that you do not go too far away. Pray for me." ²⁵Moses answered, "As soon as I leave you I will pray to the LORD that the swarms of flies may depart tomorrow from Pharaoh, his servants, and his people. Pharaoh, however, must not act deceitfully again and refuse to let the people go to sacrifice to the LORD." ²⁶When Moses left

---

* [8:12, 17] **Gnats, flies**: it is uncertain what species of troublesome insects are meant here in vv. 12–14 and then in vv. 17–27, the identification as "gnat" (vv. 12–14) and as "fly" (vv. 17–27) being based on the rendering of the Septuagint. Others suggest "lice" in vv. 12–14, while rabbinic literature renders Hebrew *'arob* in vv. 17–27 as a "mixture of wild animals." In the Hebrew of the Old Testament, the word occurs only in the context of the plagues (see also Ps 78:45 and 105:31).

† [8:15] **The finger of God**: previously the magicians had, for the most part, been able to replicate the signs and wonders Moses performed to manifest God's power—turning their staffs into snakes (7:11–12), turning water into blood (7:22), and producing frogs to overrun the land of Egypt (8:3). But now for the first time they are unable to compete, and confess a power greater than their own is at work. Cf. Lk 11:20.

‡ [8:19] **A distinction**: while some uncertainty surrounds the Hebrew here rendered as "distinction," it is clear that now the Israelites begin to be set apart from the Egyptians, a separation that reaches a climax in the death of the Egyptian firstborn (11:7).

§ [8:22] Perhaps Moses is deceiving the Pharaoh much like the "God-fearing" midwives (1:16–20), although ancient historians writing about Egypt some time after the period in which the exodus is set do note Egyptian prohibitions on sacrificing cattle or slaughtering sacred animals. As such, the Egyptians might well have fiercely resented certain sacrificial practices of the Israelites. Certain animals were held sacred in Egypt, as the representations of various deities.

a. [8:12–13] Ps 105:31.
b. [8:14] Wis 17:7.

c. [8:20] Ps 78:45; 105:31; Wis 16:9.

Pharaoh, he prayed to the LORD; **²⁷**and the LORD did as Moses had asked, removing the swarms of flies from Pharaoh, his servants, and his people. Not one remained. **²⁸**But once more Pharaoh became obstinate and would not let the people go.

CHAPTER 9

Fifth Plague: the Pestilence. ¹ Then the LORD said to Moses: Go to Pharaoh and tell him: Thus says the LORD, the God of the Hebrews: Let my people go to serve me. **²**For if you refuse to let them go and persist in holding them, **³**the hand of the LORD will strike your livestock in the field—your horses, donkeys, camels, herds and flocks— with a very severe pestilence. **⁴**But the LORD will distinguish between the livestock of Israel and that of Egypt, so that nothing belonging to the Israelites will die. **⁵**And the LORD set a definite time, saying: Tomorrow the LORD will do this in the land. **⁶**And on the next day the LORD did it. All the livestock of the Egyptians died,ᵃ but not one animal belonging to the Israelites died. **⁷**But although Pharaoh found upon inquiry that not even so much as one of the livestock of the Israelites had died, he remained obstinate and would not let the people go.

Sixth Plague: the Boils. ⁸ So the LORD said to Moses and Aaron: Each of you take handfuls of soot from a kiln, and in the presence of Pharaoh let Moses scatter it toward the sky. **⁹**It will turn into fine dust over the whole land of Egypt and cause festering boils* on human being and beast alike through- out the land of Egypt.

¹⁰So they took the soot from a kiln and appeared before Pharaoh. When Moses scattered it toward the sky, it caused festering boils on human being and beast alike. **¹¹**Because of the boils the magicians could not stand in Moses' presence, for there were boils on the magicians as well as on the rest of the Egyptians. **¹²**But the LORD hard- ened Pharaoh's heart, and he would not listen to them, just as the LORD had said to Moses.

Seventh Plague: the Hail. ¹³ Then the LORD spoke to Moses: Early tomor- row morning present yourself to Pha- raoh and say to him: Thus says the LORD, the God of the Hebrews: Let my people go to serve me, **¹⁴**for this time I will unleash all my blows upon you and your servants and your people, so that you may know that there is none like me anywhere on earth. **¹⁵**For by now I should have stretched out my hand and struck you and your people with such pestilence that you would have vanished from the earth. **¹⁶**But this is why I have let you survive: to show you† my power and to make my name resound throughout the earth!ᵇ **¹⁷**Will you continue to exalt yourself over my people and not let them go? **¹⁸**At this time tomorrow, therefore, I am going to rain down such fierce hail as there has never been in Egypt from the day it was founded up to the pres- ent. **¹⁹**Therefore, order your livestock and whatever else you have in the open fields to be brought to a place of safety. Whatever human being or ani- mal is found in the fields and is not brought to shelter will die when the hail comes down upon them. **²⁰**Those of Pharaoh's servants who feared the word of the LORD hurried their servants and their livestock off to shelter. **²¹**But those who did not pay attention to the word of the LORD left their servants and their livestock in the fields.

²²The LORD then said to Moses: Stretch out your hand toward the sky, that hail may fall upon the entire land of Egypt, on human being and beast alike and all the vegetation of the

---

* [9:9] **Boils**: the exact nature of the disease is not clear. Semitic cognates, for example, suggest the Hebrew root means "to be hot" and thus point to some sort of inflam- mation. The fact that soot taken from the kiln is the agent of the disease would point in the same direction. See further Lv 13:18–23; Dt 28:35; 2 Kgs 20:7.

a. [9:6] Ps 78:48.

† [9:16] **To show you**: some ancient versions such as the Septuagint read, "to show through you." Cf. Rom 9:17.

b. [9:16] Rom 9:17.

fields in the land of Egypt. **²³**So Moses stretched out his staff toward the sky, and the Lᴏʀᴅ sent forth peals of thunder and hail.ᶜ Lightning flashed toward the earth, and the Lᴏʀᴅ rained down hail upon the land of Egypt. **²⁴**There was hail and lightning flashing here and there through the hail, and the hail was so fierce that nothing like it had been seen in Egypt since it became a nation. **²⁵**Throughout the land of Egypt the hail struck down everything in the fields, human being and beast alike; it struck down all the vegetation of the fields and splintered every tree in the fields. **²⁶**Only in the land of Goshen, where the Israelites were, was there no hail.

²⁷Then Pharaoh sent for Moses and Aaron and said to them, "I have sinned this time! The Lᴏʀᴅ is the just one, and I and my people are the ones at fault. **²⁸**Pray to the Lᴏʀᴅ! Enough of the thunder* and hail! I will let you go; you need stay no longer." **²⁹**Moses replied to him, "As soon as I leave the city I will extend my hands to the Lᴏʀᴅ; the thunder will cease, and there will be no more hail so that you may know that the earth belongs to the Lᴏʀᴅ. **³⁰**But as for you and your servants, I know that you do not yet fear the Lᴏʀᴅ God."

³¹Now the flax and the barley were ruined, because the barley was in ear and the flax in bud. **³²**But the wheat and the spelt were not ruined, for they grow later.

³³When Moses had left Pharaoh and gone out of the city, he extended his hands to the Lᴏʀᴅ. The thunder and the hail ceased, and the rain no longer poured down upon the earth. **³⁴**But Pharaoh, seeing that the rain and the hail and the thunder had ceased, sinned again and became obstinate, both he and his servants. **³⁵**In the hardness of his heart, Pharaoh would not let the Israelites go, just as the Lᴏʀᴅ had said through Moses.

CHAPTER 10

Eighth Plague: the Locusts. **¹**Then the Lᴏʀᴅ said to Moses: Go to Pharaoh, for I have made him and his servants obstinate in order that I may perform these signs of mine among them **²**and that you may recount to your son and grandson how I made a fool of the Egyptians and what signs I did among them, so that you may know that I am the Lᴏʀᴅ.ᵃ

³So Moses and Aaron went to Pharaoh and told him, "Thus says the Lᴏʀᴅ, the God of the Hebrews: How long will you refuse to submit to me? Let my people go to serve me. **⁴**For if you refuse to let my people go, tomorrow I will bring locusts into your territory. **⁵**They will cover the surface of the earth, so that the earth itself will not be visible. They will eat up the remnant you saved undamaged from the hail, as well as all the trees that are growing in your fields. **⁶**They will fill your houses and the houses of your servants and of all the Egyptians—something your parents and your grandparents have not seen from the day they appeared on this soil until today." With that he turned and left Pharaoh.

⁷But Pharaoh's servants said to him, "How long will he be a snare for us? Let the people go to serve the Lᴏʀᴅ, their God. Do you not yet realize that Egypt is being destroyed?" **⁸**So Moses and Aaron were brought back to Pharaoh, who said to them, "Go, serve the Lᴏʀᴅ, your God. But who exactly will go?" **⁹**Moses answered, "With our young and old we must go; with our sons and daughters, with our flocks and herds we must go. It is a pilgrimage feast of the Lᴏʀᴅ for us." **¹⁰**"The Lᴏʀᴅ help you,"† Pharaoh replied, "if I let your little ones go with you! Clearly, you have some evil in mind. **¹¹**By no means! Just you men go and serve the

---

* [9:28] **Thunder:** lit., "divine voices," "voices of God," or the like.

c. [9:23–24] Ps 78:47; 105:32–33.

† [10:10] **The Lᴏʀᴅ help you** . . . : lit., "May the Lord be with you in the same way as I let you . . ."; a sarcastic blessing intended as a curse.

a. [10:2] Dt 6:20–25.

Lord.* After all, that is what you have been asking for." With that they were driven from Pharaoh's presence.

¹²ᵇThe Lord then said to Moses: Stretch out your hand over the land of Egypt for the locusts, that they may come upon it and eat up all the land's vegetation, whatever the hail has left. ¹³So Moses stretched out his staff over the land of Egypt, and the Lord drove an east wind† over the land all that day and all night. When it was morning, the east wind brought the locusts. ¹⁴The locusts came up over the whole land of Egypt and settled down over all its territory. Never before had there been such a fierce swarm of locusts, nor will there ever be again. ¹⁵They covered the surface of the whole land, so that it became black. They ate up all the vegetation in the land and all the fruit of the trees the hail had spared. Nothing green was left on any tree or plant in the fields throughout the land of Egypt.

¹⁶Pharaoh hurriedly summoned Moses and Aaron and said, "I have sinned against the Lord, your God, and against you. ¹⁷But now, do forgive me my sin only this once, and pray to the Lord, your God, only to take this death from me." ¹⁸When Moses left Pharaoh, he prayed to the Lord, ¹⁹and the Lord caused the wind to shift to a very strong west wind, which took up the locusts and hurled them into the Red Sea.‡ Not a single locust remained within the whole territory of Egypt. ²⁰Yet the Lord hardened Pharaoh's heart, and he would not let the Israelites go.

Ninth Plague: the Darkness. ²¹ᶜThen the Lord said to Moses: Stretch out your hand toward the sky, that over the land of Egypt there may be such darkness§ that one can feel it. ²²So Moses stretched out his hand toward the sky, and there was dense darkness throughout the land of Egypt for three days. ²³People could not see one another, nor could they get up from where they were, for three days. But all the Israelites had light where they lived.

²⁴Pharaoh then summoned Moses and Aaron and said, "Go, serve the Lord. Only your flocks and herds will be detained. Even your little ones may go with you." ²⁵But Moses replied, "You also must give us sacrifices and burnt offerings to make to the Lord, our God. ²⁶Our livestock also must go with us. Not an animal must be left behind, for some of them we will select for service¶ to the Lord, our God; but we will not know with which ones we are to serve the Lord until we arrive there." ²⁷But the Lord hardened Pharaoh's heart, and he was unwilling to let them go. ²⁸Pharaoh said to Moses, "Leave me, and see to it that you do not see my face again! For the day you do see my face you will die!" ²⁹Moses replied, "You are right! I will never see your face again."

CHAPTER 11

Tenth Plague: the Death of the Firstborn. ¹Then the Lord spoke to Moses: One more plague I will bring upon Pharaoh and upon Egypt. After that he will let you depart. In fact, when he finally lets you go, he will drive you away. ²ᵃInstruct the people that every man is to ask his neighbor,

---

§ [10:21] **Darkness**: commentators note that at times a storm from the south, called the *khamsin*, blackens the sky of Egypt with sand from the Sahara; the dust in the air is then so thick that the darkness can, in a sense, "be felt." But such observations should not obscure the fact that for the biblical author what transpires in each of the plagues is clearly something extraordinary, an event which witnesses to the unrivaled power of Israel's God.

¶ [10:26] **Service**: as is obvious from v. 25, the service in question here is the offering of sacrifice. The continued use of the verb *'bd* "to serve" and related nouns for both the people's bondage in Egypt and their subsequent service to the Lord dramatizes the point of the conflict between Pharaoh and the God of Israel, who demands from the Israelites an attachment which is exclusive. See Lv 25:55.

---

* [10:11] Pharaoh realized that if the men alone went they would have to return to their families. He suspected that the Hebrews had no intention of returning.

† [10:13] **East wind**: coming across the desert from Arabia, the strong east wind brings Egypt the burning sirocco and, at times, locusts. Cf. 14:21.

‡ [10:19] **The Red Sea**: the traditional translation, cf. Septuagint and other Versions; but the Hebrew literally means "sea of reeds" or "reedy sea," which could probably be applied to a number of bodies of shallow water, most likely somewhat to the north of the present deep Red Sea.

b. [10:12–15] Ps 78:46; 105:34–35.
c. [10:21–22] Ps 105:28.

a. [11:2–3] Ex 3:21–22; 12:35–36.

EX

and every woman her neighbor, for silver and gold articles and for clothing. ³The LORD indeed made the Egyptians well-disposed toward the people; Moses himself was very highly regarded by Pharaoh's servants and the people in the land of Egypt.

⁴Moses then said, "Thus says the LORD: About midnight I will go forth through Egypt.ᵇ ⁵ᶜEvery firstborn in the land of Egypt will die, from the firstborn of Pharaoh who sits on his throne to the firstborn of the slave-girl who is at the handmill,* as well as all the firstborn of the animals. ⁶Then there will be loud wailing throughout the land of Egypt, such as has never been, nor will ever be again. ⁷But among all the Israelites, among human beings and animals alike, not even a dog will growl, so that you may know that the LORD distinguishes between Egypt and Israel. ⁸All these servants of yours will then come down to me and bow down before me, saying: Leave, you and all your followers!ᵈ Then I will depart." With that he left Pharaoh's presence in hot anger.

⁹The LORD said to Moses: Pharaoh will not listen to you so that my wonders may be multiplied in the land of Egypt. ¹⁰Thus, although Moses and Aaron performed all these wonders in Pharaoh's presence, the LORD hardened Pharaoh's heart, and he would not let the Israelites go from his land.

CHAPTER 12

The Passover Ritual Prescribed.†
¹The LORD said to Moses and Aaron in the land of Egypt: ²‡This month will stand at the head of your calendar; you will reckon it the first month of the year.ᵃ ³Tell the whole community of Israel: On the tenth of this month every family must procure for itself a lamb, one apiece for each household. ⁴If a household is too small for a lamb, it along with its nearest neighbor will procure one, and apportion the lamb's cost§ in proportion to the number of persons, according to what each household consumes. ⁵Your lamb must be a year-old male and without blemish. You may take it from either the sheep or the goats. ⁶You will keep it until the fourteenth day of this month, and then, with the whole community of Israel assembled, it will be slaughtered during the evening twilight. ⁷They will take some of its blood and apply it to the two doorposts and the lintel of the houses in which they eat it. ⁸They will consume its meat that same night, eating it roasted with unleavened bread and bitter herbs. ⁹Do not eat any of it raw or even boiled in water, but roasted, with its head and shanks and inner organs. ¹⁰You must not keep any of it beyond the morning; whatever is left over in the morning must be burned up.

¹¹This is how you are to eat it: with your loins girt, sandals on your feet and your staff in hand, you will eat it in a hurry. It is the LORD's Passover. ¹²For on this same night I will go through Egypt, striking down every firstborn in the land, human being and beast alike, and executing judgment on all the gods of Egypt—I, the LORD!ᵇ ¹³But for you the blood will mark the houses where you are. Seeing the blood, I will pass over you; thereby, when I strike the land of Egypt, no destructive blow will come upon you.ᶜ

¹⁴This day will be a day of remembrance for you, which your future

---

* [11:5] **Handmill**: two pieces of stone were used to grind grain. A smaller upper stone was moved back and forth over a larger stationary stone. This menial work was done by slaves and captives.
† [12:1–20] This section, which interrupts the narrative of the exodus, contains later legislation concerning the celebration of Passover.
‡ [12:2] As if to affirm victory over Pharaoh and sovereignty over the Israelites, the Lord proclaims a new calendar for Israel. **This month**: Abib, the month of "ripe grain." Cf. 13:4; 23:15; 34:18; Dt 16:1. It occurred near the vernal equinox, March–April. Later it was known by the Babylonian name of Nisan. Cf. Neh 2:1; Est 3:7.

b. [11:4] Ex 12:12.
c. [11:5–6] Ex 12:29–30.
d. [11:8] Ex 12:31–33.

§ [12:4] **The lamb's cost**: some render the Hebrew, "reckon for the lamb the number of persons required to eat it." Cf. v. 10.

a. [12:2–20] Lv 23:5–8; Nm 9:2–5; 28:16–25; Dt 16:1–8.
b. [12:12] Nm 33:4.
c. [12:13] Heb 11:28.

generations will celebrate with pilgrimage to the LORD; you will celebrate it as a statute forever. **15**For seven days you must eat unleavened bread. From the very first day you will have your houses clear of all leaven. For whoever eats leavened bread from the first day to the seventh will be cut off* from Israel. **16**On the first day you will hold a sacred assembly, and likewise on the seventh. On these days no sort of work shall be done, except to prepare the food that everyone needs. **17**Keep, then, the custom of the unleavened bread,*d* since it was on this very day that I brought your armies out of the land of Egypt. You must observe this day throughout your generations as a statute forever. **18**From the evening of the fourteenth day of the first month until the evening of the twenty-first day of this month you will eat unleavened bread. **19**For seven days no leaven may be found in your houses; for anyone, a resident alien or a native, who eats leavened food will be cut off from the community of Israel. **20**You shall eat nothing leavened; wherever you dwell you may eat only unleavened bread.

Promulgation of the Passover. **21**Moses summoned all the elders of Israel and said to them, "Go and procure lambs for your families, and slaughter the Passover victims. **22e**Then take a bunch of hyssop,† and dipping it in the blood that is in the basin, apply some of this blood to the lintel and the two doorposts. And none of you shall go outdoors until morning. **23**For when the LORD goes by to strike down the Egyptians, seeing the blood on the lintel and the two doorposts, the LORD will pass over that door and not let the destroyer come into your houses to strike you down.

24"You will keep this practice forever as a statute for yourselves and your descendants. **25**Thus, when you have entered the land which the LORD will give you as he promised, you must observe this rite. **26f**When your children ask you, 'What does this rite of yours mean?' **27**you will reply, 'It is the Passover sacrifice for the LORD, who passed over the houses of the Israelites in Egypt; when he struck down the Egyptians, he delivered our houses.'"

Then the people knelt and bowed down, **28**and the Israelites went and did exactly as the LORD had commanded Moses and Aaron.

Death of the Firstborn. **29g**And so at midnight the LORD struck down every firstborn in the land of Egypt, from the firstborn of Pharaoh sitting on his throne to the firstborn of the prisoner in the dungeon, as well as all the firstborn of the animals. **30**Pharaoh arose in the night, he and all his servants and all the Egyptians; and there was loud wailing throughout Egypt, for there was not a house without its dead.

Permission to Depart. **31**During the night Pharaoh summoned Moses and Aaron and said, "Leave my people at once, you and the Israelites! Go and serve the LORD as you said. **32**Take your flocks, too, and your herds, as you said, and go; and bless me, too!"‡

33The Egyptians, in a hurry to send them away from the land, urged the people on, for they said, "All of us will die!" **34**The people, therefore, took their dough before it was leavened, in their kneading bowls wrapped in their cloaks on their shoulders. **35h**And the Israelites did as Moses had

---

* [12:15] **Cut off:** a common Priestly term, not easily reduced to a simple English equivalent, since its usage appears to involve a number of associated punishments, some or all of which may come into play in any instance of the term's use. These included the excommunication of the offender from the Israelite community, the premature death of the offender, the eventual eradication of the offender's posterity, and finally the loss by the offender of all ancestral holdings.

† [12:22] **Hyssop:** a plant with many small woody branches that was convenient for a sprinkling rite.

d. [12:17] Ex 13:3.
e. [12:22–23] Ex 12:7, 13.

‡ [12:32] **Bless me, too:** in a final and humiliating admission of defeat, once again Pharaoh asks Moses to intercede for him (cf. 8:24). However, Pharaoh may be speaking sarcastically.

f. [12:26–27] Ex 13:8, 14–15; Dt 6:20–25.
g. [12:29–30] Ex 11:4–6; Nm 33:4; Ps 78:51; 105:36; 136:10; Wis 18:10–16.
h. [12:35–36] Ex 3:21–22; 11:2–3; Ps 105:37–38.

commanded: they asked the Egyptians for articles of silver and gold and for clothing. ³⁶Indeed the Lord had made the Egyptians so well-disposed toward the people that they let them have whatever they asked for. And so they despoiled the Egyptians.

Departure from Egypt. ³⁷The Israelites set out from Rameses[i] for Succoth, about six hundred thousand men on foot, not counting the children. ³⁸A crowd of mixed ancestry* also went up with them, with livestock in great abundance, both flocks and herds. ³⁹The dough they had brought out of Egypt they baked into unleavened loaves. It was not leavened, because they had been driven out of Egypt and could not wait. They did not even prepare food for the journey.

⁴⁰The time the Israelites had stayed in Egypt[†] was four hundred and thirty years.[j] ⁴¹At the end of four hundred and thirty years, on this very date, all the armies of the Lord left the land of Egypt. ⁴²This was a night of vigil for the Lord, when he brought them out of the land of Egypt; so on this night all Israelites must keep a vigil for the Lord throughout their generations.

Law of the Passover. ⁴³The Lord said to Moses and Aaron: This is the Passover statute. No foreigner may eat of it. ⁴⁴However, every slave bought for money you will circumcise; then he may eat of it. ⁴⁵But no tenant or hired worker may eat of it. ⁴⁶It must be eaten in one house; you may not take any of its meat outside the house.[k] You shall not break any of its bones.[‡] ⁴⁷The whole community of Israel must celebrate this feast. ⁴⁸If any alien[l] residing among you would celebrate the Passover for the Lord, all his males must be circumcised, and then he may join in its celebration just like the natives. But no one who is uncircumcised may eat of it. ⁴⁹There will be one law[§] for the native and for the alien residing among you.

⁵⁰All the Israelites did exactly as the Lord had commanded Moses and Aaron. ⁵¹On that same day the Lord brought the Israelites out of the land of Egypt company by company.

CHAPTER 13

Consecration of Firstborn. ¹The Lord spoke to Moses and said: ²Consecrate to me every firstborn; whatever opens the womb among the Israelites,[a] whether of human being or beast, belongs to me.

³[b]Moses said to the people, "Remember this day on which you came out of Egypt, out of a house of slavery. For it was with a strong hand that the Lord brought you out from there. Nothing made with leaven may be eaten. ⁴This day on which you are going out is in the month of Abib.[¶] ⁵Therefore, when the Lord, your God, has brought you into the land of the Canaanites, the Hittites, the Amorites, the Perrizites, the Girgashites, the Hivites, and the Jebusites, which he swore to your ancestors to give you, a land flowing with milk and honey, you will perform the following service** in this month. ⁶For seven days you will eat unleavened bread, and the seventh day will also be a festival to the Lord.

* [12:38] **Mixed ancestry**: not simply descendants of Jacob; cf. Nm 11:4; Lv 24:10–11.
† [12:40] **In Egypt**: according to the Septuagint and the Samaritan Pentateuch "in Canaan and Egypt," thus reckoning from the time of Abraham. Cf. Gal 3:17.
‡ [12:46] **You shall not break any of its bones**: the application of these words to Jesus on the cross (Jn 19:36) sees the Paschal lamb as a prophetic type of Christ, sacrificed to free men and women from the bondage of sin. Cf. also 1 Cor 5:7; 1 Pt 1:19.

i. [12:37] Nm 33:3–5.
j. [12:40] Gn 15:13; Acts 7:6; Gal 3:17.
k. [12:46] Nm 9:12; Jn 19:36.

§ [12:49] **One law**: the first appearance of the word torah, traditionally translated as "law," though it can have the broader meaning of "teaching" or "instruction." Elsewhere, too, it is said that the "alien" is to be accorded the same treatment as the Israelite (e.g., Lv 19:34).
¶ [13:4] **Abib**: lit., "ear (of grain)," the old Canaanite name for this month; Israel later called it "Nisan." It was the first month in their liturgical calendar (cf. Ex 12:2).
** [13:5] **The following service**: the celebration of the feast of Unleavened Bread now constitutes the Israelites' service, in contrast to the "service" they performed for Pharaoh as his slaves.

l. [12:48] Nm 9:14.

a. [13:2] Ex 13:12–15.
b. [13:3–10] Ex 12:2–20.

EX

[7] Unleavened bread may be eaten during the seven days, but nothing leavened and no leaven may be found in your possession in all your territory. [8] And on that day you will explain to your son, 'This is because of what the LORD did for me when I came out of Egypt.' [9] It will be like a sign* on your hand and a reminder on your forehead,[c] so that the teaching of the LORD will be on your lips: with a strong hand the LORD brought you out of Egypt. [10] You will keep this statute at its appointed time from year to year.

[11] "When the LORD, your God, has brought you into the land of the Canaanites, just as he swore to you and your ancestors, and gives it to you, [12d] you will dedicate to the LORD every newborn that opens the womb; and every firstborn male of your animals will belong to the LORD. [13] Every firstborn of a donkey you will ransom with a sheep. If you do not ransom it, you will break its neck. Every human firstborn of your sons you must ransom. [14] And when your son asks you later on, 'What does this mean?' you will tell him, 'With a strong hand the LORD brought us out of Egypt, out of a house of slavery. [15] When Pharaoh stubbornly refused to let us go, the LORD killed every firstborn in the land of Egypt, the firstborn of human being and beast alike. That is why I sacrifice to the LORD every male that opens the womb, and why I ransom every firstborn of my sons.' [16] It will be like a sign on your hand and a band on your forehead that with a strong hand the LORD brought us out of Egypt."[e]

IV. THE DELIVERANCE OF THE ISRAELITES FROM PHARAOH AND VICTORY AT THE SEA

Toward the Red Sea. [17] Now, when Pharaoh let the people go, God did not lead them by way of the Philistines' land,[†] though this was the nearest; for God said: If the people see that they have to fight, they might change their minds and return to Egypt. [18] Instead, God rerouted them toward the Red Sea by way of the wilderness road, and the Israelites went up out of the land of Egypt arrayed for battle. [19] Moses also took Joseph's bones[f] with him, for Joseph had made the Israelites take a solemn oath, saying, "God will surely take care of you, and you must bring my bones up with you from here."

[20] Setting out from Succoth, they camped at Etham[g] near the edge of the wilderness.

[21h] The LORD preceded them, in the daytime by means of a column of cloud to show them the way, and at night by means of a column of fire[‡] to give them light. Thus they could travel both day and night. [22] Neither the column of cloud by day nor the column of fire by night ever left its place in front of the people.

CHAPTER 14

[1] Then the LORD spoke to Moses: [2] Speak to the Israelites: Let them turn about and camp before Pi-hahiroth, between Migdol and the sea.[a] Camp in front of Baal-zephon,[§] just opposite, by the

---

* [13:9] **Sign**: while here observance of the feast of Unleavened Bread is likened only metaphorically to a physical sign of one's piety that can be worn as a kind of badge in commemoration of the exodus, from ancient times Jews have seen in this verse also the basis for the wearing of phylacteries. These are small receptacles for copies of biblical verses which Jewish men bind to the arms and forehead as a kind of mnemonic device for the observance of the Law.

c. [13:9] Ex 13:16; Dt 6:8; 11:18.
d. [13:12–15] Ex 13:2; 22:28–29; 34:19–20; Nm 3:12–13; 8:16–17; 18:15; Dt 15:19.
e. [13:16] Ex 13:9.

† [13:17] **By way of the Philistines' land**: the most direct route from Egypt to Palestine, along the shore of the Mediterranean.
‡ [13:21] **A column of cloud . . . a column of fire**: probably one and the same extraordinary phenomenon, a central nucleus of fire surrounded by smoke; only at night was its luminous nature visible; cf. 40:38.
§ [14:2] **Pi-hahiroth . . . Migdol . . . Baal-zephon**: these places have not been definitively identified. Even the relative position of Pi-hahiroth and Baal-zephon is not clear; perhaps the former was on the west shore of the sea, where the Israelites were, and the latter on the opposite shore.

f. [13:19] Gn 50:25; Jos 24:32.
g. [13:20] Nm 33:6.
h. [13:21–22] Ex 40:38; Nm 9:15–22; Dt 1:33; Neh 9:19; Ps 78:14; 105:39; Wis 10:17.
a. [14:2] Nm 33:7–8.

sea. ³Pharaoh will then say, "The Israelites are wandering about aimlessly in the land. The wilderness has closed in on them." ⁴I will so harden Pharaoh's heart that he will pursue them. Thus I will receive glory through Pharaoh and all his army, and the Egyptians will know that I am the LORD.

This the Israelites did. ⁵ᵇWhen it was reported to the king of Egypt that the people had fled, Pharaoh and his servants had a change of heart about the people. "What in the world have we done!" they said. "We have released Israel from our service!" ⁶So Pharaoh harnessed his chariots and took his army with him. ⁷He took six hundred select chariots and all the chariots of Egypt, with officers* on all of them. ⁸The LORD hardened the heart of Pharaoh, king of Egypt, so that he pursued the Israelites while they were going out in triumph. ⁹The Egyptians pursued them—all Pharaoh's horses, his chariots, his horsemen,† and his army— and caught up with them as they lay encamped by the sea, at Pi-hahiroth, in front of Baal-zephon.

Crossing the Red Sea. ¹⁰Now Pharaoh was near when the Israelites looked up and saw that the Egyptians had set out after them. Greatly frightened, the Israelites cried out to the LORD. ¹¹To Moses they said, "Were there no burial places in Egypt that you brought us to die in the wilderness? What have you done to us, bringing us out of Egypt? ¹²Did we not tell you this in Egypt, when we said, 'Leave us alone that we may serve the Egyptians'? Far better for us to serve the Egyptians than to die in the wilderness." ¹³But Moses answered the people, "Do not fear! Stand your ground and see the victory the LORD will win for you today. For these Egyptians whom you see today you will never see again. ¹⁴The LORD will fight for you; you have only to keep still."

¹⁵Then the LORD said to Moses: Why are you crying out to me? Tell the Israelites to set out. ¹⁶And you, lift up your staff and stretch out your hand over the sea, and split it in two, that the Israelites may pass through the sea on dry land. ¹⁷But I will harden the hearts of the Egyptians so that they will go in after them, and I will receive glory through Pharaoh and all his army, his chariots and his horsemen. ¹⁸The Egyptians will know that I am the LORD, when I receive glory through Pharaoh, his chariots, and his horsemen.

¹⁹The angel of God,‡ who had been leading Israel's army, now moved and went around behind them. And the column of cloud, moving from in front of them, took up its place behind them, ²⁰so that it came between the Egyptian army and that of Israel. And when it became dark, the cloud illumined the night; and so the rival camps did not come any closer together all night long.§ ²¹ᶜThen Moses stretched out his hand over the sea; and the LORD drove back the sea with a strong east wind all night long and turned the sea into dry ground. The waters were split, ²²so that the Israelites entered into the midst of the sea on dry land, with the water as a wall to their right and to their left.

Rout of the Egyptians. ²³The Egyptians followed in pursuit after them— all Pharaoh's horses and chariots and horsemen—into the midst of the sea. ²⁴But during the watch just before dawn, the LORD looked down from a column of fiery cloud upon the Egyptian army

---

* [14:7] **Officers:** cf. 1 Kgs 9:22; Ez 23:15. The Hebrew word *shalish*, rendered in 1 Kgs 9:22 as "adjutant," has yet to have its meaning convincingly established. Given the very possible etymological connection with the number "three," others suggest the translation "three-man crew" or, less likely, the "third man in the chariot" although Egyptian chariots carried two-man crews. The author of the text may have been describing the chariots of his experience without direct historical knowledge of Egyptian ways.

† [14:9] **Horsemen:** the usage here may be anachronistic, since horsemen, or cavalry, play a part in warfare only at the end of the second millennium B.C.

b. [14:5–8] Wis 19:3; 1 Mc 4:9.

‡ [14:19] **Angel of God:** Hebrew *mal'ak ha'elohim* (Septuagint *ho angelos tou theou*) here refers not to an independent spiritual being but to God's power at work in the world; corresponding to the column of cloud/fire, the expression more clearly preserves a sense of distance between God and God's creatures. The two halves of the verse are parallel and may come from different narrative sources.

§ [14:20] The reading of the Hebrew text here is uncertain. The image is of a darkly glowing storm cloud, ominously bright, keeping the two camps apart.

c. [14:21–22] Ex 15:19; Ps 66:6; 78:13; 136:13–14; Wis 10:18; 19:7–8; Is 63:12–13; Heb 11:29.

EX

and threw it into a panic; ²⁵and he so clogged their chariot wheels that they could drive only with difficulty. With that the Egyptians said, "Let us flee from Israel, because the LORD is fighting for them against Egypt."

²⁶Then the LORD spoke to Moses: Stretch out your hand over the sea, that the water may flow back upon the Egyptians, upon their chariots and their horsemen. ²⁷So Moses stretched out his hand over the sea, and at daybreak the sea returned to its normal flow. The Egyptians were fleeing head on toward it when the LORD cast the Egyptians into the midst of the sea. ^{28d}As the water flowed back, it covered the chariots and the horsemen. Of all Pharaoh's army which had followed the Israelites into the sea, not even one escaped. ²⁹But the Israelites had walked on dry land through the midst of the sea, with the water as a wall to their right and to their left. ³⁰Thus the LORD saved Israel on that day from the power of Egypt. When Israel saw the Egyptians lying dead on the seashore ³¹and saw the great power that the LORD had shown against Egypt, the people feared the LORD. They believed in the LORD^e and in Moses his servant.

CHAPTER 15

¹Then Moses and the Israelites sang^a this song to the LORD:[*]

I will sing to the LORD, for he is
  gloriously triumphant;
  horse and chariot he has cast into
    the sea.
²My strength and my refuge is the
  LORD,
  and he has become my savior.^b
This is my God, I praise him;
  the God of my father, I extol him.
³The LORD is a warrior,
  LORD is his name!
⁴Pharaoh's chariots and army he
  hurled into the sea;
  the elite of his officers were
    drowned in the Red Sea.[†]
⁵The flood waters covered them,
  they sank into the depths like a
    stone.^c
⁶Your right hand, O LORD, magnifi-
    cent in power,
  your right hand, O LORD, shat-
    tered the enemy.
⁷In your great majesty you over-
    threw your adversaries;
  you loosed your wrath to con-
    sume them like stubble.
⁸At the blast of your nostrils the
    waters piled up,
  the flowing waters stood like a
    mound,
  the flood waters foamed in the
    midst of the sea.
⁹The enemy boasted, "I will pursue
    and overtake them;
  I will divide the spoils and have
    my fill of them;
  I will draw my sword; my hand
    will despoil them!"
¹⁰When you blew with your breath,
    the sea covered them;
  like lead they sank in the mighty
    waters.
¹¹Who is like you among the gods,
    O LORD?
  Who is like you, magnificent

---

* [15:1–21] This poem, regarded by many scholars as one of the oldest compositions in the Bible, was once an independent work. It has been inserted at this important juncture in the large narrative of Exodus to celebrate God's saving power, having miraculously delivered the people from their enemies, and ultimately leading them to the promised land.

Although the victory it describes over the Egyptians at the sea bears a superficial resemblance in v. 8 to the preceding depiction of the water standing like a wall (14:22), the poem (as opposed to the following prose verse, v. 19) suggests a different version of the victory at sea than that found in chap. 14. There is no splitting of the sea in an act reminiscent of the Lord's combat at creation with the sea monsters Rahab and Leviathan (Jb 9:13; 26:12; Ps 74:13–14; 89:11; Is 51:9–10); nor is there mention of an east wind driving the waters back so that the Israelites can cross. In this version it is by means of a storm at sea, caused by a ferocious blast from his nostrils, that the Lord achieves a decisive victory against Pharaoh and his army (vv. 1–12). The second half of the poem (vv. 13–18) describes God's guidance into the promised land.

d. [14:28–29] Dt 11:4; Ps 106:11.
e. [14:31] Ex 4:31; Ps 106:12; Wis 10:20.

a. [15:1] Ex 15:21.

† [15:4] **Red Sea**: the traditional translation of the Hebrew *yam suph*, which actually means "Sea of Reeds" or "reedy sea." The location is uncertain, though in view of the route taken by the Israelites from Egypt to Sinai, it could not have been the Red Sea, which is too far south. It was probably a smaller body of water south of the Gulf of Suez. The term occurs also in Exodus at 10:19; 13:18; and 23:31.

b. [15:2] Ps 118:14; Is 12:2.
c. [15:5] Neh 9:11.

among the holy ones?
Awe-inspiring in deeds of renown,
  worker of wonders,
  ¹²when you stretched out your
    right hand, the earth swallowed
    them!
¹³In your love* you led the people
    you redeemed;
  in your strength you guided them
    to your holy dwelling.
¹⁴The peoples heard and quaked;
  anguish gripped the dwellers in
    Philistia.
¹⁵Then were the chieftains of Edom
    dismayed,
  the nobles of Moab seized by
    trembling;
All the inhabitants of Canaan
    melted away;
  ^{16d}terror and dread fell upon
    them.
By the might of your arm they
    became silent like stone,
  while your people, Lord, passed
    over,
  while the people whom you cre-
    ated passed over.†
¹⁷You brought them in, you planted
    them
  on the mountain that is your
    own—
The place you made the base of
    your throne, Lord,
  the sanctuary, Lord, your hands
    established.
¹⁸May the Lord reign forever and
    ever!

¹⁹When Pharaoh's horses and chari-
ots and horsemen entered the sea, the
Lord made the waters of the sea flow
back upon them, though the Israelites
walked on dry land through the midst
of the sea.^{e 20}Then the prophet Miriam,
Aaron's sister, took a tambourine in
her hand, while all the women went
out after her with tambourines, dancing; ²¹and she responded‡ to them:

Sing to the Lord, for he is gloriously
    triumphant;
  horse and chariot he has cast into
    the sea.^f

V. THE JOURNEY IN THE WILDERNESS TO SINAI

At Marah and Elim. ^{22g}Then Moses
led Israel forward from the Red Sea,§
and they marched out to the wilderness of Shur. After traveling for three
days through the wilderness without
finding water, ²³they arrived at Marah,
where they could not drink its water,
because it was too bitter. Hence this
place was called Marah. ²⁴As the people grumbled against Moses, saying,
"What are we to drink?" ²⁵he cried out
to the Lord, who pointed out to him a
piece of wood. When he threw it into
the water, the water became fresh.^h

It was here that God, in making
statutes and ordinances for them, put
them to the test. ²⁶He said: If you listen closely to the voice of the Lord,
your God, and do what is right in his
eyes: if you heed his commandments
and keep all his statutes, I will not
afflict you with any of the diseases
with which I afflicted the Egyptians;ⁱ
for I, the Lord, am your healer.

²⁷Then they came to Elim, where
there were twelve springs of water and
seventy palm trees, and they camped
there near the water.^j

---

* [15:13] **Love:** the very important Hebrew term *hesed* carries a variety of nuances depending on context: love, kindness, faithfulness. It is often rendered "steadfast love."
  It implies a relationship that generates an obligation and
  therefore is at home in a covenant context. Cf. 20:6.
† [15:16] **Passed over:** an allusion to the crossing of the Jordan River
  (cf. Jos 3–5), written as if the entry into the promised land had
  already occurred. This verse suggests that at one time there was
  a ritual enactment of the conquest at a shrine near the Jordan
  River which included also a celebration of the victory at the sea.
‡ [15:21] **She responded:** Miriam's refrain echoes the first
  verse of this song and was probably sung as an antiphon
  after each verse.
§ [15:22] **Red Sea:** see note on Ex 15:4.

d. [15:16–17] Ps 78:53–55.
e. [15:19] Ex 14:21–29.
f. [15:21] Ex 15:1.
g. [15:22–23] Nm 33:8.
h. [15:25] Sir 38:5.
i. [15:26] Dt 7:15.
j. [15:27] Nm 33:9.

EX

CHAPTER 16

The Wilderness of Sin. ¹Having set out from Elim, the whole Israelite community came into the wilderness of Sin, which is between Elim and Sinai, on the fifteenth day of the second month* after their departure from the land of Egypt. ²Here in the wilderness the whole Israelite community grumbled against Moses and Aaron. ³The Israelites said to them, "If only we had died at the LORD's hand in the land of Egypt, as we sat by our kettles of meat and ate our fill of bread! But you have led us into this wilderness to make this whole assembly die of famine!"

The Quail and the Manna. ⁴Then the LORD said to Moses:ᵃ I am going to rain down bread from heaven† for you. Each day the people are to go out and gather their daily portion; thus will I test them, to see whether they follow my instructions or not. ⁵On the sixth day, however, when they prepare what they bring in, let it be twice as much as they gather on the other days. ⁶So Moses and Aaron told all the Israelites,ᵇ "At evening you will know that it was the LORD who brought you out of the land of Egypt; ⁷and in the morning you will see the glory of the LORD, when he hears your grumbling against him. But who are we that you should grumble against us?" ⁸And Moses said, "When the LORD gives you meat to eat in the evening and in the morning your fill of bread, and hears the grumbling you

utter against him, who then are we? Your grumbling is not against us, but against the LORD."

⁹Then Moses said to Aaron, "Tell the whole Israelite community: Approach the LORD, for he has heard your grumbling." ¹⁰But while Aaron was speaking to the whole Israelite community, they turned in the direction of the wilderness, and there the glory of the LORD appeared in the cloud! ¹¹The LORD said to Moses: ¹²I have heard the grumbling of the Israelites. Tell them: In the evening twilight you will eat meat, and in the morning you will have your fill of bread, and then you will know that I, the LORD, am your God.

¹³In the evening, quailᶜ came up and covered the camp. In the morning there was a layer of dew all about the camp, ¹⁴and when the layer of dew evaporated, fine flakes were on the surface of the wilderness, fine flakes like hoarfrost on the ground. ¹⁵On seeing it, the Israelites asked one another, "What is this?"‡ for they did not know what it was. But Moses told them, "It is the bread which the LORD has given you to eat.ᵈ

Regulations Regarding the Manna. ¹⁶"Now, this is what the LORD has commanded. Gather as much of it as each needs to eat, an omer§ for each person for as many of you as there are, each of you providing for those in your own tent." ¹⁷The Israelites did so. Some gathered a large and some a small amount. ¹⁸¶But when they measured it out by the omer, the one who had gathered a large amount did not have too much, and the one who had gathered a small amount did not have too little. They gathered as much as each needed to eat. ¹⁹Moses said to

---

* [16:1] **On the fifteenth day of the second month**: just one full month after their departure from Egypt. Cf. 12:2, 51; Nm 33:3–4. The Septuagint takes the date to be the beginning of the Israelites' grumbling.

† [16:4] **Bread from heaven**: as a gift from God, the manna is said to come down from the sky. Cf. Ps 78:24–25; Wis 16:20. Perhaps it was similar to a natural substance that is still found in small quantities on the Sinai peninsula—probably the honey-like resin from the tamarisk tree—but here it is, at least in part, clearly an extraordinary sign of God's providence. With reference to Jn 6:32, 49–52, the Christian tradition has regarded the manna as a type of the Eucharist. **Test**: as the text stands, it seems to leave open the question whether the test concerns trusting in God to provide them with the daily gift of food or observing the sabbath instructions.

‡ [16:15] **What is this**: the Hebrew *man hu* is thus rendered by the ancient versions, which understood the phrase as a popular etymology of the Hebrew word *man*, "manna"; but some render *man hu*, "This is manna."

§ [16:16] **Omer**: a dry measure of approximately two quarts.

¶ [16:18] Paul cites this passage as an example of equitable sharing (2 Cor 8:15).

---

a. [16:4] Ps 78:24–25; 105:40; Jn 6:31–32; 1 Cor 10:3.
b. [16:6–7] Ex 16:12.
c. [16:13] Nm 11:31; Ps 78:27–28.
d. [16:15] Dt 8:3.

EX

them, "Let no one leave any of it over until morning." **20**But they did not listen to Moses, and some kept a part of it over until morning, and it became wormy and stank. Therefore Moses was angry with them.

21Morning after morning they gathered it, as much as each needed to eat; but when the sun grew hot, it melted away. **22**On the sixth day they gathered twice as much food, two omers for each person. When all the leaders of the community came and reported this to Moses, **23**he told them, "That is what the LORD has prescribed. Tomorrow is a day of rest, a holy sabbath of the LORD. Whatever you want to bake, bake; whatever you want to boil, boil; but whatever is left put away and keep until the morning." **24**When they put it away until the morning, as Moses commanded, it did not stink nor were there worms in it. **25**Moses then said, "Eat it today, for today is the sabbath of the LORD. Today you will not find any in the field. **26**Six days you will gather it, but on the seventh day, the sabbath, it will not be there." **27**Still, on the seventh day some of the people went out to gather it, but they did not find any. **28**Then the LORD said to Moses: How long will you refuse to keep my commandments and my instructions? **29**Take note! The LORD has given you the sabbath. That is why on the sixth day he gives you food for two days. Each of you stay where you are and let no one go out on the seventh day. **30**After that the people rested on the seventh day.

31The house of Israel named this food manna.*e* It was like coriander seed,* white, and it tasted like wafers made with honey.

32Moses said, "This is what the LORD has commanded. Keep a full omer of it for your future generations, so that they may see the food I gave

you to eat in the wilderness when I brought you out of the land of Egypt." **33**Moses then told Aaron, "Take a jar† and put a full omer of manna in it. Then place it before the LORD to keep it for your future generations." **34**As the LORD had commanded Moses, Aaron placed it in front of the covenant‡ to keep it.

35The Israelites ate the manna for forty years, until they came to settled land;*f* they ate the manna until they came to the borders of Canaan. **36**(An omer is one tenth of an ephah.)§

CHAPTER 17

Water from the Rock. 1 From the wilderness of Sin the whole Israelite community journeyed by stages, as the LORD directed, and encamped at Rephidim.*a*

But there was no water for the people to drink, **2***b*and so they quarreled with Moses and said, "Give us water to drink." Moses replied to them, "Why do you quarrel with me? Why do you put the LORD to a test?" **3**Here, then, in their thirst for water, the people grumbled against Moses, saying, "Why then did you bring us up out of Egypt? To have us die of thirst with our children and our livestock?" **4**So Moses cried out to the LORD, "What shall I do with this people? A little more and they will stone me!" **5**The LORD answered Moses: Go on ahead of the people, and take along with you some of the elders of Israel, holding in your hand, as you go, the staff with which you struck the Nile. **6**I will be standing there in front of you on the rock in Horeb. Strike the rock, and the water will flow from it for the people to drink.*c* Moses did this, in the sight

---

† [16:33] **Jar:** according to the Greek translation, which is followed in Heb 9:4, this was a golden vessel.

‡ [16:34] **The covenant:** i.e., the ark of the covenant, in which were placed the two tablets of the Ten Commandments. Cf. 25:16, 21–22.

§ [16:36] **Omer . . . ephah:** see note on Is 5:10.

f. [16:35] Jos 5:12.

a. [17:1] Nm 33:12–14.
b. [17:2–7] Nm 20:2–13.
c. [17:5–6] Dt 8:15; Ps 78:15–16; 105:41; Wis 11:4; Is 43:20; 48:21.

---

* [16:31] **Coriander seed:** small, round, aromatic seeds of bright brown color; the comparison, therefore, refers merely to the size and shape, not to the taste or color of the manna.

e. [16:31] Nm 11:7.

of the elders of Israel. **7**The place was named Massah and Meribah,* because the Israelites quarreled there and tested the LORD, saying, "Is the LORD in our midst or not?"**d**

Battle with Amalek. 8 Then Amalek† came and waged war against Israel in Rephidim.**e 9**So Moses said to Joshua, "Choose some men for us, and tomorrow go out and engage Amalek in battle. I will be standing on top of the hill with the staff of God in my hand." **10**Joshua did as Moses told him: he engaged Amalek in battle while Moses, Aaron, and Hur climbed to the top of the hill. **11**As long as Moses kept his hands raised up, Israel had the better of the fight, but when he let his hands rest, Amalek had the better of the fight. **12**Moses' hands, however, grew tired; so they took a rock and put it under him and he sat on it. Meanwhile Aaron and Hur supported his hands, one on one side and one on the other, so that his hands remained steady until sunset. **13**And Joshua defeated Amalek and his people with the sword.

14Then the LORD said to Moses: Write this down in a book as something to be remembered, and recite it to Joshua:**f** I will completely blot out the memory of Amalek from under the heavens. **15**Moses built an altar there, which he named Yahweh-nissi;‡ **16**for he said, "Take up the banner of the LORD!§ The LORD has a war against Amalek through the ages."

CHAPTER 18

Meeting with Jethro. 1 Now Moses' father-in-law Jethro, the priest of Midian, heard of all that God had done for Moses and for his people Israel: how the LORD had brought Israel out of Egypt. **2**So his father-in-law Jethro took along Zipporah, Moses' wife—now this was after Moses had sent her back—¶ **3**and her two sons. One of these was named Gershom;**a** for he said, "I am a resident alien in a foreign land." **4**The other was named Eliezer; for he said, "The God of my father is my help; he has rescued me from Pharaoh's sword." **5**Together with Moses' wife and sons, then, his father-in-law Jethro came to him in the wilderness where he was encamped at the mountain of God,** **6**and he sent word to Moses, "I, your father-in-law Jethro, am coming to you, along with your wife and her two sons."

7Moses went out to meet his father-in-law, bowed down, and then kissed him. Having greeted each other, they went into the tent. **8**Moses then told his father-in-law of all that the LORD had done to Pharaoh and the Egyptians for the sake of Israel, and of all the hardships that had beset them on their journey, and how the LORD had rescued them. **9**Jethro rejoiced over all the goodness that the LORD had shown Israel in rescuing them from the power of the Egyptians. **10**"Blessed be the LORD," he said, "who has rescued you from the power of the Egyptians and of Pharaoh. **11**Now I know that the LORD is greater than all the gods; for he rescued the people from the power of the Egyptians when they treated them arrogantly." **12**Then Jethro, the father-in-law of Moses, brought a burnt

---

* [17:7] **Massah . . . Meribah:** Hebrew words meaning, respectively, "the place of the test" and "the place of strife, of quarreling."

† [17:8] **Amalek:** the Amalekites appear in the Bible as early inhabitants of southern Palestine and the Sinai peninsula prior to the appearance of the Israelites in the region. Cf. Nm 24:20.

‡ [17:15] **Yahweh-nissi:** meaning, "the Lord is my banner."

§ [17:16] **Take up the banner of the LORD:** lit., "a hand on the LORD's banner," apparently a war cry for the Israelite troops in the conduct of Holy War; however, the Hebrew text is difficult to interpret.

d. [17:7] Ps 95:8–9.
e. [17:8] Dt 25:17–19; 1 Sm 15:2.
f. [17:14] Nm 24:20; 1 Sm 15:3, 20.

¶ [18:2] **Moses had sent her back:** a later gloss which attempts to harmonize Zipporah's presence with Jethro here in this story and the account of Moses' return to Egypt with Zipporah in 4:20.

** [18:5] The allusion to meeting Moses encamped at the mountain of God, prior to the arrival of the Israelites at Sinai in chap. 19, might well suggest a different narrative context for this story from an earlier stage of the biblical tradition's development. It is noteworthy that immediately after the Sinai pericope (Ex 19:1–Nm 10:28), recounting the theophany at Sinai and the giving of the law, the narrative of Israel's march through the wilderness resumes with an apparent doublet of the visit by Moses' father-in-law (Nm 10:29–32).

a. [18:3] Ex 2:22.

offering* and sacrifices for God, and Aaron came with all the elders of Israel to share with Moses' father-in-law in the meal before God.

Appointment of Minor Judges. [13]The next day Moses sat in judgment for the people, while they stood around him from morning until evening. [14]When Moses' father-in-law saw all that he was doing for the people, he asked, "What is this business that you are conducting for the people? Why do you sit alone while all the people have to stand about you from morning till evening?" [15]Moses answered his father-in-law, "The people come to me to consult God. [16]Whenever they have a disagreement, they come to me to have me settle the matter between them and make known to them God's statutes and instructions."

[17]"What you are doing is not wise," Moses' father-in-law replied. [18]"You will surely wear yourself out, both you and these people with you. The task is too heavy for you;[b] you cannot do it alone. [19]†Now, listen to me, and I will give you some advice, and may God be with you. Act as the people's representative before God, and bring their disputes to God. [20]Enlighten them in regard to the statutes and instructions, showing them how they are to conduct themselves and what they are to do. [21]But you should also look among all the people for able and God-fearing men, trustworthy men who hate dishonest gain, and set them over the people as commanders of thousands, of hundreds, of fifties, and of tens.[c] [22]Let these render decisions for the people in all routine cases. Every important case they should refer to you, but every lesser case they can settle themselves. Lighten your burden by letting them bear it with you! [23]If you do this, and God so commands you,‡ you will be able to stand the strain, and all these people, too, will go home content."

[24]Moses listened to his father-in-law and did all that he had said. [25]He picked out able men from all Israel and put them in charge of the people as commanders of thousands, of hundreds, of fifties, and of tens. [26]They rendered decisions for the people in all routine cases. The more difficult cases they referred to Moses, but all the lesser cases they settled themselves. [27]Then Moses said farewell to his father-in-law, who went off to his own country.

VI. COVENANT AND LEGISLATION AT MOUNT SINAI

CHAPTER 19

Arrival at Sinai. [1]aIn the third month after the Israelites' departure from the land of Egypt, on the first day, they came to the wilderness of Sinai. [2]After they made the journey from Rephidim and entered the wilderness of Sinai, they then pitched camp in the wilderness.§

While Israel was encamped there in front of the mountain, [3]Moses went up to the mountain of God. Then the LORD called to him from the mountain, saying: This is what you will say to the house of Jacob; tell the Israelites: [4]You have seen how I treated the Egyptians and how I bore you up on eagles' wings

---

* [18:12] That a non-Israelite, such as Jethro, should bless Israel's God by way of acknowledging what God had done for Israel (v. 10) is not entirely surprising; but the Midianite priest's sacrifice to the God of Israel, including his presiding over a sacrificial meal with Aaron and the elders of Israel, is unusual, suggesting that he was himself already a worshiper of Yhwh, Israel's God. Note further in this connection the role Jethro takes in the following narrative (vv. 13–27) in instituting a permanent judiciary for the Israelites. **Burnt offering**: a sacrifice wholly burnt up as an offering to God.

† [18:19–20] By emphasizing Moses' mediatorial role for the people before God in regard to God's statutes and instructions, this story about the institution of Israel's judiciary prepares for Moses' role in the upcoming revelation of the law at Sinai.

b. [18:18] Nm 11:14.
c. [18:21, 25] Dt 1:15; 16:18.

‡ [18:23] **And God so commands you**: i.e., and God approves.
§ [19:2] Apparently from a different source (P) than v. 1, which notes the date, v. 2 from the J source includes a second notice of the arrival in the wilderness of Sinai. The Israelites now will be camped at Sinai from this point on all the way to Nm 10:10. This is a striking indication of the centrality and importance of the Sinai narrative in the overall composition of the Pentateuch.

a. [19:1–2] Nm 33:15.

and brought you to myself.*b* *5*Now, if you obey me completely and keep my covenant,* you will be my treasured possession among all peoples,*c* though all the earth is mine. *6*You will be to me a kingdom of priests,† a holy nation.*d* That is what you must tell the Israelites. *7*So Moses went and summoned the elders of the people. When he set before them all that the LORD had ordered him to tell them, *8*all the people answered together, "Everything the LORD has said, we will do." Then Moses brought back to the LORD the response of the people.

*9*The LORD said to Moses: I am coming to you now in a dense cloud,*e* so that when the people hear me speaking with you, they will also remain faithful to you.

When Moses, then, had reported the response of the people to the LORD, *10*the LORD said to Moses: Go to the people and have them sanctify themselves today and tomorrow. Have them wash their garments *11*and be ready for the third day; for on the third day the LORD will come down on Mount Sinai in the sight of all the people. *12*Set limits for the people all around,*f* saying: Take care not to go up the mountain, or even to touch its edge. All who touch the mountain must be put to death. *13*No hand shall touch them, but they must be stoned to death or killed with arrows. Whether human being or beast, they must not be allowed to live. Only when the ram's horn sounds may they go up on the mountain.‡ *14*Then Moses came down from the mountain to the people and had them sanctify themselves, and they washed their garments. *15*He said to the people, "Be ready for the third day. Do not approach a woman."

The Great Theophany. *16g*On the morning of the third day there were peals of thunder and lightning, and a heavy cloud over the mountain, and a very loud blast of the shofar,§ so that all the people in the camp trembled. *17*But Moses led the people out of the camp to meet God, and they stationed themselves at the foot of the mountain. *18*Now Mount Sinai was completely enveloped in smoke, because the LORD had come down upon it in fire. The smoke rose from it as though from a kiln, and the whole mountain trembled violently. *19*The blast of the shofar grew louder and louder, while Moses was speaking and God was answering him with thunder.

*20¶*When the LORD came down upon Mount Sinai, to the top of the mountain, the LORD summoned Moses to the top of the mountain, and Moses went up. *21*Then the LORD told Moses: Go down and warn the people not to break through to the LORD in order to see him; otherwise many of them will be struck down. *22*For their part, the priests, who approach the LORD must sanctify themselves; else the LORD will break out in anger against them. *23*But Moses said to the LORD, "The people

---

* [19:5] **Covenant**: while covenants between individuals and between nations are ubiquitous in the ancient Near East, the adaptation of this concept to express the relationship that will henceforth characterize God's relationship to Israel represents an important innovation of biblical faith. Other gods might "choose" nations to fulfill a special destiny or role in the world; but only Israel's God is bound to a people by covenant. Thereby Israel's identity as a people is put upon a foundation that does not depend upon the vicissitudes of Israelite statehood or the normal trappings of national existence. Israel will be a covenant people.

† [19:6] **Kingdom of priests**: inasmuch as this phrase is parallel to "holy nation," it most likely means that the whole Israelite nation is set apart from other nations and so consecrated to God, or holy, in the way priests are among the people (cf. Is 61:6; 1 Pt 2:5, 9).

b. [19:4] Dt 32:11–12.
c. [19:5] Dt 7:6; 14:2; 26:18–19; 32:8–9.
d. [19:6] 1 Pt 2:9.
e. [19:9] Ex 20:21; 24:15–18.
f. [19:12–13] Ex 34:3; Heb 12:18–19.

‡ [19:13] **May they go up on the mountain**: in vv. 12–13a, a later Priestly reshaping of an earlier version of the instructions governing how the people are to prepare for the encounter with God (vv. 10–11, 13b), the people are to be restrained from ascending the mountain, which is suffused with the holiness of God and too dangerous for their approach. In the earlier version, as v. 13b suggests, the sanctified people must come near, in order to hear God speaking with Moses (v. 9) and in this way receive confirmation of his special relationship with God.

§ [19:16] **Shofar**: a ram's horn used like a trumpet for signaling both for liturgical and military purposes.

¶ [19:20–25] At this point the Priestly additions of vv. 12–13a are elaborated with further Priestly instructions, which include the priests' sanctifying themselves apart from the people (v. 22) and Aaron accompanying Moses to the top of the mountain (v. 24).

g. [19:16–19] Dt 4:10–12.

cannot go up to Mount Sinai, for you yourself warned us, saying: Set limits around the mountain to make it sacred." [24]So the LORD said to him: Go down and come up along with Aaron. But do not let the priests and the people break through to come up to the LORD; else he will break out against them." [25]So Moses went down to the people and spoke to them.

CHAPTER 20

The Ten Commandments.[*] [1]Then God spoke all these words:

[2a]I am the LORD your God, who brought you out of the land of Egypt,[b] out of the house of slavery. [3]You shall not have other gods beside me.[†] [4]You shall not make for yourself an idol[c] or a likeness of anything[‡] in the heavens above or on the earth below or in the waters beneath the earth; [5]you shall not bow down before them or serve them.[d] For I, the LORD, your God, am a jealous God, inflicting punishment for their ancestors' wickedness on the children of those who hate me, down to the third and fourth generation[§]; [6]but showing love down to the thousandth generation of those who love me and keep my commandments.

[7]You shall not invoke the name of the LORD, your God, in vain.[¶e] For the LORD will not leave unpunished anyone who invokes his name in vain.

[8]Remember the sabbath day—keep it holy.[**] [9]Six days you may labor and do all your work, [10]but the seventh day is a sabbath of the LORD your God.[f] You shall not do any work, either you, your son or your daughter, your male or female slave, your work animal, or the resident alien within your gates. [11]For in six days the LORD made the heavens and the earth, the sea and all that is in them; but on the seventh day he rested.[g] That is why the LORD has blessed the sabbath day and made it holy.[††]

[12‡‡h]Honor your father and your mother, that you may have a long life in the land the LORD your God is giving you.[i]

---

[*] [20:1–17] The precise numbering and division of these precepts into "ten commandments" is somewhat uncertain. Traditionally among Catholics and Lutherans vv. 1–6 are considered as only one commandment, and v. 17 as two. The Anglican, Greek Orthodox, and Reformed churches count vv. 1–6 as two, and v. 17 as one. Cf. Dt 5:6–21. The traditional designation as "ten" is not found here but in 34:28 (and also Dt 4:13 and 10:4), where these precepts are alluded to literally as "the ten words." That they were originally written on two tablets appears in Ex 32:15–16; 34:28–29; Dt 4:13; 10:2–4.

The present form of the commands is a product of a long development, as is clear from the fact that the individual precepts vary considerably in length and from the slightly different formulation of Dt 5:6–21 (see especially vv. 12–15 and 21). Indeed they represent a mature formulation of a traditional morality. Why this specific selection of commands should be set apart is not entirely clear. None of them is unique in the Old Testament and all of the laws which follow are also from God and equally binding on the Israelites. Even so, this collection represents a privileged expression of God's moral demands on Israel and is here set apart from the others as a direct, unmediated communication of God to the Israelites and the basis of the covenant being concluded on Sinai.

[†] [20:3] **Beside me:** this commandment is traditionally understood as an outright denial of the existence of other gods except the God of Israel; however, in the context of the more general prohibitions in vv. 4–5, it is, more precisely, God's demand for Israel's exclusive worship and allegiance.

The Hebrew phrase underlying the translation "beside me" is, nonetheless, problematic and has been variously translated, e.g., "except me," "in addition to me," "in preference to me," "in defiance of me," and "in front of me" or "before my face." The latter translation, with its concrete, spatial nuances, has suggested to some that the prohibition once sought to exclude from the Lord's sanctuary the cult images or idols of other gods, such as the asherah, or stylized sacred tree of life, associated with the Canaanite goddess Asherah (34:13). Over the course of time, as vv. 4–5 suggest, the original scope of v. 3 was expanded.

[‡] [20:4] **Or a likeness of anything:** compare this formulation to that found in Dt 5:8, which understands this phrase and the following phrases as specifications of the prohibited idol (Hebrew *pesel*), which usually refers to an image that is carved or hewn rather than cast.

[§] [20:5] **Jealous:** demanding exclusive allegiance. **Inflicting punishment . . . the third and fourth generation:** the intended emphasis is on God's mercy by the contrast between punishment and mercy ("to the thousandth generation"—v. 6). Other Old Testament texts repudiate the idea of punishment devolving on later generations (cf. Dt 24:16; Jer 31:29–30; Ez 18:2–4). Yet it is known that later generations may suffer the punishing effects of sins of earlier generations, but not the guilt.

[¶] [20:7] **In vain:** i.e., to no good purpose, a general framing of the prohibition which includes swearing falsely, especially in the context of a legal proceeding, but also goes beyond it (cf. Lv 24:16; Prv 30:8–9).

[**] [20:8] **Keep it holy:** i.e., to set it apart from the other days of the week, in part, as the following verse explains, by not doing work that is ordinarily done in the course of a week. The special importance of this command can be seen in the fact that, together with vv. 9–11, it represents the longest of the Decalogue's precepts.

[††] [20:11] Here, in a formulation which reflects Priestly theology, the veneration of the sabbath is grounded in God's own hallowing of the sabbath in creation. Compare 31:13; Dt 5:15.

[‡‡] [20:12–17] The Decalogue falls into two parts: the preceding precepts refer to God, the following refer primarily to one's fellow Israelites.

---

a. [20:2–17] Dt 5:6–21.
b. [20:2] Lv 26:13; Ps 81:11; Hos 13:4.
c. [20:4] Ex 34:17; Lv 26:1; Dt 4:15–19; 27:15.

d. [20:5] Ex 34:7, 14; Nm 14:18; Dt 4:24; 6:15.
e. [20:7] Lv 19:12; 24:16.
f. [20:8–11] Ex 23:12; 31:13–16; 34:21; 35:2; Lv 23:3.
g. [20:11] Ex 31:17; Gn 2:2–3.
h. [20:12–16] Mt 19:18–19; Mk 10:19; Lk 18:20; Rom 13:9.
i. [20:12] Lv 20:9; Mt 15:4; Mk 7:10; Eph 6:2–3.

13 You shall not kill.[*][j]

14 You shall not commit adultery.[k]

15 You shall not steal.[l]

16 You shall not bear false witness against your neighbor.[m]

17 You shall not covet your neighbor's house. You shall not covet your neighbor's wife, his male or female slave, his ox or donkey, or anything that belongs to your neighbor.[n]

Moses Accepted as Mediator. 18 Now as all the people witnessed the thunder and lightning, the blast of the shofar and the mountain smoking, they became afraid and trembled.[o] So they took up a position farther away 19 and said to Moses, "You speak to us, and we will listen; but do not let God speak to us, or we shall die." 20 Moses answered the people, "Do not be afraid, for God has come only to test you and put the fear of him upon you so you do not sin." 21 So the people remained at a distance, while Moses approached the dark cloud where God was.

The Covenant Code. 22 [†]The LORD said to Moses: This is what you will say to the Israelites: You have seen for yourselves that I have spoken to you from heaven. 23 You shall not make alongside of me gods of silver, nor shall you make for yourselves gods of gold.[p] 24 An altar of earth make for me, and sacrifice upon it your burnt offerings and communion sacrifices, your sheep and your oxen.[q] In every place where I cause my name to be invoked[‡] I will come to you and bless you. 25 But if you make an altar of stone for me,[r] do not build it of cut stone, for by putting a chisel to it you profane it. 26 You shall not ascend to my altar by steps, lest your nakedness be exposed.

CHAPTER 21

Laws Regarding Slaves. 1 These are the ordinances[§] you shall lay before them. 2 [a]When you purchase a Hebrew slave,[¶] he is to serve you for six years, but in the seventh year he shall leave as a free person without any payment. 3 If he comes into service alone, he shall leave alone; if he comes with a wife, his wife shall leave with him. 4 But if his master gives him a wife and she bears him sons or daughters, the woman and her children belong to her master and the man shall leave alone. 5 If, however, the slave declares, 'I love my master and my wife and children; I will not leave as a free person,' 6 his master shall bring him to God[**] and there, at the door or doorpost, he shall

* [20:13] **Kill**: as frequent instances of killing in the context of war or certain crimes (see vv. 12–18) demonstrate in the Old Testament, not all killing comes within the scope of the commandment. For this reason, the Hebrew verb translated here as "kill" is often understood as "murder," although it is in fact used in the Old Testament at times for unintentional acts of killing (e.g., Dt 4:41; Jos 20:3) and for legally sanctioned killing (Nm 35:30). The term may originally have designated any killing of another Israelite, including acts of manslaughter, for which the victim's kin could exact vengeance. In the present context, it denotes the killing of one Israelite by another, motivated by hatred or the like (Nm 35:20; cf. Hos 6:9).

† [20:22–23:33] This collection consists of the civil and religious laws, both apodictic (absolute) and casuistic (conditional), which were given to the people through the mediation of Moses. They will be written down by Moses in 24:4.

‡ [20:24] **Where I cause my name to be invoked**: i.e., at the sacred site where God wishes to be worshiped. Dt 12 will demand the centralization of all sacrificial worship in one place chosen by God.

§ [21:1] **Ordinances**: judicial precedents to be used in settling questions of law and custom. More than half of the civil and religious laws in this collection (20:22–23:33), designated in 24:7 as "the book of the covenant," have parallels in the cuneiform laws of the ancient Near East. It is clear that Israel participated in a common legal culture with its neighbors.

¶ [21:2] **Slave**: an Israelite could become a slave of another Israelite as a means of paying a debt, or an Israelite could be born into slavery due to a parent's status as a slave. Here a time limit is prescribed for such slavery; other stipulations (vv. 20–21, 26–27) tried to reduce the evils of slavery, but slavery itself is not condemned in the Old Testament.

** [21:6] **To God**: the ritual of the piercing of the slave's ear, which signified a lifetime commitment to the master, probably took place at the door of the household, where God as protector of the household was called upon as a witness. Another possible location for the ritual would have been the door of the sanctuary, where God or judges would have witnessed the slave's promise of lifetime obedience to his master.

j. [20:13] Mt 5:21.
k. [20:14] Lv 18:20; 20:10; Dt 22:22; Mt 5:27.
l. [20:15] Lv 19:11.
m. [20:16] Ex 23:1; Dt 19:16–19; Prv 19:5, 9; 24:28.
n. [20:17] Rom 7:7.
o. [20:18–21] Dt 4:11; 5:22–27; 18:16; Heb 12:18–19.
p. [20:23] Ex 20:3–4.
q. [20:24] Dt 12:5, 11; 14:23; 16:6.
r. [20:25] Dt 27:5; Jos 8:31.
a. [21:2–6] Lv 25:39–55; Dt 15:12–18; Jer 34:14.

pierce his ear with an awl, thus keeping him as his slave forever.

⁷When a man sells his daughter as a slave, she shall not go free as male slaves do. ⁸But if she displeases her master, who had designated her* for himself, he shall let her be redeemed. He has no right to sell her to a foreign people, since he has broken faith with her. ⁹If he designates her for his son, he shall treat her according to the ordinance for daughters. ¹⁰If he takes another wife, he shall not withhold her food, her clothing, or her conjugal rights. ¹¹If he does not do these three things for her, she may leave without cost, without any payment.

Personal Injury. ¹²†Whoever strikes someone a mortal blow must be put to death.*ᵇ* ¹³However, regarding the one who did not hunt another down, but God caused death to happen by his hand, I will set apart for you a place to which that one may flee. ¹⁴But when someone kills a neighbor after maliciously scheming to do so, you must take him even from my altar and put him to death. ¹⁵Whoever strikes father or mother shall be put to death.‡

¹⁶A kidnaper, whether he sells the person or the person is found in his possession, shall be put to death.*ᶜ*

¹⁷Whoever curses§ father or mother shall be put to death.*ᵈ*

¹⁸When men quarrel and one strikes the other with a stone or with his fist, not mortally, but enough to put him in bed, ¹⁹the one who struck the blow shall be acquitted, provided the

other can get up and walk around with the help of his staff. Still, he must compensate him for his recovery time and make provision for his complete healing.

²⁰When someone strikes his male or female slave with a rod so that the slave dies under his hand, the act shall certainly be avenged. ²¹If, however, the slave survives for a day or two, he is not to be punished, since the slave is his own property.

²²¶When men have a fight and hurt a pregnant woman, so that she suffers a miscarriage, but no further injury, the guilty one shall be fined as much as the woman's husband demands of him, and he shall pay in the presence of the judges. ²³*ᵉ*But if injury ensues, you shall give life for life, ²⁴eye for eye, tooth for tooth, hand for hand, foot for foot, ²⁵burn for burn, wound for wound, stripe for stripe.

²⁶When someone strikes his male or female slave in the eye and destroys the use of the eye, he shall let the slave go free in compensation for the eye. ²⁷If he knocks out a tooth of his male or female slave, he shall let the slave go free in compensation for the tooth.

²⁸When an ox gores a man or a woman to death, the ox must be stoned; its meat may not be eaten. The owner of the ox, however, shall be free of blame. ²⁹But if an ox was previously in the habit of goring people and its owner, though warned, would not watch it; should it then kill a man or a woman, not only must the ox be stoned, but its owner also must be put to death. ³⁰If, however, a fine is imposed on him, he must pay in

---

* [21:8] **Designated her:** intended her as a wife of second rank.
† [21:12–14] Unintentional homicide is to be punished differently from premeditated, deliberate murder. One who kills unintentionally can seek asylum by grasping the horns of the altar at the local sanctuary. In later Israelite history, when worship was centralized in Jerusalem, cities throughout the realm were designated as places of refuge. Apparently the leaders of the local community were to determine whether or not the homicide was intentional.
‡ [21:15] The verb used most often signifies a violent, sometimes deadly, attack. The severe penalty assigned is intended to safeguard the integrity of the family.
§ [21:17] **Curses:** not merely an angrily uttered expletive at one's parents, but a solemn juridical formula of justifiable retribution which was considered to be legally binding and guaranteed by God.

b. [21:12] Lv 24:17; Nm 35:15–29; Dt 4:41–42; 19:2–5.
c. [21:16] Dt 24:7.
d. [21:17] Lv 20:9; Prv 20:20; Mt 15:4; Mk 7:10.

¶ [21:22–25] This law of talion is applied here in the specific case of a pregnant woman who, as an innocent bystander, is injured by two fighting men. The law of talion is not held up as a general principle to be applied throughout the book of the covenant. (But see note on Lv 24:19–20.) Here this principle of rigorous accountability aimed to prevent injury to a woman about to give birth by apparently requiring the assailant to have his own wife injured as she was about to bring new life into his family. However, it is debatable whether talion was ever understood or applied literally in Israel. In his Sermon on the Mount, Jesus challenges his audience to find a deeper form of justice than the supposed equilibrium offered by talion (Mt 5:38–40).

e. [21:23–25] Lv 24:18–21; Dt 19:21; Mt 5:38.

ransom* for his life whatever amount is imposed on him. ³¹This ordinance applies if it is a boy or a girl that the ox gores. ³²But if it is a male or a female slave that it gores, he must pay the owner of the slave thirty shekels of silver, and the ox must be stoned.

Property Damage. ³³When someone uncovers or digs a cistern and does not cover it over again, should an ox or a donkey fall into it, ³⁴the owner of the cistern must make good by restoring the value of the animal to its owner, but the dead animal he may keep.

³⁵When one man's ox hurts another's ox and it dies, they shall sell the live ox and divide this money as well as the dead animal equally between them. ³⁶But if it was known that the ox was previously in the habit of goring and its owner would not watch it, he must make full restitution, an ox for an ox; but the dead animal he may keep.

³⁷When someone steals an ox or a sheep and slaughters or sells it, he shall restore five oxen for the one ox, and four sheep for the one sheep.ᶠ

CHAPTER 22

¹[If a thief is caught† in the act of housebreaking and beaten to death, there is no bloodguilt involved. ²But if after sunrise he is thus beaten, there is bloodguilt.] He must make full restitution. If he has nothing, he shall be sold to pay for his theft. ³If what he stole is found alive in his possession, be it an ox, a donkey or a sheep, he shall make twofold restitution.

⁴When someone causes a field or a vineyard to be grazed over, by sending his cattle to graze in another's field, he must make restitution with the best produce of his own field or vineyard. ⁵If a fire breaks out, catches on to thorn bushes, and consumes shocked grain, standing grain, or the field itself, the one who started the fire must make full restitution.

Trusts and Loans. ⁶When someone gives money or articles to another for safekeeping and they are stolen from the latter's house, the thief, if caught, must make twofold restitution. ⁷If the thief is not caught, the owner of the house shall be brought to God,‡ to swear that he himself did not lay hands on his neighbor's property. ⁸In every case of dishonest appropriation, whether it be about an ox, or a donkey, or a sheep, or a garment, or anything else that has disappeared, where another claims that the thing is his, the claim of both parties shall be brought before God; the one whom God convicts must make twofold restitution to the other.

⁹When someone gives an ass, or an ox, or a sheep, or any other animal to another for safekeeping, if it dies, or is maimed or snatched away, without anyone witnessing the fact, ¹⁰there shall be an oath before the LORD between the two of them that the guardian did not lay hands on his neighbor's property; the owner must accept the oath, and no restitution is to be made. ¹¹But if the guardian has actually stolen from it, then he must make restitution to the owner. ¹²If it has been killed by a wild beast, let him bring it as evidence; he need not make restitution for the mangled animal.ᵃ

¹³When someone borrows an animal from a neighbor, if it is maimed or dies while the owner is not present, that one must make restitution. ¹⁴But if the owner is present, that one need not make restitution. If it was hired, this was covered by the price of its hire.

---

* [21:30] **Ransom**: the amount of money or material goods required to restore the relationship between the relatives of the victim and the negligent owner of the goring ox.

† [22:1–2] **If a thief is caught**: this seems to be a fragment of what was once a longer law on housebreaking, which has been inserted here into the middle of a law on stealing animals. At night the householder would be justified in killing a burglar outright, but not so in the daytime, when the burglar could more easily be caught alive. **He must make full restitution**: this stood originally immediately after 21:37.

f. [21:37] 2 Sm 12:6.

‡ [22:7] **Brought to God**: either within the household or at the sanctuary, the owner of the house is required to take an oath before God.

a. [22:12] Gn 31:39.

Social Laws. ¹⁵ᵇWhen a man seduces a virgin who is not betrothed, and lies with her, he shall make her his wife by paying the bride price. ¹⁶If her father refuses to give her to him, he must still pay him the bride price for virgins.*

¹⁷You shall not let a woman who practices sorcery live.ᶜ

¹⁸Anyone who lies with an animal shall be put to death.ᵈ

¹⁹Whoever sacrifices to any god, except to the Lᴏʀᴅ alone, shall be put under the ban.ᵉ

²⁰You shall not oppress or afflict a resident alien, for you were once aliens residing in the land of Egypt.ᶠ ²¹You shall not wrong any widow or orphan. ²²If ever you wrong them and they cry out to me, I will surely listen to their cry. ²³My wrath will flare up, and I will kill you with the sword; then your own wives will be widows, and your children orphans.

²⁴ᵍIf you lend money to my people, the poor among you, you must not be like a money lender; you must not demand interest from them. ²⁵If you take your neighbor's cloak as a pledge, you shall return it to him before sunset; ²⁶for this is his only covering; it is the cloak for his body. What will he sleep in? If he cries out to me, I will listen; for I am compassionate.ʰ

²⁷You shall not despise God,† nor curse a leader of your people.ⁱ

²⁸You shall not delay the offering of your harvest and your press. You shall give me the firstborn of your sons. ²⁹You must do the same with your oxen and your sheep; for seven days the firstling may stay with its mother, but on the eighth day you must give it to me.ʲ

³⁰You shall be a people sacred to me. Flesh torn to pieces in the field you shall not eat; you must throw it to the dogs.ᵏ

CHAPTER 23

¹You shall not repeat a false report. Do not join your hand with the wicked to be a witness supporting violence.ᵃ ²You shall not follow the crowd in doing wrong. When testifying in a lawsuit, you shall not follow the crowd in perverting justice. ³You shall not favor the poor in a lawsuit.ᵇ

⁴When you come upon your enemy's ox or donkey going astray, you must see to it that it is returned.ᶜ ⁵When you notice the donkey of one who hates you lying down under its burden, you should not desert him; you must help him with it.

⁶You shall not pervert justice for the needy among you in a lawsuit. ⁷You shall keep away from anything dishonest. The innocent and the just you shall not put to death, for I will not acquit the guilty. ⁸Never take a bribe, for a bribe blinds the clear-sighted and distorts the words of the just.ᵈ ⁹You shall not oppress a resident alien; you well know how it feels to be an alien, since you were once aliens yourselves in the land of Egypt.ᵉ

Religious Laws. ¹⁰ᶠFor six years you may sow your land and gather in its produce. ¹¹But the seventh year you shall let the land lie untilled and fallow, that the poor of your people may eat of it and their leftovers the wild animals may eat. So also shall you do in regard to your vineyard and your olive grove.

¹²For six days you may do your work, but on the seventh day you must

---

* [22:16] **The bride price for virgins:** fifty shekels according to Dt 22:29.
† [22:27] **Despise God:** a turning away from God's authority and so failing to honor God (cf. 1 Sm 2:30).

b. [22:15–16] Dt 22:28–29.
c. [22:17] Lv 19:26, 31; 20:6, 27; Dt 18:10–11.
d. [22:18] Lv 18:23; Dt 27:21.
e. [22:19] Dt 13; 17:2–7.
f. [22:20–23] Ex 23:9; Lv 19:33–34; Dt 10:18–19; 24:17–18; 27:19; Zec 7:10.
g. [22:24] Lv 25:35–38; Dt 23:19–20; 24:10–13; Ez 18:7–8, 17–18.
h. [22:25–26] Dt 24:10–13; Jb 22:6; Prv 20:16; 27:13; Am 2:8.
i. [22:27] Acts 23:5.
j. [22:29] Ex 13:2; 34:19; Lv 22:27; Dt 15:19.

k. [22:30] Lv 7:24; 17:15; 22:8.

a. [23:1–2] Dt 19:16–21.
b. [23:3] Lv 19:15.
c. [23:4] Dt 22:1–4.
d. [23:8] Dt 16:19; 27:25; Sir 20:28.
e. [23:9] Ex 22:20.
f. [23:10–11] Lv 25:3–7.

rest,^{g} that your ox and your donkey may have rest, and that the son of your maidservant and the resident alien may be refreshed. ^{13}Give heed to all that I have told you.

You shall not mention the name of any other god; it shall not be heard from your lips.

^{14h}Three times a year you shall celebrate a pilgrim feast to me.* ^{15}You shall keep the feast of Unleavened Bread. As I have commanded you, you must eat unleavened bread for seven days at the appointed time in the month of Abib, for it was then that you came out of Egypt. No one shall appear before me† empty-handed. ^{16}You shall also keep the feast of the grain harvest with the first fruits of the crop that you sow in the field; and finally, the feast of Ingathering at the end of the year, when you collect your produce from the fields. ^{17}Three times a year shall all your men appear before the LORD God.

^{18}You shall not offer the blood of my sacrifice with anything leavened;^{i} nor shall the fat of my feast be kept overnight till the next day. ^{19}The choicest first fruits of your soil you shall bring to the house of the LORD, your God.

You shall not boil a young goat in its mother's milk.‡

Reward of Fidelity. ^{20}See, I am sending an angel^j before you, to guard you on the way and bring you to the place I have prepared. ^{21}Be attentive to him and obey him. Do not rebel against him, for he will not forgive your sin. My authority is within him.§ ^{22}If you obey him and carry out all I tell you, I will be an enemy to your enemies and a foe to your foes.

^{23}My angel will go before you and bring you to the Amorites, Hittites, Perizzites, Canaanites, Hivites and Jebusites; and I will wipe them out. ^{24}Therefore, you shall not bow down to their gods and serve them, nor shall you act as they do; rather, you must demolish them and smash their sacred stones.^{¶k} ^{25}You shall serve the LORD, your God; then he will bless your food and drink, and I will remove sickness from your midst; ^{26}no woman in your land will be barren or miscarry; and I will give you a full span of life.

^{27}I will have the terror of me precede you, so that I will throw into panic every nation you reach.^{l} I will make all your enemies turn from you in flight, ^{28}and ahead of you I will send hornets** to drive the Hivites, Canaanites and Hittites out of your way. ^{29}But I will not drive them all out before you in one year, lest the land become desolate and the wild animals multiply against you. ^{30}Little by little I will drive them out before you, until you have grown numerous enough to take possession of the land. ^{31m}I will set your boundaries from the Red Sea to the sea of the Philistines,†† and from the wilderness to the Euphrates; all who dwell in this land I will hand over to you and you shall drive them out before you. ^{32}You shall not make a covenant with them or their gods. ^{33}They must not live in your land. For if you serve their gods, this will become a snare to you.^{n}

---

* [23:14] These feasts—Passover/Unleavened Bread, Weeks (Pentecost), and Booths (Tabernacles or Succoth/Sukkoth)—are also listed in 34:18–26; Lv 23; Dt 16.

† [23:15] **Appear before me**: the original expression was "see my face"; so also in several other places, as 23:17; 34:23–24; Dt 16:16; 31:11.

‡ [23:19] **Boil a young goat in its mother's milk**: this command, repeated in 34:26 and Dt 14:21, is difficult to understand. It may originate from a taboo that forbade killing the young that were still nursing from the mother, or that forbade the mixing of life and death: the slaughtered young goat with the milk that previously had nourished its life. The Jewish dietary custom of keeping meat and dairy products separate is based on this command.

§ [23:21] **My authority is within him**: lit., "My name is within him."

g. [23:12] Ex 20:8–10.
h. [23:14–17] Ex 34:18, 22–24; Lv 23; Dt 16:1–17.
i. [23:18–19] Ex 34:25–26.
j. [23:20] Ex 14:19; 32:34; 33:2.

¶ [23:24] **Sacred stones**: objects that symbolized the presence of Canaanite deities. In general, standing stones served as memorials for deities, persons, or significant events such as military victories or covenant-making. See 24:4.

** [23:28] **Hornets**: the Hebrew *sir'ah* is a disputed term, but according to ancient interpreters it refers to hornets that were unleashed against the enemy to sting them and cause panic (cf. Dt 7:20; Jos 24:12; Wis 12:8). Others associate the word with plagues or troublesome afflictions.

†† [23:31] **The sea of the Philistines**: the Mediterranean. Only in the time of David and Solomon did the territory of Israel come near to reaching such distant borders.

k. [23:23–24] Ex 34:10–16; Nm 33:51–52; Dt 7:24–26.
l. [23:27–30] Dt 2:25; 7:20–22.
m. [23:31] Gn 15:18; Dt 11:24; Jos 1:4.
n. [23:32–33] Ex 34:12–16; Dt 7:2–6.

EX

CHAPTER 24

Ratification of the Covenant. ¹Moses himself was told: Come up to the LORD, you and Aaron, with Nadab, Abihu, and seventy of the elders of Israel. You shall bow down at a distance. ²Moses alone is to come close to the LORD; the others shall not come close, and the people shall not come up with them.

³When Moses came to the people and related all the words and ordinances of the LORD, they all answered with one voice, "We will do everything that the LORD has told us."ᵃ ⁴Moses then wrote down all the words of the LORD and, rising early in the morning, he built at the foot of the mountain an altar and twelve sacred stones* for the twelve tribes of Israel. ⁵ᵇThen, having sent young men of the Israelites to offer burnt offerings and sacrifice young bulls as communion offerings to the LORD, ⁶Moses took half of the blood and put it in large bowls; the other half he splashed on the altar. ⁷Taking the book of the covenant, he read it aloud to the people, who answered, "All that the LORD has said, we will hear and do." ⁸Then he took the blood and splashed it on the people, saying, "This is the blood of the covenant which the LORD has made with you according to all these words."

⁹Moses then went up with Aaron, Nadab, Abihu, and seventy elders of Israel, ¹⁰and they beheld the God of Israel. Under his feet there appeared to be sapphire tilework, as clear as the sky itself. ¹¹Yet he did not lay a hand on these chosen Israelites. They saw God,† and they ate and drank.

Moses on the Mountain. ¹²The LORD said to Moses: Come up to me on the mountain and, while you are there, I will give you the stone tabletsᶜ on which I have written the commandments intended for their instruction. ¹³So Moses set out with Joshua, his assistant, and went up to the mountain of God. ¹⁴He told the elders, "Wait here for us until we return to you. Aaron and Hur are with you. Anyone with a complaint should approach them." ¹⁵Moses went up the mountain. Then the cloud covered the mountain. ¹⁶The glory of the LORD settled upon Mount Sinai. The cloud covered it for six days, and on the seventh day he called to Moses from the midst of the cloud.ᵈ ¹⁷To the Israelites the glory of the LORD was seen as a consuming fire on the top of the mountain.ᵉ ¹⁸But Moses entered into the midst of the cloud and went up on the mountain. He was on the mountain for forty days and forty nights.ᶠ

CHAPTER 25

Collection of Materials. ¹The LORD spoke to Moses:ᵃ ²Speak to the Israelites: Let them receive contributions for me. From each you shall receive the contribution that their hearts prompt them to give me. ³These are the contributions you shall accept from them: gold, silver, and bronze;ᵇ ⁴violet, purple, and scarlet yarn; fine linen and goat hair; ⁵rams' skins dyed red, and tahash‡ skins; acacia wood; ⁶oil for the light; spices for the anointing oil and for the fragrant incense; ⁷onyx stones and other gems for mounting on the ephod and the breastpiece. ⁸They are to make a sanctuary for me, that I may dwell in their midst.ᶜ ⁹According to all that I show you regarding the pattern

---

* [24:4] **Sacred stones**: stone shafts or slabs, erected as symbols of the fact that each of the twelve tribes had entered into this covenant with God; see 23:24; Gn 28:18.
† [24:11] **They saw God**: the ancients thought that the sight of God would bring instantaneous death. Cf. 33:20; Gn 16:13; 32:31; Jgs 6:22–23; 13:22. **Ate and drank**: partook of the sacrificial meal.

a. [24:3] Ex 19:8.
b. [24:5–8] Heb 9:18–20.

‡ [25:5] **Tahash**: perhaps a kind of specially finished leather. The Greek and Latin versions took it for the color hyacinth.

c. [24:12] Ex 31:18; 32:15–16; Dt 5:22.
d. [24:16] Sir 45:5.
e. [24:17] Ex 19:18; Heb 12:18.
f. [24:18] Ex 34:28; Dt 9:9.

a. [25:1–7] Ex 35:4–9, 20–29.
b. [25:3] Ex 35:4–9.
c. [25:8–9] Ex 26:1–30; 36:8–38.

of the tabernacle and the pattern of its furnishings, so you are to make it.*d*

Plan of the Ark. ¹⁰You shall make an ark of acacia wood,*e* two and a half cubits* long, one and a half cubits wide, and one and a half cubits high. ¹¹Plate it inside and outside with pure gold, and put a molding of gold around the top of it. ¹²Cast four gold rings and put them on the four supports of the ark, two rings on one side and two on the opposite side. ¹³Then make poles of acacia wood and plate them with gold. ¹⁴These poles you are to put through the rings on the sides of the ark, for carrying it; ¹⁵they must remain in the rings of the ark and never be withdrawn. ¹⁶In the ark you are to put the covenant which I will give you.

¹⁷You shall then make a cover† of pure gold, two and a half cubits long, and one and a half cubits wide. ¹⁸Make two cherubim‡ of beaten gold for the two ends of the cover; ¹⁹make one cherub at one end, and the other at the other end, of one piece with the cover, at each end. ²⁰The cherubim shall have their wings spread out above, sheltering the cover with them; they shall face each other, with their faces looking toward the cover. ²¹This cover you shall then place on top of the ark. In the ark itself you are to put the covenant which I will give you. ²²There I will meet you and there, from above the cover, between the two cherubim on the ark of the covenant, I will tell you all that I command you regarding the Israelites.

The Table. ²³You shall also make a table of acacia*f* wood, two cubits long, a cubit wide, and a cubit and a half high. ²⁴Plate it with pure gold and make a molding of gold around it. ²⁵Make a frame§ for it, a handbreadth high, and make a molding of gold around the frame. ²⁶You shall also make four rings of gold for it and fasten them at the four corners, one at each leg. ²⁷The rings shall be alongside the frame as holders for the poles to carry the table. ²⁸These poles for carrying the table you shall make of acacia wood and plate with gold. ²⁹You shall make its plates¶ and cups, as well as its pitchers and bowls for pouring libations; make them of pure gold. ³⁰On the table you shall always keep showbread set before me.*g*

The Menorah. ³¹You shall make a menorah** of pure beaten gold*h*—its shaft and branches—with its cups and knobs and petals springing directly from it. ³²Six branches are to extend from its sides, three branches on one side, and three on the other. ³³††On one branch there are to be three cups, shaped like almond blossoms, each with its knob and petals; on the opposite branch there are to be three cups, shaped like almond blossoms, each with its knob and petals; and so for the six branches that extend from the menorah. ³⁴On the menorah there are to be four cups,‡‡ shaped like almond

---

§ [25:25] **A frame**: probably placed near the bottom of the legs to keep them steady. The golden table of Herod's Temple is pictured thus on the Arch of Titus.

¶ [25:29–30] The plates held the showbread, that is, the holy bread which was placed upon the table every sabbath as an offering to God, and was later eaten by the priests. The cups held the incense which was strewn upon the bread. Cf. Lv 24:5–9. The libation wine was poured from the pitchers into the bowls. All these vessels were kept on the golden table.

** [25:31] **Menorah**: this traditional lampstand is still used today in Jewish liturgy.

†† [25:33] In keeping with the arrangement of the ornaments on the shaft, the three sets of ornaments on each branch were probably so placed that one was at the top and the other two equally spaced along the length of the branch. **Knob**: the cup-shaped seed capsule at the base of a flower.

‡‡ [25:34–35] Of the four ornaments on the shaft, one was at the top and one was below each of the three sets of side branches.

f. [25:23–30] Ex 37:10–16.
g. [25:30] Lv 24:5–9.
h. [25:31–40] Ex 37:17–24.

---

* [25:10] **Cubits**: the distance between the elbow and tip of the middle finger of an average-size person, about eighteen inches. The dimensions of the ark of the covenant were approximately 3 3/4 feet long, 2 1/4 feet wide, and 2 1/4 feet high.

† [25:17] **Cover**: the Hebrew term, *kapporet*, has been connected with *kippur*, as in the feast of Yom Kippur or Day of Atonement (Lv 16; 23:26–32): hence, influenced by the Greek and Latin versions, and Luther's German, English translations have rendered it "propitiatory," "mercy seat," and the like.

‡ [25:18–20] **Cherubim**: probably in the form of human-headed winged lions. The cherubim over the ark formed the throne for the invisible Lord. Cf. Ps 80:2. For a more detailed description of the somewhat different cherubim in the Temple of Solomon, see 1 Kgs 6:23–28; 2 Chr 3:10–13.

d. [25:9] Acts 7:44.
e. [25:10–22] Ex 37:1–9; Heb 9:1–5.

blossoms, with their knobs and petals. ³⁵The six branches that go out from the menorah are to have a knob under each pair. ³⁶Their knobs and branches shall so spring from it that the whole will form a single piece of pure beaten gold. ^{37*}You shall then make seven lampsⁱ for it and so set up the lamps that they give their light on the space in front of the menorah. ³⁸These, as well as the trimming shears and trays,[†] must be of pure gold. ³⁹Use a talent[‡] of pure gold for the menorah and all these utensils. ⁴⁰See that you make them according to the pattern shown you on the mountain.^j

CHAPTER 26

The Tent Cloth. ¹The tabernacle itself you shall make out of ten sheets[§] woven of fine linen twined and of violet, purple, and scarlet yarn, with cherubim embroidered on them.^a ²The length of each shall be twenty-eight cubits, and the width four cubits; all the sheets shall be of the same size. ³Five of the sheets are to be joined one to another; and the same for the other five. ⁴Make loops of violet yarn along the edge of the end sheet in one set, and the same along the edge of the end sheet in the other set. ⁵Make fifty loops along the edge of the end sheet in the first set, and fifty loops along the edge of the corresponding sheet in the second set, and so placed that the loops are directly opposite each other. ⁶Then make fifty clasps of gold and join the

two sets of sheets, so that the tabernacle forms one whole.

⁷Also make sheets woven of goat hair for a tent[¶] over the tabernacle. Make eleven such sheets; ⁸the length of each shall be thirty cubits, and the width four cubits: all eleven sheets shall be of the same size. ⁹Join five of the sheets into one set, and the other six sheets into another set. Use the sixth sheet double at the front of the tent.^{**} ¹⁰Make fifty loops along the edge of the end sheet in one set, and fifty loops along the edge of the end sheet in the second set. ¹¹Also make fifty bronze clasps and put them into the loops, to join the tent into one whole. ¹²There will be an extra half sheet of tent covering, which shall be allowed to hang down over the rear of the tabernacle. ¹³Likewise, the sheets of the tent will have an extra cubit's length to be left hanging down on either side of the tabernacle to cover it. ¹⁴Over the tent itself make a covering of rams' skins dyed red, and above that, a covering of tahash skins.

The Framework. ^{15b}You shall make frames for the tabernacle, acacia-wood uprights. ¹⁶The length of each frame is to be ten cubits, and its width one and a half cubits. ¹⁷Each frame shall have two arms^{††} joined one to another; so you are to make all the frames of the tabernacle. ¹⁸Make the frames of the tabernacle as follows: twenty frames on the south side, ¹⁹with forty silver pedestals under the twenty frames, two pedestals under each frame for its two arms; ²⁰twenty frames on the other side of the tabernacle, the north side, ²¹with their forty silver pedestals, two pedestals under each frame. ²²At the rear of the tabernacle, to the west,

---

* [25:37] The lamps were probably shaped like small boats, with the wick at one end; the end with the wick was turned toward the front of the menorah.

† [25:38] **Trays:** small receptacles for the burnt-out wicks.

‡ [25:39] **Talent:** Heb. *kikkar.* The largest unit of weight used in the Bible, equivalent to 3,000 shekels (see 38:24). It is difficult to be precise about biblical weights; the Israelite talent may have weighed between 75–80 pounds.

§ [26:1] **Sheets:** strips of tapestry, woven of white linen, the colored threads being used for the cherubim which were embroidered on them. These sheets were stretched across the top of the tabernacle to form a roof, their free ends hanging down inside the framework that formed the walls.

i. [25:37] Lv 24:2–4; Nm 8:2.

j. [25:40] Heb 8:5.

a. [26:1–14] Ex 36:8–19.

¶ [26:7] **Tent:** the cloth made of sheets of goat hair to cover the tabernacle.

** [26:9] Half the width of the end strip was folded back at the front of the tabernacle, thus leaving another half-strip to hang down at the rear. Cf. v. 12.

†† [26:17] **Arms:** lit., "hands." According to some, they served as "tongue and groove" to mortise the structural elements; according to others, they were pegs that fitted into sockets in the pedestals.

b. [26:15–30] Ex 36:20–34.

six frames, ²³and two frames for the corners of the tabernacle, at its rear. ²⁴These two shall be double at the bottom, and likewise double at the top, to the first ring. That is how both corner frames are to be made. ²⁵Thus, there shall be eight frames, with their sixteen silver pedestals, two pedestals under each frame. ²⁶Also make bars of acacia wood: five for the frames on one side of the tabernacle, ²⁷five for those on the other side, and five for those at the rear, to the west. ²⁸The center bar, at the middle of the frames, shall reach across from end to end. ²⁹Plate the frames with gold, and make gold rings on them as holders for the bars, which are also to be plated with gold. ³⁰You shall set up the tabernacle according to its plan, which you were shown on the mountain.

The Veils. ³¹You shall make a veil woven of violet, purple, and scarlet yarn,^c and of fine linen twined, with cherubim embroidered on it.^d ³²It is to be hung on four gold-plated columns of acacia wood, which shall have gold hooks[*] and shall rest on four silver pedestals. ³³Hang the veil from clasps. The ark of the covenant you shall bring inside, behind this veil which divides the holy place from the holy of holies. ³⁴Set the cover on the ark of the covenant in the holy of holies.

³⁵Outside the veil you shall place the table and the menorah, the latter on the south side of the tabernacle, opposite the table, which is to be put on the north side. ³⁶For the entrance of the tent make a variegated[†] curtain of violet, purple, and scarlet yarn and of fine linen twined. ³⁷Make five columns of acacia wood for this curtain; plate them with gold, with their hooks of gold; and cast five bronze pedestals for them.

CHAPTER 27

The Altar for Burnt Offerings. ¹You shall make an altar^a of acacia wood, on a square, five cubits long and five cubits wide; it shall be three cubits high. ²At the four corners make horns[‡] that are of one piece with the altar. You shall then plate it with bronze. ³Make pots for removing the ashes, as well as shovels, basins, forks, and fire pans; all these utensils you shall make of bronze. ⁴Make for it a grating,[§] a bronze network; make four bronze rings for it, one at each of its four corners. ⁵Put it down around the altar, on the ground. This network is to be half as high as the altar. ⁶You shall also make poles of acacia wood for the altar, and plate them with bronze. ⁷These poles are to be put through the rings, so that they are on either side of the altar when it is carried. ⁸Make the altar itself in the form of a hollow[¶] box. Just as it was shown you on the mountain, so it is to be made.

Court of the Tabernacle. ⁹^bYou shall also make a court for the tabernacle. On the south side the court shall have hangings, of fine linen twined, a hundred cubits long, ¹⁰with twenty columns and twenty pedestals of bronze; the hooks and bands on the columns shall be of silver. ¹¹On the north side there shall be similar hangings, a hundred cubits long, with twenty columns and twenty pedestals of bronze; the hooks and bands on the columns shall be of silver. ¹²On the west side, across the width of the court, there shall be hangings, fifty cubits long, with ten columns and ten pedestals.

---

‡ [27:2] **Horns:** the horn of a ram, goat or ox is a common Old Testament figure for strength and dignity; they represent the divine character of the altar itself or the deity worshiped there.

§ [27:4] **Grating:** it is not clear whether this was flush with the altar or at some small distance from it; in the latter case the space between the altar and the grating would be filled with stones and serve as a platform around the altar, which would otherwise be too high for the priest to reach conveniently.

¶ [27:8] **Hollow:** probably filled with earth or stones when in use. Cf. 20:24–25.

---

* [26:32] **Hooks:** probably placed near the tops of the columns, to hold the rope from which the veils and curtains hung.

† [26:36] **Variegated:** without definite designs such as the cherubim on the inner veil.

c. [26:31] 2 Chr 3:14.
d. [26:31] Ex 36:35–38.

a. [27:1–8] Ex 38:1–7.
b. [27:9–19] Ex 38:9–20.

EX

¹³The width of the court on the east side shall be fifty cubits. ¹⁴On one side there shall be hangings to the extent of fifteen cubits, with three columns and three pedestals; ¹⁵on the other side there shall be hangings to the extent of fifteen cubits, with three columns and three pedestals.

¹⁶At the gate of the court there shall be a variegated curtain, twenty cubits long, woven of violet, purple, and scarlet yarn and of fine linen twined. It shall have four columns and four pedestals.

¹⁷All the columns around the court shall have bands and hooks of silver, and pedestals of bronze. ¹⁸The court is to be one hundred cubits long, fifty cubits wide, and five cubits high. Fine linen twined must be used, and the pedestals must be of bronze. ¹⁹All the fittings of the tabernacle, whatever be their use, as well as all its tent pegs and all the tent pegs of the court, must be of bronze.

Oil for the Lamps. ²⁰You shall command the Israelites to bring you clear oil of crushed olives, to be used for the light, so that you may keep lamps burning always.^c ²¹From evening to morning Aaron and his sons shall maintain them before the LORD in the tent of meeting, outside the veil which hangs in front of the covenant. This shall be a perpetual statute for the Israelites throughout their generations.

CHAPTER 28

The Priestly Vestments. ^{1a}Have your brother Aaron, and with him his sons, brought to you, from among the Israelites, that they may be my priests: Nadab and Abihu, Eleazar and Ithamar, Aaron's sons. ²For the glorious adornment of your brother Aaron you shall have sacred vestments made. ³Therefore, tell the various artisans whom I have endowed with skill* to make vestments for Aaron to consecrate him as my priest. ⁴These are the vestments they shall make: a breastpiece, an ephod, a robe, a brocade tunic, a turban, and a sash. In making these sacred vestments which your brother Aaron and his sons are to wear in serving as my priests, ⁵they shall use gold, violet, purple, and scarlet yarn and fine linen.

The Ephod and Breastpiece. ⁶The ephod[†] they shall make of gold thread and of violet, purple, and scarlet yarn, embroidered on cloth of fine linen twined.^b ⁷It shall have a pair of shoulder straps joined to its two upper ends. ⁸The embroidered belt of the ephod shall extend out from it and, like it, be made of gold thread, of violet, purple, and scarlet yarn, and of fine linen twined.

⁹Get two onyx stones and engrave on them the names of the sons of Israel: ¹⁰six of their names on one stone, and the names of the remaining six on the other stone, in the order of their birth. ¹¹As a gem-cutter engraves a seal, so shall you have the two stones engraved with the names of the sons of Israel and then mounted in gold filigree work. ¹²Set these two stones on the shoulder straps of the ephod as memorial stones of the sons of Israel. Thus Aaron shall bear their names on his shoulders as a reminder before the LORD. ¹³Make filigree rosettes of gold,^c ¹⁴as well as two chains of pure gold, twisted like cords, and fasten the cordlike chains to the filigree rosettes.

^{15d}The breastpiece[‡] of decision you shall also have made, embroidered like

† [28:6] **Ephod:** this Hebrew word is retained in the translation because it is the technical term for a peculiar piece of the priestly vestments, the exact nature of which is uncertain. It seems to have been a sort of apron that hung from the shoulders of the priest by shoulder straps (v. 7) and was tied around his waist by the loose ends of the attached belt (v. 8).

‡ [28:15–30] **Breastpiece:** an approximately nine-inch square, pocketlike receptacle for holding the Urim and Thummim (v. 30). It formed an integral part of the ephod, to which it was attached by an elaborate system of rings and chains. Both the ephod and its breastpiece were made of brocaded linen. **Span:** Heb. *zeret*, the distance between the top of the little finger and the thumb; one half a cubit, approximately nine inches.

* [28:3] **Artisans . . . endowed with skill:** lit., "wise of heart," and "filled with a spirit of wisdom." In Hebrew wisdom includes practical skills. Cf. 35:35; 36:1–2.

c. [27:20–21] Lv 24:1–4.

a. [28:1–5] Ex 39:1; Sir 45:7.

b. [28:6–12] Ex 39:2–7; Sir 45:8–14.
c. [28:13–14] Ex 28:22, 25; 39:15, 18.
d. [28:15–21] Ex 39:15–21.

the ephod with gold thread and violet, purple, and scarlet yarn on cloth of fine linen twined. ¹⁶It is to be square when folded double, a span high and a span wide. ¹⁷ˑOn it you shall mount four rows of precious stones: in the first row, a carnelian, a topaz, and an emerald; ¹⁸in the second row, a garnet, a sapphire, and a beryl; ¹⁹in the third row, a jacinth, an agate, and an amethyst; ²⁰in the fourth row, a chrysolite, an onyx, and a jasper. These stones are to be mounted in gold filigree work, ²¹twelve of them to match the names of the sons of Israel, each stone engraved like a seal with the name of one of the twelve tribes.

²²When the chains of pure gold, twisted like cords, have been made for the breastpiece, ²³you shall then make two rings of gold for it and fasten them to the two upper ends of the breastpiece. ²⁴The gold cords are then to be fastened to the two rings at the upper ends of the breastpiece, ²⁵the other two ends of the cords being fastened in front to the two filigree rosettes which are attached to the shoulder straps of the ephod. ²⁶Make two other rings of gold and put them on the two lower ends of the breastpiece, on its edge that faces the ephod. ²⁷Then make two more rings of gold and fasten them to the bottom of the shoulder straps next to where they join the ephod in front, just above its embroidered belt. ²⁸Violet ribbons shall bind the rings of the breastpiece to the rings of the ephod, so that the breastpiece will stay right above the embroidered belt of the ephod and not swing loose from it.

²⁹Whenever Aaron enters the sanctuary, he will thus bear the names of the sons of Israel on the breastpiece of decision over his heart as a constant reminder before the Lord. ³⁰In this breastpiece of decisionᵉ you shall put the Urim and Thummim,† that they may be over Aaron's heart whenever he enters the presence of the Lord. Thus he shall always bear the decisions for the Israelites over his heart in the presence of the Lord.

Other Vestments. ³¹The robe of the ephodᶠ you shall make entirely of violet material. ³²It shall have an opening for the head in the center, and around this opening there shall be a selvage, woven as at the opening of a shirt, to keep it from being torn. ³³At the hem at the bottom you shall make pomegranates, woven of violet, purple, and scarlet yarn and fine linen twined, with gold bells between them; ³⁴a gold bell, a pomegranate, a gold bell, a pomegranate, all around the hem of the robe. ³⁵Aaron shall wear it when ministering, that its sound may be heard as he enters and leaves the Lord's presence in the sanctuary; else he will die.

³⁶You shall also make a plate of pure gold and engrave on it, as on a seal engraving, "Sacred to the Lord." ³⁷This plate is to be tied over the turban with a violet ribbon in such a way that it rests on the front of the turban,ᵍ ³⁸over Aaron's forehead. Since Aaron bears whatever guilt the Israelites may incur in consecrating any of their sacred gifts, this plate must always be over his forehead, so that they may find favor with the Lord.

³⁹ʰThe tunic of fine linen shall be brocaded. The turban shall be made of fine linen. The sash shall be of variegated work.

⁴⁰Likewise, for the glorious adornment of Aaron's sons you shall have tunics and sashes and skullcaps made, for glorious splendor. ⁴¹With these you shall clothe your brother Aaron

---

* [28:17–20] The translation of the Hebrew names of some of these gems is quite conjectural.

e. [28:30] Lv 8:8; Sir 45:11.

† [28:30] **Urim and Thummim:** both the meaning of these Hebrew words and the exact nature of the objects so designated are uncertain. They were apparently lots of some kind which were drawn or cast by the priest to ascertain God's decision on particular questions. Hence, the pocket in which they were kept was called "the breastpiece of decision."

f. [28:31–35] Ex 39:20–25; Lv 8:9; Sir 45:10.
g. [28:37] Ex 39:31; Lv 8:9.
h. [28:39–43] Ex 39:27–31.

and his sons. Anoint and install them,* consecrating them as my priests. ⁴²You must also make linen pants for them, to cover their naked flesh from their loins to their thighs.ⁱ ⁴³Aaron and his sons shall wear them whenever they go into the tent of meeting or approach the altar to minister in the sanctuary, lest they incur guilt and die. This shall be a perpetual ordinance for him and for his descendants.

CHAPTER 29

Consecration of the Priests. ¹This is the rite you shall perform in conse-crating them as my priests.ᵃ Procure a young bull and two unblemished rams. ²With bran flour make unleav-ened cakes mixed with oil, and unleav-ened wafers spread with oil, ³and put them in a basket. Take the basket of them along with the bull and the two rams. ⁴Aaron and his sons you shall also bring to the entrance of the tent of meeting, and there wash them with water. ⁵Take the vestments and clothe Aaron with the tunic, the robe of the ephod, the ephod itself, and the breastpiece, fastening the embroidered belt of the ephod around him. ⁶Put the turban on his head, the sacred diadem on the turban. ⁷Then take the anoint-ing oil and pour it on his head, and anoint him. ⁸Bring forward his sons also and clothe them with the tunics, ⁹gird them with the sashes, and tie the skullcaps on them.ᵇ Thus shall the priesthood be theirs by a perpet-ual statute, and thus shall you install Aaron and his sons.

Installation Sacrifices. ¹⁰ᶜNow bring forward the bull in front of the tent of meeting. There Aaron and his sons shall lay their hands on its head. ¹¹Then slaughter the bull before the Lord, at the entrance of the tent of

meeting. ¹²Take some of its blood and with your finger put it on the horns of the altar. All the rest of the blood you shall pour out at the base of the altar. ¹³All the fat that covers its inner organs, as well as the lobe of its liver and its two kidneys, together with the fat that is on them, you shall take and burn on the altar. ¹⁴But the meat and hide and dung of the bull you must burn up outside the camp, since this is a purification offering.ᵈ

¹⁵Then take one of the rams, and after Aaron and his sons have laid their hands on its head, ¹⁶slaughter it. The blood you shall take and splash on all the sides of the altar. ¹⁷Cut the ram into pieces; you shall wash its inner organs and shanks and put them with the pieces and with the head. ¹⁸Then you shall burn the entire ram on the altar, since it is a burnt offering, a sweet-smelling oblation to the Lord.

¹⁹After this take the other ram, and when Aaron and his sons have laid their hands on its head, ²⁰slaughter it. Some of its blood you shall take and put on the tip of Aaron's right ear and on the tips of his sons' right ears and on the thumbs of their right hands and the great toes of their right feet. Splash the rest of the blood on all the sides of the altar. ²¹Then take some of the blood that is on the altar, together with some of the anointing oil, and sprinkle this on Aaron and his vest-ments, as well as on his sons and their vestments, that he and his sons and their vestments may be sacred.

²²Now, from this ram you shall take its fat: its fatty tail,† the fat that covers its inner organs, the lobe of its liver, its two kidneys with the fat that is on them, and its right thigh, since this is the ram for installation; ²³then, out of the basket of unleavened food that you have set before the Lord, you shall take one of the loaves of bread, one of the cakes made with oil, and one of

* [28:41] **Install them:** lit., "fill their hands," a technical expression used for the installation of priests.

i. [28:42] Ez 44:18.

a. [29:1–8] Lv 8:1–9.
b. [29:9] Lv 8:13.
c. [29:10–26] Lv 8:14–30.

† [29:22] **Fatty tail:** the thick layer of fat surrounding the tails of sheep and rams bred in the Middle East. It is regarded as a choice food. Cf. Lv 3:9.

d. [29:14] Heb 13:11.

EX

the wafers. **24**All these things you shall put into the hands of Aaron and his sons, so that they may raise them as an elevated offering* before the LORD. **25**After you receive them back from their hands, you shall burn them on top of the burnt offering on the altar as a sweet-smelling oblation to the LORD. **26**Finally, take the brisket of Aaron's installation ram and raise it as an elevated offering before the LORD; this is to be your own portion.

27†Thus shall you set aside the brisket of whatever elevated offering is raised,*e* as well as the thigh of whatever contribution is raised up, whether this be the installation ram or anything else belonging to Aaron or to his sons. **28**Such things are due to Aaron and his sons from the Israelites by a perpetual statute as a contribution. From their communion offerings, too, the Israelites shall make a contribution, their contribution to the LORD.

29The sacred vestments*f* of Aaron shall be passed down to his sons after him, that in them they may be anointed and installed. **30**The son who succeeds him as priest and who is to enter the tent of meeting to minister in the sanctuary shall be clothed with them for seven days.

31*g*You shall take the installation ram and boil its meat in a holy place. **32**At the entrance of the tent of meeting Aaron and his sons shall eat the meat of the ram and the bread that is in the basket. **33**They themselves are to eat of these things by which atonement was made at their installation and consecration; but no unauthorized person may eat of them, since they are sacred. **34**If some of the meat of the installation sacrifice or some of the bread remains over on the next day, this remnant you must burn up; it is not to be eaten, since it is sacred.

35Carry out all these commands in regard to Aaron and his sons just as I have given them to you.*h* Seven days you shall spend installing them, **36***i*sacrificing a bull each day as a purification offering, to make atonement. Thus you shall purify the altar‡ by purging it, and you shall anoint it in order to consecrate it. **37**Seven days you shall spend in purging the altar and in consecrating it. Then the altar will be most sacred, and whatever touches it will become sacred.

38§Now, this is what you shall regularly offer on the altar: two yearling lambs*j* as the sacrifice established for each day; **39**one lamb in the morning and the other lamb at the evening twilight. **40**With the first lamb there shall be a tenth of an ephah of bran flour mixed with a fourth of a hin¶ of oil of crushed olives and, as its libation, a fourth of a hin of wine. **41**The other lamb you shall offer at the evening twilight, with the same grain offering and libation as in the morning. You shall offer this as a sweet-smelling oblation to the LORD. **42**Throughout your generations this regular burnt offering shall be made before the LORD at the entrance of the tent of meeting, where I will meet you and speak to you.

43There, at the altar, I will meet the Israelites; hence, it will be made sacred by my glory.*k* **44**Thus I will consecrate the tent of meeting and the altar, just as I also consecrate Aaron and his sons to be my priests. **45**I will dwell in the midst of the Israelites and will be

---

* [29:24–26] **Elevated offering:** the portions of a communion offering, brisket and right thigh, which the officiating priest raised in the presence of the Lord. They were reserved for Aaron and his sons.

† [29:27–30] These verses are a parenthetical interruption of the installation ritual; v. 31 belongs logically immediately after v. 26.

‡ [29:36–37] **Purify the altar:** the purpose of the purification offering here is to cleanse, or purify, the newly constructed altar of any defilement resulting from presumably minor and inadvertent sins, but the text is not explicit about what the offenses were or who committed them. So various theories have been proposed to explain the cause of the altar's contamination. Note, however, that the offering appears to be demanded of Aaron and his sons; they are the ones who lay hands upon it (v. 10).

§ [29:38–42] A parenthesis inserted into the rubrics for consecrating the altar; v. 43 belongs directly after v. 37.

¶ [29:40] **Hin:** see note on Ez 45:24.

---

e. [29:27–28] Lv 7:31–34; 10:14–15; Nm 18:18–19; Dt 18:3.
f. [29:29] Nm 20:26, 28.
g. [29:31–34] Lv 8:31–32.
h. [29:35] Lv 8:36.
i. [29:36–37] Lv 8:33–35.
j. [29:38–42] Nm 28:3–8.
k. [29:43] Ex 25:22.

their God. [46]They shall know that I, the LORD, am their God who brought them out of the land of Egypt, so that I, the LORD, their God, might dwell among them.

CHAPTER 30

Altar of Incense. [1]For burning incense you shall make an altar of acacia wood,[a] [2]with a square surface, a cubit long, a cubit wide, and two cubits high, with horns that are of one piece with it. [3]Its grate on top, its walls on all four sides, and its horns you shall plate with pure gold. Put a gold molding around it, [4]Underneath the molding you shall put gold rings, two on one side and two on the opposite side, as holders for the poles used in carrying it. [5]Make the poles, too, of acacia wood and plate them with gold. [6]This altar you are to place in front of the veil that hangs before the ark of the covenant where I will meet you.[b]

[7]On it Aaron shall burn fragrant incense. Morning after morning, when he prepares the lamps, [8]and again in the evening twilight, when he lights the lamps, he shall burn incense. Throughout your generations this shall be the regular incense offering before the LORD. [9]On this altar you shall not offer up any profane incense, or any burnt offering or grain offering; nor shall you pour out a libation upon it. [10]Once a year Aaron shall purge its horns.[c] Throughout your generations he is to purge it once a year with the blood of the atoning purification offering. This altar is most sacred to the LORD.

Census Tax. [11]The LORD also told Moses: [12]When you take a census[d] of the Israelites who are to be enrolled, each one, as he is enrolled, shall give the LORD a ransom for his life, so that no plague may come upon them for being enrolled. [13]This is what

everyone who is enrolled must pay: a half-shekel, according to the standard of the sanctuary shekel—twenty gerahs to the shekel—a half-shekel contribution to the LORD.[e] [14]Everyone who is enrolled, of twenty years or more, must give the contribution to the LORD. [15]The rich need not give more, nor shall the poor give less, than a half-shekel in this contribution to the LORD to pay the ransom for their lives. [16]When you receive this ransom money from the Israelites, you shall donate it to the service of the tent of meeting, that there it may be a reminder of the Israelites before the LORD of the ransom paid for their lives.

The Basin. [17]The LORD told Moses: [18]For ablutions you shall make a bronze basin with a bronze stand. Place it between the tent of meeting and the altar, and put water in it.[g] [19]Aaron and his sons shall use it in washing their hands and feet.[h] [20]When they are about to enter the tent of meeting, they must wash with water, lest they die. Likewise when they approach the altar to minister, to offer an oblation to the LORD, [21]they must wash their hands and feet, lest they die. This shall be a perpetual statute for him and his descendants throughout their generations.

The Anointing Oil. [22]The LORD told Moses: [23]Take the finest spices: five hundred shekels of free-flowing myrrh; half that amount, that is, two hundred and fifty shekels, of fragrant cinnamon; two hundred and fifty shekels of fragrant cane; [24]five hundred shekels of cassia—all according to the standard of the sanctuary shekel; together with a hin of olive oil; [25]and blend them into sacred anointing oil,[i] perfumed ointment expertly prepared.[j] With this sacred anointing oil [26]you shall anoint the tent of meeting and the ark

a. [30:1–5] Ex 37:25–28.
b. [30:6] Ex 40:26.
c. [30:10] Lv 16:18.
d. [30:12] Nm 1:2–3; 26:2.
e. [30:13] Mt 17:24–27.
f. [30:16] Ex 38:25.
g. [30:18] Ex 38:8; 40:7, 30.
h. [30:19–21] Ex 40:31–32.
i. [30:25] Ex 37:29.
j. [30:25–29] Ex 40:9–11; Lv 8:10; Nm 7:1.

of the covenant, ²⁷the table and all its utensils, the menorah and its utensils, the altar of incense ²⁸and the altar for burnt offerings with all its utensils, and the basin with its stand. ²⁹When you have consecrated them, they shall be most sacred; whatever touches them shall be sacred. ³⁰Aaron and his sons you shall also anoint and consecrate as my priests.^k ³¹Tell the Israelites: As sacred anointing oil this shall belong to me throughout your generations. ³²It may not be used in any ordinary anointing of the body, nor may you make any other oil of a like mixture. It is sacred, and shall be treated as sacred by you. ³³Whoever prepares a perfume like this, or whoever puts any of this on an unauthorized person, shall be cut off from his people.

The Incense. ³⁴*l*The LORD told Moses: Take these aromatic substances: storax and onycha and galbanum, these and pure frankincense in equal parts; ³⁵and blend them into incense. This fragrant powder, expertly prepared, is to be salted and so kept pure and sacred. ³⁶Grind some of it into fine dust and put this before the covenant in the tent of meeting where I will meet you. This incense shall be treated as most sacred by you. ³⁷You may not make incense of a like mixture for yourselves; you must treat it as sacred to the LORD. ³⁸Whoever makes an incense like this for his own enjoyment of its fragrance, shall be cut off from his people.

CHAPTER 31

Choice of Artisans. ¹*a*The LORD said to Moses: ²See, I have singled out* Bezalel, son of Uri, son of Hur, of the tribe of Judah, ³and I have filled him with a divine spirit of skill and understanding and knowledge in every craft: ⁴in the production of embroidery,

in making things of gold, silver, or bronze, ⁵in cutting and mounting precious stones, in carving wood, and in every other craft. ⁶As his assistant I myself have appointed Oholiab, son of Ahisamach, of the tribe of Dan. I have also endowed all the experts with the necessary skill to make all the things I have commanded you: ⁷*b*the tent of meeting, the ark of the covenant with its cover, all the furnishings of the tent, ⁸the table with its utensils, the pure gold menorah with all its utensils, the altar of incense, ⁹the altar for burnt offerings with all its utensils, the basin with its stand, ¹⁰the service cloths,[†] the sacred vestments for Aaron the priest, the vestments for his sons in their ministry, ¹¹the anointing oil, and the fragrant incense for the sanctuary. According to all I have commanded you, so shall they do.

Sabbath Laws. ¹²*c*The LORD said to Moses: ¹³You must also tell the Israelites: Keep my sabbaths, for that is to be the sign between you and me throughout the generations, to show that it is I, the LORD, who make you holy. ¹⁴‡Therefore, you must keep the sabbath for it is holiness for you. Whoever desecrates it shall be put to death. If anyone does work on that day, that person must be cut off from the people. ¹⁵Six days there are for doing work, but the seventh day is the sabbath of complete rest, holy to the LORD. Anyone who does work on the sabbath day shall be put to death. ¹⁶So shall the Israelites observe the sabbath, keeping it throughout their generations as an everlasting covenant. ¹⁷Between me and the Israelites it is to be an everlasting sign; for in six days the LORD made the heavens and the earth, but on the seventh day he rested at his ease.

---

* [31:2] **Singled out**: lit., "called by name"; cf. 35:30.

k. [30:30] Ex 29:7; Lv 8:12.
l. [30:34–38] Ex 25:6; 37:29.

a. [31:1–6] Ex 35:30–35.

† [31:10] **The service cloths**: so the Greek. They were perhaps the colored cloths mentioned in Nm 4:4–15.
‡ [31:14–15] For the distinction between work proscribed on certain festivals and weekly Sabbaths, see note on Lv 23:3.

b. [31:7–11] Ex 35:10–19.
c. [31:12–17] Ex 20:8–11; 35:1–3.

¹⁸When the Lord had finished speaking to Moses on Mount Sinai, he gave him the two tablets of the covenant, the stone tablets inscribed by God's own finger.ᵈ

VII. ISRAEL'S APOSTASY AND GOD'S RENEWAL OF THE COVENANT

CHAPTER 32

The Golden Calf. ¹When the people saw that Moses was delayed in coming down from the mountain, they gathered around Aaron and said to him, "Come, make us a god who will go before us; as for that man Moses who brought us out of the land of Egypt, we do not know what has happened to him."ᵃ ²Aaron replied, "Take off the golden earrings that your wives, your sons, and your daughters are wearing, and bring them to me." ³So all the people took off their earrings and brought them to Aaron. ⁴He received their offering, and fashioning it with a tool, made a molten calf. Then they cried out, "These are your gods, Israel, who brought you* up from the land of Egypt."ᵇ ⁵On seeing this, Aaron built an altar in front of the calf and proclaimed, "Tomorrow is a feast of the Lord." ⁶Early the next day the people sacrificed burnt offerings and brought communion sacrifices. Then they sat down to eat and drink, and rose up to revel.ᶜ

⁷ᵈThen the Lord said to Moses: Go down at once because your people, whom you brought out of the land of Egypt, have acted corruptly. ⁸They have quickly turned aside from the way I commanded them, making for themselves a molten calf and bowing down to it, sacrificing to it and crying out, "These are your gods, Israel, who brought you up from the land of Egypt!" ⁹ᵉI have seen this people, how stiff-necked they are, continued the Lord to Moses. ¹⁰Let me alone, then, that my anger may burn against them to consume them. Then I will make of you a great nation.

¹¹†But Moses implored the Lord, his God, saying,ᶠ "Why, O Lord, should your anger burn against your people, whom you brought out of the land of Egypt with great power and with a strong hand? ¹²Why should the Egyptians say, 'With evil intent he brought them out, that he might kill them in the mountains and wipe them off the face of the earth'? Turn from your burning wrath; change your mind about punishing your people. ¹³Remember your servants Abraham, Isaac, and Israel, and how you swore to them by your own self, saying,ᵍ 'I will make your descendants as numerous as the stars in the sky; and all this land that I promised, I will give your descendants as their perpetual heritage.'" ¹⁴So the Lord changed his mind about the punishment he had threatened to inflict on his people.

¹⁵Moses then turned and came down the mountain with the two tablets of the covenant in his hands,ʰ tablets that were written on both sides, front and back. ¹⁶The tablets were made by God; the writing was the writing of God, engraved on the tablets.ⁱ ¹⁷Now, when Joshua heard the noise of the people

---

* [32:4–5] **Who brought you . . . a feast of the Lord:** it seems that the golden calf was intended as an image, not of another god, but of the Lord, whose strength was symbolized by the strength of a young bull. The Israelites, however, had been forbidden to represent the Lord under any visible form. Cf. 20:4. In the tenth century Jeroboam made golden calves for the shrines at Bethel and Dan, presumably to function as thrones for the Lord as the ark did in Jerusalem (see 1 Kgs 12:27–30).

d. [31:18] Ex 24:12; 32:15–16; Dt 5:22.

a. [32:1] Ex 32:23; Acts 7:40.
b. [32:4] Ex 32:8; 1 Kgs 12:28.
c. [32:6] 1 Cor 10:7.
d. [32:7–8] Dt 9:12, 16.

† [32:11–13] Moses uses three arguments to persuade the Lord to remain faithful to the Sinai covenant even though the people have broken it: (1) they are God's own people, redeemed with God's great power; (2) God's reputation will suffer if they are destroyed; (3) the covenant with Abraham still stands. The Lord's change of mind is a testimony to Israel's belief in the power of intercessory prayer.

e. [32:9–10] Dt 9:13.
f. [32:11–12] Nm 14:13–19; Dt 9:28–29; Ps 106:23.
g. [32:13] Gn 22:16–17.
h. [32:15] Dt 9:15.
i. [32:16] Ex 31:18.

shouting, he said to Moses, "That sounds like a battle in the camp." **18**But Moses answered,

> "It is not the noise of victory,
> it is not the noise of defeat;
> the sound I hear is singing."

19As he drew near the camp, he saw the calf and the dancing. Then Moses' anger burned, and he threw the tablets down and broke them on the base of the mountain.*j* **20**Taking the calf they had made, he burned it in the fire and then ground it down to powder, which he scattered on the water* and made the Israelites drink.*k*

21†Moses asked Aaron, "What did this people do to you that you should lead them into a grave sin?" **22**Aaron replied, "Do not let my lord be angry. You know how the people are prone to evil. **23**They said to me, 'Make us a god to go before us; as for this man Moses who brought us out of the land of Egypt, we do not know what has happened to him.' **24**So I told them, 'Whoever is wearing gold, take it off.' They gave it to me, and I threw it into the fire, and this calf came out."

25Moses saw that the people were running wild because Aaron had lost control—to the secret delight of their foes. **26**Moses stood at the gate of the camp and shouted, "Whoever is for the LORD, come to me!" All the Levites*l* then rallied to him, **27**and he told them, "Thus says the LORD, the God of Israel: Each of you put your sword on your hip! Go back and forth through the camp, from gate to gate, and kill your brothers, your friends, your neighbors!" **28**The Levites did as Moses had commanded, and that day about three thousand of the people fell. **29**Then Moses said, "Today you

are installed as priests‡ for the LORD, for you went against your own sons and brothers, to bring a blessing upon yourselves this day."

The Atonement. **30**On the next day Moses said to the people,*m* "You have committed a grave sin. Now I will go up to the LORD; perhaps I may be able to make atonement for your sin." **31**So Moses returned to the LORD and said, "Ah, this people has committed a grave sin in making a god of gold for themselves! **32**Now if you would only forgive their sin! But if you will not, then blot me out of the book that you have written."§ **33**The LORD answered Moses: Only the one who has sinned against me will I blot out of my book. **34**Now, go and lead the people where I have told you. See, my angel will go before you. When it is time for me to punish, I will punish them for their sin.

35Thus the LORD struck the people for making the calf, the one that Aaron made.

CHAPTER 33

1The LORD spoke to Moses: Go! You and the people whom you have brought up from the land of Egypt are to go up from here to the land about which I swore to Abraham, Isaac, and Jacob: I will give it to your descendants.*a* **2**Driving out the Canaanites, Amorites, Hittites, Perizzites, Hivites and Jebusites, I will send an angel before you*b* **3**to a land flowing with milk and honey. But I myself will not go up in your company, because you are a stiff-necked people; otherwise I might consume you on the way. **4**When the people heard this painful

---

* [32:20] **The water:** according to Dt 9:21, this was the stream that flowed down Mount Sinai.

† [32:21–24] Aaron attempts to persuade Moses not to act in anger, just as Moses persuaded the Lord. He also shifts the blame from himself to the people.

j. [32:19] Dt 9:16–17.
k. [32:20] Dt 9:21.
l. [32:26–29] Dt 33:8–9.

‡ [32:29] **Installed as priests:** lit., "fill your hands," a term for the ordination of priests (see 28:41; 29:9, 29, 33, 35; Nm 3:3). Because of their zeal for the true worship of the Lord, the Levites were chosen to be special ministers of the ritual service.

§ [32:32] **The book that you have written:** a symbolic reference to the list of God's faithful people.

m. [32:30–34] Dt 9:18–19.

a. [33:1] Gn 12:7.
b. [33:2] Ex 23:23.

news, they mourned, and no one wore any ornaments.

⁵The Lᴏʀᴅ spoke to Moses: Speak to the Israelites: You are a stiff-necked people. Were I to go up in your company even for a moment, I would destroy you. Now off with your ornaments! Let me think what to do with you. ⁶So, from Mount Horeb onward, the Israelites stripped off their ornaments.

Moses' Intimacy with God. ⁷Moses used to pitch a tent*ᶜ* outside the camp at some distance. It was called the tent of meeting. Anyone who wished to consult the Lᴏʀᴅ would go to the tent of meeting outside the camp. ⁸Whenever Moses went out to the tent, the people would all rise and stand at the entrance of their own tents, watching Moses until he entered the tent. ⁹As Moses entered the tent, the column of cloud would come down and stand at its entrance while the Lᴏʀᴅ spoke with Moses. ¹⁰On seeing the column of cloud stand at the entrance of the tent, all the people would rise and bow down at the entrance of their own tents. ¹¹The Lᴏʀᴅ used to speak to Moses face to face,*ᵈ* as a person speaks to a friend. Moses would then return to the camp, but his young assistant, Joshua, son of Nun, never left the tent. ¹²Moses said to the Lᴏʀᴅ, "See, you are telling me: Lead this people.*ᵉ* But you have not let me know whom you will send with me. Yet you have said: You are my intimate friend;* You have found favor with me. ¹³Now, if I have found favor with you, please let me know your ways so that, in knowing you, I may continue to find favor with you. See, this nation is indeed your own people. ¹⁴The Lᴏʀᴅ answered: I myself† will go along, to give you rest.

¹⁵Moses replied, "If you are not going yourself, do not make us go up from here. ¹⁶For how can it be known that I and your people have found favor with you, except by your going with us? Then we, your people and I, will be singled out from every other people on the surface of the earth." ¹⁷The Lᴏʀᴅ said to Moses: This request, too, which you have made, I will carry out, because you have found favor with me and you are my intimate friend.

¹⁸Then Moses said, "Please let me see your glory!" ¹⁹The Lᴏʀᴅ answered: I will make all my goodness pass before you, and I will proclaim my name, "Lᴏʀᴅ," before you; I who show favor to whom I will, I who grant mercy to whom I will.*ᶠ* ²⁰But you cannot see my face,*ᵍ* for no one can see me and live.‡ ²¹Here, continued the Lᴏʀᴅ, is a place near me where you shall station yourself on the rock. ²²When my glory passes I will set you in the cleft of the rock and will cover you with my hand until I have passed by. ²³Then I will remove my hand, so that you may see my back; but my face may not be seen.

CHAPTER 34

Renewal of the Tablets. ¹The Lᴏʀᴅ said to Moses: "Cut two stone tablets like the former,*ᵃ* that I may write on them the words§ which were on the former tablets that you broke. ²Get ready for tomorrow morning, when you are to go up Mount Sinai and there present yourself to me on the top of the mountain. ³No one shall come up with you, and let no one even be seen on any part of the mountain;*ᵇ* even the sheep and the cattle are not to graze in

---

‡ [33:20] **No one can see me and live**: reflecting the tradition that to see God meant instant death. This is contradicted by the statements that Hagar (Gn 16:13), Jacob (Gn 32:31), and Manoah and his wife (Jgs 13:22) all "see God" and yet live (see also Ex 24:10–11).

§ [34:1] **Words**: a common term for commandments, especially the Decalogue (see v. 28). In v. 27 "words" connotes the commands given in vv. 11–26.

f. [33:19] Rom 9:15.
g. [33:20] Jn 1:18; 1 Tm 6:16.

a. [34:1] Dt 10:1–2.
b. [34:3] Ex 19:12–13, 21.

---

* [33:12] **Intimate friend**: lit., "know by name." The root word meaning "know" or "make known" appears four times in vv. 12–13.

† [33:14] **I myself**: lit., "my face," that is, "my presence." The making of the calf (32:1–4) is an attempt to control the Lord's presence. In response the Lord refuses to accompany the people (33:3) until Moses persuades him.

c. [33:7] Ex 29:42–43.
d. [33:11] Nm 12:8; Dt 34:10; Sir 45:4–5.
e. [33:12] Ex 32:34.

veil; ¹³the table, with its poles and all its utensils, and the showbread; ¹⁴the menorah, with its utensils, the lamps, and the oil for the light; ¹⁵the altar of incense, with its poles; the anointing oil, and the fragrant incense; the entrance curtain for the entrance of the tabernacle; ¹⁶the altar for burnt offerings, with its bronze grating, its poles, and all its utensils; the basin, with its stand; ¹⁷the hangings of the court, with their columns and pedestals; the curtain for the gate of the court; ¹⁸the tent pegs for the tabernacle and for the court, with their ropes; ¹⁹the service cloths for use in the sanctuary; the sacred vestments for Aaron, the priest, and the vestments for his sons in their ministry."

The Contribution. ²⁰When the whole Israelite community left Moses' presence, ²¹all, as their hearts moved them and their spirit prompted, brought a contribution to the LORD for the work of the tent of meeting, for all its services, and for the sacred vestments. ²²Both the men and the women, all as their heart prompted them, brought brooches, earrings, rings, necklaces, and various other gold articles.ᵈ Everyone who could presented an offering of gold to the LORD. ²³Everyone who happened to have violet, purple, or scarlet yarn, fine linen or goat hair, rams' skins dyed red or tahash skins, brought them. ²⁴Whoever could make a contribution of silver or bronze offered it to the LORD; and everyone who happened to have acacia wood for any part of the work, brought it. ²⁵All the women who were expert spinners brought hand-spun violet, purple, and scarlet yarn and fine linen thread. ²⁶All the women, as their hearts and skills moved them, spun goat hair. ²⁷The tribal leaders brought onyx stones and other gems for mounting on the ephod and on the breastpiece; ²⁸as well as spices, and oil for the light, anointing oil, and fragrant incense. ²⁹Every Israelite man and woman brought to the

LORD such voluntary offerings as they thought best, for the various kinds of work which the LORD, through Moses, had commanded to be done.

The Artisans. ³⁰Moses said to the Israelites:ᵉ "See, the LORD has singled out Bezalel, son of Uri, son of Hur, of the tribe of Judah, ³¹and has filled him with a divine spirit of skill and understanding and knowledge in every craft: ³²in the production of embroidery, in making things of gold, silver, or bronze, ³³in cutting and mounting precious stones, in carving wood, and in every other craft. ³⁴He has also given both him and Oholiab, son of Ahisamach, of the tribe of Dan, the ability to teach others. ³⁵He has endowed them with skill to execute all types of work: engraving, embroidering, the making of variegated cloth of violet, purple, and scarlet yarn and fine linen thread, weaving, and all other arts and crafts.

CHAPTER 36

¹"Bezalel, therefore, will set to work with Oholiab and with all the artisans whom the LORD has endowed with skill and understanding in knowing how to do all the work for the service of the sanctuary, just as the LORD has commanded."ᵃ

²Moses then called Bezalel and Oholiab and all the other artisans whom the LORD had endowed with skill, men whose hearts moved them to come and do the work. ³They received from Moses all the contributions which the Israelites had brought for the work to be done for the sanctuary service. Still, morning after morning the people continued to bring their voluntary offerings to Moses. ⁴Thereupon all the artisans who were doing the work for the sanctuary came from the work each was doing, ⁵and told Moses, "The people are bringing much more than is needed to carry out the work which

---

d. [35:22–28] Ex 25:3–7.

e. [35:30–35] Ex 31:1–6.

a. [36:1–2] Ex 31:1, 6.

the LORD has commanded us to do." [6]Moses, therefore, ordered a proclamation to be made throughout the camp: "Let neither man nor woman make any more contributions for the sanctuary." So the people stopped bringing their offerings; [7]there was already enough at hand, and more than enough, to complete the work to be done.

The Tent Cloth and Coverings. [8][b]The various artisans who were doing the work made the tabernacle with its ten sheets woven of fine linen twined, having cherubim embroidered on them with violet, purple, and scarlet yarn. [9]The length of each sheet was twenty-eight cubits, and the width four cubits; all the sheets were the same size. [10]Five of the sheets were joined together, edge to edge; and the other five sheets likewise, edge to edge. [11]Loops of violet yarn were made along the edge of the end sheet in the first set, and the same along the edge of the end sheet in the second set. [12]Fifty loops were thus put on one inner sheet, and fifty loops on the inner sheet in the other set, with the loops directly opposite each other. [13]Then fifty clasps of gold were made, with which the sheets were joined so that the tabernacle formed one whole.

[14]Sheets of goat hair were also woven as a tent over the tabernacle. Eleven such sheets were made. [15]The length of each sheet was thirty cubits and the width four cubits; all eleven sheets were the same size. [16]Five of these sheets were joined into one set, and the other six sheets into another set. [17]Fifty loops were made along the edge of the end sheet in one set, and fifty loops along the edge of the corresponding sheet in the other set. [18]Fifty bronze clasps were made with which the tent was joined so that it formed one whole. [19]A covering for the tent was made of rams' skins dyed red and, above that, a covering of tahash skins.

The Framework. [20][c]Frames were made for the tabernacle, acacia-wood uprights. [21]The length of each frame was ten cubits, and the width one and a half cubits. [22]Each frame had two arms, fastening them one to another. In this way all the frames of the tabernacle were made. [23]The frames for the tabernacle were made as follows: twenty frames on the south side, [24]with forty silver pedestals under the twenty frames, two pedestals under each frame for its two arms; [25]twenty frames on the other side of the tabernacle, the north side, [26]with their forty silver pedestals, two pedestals under each frame. [27]At the rear of the tabernacle, to the west, six frames were made, [28]and two frames were made for the corners of the tabernacle, at its rear. [29]These were double at the bottom, and likewise double at the top, to the first ring. That is how both corner frames were made. [30]Thus, there were eight frames, with their sixteen silver pedestals, two pedestals under each frame. [31]Bars of acacia wood were also made, five for the frames on one side of the tabernacle, [32]five for those on the other side, and five for those at the rear, to the west. [33]The center bar, at the middle of the frames, was made to reach across from end to end. [34]The frames were plated with gold, and gold rings were made on them as holders for the bars, which were also plated with gold.

The Veil. [35][d]The veil was made of violet, purple, and scarlet yarn, and of fine linen twined, with cherubim embroidered on it. [36]Four gold-plated columns of acacia wood, with gold hooks, were made for it, and four silver pedestals were cast for them.

[37]The curtain for the entrance of the tent was made of violet, purple, and scarlet yarn, and of fine linen twined, woven in a variegated manner. [38]Its five columns, with their hooks as well as their capitals and bands, were

---

b. [36:8–19] Ex 26:1–14.

c. [36:20–34] Ex 26:15–29.
d. [36:35–38] Ex 26:31–37.

plated with gold; their five pedestals were of bronze.

CHAPTER 37

The Ark. [1]Bezalel made the ark of acacia wood, two and a half cubits long, one and a half cubits wide, and one and a half cubits high. [2]The inside and outside were plated with gold, and a molding of gold was put around it. [3]Four gold rings were cast for its four supports, two rings on one side and two on the opposite side. [4]Poles of acacia wood were made and plated with gold; [5]these poles were put through the rings on the sides of the ark, for carrying it.

[6]The cover was made of pure gold, two and a half cubits long and one and a half cubits wide. [7]Two cherubim of beaten gold were made for the two ends of the cover; [8]one cherub was at one end, the other at the other end, made of one piece with the cover, at each end. [9]The cherubim had their wings spread out above, sheltering the cover. They faced each other, with their faces looking toward the cover.[a]

The Table. [10][b]The table was made of acacia wood, two cubits long, a cubit wide, and a cubit and a half high. [11]It was plated with pure gold, and a molding of gold was put around it. [12]A frame a handbreadth high was also put around it, with a molding of gold around the frame. [13]Four rings of gold were cast for it and fastened at the four corners, one at each leg. [14]The rings were alongside the frame as holders for the poles to carry the table. [15]These poles for carrying the table were made of acacia wood and plated with gold. [16]The vessels that were set on the table, its plates and cups, as well as its pitchers and bowls for pouring libations, were made of pure gold.

The Menorah. [17][c]The menorah was made of pure beaten gold—its shaft and branches—with its cups and knobs and petals springing directly from it. [18]Six branches extended from its sides, three branches on one side and three on the other. [19]On one branch there were three cups, shaped like almond blossoms, each with its knob and petals; on the opposite branch there were three cups, shaped like almond blossoms, each with its knob and petals; and so for the six branches that extended from the menorah. [20]On the menorah there were four cups, shaped like almond blossoms, with their knobs and petals. [21]The six branches that went out from the menorah had a knob under each pair. [22]The knobs and branches so sprang from it that the whole formed but a single piece of pure beaten gold. [23]Its seven lamps, as well as its trimming shears and trays, were made of pure gold. [24]A talent of pure gold was used for the menorah and its various utensils.

The Altar of Incense. [25][d]The altar of incense was made of acacia wood, on a square, a cubit long, a cubit wide, and two cubits high, having horns that sprang directly from it. [26]Its grate on top, its walls on all four sides, and its horns were plated with pure gold; and a gold molding was put around it. [27]Underneath the molding gold rings were placed, two on one side and two on the opposite side, as holders for the poles used in carrying it. [28]The poles, too, were made of acacia wood and plated with gold.

[29]The sacred anointing oil and the fragrant incense were prepared in their pure form by a perfumer.[e]

CHAPTER 38

The Altar for Burnt Offerings. [1]The altar for burnt offerings[a] was made of acacia wood, on a square, five cubits long and five cubits wide; its height was three cubits. [2]At the four corners

a. [37:1–9] Ex 25:10–22.
b. [37:10–16] Ex 25:23–30.
c. [37:17–24] Ex 25:31–39.

d. [37:25–28] Ex 30:1–5.
e. [37:29] Ex 30:23–25, 34–36.

a. [38:1–7] Ex 27:1–8; 2 Chr 1:5.

horns were made that sprang directly from the altar. It was then plated with bronze. ³All the utensils of the altar, the pots, shovels, basins, forks and fire pans, were likewise made of bronze. ⁴A grating, a bronze network, was made for the altar and placed around it, on the ground, half as high as the altar itself. ⁵Four rings were cast for the four corners of the bronze grating, as holders for the poles, ⁶which were made of acacia wood and plated with bronze. ⁷The poles were put through the rings on the sides of the altar for carrying it. The altar was made in the form of a hollow box.

⁸The bronze basin,^b with its bronze stand, was made from the mirrors of the women who served* at the entrance of the tent of meeting.

The Court of the Tabernacle. ⁹^cThe court was made as follows. On the south side the hangings of the court were of fine linen twined, a hundred cubits long, ¹⁰with twenty columns and twenty pedestals of bronze, the hooks and bands of the columns being of silver. ¹¹On the north side there were similar hangings, a hundred cubits long, with twenty columns and twenty pedestals of bronze; the hooks and bands of the columns were of silver. ¹²On the west side there were hangings, fifty cubits long, with ten columns and ten pedestals; the hooks and bands of the columns were of silver. ¹³On the east side the court was fifty cubits. ¹⁴On one side there were hangings to the extent of fifteen cubits, with three columns and three pedestals; ¹⁵on the other side, beyond the gate of the court, there were likewise hangings to the extent of fifteen cubits, with three columns and three pedestals. ¹⁶The hangings on all sides of the court were woven of fine linen twined. ¹⁷The pedestals of the columns were of bronze, while the hooks and bands of

the columns were of silver; the capitals were silver-plated, and all the columns of the court were banded with silver.

¹⁸At the gate of the court there was a variegated curtain, woven of violet, purple, and scarlet yarn and of fine linen twined, twenty cubits long and five cubits wide, in keeping with the hangings of the court. ¹⁹There were four columns and four pedestals of bronze for it, while their hooks were of silver, and their capitals and their bands silver-plated. ²⁰All the tent pegs for the tabernacle and for the court around it were of bronze.

Amount of Metal Used. ²¹The following is an account of the various amounts used on the tabernacle, the tabernacle of the covenant, drawn up at the command of Moses by the Levites under the direction of Ithamar, son of Aaron the priest. ²²However, it was Bezalel, son of Uri,^d son of Hur, of the tribe of Judah, who made all that the Lord commanded Moses, ²³and he was assisted by Oholiab, son of Ahisamach, of the tribe of Dan, who was an engraver, an embroiderer, and a weaver of variegated cloth of violet, purple, and scarlet yarn and of fine linen.

²⁴All the gold used in the entire construction of the sanctuary, having previously been given as an offering, amounted to twenty-nine talents and seven hundred and thirty shekels, according to the standard of the sanctuary shekel. ²⁵The silver of those of the community who were enrolled was one hundred talents and one thousand seven hundred and seventy-five shekels, according to the standard of the sanctuary shekel; ²⁶one bekah apiece, that is, a half-shekel, according to the standard of the sanctuary shekel, was received from everyone who was enrolled, of twenty years or more, namely, six hundred and three thousand five hundred and fifty men.^e ²⁷One hundred talents of silver were

* [38:8] The reflecting surface of ancient mirrors was usually of polished bronze. **The women who served:** cf. 1 Sm 2:22.

b. [38:8] Ex 30:18–21.
c. [38:9–20] Ex 27:9–19.

d. [38:22–23] Ex 31:2, 6; 35:30, 34; 36:1.
e. [38:26] Nm 1:46.

used for casting the pedestals of the sanctuary and the pedestals of the veil, one talent for each pedestal, or one hundred talents for the one hundred pedestals. **28**The remaining one thousand seven hundred and seventy-five shekels were used for making the hooks on the columns, for plating the capitals, and for banding them with silver. **29**The bronze, given as an offering, amounted to seventy talents and two thousand four hundred shekels. **30**With this were made the pedestals at the entrance of the tent of meeting, the bronze altar with its bronze gratings, and all the utensils of the altar, **31**the pedestals around the court, the pedestals at the gate of the court, and all the tent pegs for the tabernacle and for the court around it.

CHAPTER 39

The Priestly Vestments. 1 With violet, purple, and scarlet yarn were woven the service cloths for use in the sanctuary, as well as the sacred vestments**a** for Aaron, as the Lord had commanded Moses.

2bThe ephod was woven of gold thread and of violet, purple, and scarlet yarn and of fine linen twined. **3**Gold was first hammered into gold leaf and then cut up into threads, which were woven with the violet, purple, and scarlet yarn into an embroidered pattern on the fine linen. **4**Shoulder straps were made for it and joined to its two upper ends. **5**The embroidered belt on the ephod extended out from it, and like it, was made of gold thread, of violet, purple, and scarlet yarn, and of fine linen twined, as the Lord had commanded Moses. **6**The onyx stones were prepared and mounted in gold filigree work; they were engraved like seal engravings with the names of the sons of Israel. **7**These stones were set on the shoulder straps of the ephod as memorial stones of the sons of Israel, just as the Lord had commanded Moses.

8cThe breastpiece was embroidered like the ephod, with gold thread and violet, purple, and scarlet yarn on cloth of fine linen twined. **9**It was square and folded double, a span high and a span wide in its folded form. **10**Four rows of precious stones were mounted on it: in the first row a carnelian, a topaz, and an emerald; **11**in the second row, a garnet, a sapphire, and a beryl; **12**in the third row a jacinth, an agate, and an amethyst; **13**in the fourth row a chrysolite, an onyx, and a jasper. They were mounted in gold filigree work. **14**These stones were twelve, to match the names of the sons of Israel, and each stone was engraved like a seal with the name of one of the twelve tribes.

15d Chains of pure gold, twisted like cords, were made for the breastpiece, **16**together with two gold filigree rosettes and two gold rings. The two rings were fastened to the two upper ends of the breastpiece. **17**The two gold chains were then fastened to the two rings at the ends of the breastpiece. **18**The other two ends of the two chains were fastened in front to the two filigree rosettes, which were attached to the shoulder straps of the ephod. **19**Two other gold rings were made and put on the two lower ends of the breastpiece, on the edge facing the ephod. **20**Two more gold rings were made and fastened to the bottom of the two shoulder straps next to where they joined the ephod in front, just above its embroidered belt. **21**Violet ribbons bound the rings of the breastpiece to the rings of the ephod, so that the breastpiece stayed right above the embroidered belt of the ephod and did not swing loose from it. All this was just as the Lord had commanded Moses.

Other Vestments. 22 The robe of the ephod was woven entirely of violet yarn, **23**with an opening in its center like the opening of a shirt, with selvage around the opening to keep it

---

a. [39:1] Ex 31:10.
b. [39:2–10] Ex 28:6–12.
c. [39:8–14] Ex 28:15–21.
d. [39:15–21] Ex 28:31–35.

from being torn. ²⁴At the hem of the robe pomegranates were made of violet, purple, and scarlet yarn and of fine linen twined; ²⁵bells of pure gold were also made and put between the pomegranates all around the hem of the robe: ²⁶a bell, a pomegranate, a bell, a pomegranate, all around the hem of the robe which was to be worn in performing the ministry—all this, just as the LORD had commanded Moses.

²⁷For Aaron and his sons there were also woven tunics of fine linen;^e ²⁸the turban of fine linen; the ornate skullcaps of fine linen; linen pants of fine linen twined; ²⁹and sashes of variegated work made of fine linen twined and of violet, purple, and scarlet yarn, as the LORD had commanded Moses. ^{30f}The plate of the sacred diadem was made of pure gold and inscribed, as on a seal engraving: "Sacred to the LORD." ³¹It was tied over the turban with a violet ribbon, as the LORD had commanded Moses.

Presentation of the Work to Moses. ³²Thus the entire work of the tabernacle of the tent of meeting was completed. The Israelites did the work just as the LORD had commanded Moses; so it was done. ³³They then brought to Moses the tabernacle, the tent with all its furnishings, the clasps, the frames, the bars, the columns, the pedestals, ³⁴the covering of rams' skins dyed red, the covering of tahash skins, the curtain veil; ³⁵the ark of the covenant with its poles, the cover, ³⁶the table with all its utensils and the showbread, ³⁷the pure gold menorah with its lamps set up on it and with all its utensils, the oil for the light, ³⁸the golden altar, the anointing oil, the fragrant incense; the curtain for the entrance of the tent, ³⁹the altar of bronze with its bronze grating, its poles and all its utensils, the basin with its stand, ⁴⁰the hangings of the court with their columns and pedestals, the curtain for the gate of the court with its ropes and tent

pegs, all the equipment for the service of the tabernacle of the tent of meeting; ⁴¹the service cloths for use in the sanctuary, the sacred vestments for Aaron the priest, and the vestments to be worn by his sons in their ministry. ⁴²Just as the LORD had commanded Moses, so the Israelites had carried out all the work. ⁴³So when Moses saw that all the work was done just as the LORD had commanded, he blessed them.

CHAPTER 40

Setting up the Tabernacle. ¹Then the LORD said to Moses: ^{2a}On the first day of the first month[*] you shall set up the tabernacle of the tent of meeting.^b ³Put the ark of the covenant in it, and screen off the ark with the veil.^c ⁴Bring in the table and set it. Then bring in the menorah and set up the lamps on it. ⁵Put the golden altar of incense in front of the ark of the covenant, and hang the curtain at the entrance of the tabernacle. ⁶Put the altar for burnt offerings in front of the entrance of the tabernacle of the tent of meeting. ⁷Place the basin between the tent of meeting and the altar, and put water in it. ⁸Set up the court round about, and put the curtain at the gate of the court.

^{9d}Take the anointing oil and anoint the tabernacle and everything in it, consecrating it and all its furnishings, so that it will be sacred. ¹⁰Anoint the altar for burnt offerings and all its utensils, consecrating it, so that it will be most sacred. ¹¹Likewise, anoint the basin with its stand, and thus consecrate it.

^{12e}Then bring Aaron and his sons to the entrance of the tent of meeting, and there wash them with water. ¹³Clothe Aaron with the sacred vestments and anoint him, thus consecrating him as my priest. ¹⁴Bring forward his sons

* [40:2] **On the first day of the first month:** almost a year after the departure of the Israelites from Egypt. Cf. v. 17.

a. [40:2–8] Ex 40:16–33.
b. [40:2] Ex 26:30.
c. [40:3–8] Ex 26:33–37.
d. [40:9–11] Ex 30:26–29.
e. [40:12–15] Ex 28:41; 29:4–9; Lv 8:1–13.

e. [39:27–29] Ex 28:39–42.
f. [39:30–31] Ex 28:36–37.

also, and clothe them with the tunics. ¹⁵As you have anointed their father, anoint them also as my priests. Thus, by being anointed, shall they receive a perpetual priesthood throughout all future generations.

¹⁶Moses did just as the LORD had commanded him. ¹⁷On the first day of the first month of the second year the tabernacle was set up. ¹⁸It was Moses who set up the tabernacle. He placed its pedestals, set up its frames, put in its bars, and set up its columns. ¹⁹He spread the tent over the tabernacle and put the covering on top of the tent, as the LORD had commanded him. ^{20f}He took the covenant and put it in the ark; he placed poles alongside the ark and set the cover upon it. ²¹He brought the ark into the tabernacle and hung the curtain veil, thus screening off the ark of the covenant, as the LORD had commanded him. ²²He put the table in the tent of meeting, on the north side of the tabernacle, outside the veil, ²³and arranged the bread on it before the LORD, as the LORD had commanded him.^g ²⁴He placed the menorah in the tent of meeting, opposite the table, on the south side of the tabernacle, ²⁵and he set up the lamps before the LORD, as the LORD had commanded him. ²⁶He placed the golden altar in the tent of meeting, in front of the veil, ²⁷and on it he burned fragrant incense, as the LORD had commanded him. ²⁸He hung the curtain at the entrance of the tabernacle. ²⁹He put the altar for burnt offerings in front of the entrance of the tabernacle of the tent of meeting, and sacrificed burnt offerings and grain offerings on it, as the LORD had commanded him. ^{30h}He placed the basin between the tent of meeting and the altar, and put water in it for washing. ³¹Moses and Aaron and his sons used to wash their hands and feet there, ³²for they washed themselves whenever they went into the tent of meeting or approached the altar, as the LORD had commanded Moses. ³³Finally, he set up the court around the tabernacle and the altar and hung the curtain at the gate of the court.

Thus Moses finished all the work.

God's Presence in the Tabernacle. ³⁴ⁱThen the cloud covered the tent of meeting, and the glory of the LORD filled the tabernacle. ³⁵Moses could not enter the tent of meeting, because the cloud settled down upon it and the glory of the LORD filled the tabernacle. ³⁶Whenever the cloud rose from the tabernacle, the Israelites would set out on their journey. ³⁷But if the cloud did not lift, they would not go forward; only when it lifted did they go forward. ³⁸The cloud of the LORD was over the tabernacle by day, and fire in the cloud at night, in the sight of the whole house of Israel in all the stages of their journey.

EX

f. [40:20–29] Ex 25:16, 21; 26:33–37.
g. [40:23] Ex 25:30.
h. [40:30–32] Ex 30:18–21.
i. [40:34–38] Nm 9:15–22.

THE BOOK OF LEVITICUS

Introduction

The name "Leviticus" was given to the third book of the Pentateuch by the ancient Greek translators because a good part of this book deals with concerns of the priests, who are of the tribe of Levi.

The book mainly treats cultic matters (i.e., sacrifices and offerings, purity and holiness, the priesthood, the operation of the sanctuary, and feast days) but is also interested in various behavioral, ethical, and economic issues (e.g., sexual practices, idolatrous worship, treatment of others, the sale of land, slavery). The goal of the laws is not merely legislative. For the most part they cohere as a system and attempt to inculcate a way of life in the book's hearers and readers. In addition to these concerns, Leviticus, comprising as it does the center of the Pentateuch, carries forward the narrative of Exodus (cf. chaps. 1, 8–9, 10, 16, 24).

The book is part of the Priestly tradition (P) of the Pentateuch, to which belong various narratives and legal passages (e.g., Gn 1:1–2:4; 9:1–17; 17:1–27; Ex 12:1–20, 40–50; 25:1–31:18; 35:1–40:38; Nm 1:1–10:28; 15:1–14; 17:1–19:22; 25:6–31:54). Within the Priestly material itself there are signs of variant traditions and development.

The main divisions of Leviticus are:

I. Ritual of Sacrifices (1:1–7:38)
  A. Instructions for the Israelites (1:1–5:26)
  B. Instructions for the Priests (6:1–7:38)
II. Ceremony of Ordination (8:1–10:20)
III. Laws Regarding Ritual Purity (11:1–16:34)
IV. Holiness Laws (17:1–26:46)
V. Redemption of Offerings (27:1–34) ✠

I. RITUAL OF SACRIFICES

A. INSTRUCTIONS FOR THE ISRAELITES

CHAPTER 1

Burnt Offerings. [1]The Lord called Moses, and spoke to him from the tent of meeting:[a] [2]Speak to the Israelites and tell them: When any one of you* brings an offering of livestock to the Lord, you shall bring your offering from the herd or from the flock.[b]

[3][t][c]If a person's offering is a burnt offering[‡] from the herd, the offering must be a male without blemish.[d] The individual shall bring it to the entrance of the tent of meeting to find favor with the Lord, [4]and shall lay a hand[§] on the head[e] of the burnt offering, so that it may be acceptable[f] to make atonement[g] for the one who offers it. [5]The bull shall then be slaughtered[¶] before the Lord, and Aaron's sons, the priests, shall offer its blood by splashing it on all the sides of the altar which is at the entrance of the tent of meeting.[h] [6]Then the burnt offering shall be flayed and cut into pieces. [7]After Aaron's sons, the priests, have put burning embers on the altar and laid wood on them, [8]they shall lay the pieces of meat, together with the head and the suet, on top of the wood and the embers on the altar; [9]but the inner organs and the shanks shall be washed with water. The priest shall then burn all of it on the altar as a burnt offering, a sweet-smelling oblation to the Lord.[i]

[10]If a person's burnt offering is from the flock, that is, a sheep or a goat, the offering must be a male without blemish. [11]It shall be slaughtered on the north side of the altar before the Lord, and Aaron's sons, the priests, shall splash its blood on all the sides of the altar. [12]When it has been cut into pieces, the priest shall lay these, together with the head and suet, on top of the wood and the embers on the altar; [13]but the inner organs and the shanks shall be washed with water. The priest shall then offer all of it, burning it on the altar. It is a burnt offering, a sweet-smelling oblation to the Lord.

[14]If a person offers a bird as a burnt offering to the Lord, the offering brought must be a turtledove or a pigeon.[j] [15]Having brought it to the altar, the priest shall wring its head off and burn it on the altar. The blood shall be drained out against the side of the altar.[k] [16]He shall remove its crissum** by means of its feathers and throw it on the ash heap at the east side of the altar. [17]Then, having torn the bird open by its wings without separating the halves, the priest shall burn it on the altar, on the wood and the

---

* [1:2] **Any one of you**: women as well as men bring sacrifices (see 12:6–8; 15:28–30) and are explicitly obligated in other ritual matters (e.g., 13:29, 38; Nm 5:6; 6:2; Lk 2:24). Thus, though the Hebrew formulates sacrificial and other law with male reference, the translation reflects the inclusion of women in ritual requirements. **From the herd or from the flock**: the only animals which could be used as sacrificial victims were domestic animals either of the bovine class (bulls, cows and calves) or the ovine class (sheep and lambs, goats and kids). Excluded, therefore, were not only all wild animals, but also such "unclean" domestic animals as the camel and the donkey (cf. 11:1–47; 27:26–27).

† [1:3–5] **Entrance of the tent of meeting . . . before the Lord**: probably the forecourt from the entrance of the court to the entrance of the tent (cf. Ex 27). Thus the altar in front of the tent was entirely accessible to the laity.

‡ [1:3] The burnt offering is used for regular daily (6:1–6) offerings, public festivals (Nm 28–29), purification rituals (Lv 12:6–8; 14:19–20; 15:15, 30), and individuals' vows and voluntary offerings (22:18–20).

§ [1:4] **Lay a hand**: the imposition of a single hand for the sacrifices in chaps. 1–5 may be a means of designating the animal as belonging to the offerer. See note on 16:21. **Atonement**: see note on 16:6.

¶ [1:5] **Shall then be slaughtered**: lit., "he shall slaughter the bull." Slaughtering is not something the offerer must do (as opposed to, for example, hand placement [v. 4] or the presentation of sacrificial portions as an elevated offering [7:29–34]). Thus the verb is construed impersonally here.

---

a. [1:1] Ex 40.
b. [1:2] Lv 1:3, 10; 3:1, 6, 12.
c. [1:3] Lv 6:1–6; 22:18–19;
d. [1:3] Lv 22:17–25; Ex 12:5.
e. [1:4] Lv 3:2, 8, 13; 4:4, 15, 24, 29, 33; 8:14, 18, 22; Nm 8:12; 2 Chr 29:23; cf. Lv 16:21; 24:14; Nm 27:18, 23; Dt 34:9.
f. [1:4] Lv 19:5; 22:19–29; Gn 4:3–5; Mal 1:8–14.
g. [1:4] Lv 9:7; 14:20; Jb 1:5; 42:8; cf. Gn 32:21; Ex 29:36–37; 30:15; Lv 16:16–20; 17:11; Ez 43:20, 26.

** [1:16] **Crissum**: the area around the anus of the bird, lying beneath the bird's tail.

---

h. [1:5] Lv 1:11, 15; 3:2, 8, 13; cf. Lv 4:5–7, 25.
i. [1:9] Lv 2:2; 3:5; 4:31; 26:31; Gn 8:20–21; Nm 28:2; cf. Lv 3:11; 21:6; 21; 22:25.
j. [1:14] Lv 5:7; 12:8; 15:14–15; Lk 2:24.
k. [1:15] Lv 5:8–9.

embers. It is a burnt offering, a sweet-smelling oblation to the LORD.

CHAPTER 2

Grain Offerings. **1*****a**When anyone brings a grain offering to the LORD, the offering must consist of bran flour. The offerer shall pour oil on it and put frankincense**b** over it, **2**and bring it to Aaron's sons, the priests. A priest shall take a handful of the bran flour and oil, together with all the frankincense, and shall burn it on the altar as a token of the offering,**†** a sweet-smelling oblation to the LORD.**c** **3**The rest of the grain offering belongs to Aaron and his sons,**d** a most holy**e** portion from the oblations to the LORD.

4When you offer a grain offering baked in an oven, it must be in the form of unleavened cakes made of bran flour mixed with oil, or of unleavened wafers spread with oil.**f** **5**If your offering is a grain offering that is fried on a griddle,**g** it must be of bran flour mixed with oil and unleavened. **6**Break it into pieces, and pour oil over it. It is a grain offering. **7**If your offering is a grain offering that is prepared in a pan, it must be made of bran flour, fried in oil. **8**A grain offering that is made in any of these ways you shall bring to the LORD. It shall be presented to the priest, who shall take it to the altar. **9**The priest shall then remove from the grain offering a token and burn it on the altar as a sweet-smelling oblation to the LORD. **10**The rest of the

grain offering belongs to Aaron and his sons, a most holy portion from the oblations to the LORD.

11‡Every grain offering that you present to the LORD shall be unleavened, for you shall not burn any leaven or honey as an oblation to the LORD.**h** **12**Such you may present to the LORD in the offering of the first produce that is processed,**i** but they are not to be placed on the altar for a pleasing odor. **13**You shall season all your grain offerings with salt. Do not let the salt of the covenant with your God**§** be lacking from your grain offering. On every offering you shall offer salt.**j**

14If you offer a grain offering of first ripe fruits to the LORD, you shall offer it in the form of fresh early grain, roasted by fire and crushed as a grain offering of your first ripe fruits. **15**You shall put oil on it and set frankincense on it. It is a grain offering. **16**The priest shall then burn some of the groats and oil, together with all the frankincense, as a token of the offering, an oblation to the LORD.

CHAPTER 3

Communion Sacrifices. **1**¶aIf a person's offering is a communion sacrifice, if it is brought from the herd, be it a male or a female animal, it must be presented without blemish**b** before the LORD. **2**The one offering it shall lay a hand on the head**c** of the offering. It shall then be slaughtered at

---

* [2:1] Grain offerings are used as independent offerings (those in this chapter and cf. 6:12–16; 8:26–27; 23:10–11), as substitutes for other offerings in a case of poverty (5:11–13), and as accompaniments to animal offerings (cf. Nm 15:1–12; 28:1–29:39; Lv 14:20; 23:12, 18, 37). Chapter 2 describes two basic types of grain offering: uncooked (vv. 1–3) and cooked (vv. 4–10). The flour (*sōlet*) used was made of wheat (Ex 29:2) and Jewish tradition and Semitic cognates indicate that it is a coarse rather than a fine flour.
† [2:2] **Token of the offering:** lit., "reminder." Instead of burning the whole grain offering, only this part is burned on the altar.

a. [2:1] Lv 5:11–13; 6:7–16; 7:9–14; 24:5–9; Nm 15:1–21; cf. Gn 4:3–5.
b. [2:1] Cf. Ex 30:1–10; Lv 16:11–13; Prv 27:9.
c. [2:2] Lv 1:9.
d. [2:3] Lv 6:9; 7:9–10.
e. [2:3] Lv 6:10, 18, 22; 10:12, 17; 24:9.
f. [2:4] 1 Chr 23:29.
g. [2:5] Lv 6:14.

‡ [2:11–12] No grain offering that is leavened can be offered on the altar. Those in 7:13 and 23:17 are leavened but not offered on the altar. The Hebrew word for "honey" may refer to fruit syrup as well as to bee honey.
§ [2:13] **The salt of the covenant with your God:** partaking of salt in common was an ancient symbol of friendship and alliance. Cf. Mark 9:49–50 and Col 4:6.
¶ [3:1] The exact meaning of Hebrew *shelamim*, "communion sacrifice," is not clear. It has also been rendered "gift," "(re)payment," "peace," "well-being," or "covenant" offering. This offering may be brought for a vow or voluntary offering (cf. 22:21). A distinct version of the communion sacrifice is the thanksgiving offering (7:11–15 vis-à-vis vv. 16–18).

h. [2:11] Mt 16:12; Mk 8:15; Lk 12:1; 1 Cor 5:7; Gal 5:9.
i. [2:12] Nm 18:12–13, 27; 15:20–21.
j. [2:13] Nm 18:19; Ezr 6:9; 7:22; Ez 43:24.

a. [3:1] Lv 7:11–36.
b. [3:1] Lv 22:21.
c. [3:2] Lv 1:4.

the entrance of the tent of meeting. Aaron's sons, the priests, shall splash its blood on all the sides of the altar. ^{3d}From the communion sacrifice the individual shall offer as an oblation to the LORD the fat* that covers the inner organs, and all the fat that adheres to them, ⁴as well as the two kidneys, with the fat on them near the loins, and the lobe of the liver, which is removed with the kidneys. ⁵Aaron's sons shall burn this on the altar with the burnt offering that is on the wood and the embers, as a sweet-smelling oblation to the LORD.^e

⁶If the communion sacrifice one offers to the LORD is from the flock, be it a male or a female animal, it must be presented without blemish. ⁷If one presents a lamb as an offering, that person shall bring it before the LORD, ⁸and after laying a hand on the head of the offering, it shall then be slaughtered before the tent of meeting. Aaron's sons shall splash its blood on all the sides of the altar. ⁹From the communion sacrifice the individual shall present as an oblation to the LORD its fat: the whole fatty tail, which is removed close to the spine, the fat that covers the inner organs, and all the fat that adheres to them, ¹⁰as well as the two kidneys, with the fat on them near the loins, and the lobe of the liver, which is removed with the kidneys. ¹¹The priest shall burn this on the altar as food,^f an oblation to the LORD.

¹²If a person's offering is a goat, the individual shall bring it before the LORD, ¹³and after laying a hand on its head, it shall then be slaughtered before the tent of meeting. Aaron's sons shall splash its blood on all the sides of the altar. ¹⁴From this the one sacrificing shall present an offering

as an oblation to the LORD: the fat that covers the inner organs, and all the fat that adheres to them, ¹⁵as well as the two kidneys, with the fat on them near the loins, and the lobe of the liver, which is removed with the kidneys. ¹⁶The priest shall burn these on the altar as food, a sweet-smelling oblation.

All the fat belongs to the LORD. ¹⁷This shall be a perpetual ordinance for your descendants wherever they may dwell. You shall not eat any fat or any blood.^{†g}

CHAPTER 4

Purification Offerings. ¹The LORD said to Moses: ^{2a}Tell the Israelites: When a person inadvertently‡ does wrong by violating any one of the LORD's prohibitions—

For the Anointed Priest. ³If it is the anointed priest§ who thus does wrong and thereby makes the people guilty, he shall offer to the LORD an unblemished bull of the herd as a purification offering for the wrong he committed. ⁴Bringing the bull to the entrance of the tent of meeting, before the LORD, he shall lay his hand on its head^b and slaughter it before the LORD. ^{5¶}The

---

† [3:17] **Any fat or any blood**: this prohibition is mentioned here because portions of this offering could be eaten by lay Israelites, who may not be entirely familiar with the prohibition (cf. 7:22–27; 19:26). The fat prohibited is only the visceral fat mentioned in 3:9–10, 14–15, not muscular fat.

‡ [4:2] **Inadvertently**: the concern in this chapter, and much of chap. 5, is wrongs done unintentionally. Intentional ("high-handed") sins are punished with being "cut off" from the people (Nm 15:30–31). See note on Lv 7:20. **LORD's prohibitions**: not included in the faults figured here is failure to perform positive commandments. Failing to perform positive commands, however, still renders the individual liable to other punishment (e.g., failing to observe the Passover, Nm 9:13). Cf. Nm 15:22–31.

§ [4:3] **The anointed priest**: the chapter presents four cases of inadvertent wrong, arranged in descending order according to the status of the wrongdoer: high priest (vv. 3–12), entire community (vv. 13–21), tribal leader (vv. 22–26), and general populace (vv. 27–35). The higher one's position, the more deeply the sin affects the sanctuary (vv. 5–7, 17–18 versus vv. 25, 29, 34). See note on 16:6. **Purification offering**: the Hebrew verb *hittē'* means "remove sin, purify" (Lv 8:15; Ez 43:20–23; 45:18–19; cf. Ex 29:36). The offering cleansed the various places to which the blood was applied or the rooms in which it was sprinkled.

¶ [4:5–7] On the structure of the sanctuary, see Ex 26–27.

---

* [3:3–5] **Fat**: only part of the offering is devoted to God, as opposed to the burnt offering (chap. 1), which is wholly burnt (except for the skin). The meat is distributed among the offerer (and the offerer's party) and the priests (cf. 7:11–36).

d. [3:3–5] Lv 3:9–10, 14–16; 4:8–9, 31, 35; 6:5; 7:3–4, 30–31; 8:16, 25; 16:25; 17:6; Ex 29:13, 22; cf. Ez 44:15.

e. [3:5] Lv 1:9.

f. [3:11] Lv 9:19.

g. [3:17] Lv 17:10.

a. [4:2] Lv 6:17–23; Nm 15:22–31.

b. [4:4] Lv 1:4.

anointed priest shall then take some of the bull's blood and bring it into the tent of meeting, [6]where, dipping his finger in the blood, he shall sprinkle some of it seven times before the LORD, toward the veil of the sanctuary.[c] [7]The priest shall also put some of the blood on the horns of the altar of fragrant incense which stands before the LORD in the tent of meeting. The rest of the bull's blood he shall pour out at the base of the altar for burnt offerings which is at the entrance of the tent of meeting. [8]He shall remove all the fat of the bull of the purification offering: the fat that covers the inner organs, and all the fat that adheres to them, [9]as well as the two kidneys, with the fat on them near the loins, and the lobe of the liver, which is removed with the kidneys, [10]just as the fat pieces are removed from the ox of the communion sacrifice.[d] The priest shall burn these on the altar for burnt offerings. [11]*But the hide of the bull and its meat, with its head, shanks, inner organs and dung, [12]that is, the whole bull, shall be brought outside the camp to a clean place[†] where the ashes are deposited and there be burned in a wood fire. At the place of the ash heap, there it must be burned.[e]

For the Community. [13]If the whole community of Israel errs[‡] inadvertently and without even being aware of it violates any of the LORD's prohibitions, and thus are guilty, [14]when the wrong that was committed becomes known, the community shall offer a bull of the herd as a purification offering. They shall bring it before the tent of meeting. [15]The elders of the community shall lay their hands on the bull's head before the LORD. When the bull has been slaughtered before the LORD, [16]the anointed priest shall bring some of its blood into the tent of meeting, [17]and dipping his finger in the blood, he shall sprinkle it seven times before the LORD, toward the veil. [18]He shall also put some of the blood on the horns of the altar which is before the LORD in the tent of meeting. The rest of the blood he shall pour out at the base of the altar for burnt offerings which is at the entrance of the tent of meeting. [19]He shall remove all of its fat and burn it on the altar, [20]doing with this bull just as he did with the other bull of the purification offering; he will do the same thing. Thus the priest shall make atonement[f] on their behalf, that they may be forgiven. [21]This bull shall also be brought outside the camp and burned,[g] just as the first bull. It is a purification offering for the assembly.

For the Tribal Leader. [22]Should a tribal leader[h] do wrong inadvertently by violating any one of the prohibitions of the LORD his God, and thus be guilty, [23]when he learns of the wrong he committed, he shall bring as his offering an unblemished male goat. [24]He shall lay his hand on its head and it shall be slaughtered in the place where the burnt offering is slaughtered, before the LORD. It is a purification offering. [25]The priest shall then take some of the blood of the purification offering on his finger and put it on the horns[i] of the altar for burnt offerings. The rest of the blood he shall pour out at the base of the altar. [26]All of its fat he shall burn on the altar like the fat of the communion sacrifice. Thus the priest shall make atonement on the tribal leader's behalf for his wrong, that he may be forgiven.

For the General Populace. [27]If anyone of the general populace does wrong inadvertently by violating one of the LORD's prohibitions, and

---

* [4:11–12] See note on 6:17–23.

† [4:12] **Clean place:** i.e., ritually "clean" or pure. It has nothing to do with the presence of dirt or waste. See 6:4.

‡ [4:13] **Whole community . . . errs:** this case probably complements that of vv. 3–12. There the high priest sins so that the people become guilty. Those verses deal with his requirements for atonement; vv. 13–21 deal with the people's requirements.

c. [4:6–7] Lv 4:17–18; 16:16; cf. 4:25.
d. [4:10] Lv 3:3.
e. [4:12] Lv 6:23.

f. [4:20] Lv 1:4.
g. [4:21] Lv 6:23.
h. [4:22] Nm 10:4; 25:14.
i. [4:25] Lv 4:30, 34; 8:15; 9:9; 16:18; Ex 29:12; Ez 43:20; cf. Lv 4:7.

thus is guilty, [28]upon learning of the wrong committed, that person shall bring an unblemished she-goat as the offering for the wrong committed. [29]The wrongdoer shall lay a hand on the head of the purification offering, and the purification offering shall be slaughtered at the place of the burnt offerings. [30]The priest shall then take some of its blood on his finger and put it on the horns of the altar for burnt offerings. The rest of the blood he shall pour out at the base of the altar. [31]He shall remove all the fat, just as the fat is removed from the communion sacrifice. The priest shall burn it on the altar for a sweet odor to the LORD. Thus the priest shall make atonement, so that the individual may be forgiven.

[32]If, however, a person brings a lamb as a purification offering, that person shall bring an unblemished female, and [33]lay a hand on its head. It shall be slaughtered as a purification offering in the place where the burnt offering is slaughtered. [34]The priest shall then take some of the blood of the purification offering on his finger and put it on the horns of the altar for burnt offerings. The rest of the blood he shall pour out at the base of the altar. [35]He shall remove all its fat just as the fat is removed from the lamb of the communion sacrifice. The priest shall burn these on the altar with the other oblations for the LORD. Thus the priest shall make atonement on the person's behalf for the wrong committed, that the individual may be forgiven.

CHAPTER 5

Special Cases for Purification Offerings.[*] [1]If a person, either having seen or come to know something, does wrong by refusing as a witness under oath to give information,[a] that individual shall bear the penalty; [2]or if someone, without being aware of it, touches any unclean thing, such as the carcass of an unclean wild animal, or an unclean domestic animal, or an unclean swarming creature,[†] and thus is unclean and guilty;[b] [3]or if someone, without being aware of it, touches some human uncleanness,[c] whatever kind of uncleanness this may be, and then subsequently becomes aware of guilt; [4]or if someone, without being aware of it, rashly utters an oath with bad or good intent,[d] whatever kind of oath this may be, and then subsequently becomes aware of guilt in regard to any of these matters— [5]when someone is guilty in regard to any of these matters, that person shall confess the wrong committed, [6]and make reparation to the LORD for the wrong committed: a female animal from the flock, a ewe lamb or a she-goat, as a purification offering. Thus the priest shall make atonement on the individual's behalf for the wrong.

[7]If, however, the person cannot afford an animal of the flock,[e] that person shall bring to the LORD as reparation for the wrong committed two turtledoves or two pigeons, one for a purification offering and the other for a burnt offering. [8]The guilty party shall bring them to the priest, who shall offer the one for the purification offering first.[f] Wringing its head at the neck, yet without breaking it off, [9]he shall sprinkle some of the blood of the purification offering against the side of the altar. The rest of the blood shall be drained out against the base of the altar. It is a purification offering. [10]The other bird he shall offer as a

---

† [5:2] **Swarming creature:** a rather imprecise categorization that includes various small creatures in the seas, such as fish that go about in large groups or swarms (Gn 1:20; Lv 11:10); or, similarly, various winged insects that mass in the skies (Lv 11:20; Dt 14:19); and, finally, various small creatures that move in swarms on land, whether crawlers, quadrupeds, or of the multilegged variety (Lv 11:41–42). According to 11:29–30, even various rodents and lizards can be included in this category.

b. [5:2] Lv 11:1–45; 15:31; 17:15–16.
c. [5:3] Lv 12:4; 13:35–36; 15:2–12, 19–27; Nm 19:14–22.
d. [5:4] Nm 30:3; Jgs 11:30–36; 1 Sm 14:24–30; Mk 6:23–26; Acts 23:12.
e. [5:7] Cf. Lv 5:11; 12:8; 14:21.
f. [5:8] Lv 1:14–17.

---

* [5:1–13] This differs from the prescriptions for purification offerings in chap. 4 by listing four specific wrongs for which a purification offering is brought and allowing the substitution of birds and grain offerings in the case of poverty.

a. [5:1] Jgs 17:2–3; Prv 29:24.

burnt offering according to procedure. Thus the priest shall make atonement on the person's behalf for the wrong committed, so that the individual may be forgiven. ¹¹If the person is unable to afford even two turtledoves or two pigeons, that person shall bring as an offering for the wrong committed one tenth of an ephah* of bran flour for a purification offering. The guilty party shall not put oil or place frankincense on it, because it is a purification offering.ᵍ ¹²The individual shall bring it to the priest, who shall take a handful as a token of the offering and burn it on the altar with the other oblations for the Lord. It is a purification offering. ¹³Thus the priest shall make atonement on the person's behalf for the wrong committed in any of the above cases, so that the individual may be forgiven. The rest of the offering, like the grain offering, shall belong to the priest.

Reparation Offerings.† ¹⁴The Lord said to Moses: ¹⁵ʰWhen a person commits sacrilege by inadvertently misusing any of the Lord's sacred objects,ⁱ the wrongdoer shall bring to the Lord as reparation an unblemished ram from the flock, at the established value‡ in silver shekels according to the sanctuary shekel, as a reparation offering. ¹⁶The wrongdoer shall also restore what has been misused of the sacred objects, adding a fifth of its value,ʲ and give this to the priest. Thus the priest shall make atonement for the person

with the ram of the reparation offering, so that the individual may be forgiven. ¹⁷If someone does wrong and violates one of the Lord's prohibitions without realizing it, that person is guiltyᵏ and shall bear the penalty. ¹⁸The individual shall bring to the priest an unblemished ram of the flock, at the established value, for a reparation offering. The priest shall then make atonement on the offerer's behalf for the error inadvertently and unknowingly committed so that the individual may be forgiven. ¹⁹It is a reparation offering. The individual must make reparation to the Lord.

²⁰The Lord said to Moses: ²¹When someone does wrong and commits sacrilege against the Lord by deceivingˡ a neighbor about a deposit or a pledge or a stolen article, or by otherwise retaining a neighbor's goods unjustly;ᵐ ²²or if, having found a lost article, the person lies about it, swearing falsely about any of the things that a person may do wrong— ²³when someone has thus done wrong and is guilty, that person shall restore the thing that was stolen, the item unjustly retained, the item left as deposit, or the lost article that was found ²⁴or whatever else the individual swore falsely about. That person shall make full restitution of the thing itself, and add one fifth of its value to it, giving it to its owner at the time of reparation. ²⁵Then that person shall bring to the priest as reparation to the Lord an unblemished ram of the flock, at the established value, as a reparation offering. ²⁶The priest shall make atonement on the person's behalf before the Lord, so that the individual may be forgiven for whatever was done to incur guilt.

---

* [5:11] **Ephah**: see note on Is 5:10.
† [5:14–26] This last half of the chapter deals with a distinct sacrifice, the reparation offering (Heb. 'asham). The Hebrew root for this term has a basic meaning of "be guilty." The noun can have a consequential sense of "that which is due from guilt," i.e., "compensation, indemnification, reparation"; hence the translation "reparation offering," rather than the alternatives "guilt offering" or "trespass offering." This offering is brought most often in cases of sacrilege.
‡ [5:15] **At the established value**: the Hebrew term 'erkĕkā, which in context means "(established) value," may indicate that a person could bring the monetary equivalent of a ram instead of an actual animal. See vv. 18, 25.

g. [5:11] Lv 2:1–3; Nm 5:15.
h. [5:15] Lv 7:1–6; Nm 5:5–8.
i. [5:15] Lv 22:14.
j. [5:16] Lv 22:14; 27:13, 15, 19, 27.

k. [5:17] Ps 19:13; Jb 1:5.
l. [5:21] Ps 59:13; Hos 4:2.
m. [5:21] Ex 22:6–12.

B. INSTRUCTIONS FOR THE PRIESTS

CHAPTER 6

The Daily Burnt Offering. ¹The LORD said to Moses: ²*ᵃGive Aaron and his sons the following command: This is the ritual† for the burnt offering—the burnt offering that is to remain on the hearth of the altar all night until the next morning, while the fire is kept burning on the altar. ³The priest, clothed in his linen robe and wearing linen pants underneath, shall take away the ashes to which the fire has reduced the burnt offering on the altar, and lay them at the side of the altar. ⁴Then, having taken off these garments and put on other garments, he shall carry the ashes to a clean place outside the camp. ⁵The fire on the altar is to be kept burning; it must not go out. Every morning the priest shall put firewood on it. On this he shall lay out the burnt offeringᵇ and burn the fat of the communion offering. ⁶The fire is to be kept burning continuously on the altar; it must not go out.

The Grain Offering.‡ ⁷This is the ritual of the grain offering. Aaron's sons shall offer it before the LORD, in front of the altar. ⁸A priest shall then take from the grain offering a handful of bran flour and oil, together with all the frankincense that is on it,ᶜ and this he shall burn on the altar as a token of the offering, a sweet aroma to the LORD. ⁹The rest of it Aaron and his sons may eat; but it must be eaten unleavened in a sacred place:ᵈ in the court of the tent of meeting they shall eat it. ¹⁰It shall not be baked with leaven. I have given it to them as their portion from the oblations for the LORD; it is most holy,ᵉ like the purification offering and the reparation offering. ¹¹Every male of Aaron's descendants may eat of it perpetually throughout your generations as their rightful due from the oblations for the LORD. Whatever touches the oblations becomes holy.

High Priest's Daily Grain Offering.§ ¹²The LORD said to Moses: ¹³This is the offering that Aaron and his sons shall present to the LORD on the day he is anointed: one tenth of an ephah of bran flour for the regular grain offering, half of it in the morning and half of it in the evening. ¹⁴You shall bring it well kneaded and fried in oil on a griddle.ᶠ Having broken the offering into pieces, you shall present it as a sweet aroma to the LORD. ¹⁵The anointed priest descended from Aaron who succeeds him shall do likewise. This is the LORD's due forever. The offering shall be wholly burned.ᵍ ¹⁶Every grain offering of a priest shall be a whole offering; it may not be eaten.

Purification Offerings.¶ ¹⁷The LORD said to Moses: ¹⁸ʰTell Aaron and his sons: This is the ritual for the purification offering. At the place where the burnt offering is slaughtered, there also, before the LORD, shall the purification offering be slaughtered. It is

* [6:2–6] This passage may have reference to the burnt offering that is offered in the morning and late afternoon each day (cf. Ex 29:38–42; Nm 28:3–8).
† [6:2] **Ritual**: Hebrew *torah*, which also has the broader meaning of "instruction." The treatment of sacrifices in chaps. 6–7 recapitulates the offerings treated in 1–5 but now with more emphasis on priestly duties and prerogatives.
‡ [6:7–11] The passage is apparently concerned with the raw grain offering of 2:1–3.
§ [6:12–16] This seems to refer to a grain offering offered twice daily by the high priest, perhaps identical to the regular grain offering in Nm 4:16 (cf. Neh 10:34). This offering is distinct from the grain offering that accompanies the daily burnt offering.
¶ [6:17–23] There are two types of purification offering: one whose blood is used inside the tent sanctuary (4:1–12, 13–21) and another whose blood was only used at the outer sacrificial altar (4:22–26, 27–31, 32–35). The carcasses of the former, as well as of purification offerings brought by the priests themselves (cf. 8:14–17; 9:8–11), are not eaten by priests but disposed of at the ash heap outside the camp, which itself is set up around the sanctuary (Ex 29:14; Lv 4:11–12, 21; 6:23; 8:17; 9:11; 16:27). The Letter to the Hebrews compares Jesus' suffering "outside the gate" to the disposal of purification offering carcasses outside the camp (Heb 13:11–13).

a. [6:2] Lv 1.
b. [6:5] Lv 9:17.
c. [6:8] Lv 2:1–3.
d. [6:9] Lv 6:19; 7:6; 10:13, 17; 24:9.
e. [6:10] Lv 2:3.
f. [6:14] Lv 2:5.
g. [6:15] Lv 2:9.
h. [6:18] Lv 4:1–5:13.

most holy.[i] [19]The priest who offers the purification offering shall eat of it; it shall be eaten in a sacred place,[j] in the court of the tent of meeting. [20]Whatever touches its flesh becomes holy. If any of its blood spatters on a garment, the stained part must be washed in a sacred place. [21]A clay vessel in which it has been boiled shall be broken; if it is boiled in a copper vessel, this shall be scoured afterward and rinsed with water.[k] [22]Every male of the priestly line may eat it. It is most holy. [23]But no purification offering of which some blood has been brought into the tent of meeting[l] to make atonement in the sanctuary shall be eaten; it must be burned with fire.[m]

CHAPTER 7

Reparation Offerings. [1][a]This is the ritual for the reparation offering. It is most holy. [2]At the place where the burnt offering is slaughtered, the reparation offering shall also be slaughtered.[b] Its blood shall be splashed on all the sides of the altar. [3][c]All of its fat shall be offered: the fatty tail, the fat that covers the inner organs, and all the fat that adheres to them, [4]as well as the two kidneys with the fat on them near the loins, and the lobe of the liver, which is removed with the kidneys. [5]The priest shall burn these on the altar as an oblation to the Lord. It is a reparation offering. [6]Every male of the priestly line may eat of it; but it must be eaten in a sacred place.[d] It is most holy.[e]

[7]Because the purification offering and the reparation offering are alike,

both have the same ritual. The reparation offering belongs to the priest who makes atonement with it. [8]As for the priest who offers someone's burnt offering, to him belongs the hide of the burnt offering that is offered. [9][†f]Also, every grain offering that is baked in an oven or made in a pan or on a griddle shall belong to the priest who offers it, [10]whereas all grain offerings[g] that are mixed with oil or are dry shall belong to all of Aaron's sons without distinction.

Communion Sacrifices.[‡] [11][h]This is the ritual for the communion sacrifice that is offered to the Lord. [12][§]If someone offers it for thanksgiving, that person shall offer it with unleavened cakes mixed with oil, unleavened wafers spread with oil, and cakes made of bran flour mixed with oil and well kneaded. [13]One shall present this offering together with loaves of leavened bread along with the thanksgiving communion sacrifice. [14]From this the individual shall offer one bread of each type of offering as a contribution[¶] to the Lord; this shall belong to the priest who splashes the blood of the communion offering.

[15][**][i]The meat of the thanksgiving communion sacrifice shall be eaten on the day it is offered; none of it may be kept till the next morning.[j] [16]However,

---

* [7:1–6] These prescriptions may appear here rather than in 5:14–26 where this offering is first treated because the monetary equivalent of the offering might have been brought instead of an actual animal. See note on 5:15.

i. [6:18] Lv 2:3.
j. [6:19] Lv 6:9.
k. [6:21] Lv 11:32–33; 15:12.
l. [6:23] Lv 4:5; Heb 13:11.
m. [6:23] Lv 4:11–12, 21; 8:17; 9:11; 16:27.

a. [7:1] Lv 5:14–26.
b. [7:2] Lv 6:18.
c. [7:3] Lv 3:4.
d. [7:6] Lv 6:9.
e. [7:6] Lv 2:3.

† [7:9–10] For the distinction between uncooked and cooked grain offerings, see 2:1–10 and note on 2:1. The contradiction between v. 9 and 2:10 may reflect a development in custom, with the distribution in v. 9 coming from earlier times, when sanctuary personnel was more limited.

‡ [7:11–36] This section discusses three types of communion sacrifice: the thanksgiving offering (vv. 12–15), a votive offering, and a voluntary offering (vv. 16–18). The latter two are similar and are thus mentioned together. Verses 19–36 apply to all types of communion sacrifice.

§ [7:12–13] Four types of breads accompany the thanksgiving offering. Three types are cooked grain offerings comparable to those in 2:4–10. Also required are loaves of leavened bread (see 2:11).

¶ [7:14] Contribution: Hebrew terumah. This does not indicate a particular ritual action. The word simply means "gift, something set apart."

** [7:15–18] Sacrifices must be properly consumed for them to be effective (cf. also 19:5–8; 22:30). Similar rules obtain for the Passover offering (Ex 12:10; Nm 9:12; cf. Ex 23:18; 34:25; Dt 16:4) and the ordination offering (Ex 29:34; Lv 8:32).

f. [7:9] Lv 2:3–10; Nm 18:9; Ez 44:29.
g. [7:10] Lv 2:14–15.
h. [7:11] Lv 3.
i. [7:15] Lv 19:6–7.
j. [7:15] Lv 22:29–30.

if the sacrifice offered is a votive or a voluntary offering,* it shall be eaten on the day the sacrifice is offered, and on the next day what is left over may be eaten.[k] 17 But what is left over of the meat of the sacrifice on the third day must be burned in the fire. 18 If indeed any of the flesh of the communion sacrifice is eaten on the third day, it shall not be accepted; it will not be reckoned to the credit of the one offering it. Rather it becomes a desecrated meat. Anyone who eats of it shall bear the penalty.†

19 ‡Should the meat touch anything unclean, it may not be eaten, but shall be burned in the fire.[l] As for other meat, all who are clean may eat of it. 20 If, however, someone in a state of uncleanness eats the meat of a communion sacrifice belonging to the LORD, that person shall be cut off§[m] from the people. 21 Likewise, if someone touches anything unclean, whether it be human uncleanness or an unclean animal or an unclean loathsome creature, and then eats the meat of the communion sacrifice belonging to the LORD, that person, too, shall be cut off from the people.

Prohibition Against Blood and Fat. 22 The LORD said to Moses: 23 Tell the Israelites: You shall not eat the fat of any ox or sheep or goat.[n] 24 Although the fat of an animal that has died a natural death or has been killed by wild beasts may be put to any other use, you may not eat it.[o] 25 If anyone eats the fat of an animal from which an oblation is made to the LORD, that person shall be cut off from the people. 26 [p]Wherever you dwell, you shall not eat any blood, whether of bird or of animal. 27 Every person who eats any blood shall be cut off from the people.

Portions from the Communion Sacrifice for Priests. 28 The LORD said to Moses: 29 Tell the Israelites: The person who offers a communion sacrifice to the LORD shall be the one to bring from it the offering to the LORD. 30 The offerer's own hands shall carry the oblations for the LORD: the person shall bring the fat together with the brisket, which is to be raised as an elevated[q] offering¶ before the LORD. 31 The priest shall burn the fat on the altar,[r] but the brisket belongs to Aaron and his sons. 32 Moreover, from your communion sacrifices you shall give to the priest the right leg as a contribution. 33 The one among Aaron's sons who offers the blood and the fat of the communion offering shall have the right leg as his portion, 34 for from the communion sacrifices of the Israelites I have taken the brisket that is elevated and the leg that is a contribution, and I have given them to Aaron, the priest, and to his sons as their due from the Israelites forever.[s]

35 This is the priestly share from the oblations for the LORD, allotted to Aaron and his sons on the day they were brought forth to be the priests of the LORD, 36 which the LORD ordered to be given them from the Israelites on the day they were anointed, as their due throughout their generations forever.

* [7:16] **Votive or a voluntary offering**: these are not specific types of offerings but rather motivations for bringing the communion sacrifice (cf. 22:18). A votive offering is brought as the consequence of a promise (vow) made to God. A voluntary offering is a spontaneous gift to God independent of a prior promise. See note on 27:2–13.

† [7:18] **Bear the penalty**: this refers in many cases to punishment by God (cf. 17:16; 19:8; 20:17, 19; Nm 18:1, 23; 30:16).

‡ [7:19–21] For ritual impurity, see note on 11:1–15:33.

§ [7:20] **Cut off**: a common term in the Priestly source that cannot always be reduced to a simple English equivalent, since its usage appears to involve a number of associated punishments, some or all of which may come into play in any one instance (see Ex 12:15 and note). All the same, as a punishment from God, to be "cut off" (from one's people) frequently appears to refer to termination of the offender's family line (and perhaps in some cases an early death); see Lv 20:2–3, 20–21; Ru 4:10; Ps 109:13; Mal 2:12.

¶ [7:30] **Raised as an elevated offering**: these portions of the sacrifices were specially dedicated by lifting them in presentation before God's abode. The sanctifying effect of this action is clearly seen in 23:17–20; Nm 6:19–20.

k. [7:16] Lv 19:5–8.
l. [7:19] Lv 12:4.
m. [7:20] Lv 17:4, 9–10, 14; 18:29; 20:3, 5–6, 17–18; Gn 17:14; Ex 30:33; Nm 15:31; Ps 37:9, 28, 34; 109:13.
n. [7:23] Lv 3:17.
o. [7:24] Lv 22:8.
p. [7:26] Lv 17:10.
q. [7:30] Lv 8:27, 29; 9:21; 10:15; 14:12, 21, 24; 23:17, 20; Nm 6:20; 8:13; 18:18.
r. [7:31] Lv 3:11, 16.
s. [7:34] Ex 29:27–28.

Summary. [37]This is the ritual for the burnt offering, the grain offering, the purification offering, the reparation offering, the ordination offering,[t] and the communion sacrifice, [38]which the LORD enjoined on Moses at Mount Sinai at the time when he commanded the Israelites in the wilderness of Sinai to bring their offerings to the LORD.[u]

II. CEREMONY OF ORDINATION

CHAPTER 8

Ordination of Aaron and His Sons.[*] [1][a]The LORD said to Moses: [2]Take Aaron along with his sons, the vestments, the anointing oil, the bull for a purification offering, the two rams, and the basket of unleavened bread, [3]then assemble the whole community[†] at the entrance of the tent of meeting. [4]Moses did as the LORD had commanded. When the community[b] had assembled at the entrance of the tent of meeting, [5]Moses told them: "This is what the LORD has ordered to be done." [6]Bringing forward Aaron and his sons, Moses first washed them with water. [7][‡]Then he put the tunic on Aaron,[c] girded him with the sash, clothed him with the robe, placed the ephod on him, and girded him with the ephod's embroidered belt, fastening the ephod on him with it. [8]He then set the breastpiece on him, putting the Urim and Thummim[§] in it. [9]He put the turban on his head, attaching the gold medallion, the sacred headband,[¶] on the front of the turban, as the LORD had commanded Moses to do.

[10][**]Taking the anointing oil, Moses anointed and consecrated the tabernacle and all that was in it.[d] [11]Then he sprinkled some of the oil seven times on the altar, and anointed the altar, with all its utensils, and the laver, with its base, to consecrate them. [12]He also poured some of the anointing oil on Aaron's head and anointed him, to consecrate him.[e] [13]Moses likewise brought forward Aaron's sons, clothed them with tunics, girded them with sashes, and put skullcaps on them, as the LORD had commanded him to do.

Ordination Sacrifices. [14]He brought forward the bull for a purification offering, and Aaron and his sons laid their hands on its head. [15]When it was slaughtered, Moses took the blood[††] and with his finger he put it on the horns around the altar, thus purifying the altar.[f] He poured out the rest of the blood at the base of the altar. Thus he consecrated it so that atonement could be made on it. [16]Taking all the fat that was over the inner organs, as well as the lobe of the liver and the two kidneys with their fat,[g] Moses burned them on the altar. [17]The bull, however, with its hide and flesh and dung he burned in the fire outside the camp, as the LORD had commanded Moses to do.[h]

---

* [8:1–2] This chapter presents the fulfillment of the commands in Ex 28–29; 30:26–30; and 40:9–15.
† [8:3–4] **Community**: this word (Heb. *'edah*) may refer to tribal leaders, all adult males, or the entire nation. The last is probably intended here.
‡ [8:7–9, 13] On the priestly clothing, see Ex 28–29. **Ephod**: according to Ex 28:6–14, the term for one of Aaron's special vestments made of gold thread, with multicolored woolen thread woven into it as well as fine linen. In appearance it resembled a kind of apron, hung on the priest by shoulder straps and secured by an embroidered belt. A somewhat simpler "apron" was presumably worn by other priests (1 Sm 22:18).

t. [7:37] Lv 8:22.
u. [7:38] Lv 26:46; 27:34.

a. [8:1] Cf. Ex 28–29; 39; 40:12–15.
b. [8:4] Nm 27:19.
c. [8:7–9] Sir 45:8–13; Heb 5:1–4; 7:1–28.

§ [8:8] **The Urim and Thummim**: see Ex 28:30 and note there. Although these terms and the object(s) they refer to are still unexplained, they appear to be small objects that functioned like dice or lots to render a decision for those making an inquiry of God, perhaps originally in legal cases where the guilt of the accused could not otherwise be determined (cf. Ex 28:30; Nm 27:21; Dt 33:8; 1 Sm 28:6; Ezr 2:63; Neh 7:65).
¶ [8:9] **Headband**: see Ex 39:30–31. The gold medallion, together with its cords, comprises the sacred headband.
** [8:10–12] Anointing with the specially prepared oil (cf. Ex 30:22–33) is one of the means of making objects and persons holy by setting them apart for a special function or purpose.
†† [8:15] **Moses took the blood**: Moses is acting as a priest in this chapter.

d. [8:10] Ex 30:26.
e. [8:12] Sir 45:15.
f. [8:15] Heb 9:22.
g. [8:16–17] Lv 3:4–5; 4:8–11.
h. [8:17] Lv 6:23.

¹⁸He next brought forward the ram of the burnt offering,^{*i*} and Aaron and his sons laid their hands on its head. ¹⁹When it was slaughtered, Moses splashed the blood on all sides of the altar. ²⁰After the ram was cut up into pieces, Moses burned the head, the cut-up pieces and the suet. ²¹After the inner organs and the shanks were washed with water, Moses burned these remaining parts of the ram on the altar. It was a burnt offering for a sweet aroma, an oblation to the L<small>ORD</small>, as the L<small>ORD</small> had commanded Moses.

^{22*}Then he brought forward the second ram, the ordination ram,^{*j*} and Aaron and his sons laid their hands on its head. ²³When it was slaughtered, Moses took some of its blood and put it on the lobe of Aaron's right ear, on the thumb of his right hand, and on the big toe[†] of his right foot.^{*k*} ²⁴Moses had the sons of Aaron also come forward, and he put some of the blood on the lobes of their right ears, on the thumbs of their right hands, and on the big toes of their right feet. The rest of the blood he splashed on all the sides of the altar. ²⁵He then took the fat: the fatty tail and all the fat over the inner organs, the lobe of the liver and the two kidneys with their fat, and likewise the right thigh; ²⁶from the basket of unleavened bread that was set before the L<small>ORD</small> he took one unleavened cake, one loaf of bread made with oil, and one wafer; these he placed on top of the portions of fat and the right thigh. ²⁷He then put all these things upon the palms of Aaron and his sons, whom he had raise them as an elevated offering before the L<small>ORD</small>.^{*l*} ²⁸When Moses had removed them from their palms, he burned them on the altar with the burnt offering. They were an ordination offering for a sweet aroma, an oblation to the L<small>ORD</small>. ²⁹He then took the brisket and raised it as an elevated offering before the L<small>ORD</small>; this was Moses' own portion of the ordination ram, as the L<small>ORD</small> had commanded Moses. ³⁰Taking some of the anointing oil and some of the blood that was on the altar, Moses sprinkled it upon Aaron and his vestments, as well as his sons and their vestments, thus consecrating both Aaron and his vestments and his sons and their vestments.^{*m*}

³¹Moses said to Aaron and his sons, "Boil the meat at the entrance of the tent of meeting, and there eat it with the bread that is in the basket of the ordination offering, in keeping with the command I have received: 'Aaron and his sons shall eat of it.' ³²What is left over of the meat and the bread you shall burn in the fire. ³³Moreover, you are not to depart[‡] from the entrance of the tent of meeting for seven days, until the days of your ordination are completed; for your ordination is to last for seven days. ³⁴What has been done today the L<small>ORD</small> has commanded be done, to make atonement for you. ³⁵You must remain at the entrance of the tent of meeting day and night for seven days, carrying out the prescriptions of the L<small>ORD</small>, so that you do not die, for this is the command I have received."^{*n*} ³⁶So Aaron and his sons did all that the L<small>ORD</small> had commanded through Moses.

CHAPTER 9

Octave of the Ordination. ¹On the eighth day^{§*a*} Moses summoned Aaron

---

* [8:22–32] The priestly ordination offering is a unique type of sacrifice but similar in many respects to the communion sacrifice (chap. 3; 7:11–34).

† [8:23–24] **Lobe . . . thumb . . . toe:** these parts of the body are meant to represent the body as a whole. The application of the blood symbolizes the priests' passing from a profane to a holy state. Cf. 14:14–17.

i. [8:18] Lv 1:10–13.
j. [8:22] Lv 7:37.
k. [8:23] Lv 14:14, 17.
l. [8:27] Lv 7:30.

‡ [8:33–35] **You are not to depart:** the tenor and context of this requirement in vv. 33 and 35 seem to indicate that the priests are not to leave the sanctuary precincts for any reason. **Your ordination is to last for seven days . . . what has been done today . . . be done:** the consecration rites in Exodus are to be performed every day for seven days (cf. Ex 29:30, 35–37).

§ [9:1] **Eighth day:** this is the conclusion of the priestly initiation ceremony.

m. [8:30] Ex 40:15.
n. [8:35] Lv 10:7.

a. [9:1] Lv 8:33.

and his sons, together with the elders of Israel, ²and said to Aaron, "Take a calf of the herd for a purification offering and a ram for a burnt offering, both without blemish, and offer them before the LORD. ³*Tell the Israelites, too: Take a he-goat for a purification offering, a calf and a lamb, both unblemished yearlings, for a burnt offering, ⁴and an ox and a ram for a communion sacrifice, to sacrifice before the LORD, along with a grain offering mixed with oil; for today the LORD will appear to you." ⁵So they brought what Moses had ordered before the tent of meeting. When the whole community had come forward and stood before the LORD, ⁶†Moses said, "This is what the LORD orders you to do, that the glory of the LORD may appear to you. ⁷Approach the altar," Moses then told Aaron, "and make your purification offering and your burnt offering in atonement for yourself and for your household;‡ then make the offering of the people in atonement for them, as the LORD has commanded."ᵇ

⁸Approaching the altar, Aaron first slaughtered the calf of the purification offering that was his own offering. ⁹When his sons presented the blood to him, he dipped his finger in the blood and put it on the horns of the altar.ᶜ The rest of the blood he poured out at the base of the altar. ¹⁰He then burned on the altar the fat, the kidneys and the lobe of the liver from the purification offering, as the LORD had commanded Moses; ¹¹but the flesh and the hide he burned in the fire outside the camp.ᵈ ¹²Then Aaron slaughtered the burnt offering. When his sons brought him the blood, he splashed it on all sides of the altar. ¹³They then brought him the

pieces and the head of the burnt offering, and he burned them on the altar. ¹⁴Having washed the inner organs and the shanks, he burned these also with the burnt offering on the altar.ᵉ

¹⁵Then he had the people's offering brought. Taking the goat that was for the people's purification offering, he slaughtered it and offered it as a purification offering as before. ¹⁶Then he brought forward the burnt offering and offered it according to procedure. ¹⁷He then presented the grain offering; taking a handful of it, he burned it on the altar, in addition to the morning burnt offering.ᶠ ¹⁸Finally he slaughtered the ox and the ram, the communion sacrifice of the people. When his sons brought him the blood, Aaron splashed it on all sides of the altar.ᵍ ¹⁹The portions of fat from the ox and from the ram, the fatty tail, the covering fat, the kidneys, and the lobe of the liver ²⁰they placed on top of the briskets. Aaron burned the fat pieces on the altar, ²¹but the briskets and the right thigh he raised as an elevated offeringʰ before the LORD, as the LORD had commanded Moses.

Revelation of the Lord's Glory.

²²§Aaron then raised his hands over the people and blessedⁱ them. When he came down from offering the purification offering, the burnt offering, and the communion offering, ²³Moses and Aaron went into the tent of meeting. On coming out they blessed the people. Then the glory of the LORD appeared to all the people. ²⁴¶Fire came forth from the LORD's presence and consumed the burnt offering

---

§ [9:22–23] The people are blessed twice. For the possible content of the blessing, compare the priestly blessing in Nm 6:22–27. Solomon offers a double blessing at the dedication of the Temple (1 Kgs 8:14–21, 55–61).

¶ [9:24] The theophany consists of a fire that apparently comes from the tent of meeting. God's fiery glory is also manifested in the pillar of cloud and fire that led the Israelites and rested over the tent of meeting (Ex 13:21; 40:38; Nm 9:15–23; 10:11). On God's fiery glory, see also Ex 24:17; Ez 1:27–28.

---

* [9:3–4] The seven-day consecration of the priests in chap. 8 did not require sacrifices from the community. Now communal sacrifices as well as priestly sacrifices are required.

† [9:6–21] Aaron and his sons now perform the offerings, instead of Moses (see note on 8:15).

‡ [9:7] **For your household:** unlike the Septuagint, the Hebrew reads be'ad ha'am, "for the people."

b. [9:7] Lv 16:3–5.
c. [9:9] Lv 4:25, 30, 34.
d. [9:11] Lv 6:23.

e. [9:14] Lv 1:5–9.
f. [9:17] Nm 28:23; 2 Kgs 16:15; Ez 46:13–15.
g. [9:18] Lv 3:2.
h. [9:21] Lv 7:30–34.
i. [9:22] Nm 6:22–27.

and the fat on the altar.*ʲ* Seeing this, all the people shouted with joy and fell prostrate.

CHAPTER 10

Nadab and Abihu. ¹*Aaron's sons Nadab and Abihu took their censers and, putting incense on the fire they had set in them,*ᵃ* they offered before the LORD unauthorized fire, such as he had not commanded. ²Fire therefore came forth from the LORD's presence and consumed them,*ᵇ* so that they died in the LORD's presence. ³Moses then said to Aaron, "This is as the LORD said:

Through those near to me I will be sanctified;
in the sight of all the people I will obtain glory."†*ᶜ*

But Aaron said nothing. ⁴‡Then Moses summoned Mishael and Elzaphan, the sons of Aaron's uncle Uzziel, with the order, "Come, carry your kinsmen from before the sanctuary to a place outside the camp." ⁵So they drew near and carried them by means of their tunics outside the camp, as Moses had commanded.

Conduct of the Priests. ⁶Moses said to Aaron and his sons Eleazar and Ithamar, "Do not dishevel your hair*ᵈ* or tear your garments,*ᵉ* lest you die and bring God's wrath also on the whole community. While your kindred, the rest of the house of Israel, may mourn for those whom the LORD's fire has burned up, ⁷you shall not go beyond the entrance of the tent of meeting,*ᶠ* else you shall die; for the anointing oil of the LORD is upon you." So they did as Moses told them.

⁸The LORD said to Aaron: ⁹When you are to go to the tent of meeting, you and your sons are forbidden, by a perpetual statute throughout your generations, to drink any wine or strong drink, lest you die.*ᵍ* ¹⁰You must be able to distinguish between what is sacred and what is profane, and between what is clean and what is unclean;§*ʰ* ¹¹and you must be able to teach the Israelites all the statutes that the LORD has given them through Moses.

The Eating of the Priestly Portions. ¹²Moses said to Aaron and his surviving sons, Eleazar and Ithamar, "Take the grain offering¶ left over from the oblations to the LORD, and eat it beside the altar in the form of unleavened cakes, since it is most holy. ¹³You must eat it in a sacred place because it is your and your sons' due from the oblations to the LORD; such is the command I have received. ¹⁴*ⁱThe brisket of the elevated offering and the leg** of the contribution, however, you and your sons and daughters may eat, in a clean place; for these have been assigned to you and your children as your due from the communion sacrifices of the Israelites. ¹⁵The leg of the contribution and the brisket of the elevated offering shall be brought in with the oblations of fat to be raised as an elevated offering before the LORD. They shall belong to you and your children as your due forever, as the LORD has commanded."

---

* [10:1–2] Nadab and Abihu are the older sons of Aaron (Ex 6:23–24). Their sin apparently involves using embers from an unapproved source instead of the altar (cf. 16:12). The fire that destroys them is the same type found in 9:24.
† [10:3] The explanation for the divine reaction indicates that improper cultic actions desecrate God and compromise God's glory. Desecration evokes divine punishment (cf. Ex 28:43; Nm 4:15, 19–20). **Those near to me:** i.e., cultic officials.
‡ [10:4–5] Moses has lay people remove the bodies so that the priests can continue their cultic activities free of contamination by a corpse (cf. Nm 19).

---

j. [9:24] 1 Kgs 18:38; 2 Chr 7:1; 2 Mc 2:10; cf. Ex 24:16–17.

a. [10:1] Lv 16:1; Nm 3:4; 26:61; 1 Chr 24:2.
b. [10:2] Nm 16:35; cf. Lv 9:24.
c. [10:3] Lv 21:17, 21; Nm 20:12.
d. [10:6] Lv 13:45.
e. [10:6] Lv 21:5–6, 10–12.

---

§ [10:10] **Sacred and . . . profane . . . clean and . . . unclean:** something or someone may be either sacred or profane (i.e., ordinary, not set apart), and at the same time clean or unclean. Priests would be particularly concerned about keeping what is unclean away from the sacred.
¶ [10:12–13] **Grain offering:** this is the grain offering of the people of 9:4, 17. Only the token offering had been offered; the rest was for the priests' consumption.
** [10:14] **Brisket . . . leg:** these are from the Israelites' communion sacrifices in 9:4, 18–21.

---

f. [10:7] Lv 8:33–35; 21:12.
g. [10:9] Ez 44:21.
h. [10:10] Lv 11:47; 20:25; Ez 22:26; 44:23.
i. [10:14] Lv 7:34.

LV

¹⁶Moses inquired closely about the goat of the purification offering* and discovered that it had all been burned. So he was angry with the surviving sons of Aaron, Eleazar and Ithamar, and said, ^{17j}"Why did you not eat the purification offering in the sacred place, since it is most holy? It has been given to you that you might remove the guilt of the community and make atonement for them before the Lord. ¹⁸Since its blood was not brought inside the sanctuary, you should certainly have eaten the offering in the sanctuary, as I was commanded." ¹⁹Aaron answered Moses, "Even though they presented their purification offering and burnt offering before the Lord today, still this misfortune has befallen me. Had I then eaten of the purification offering today, would it have been pleasing to the Lord?" ²⁰On hearing this, Moses was satisfied.

III. LAWS REGARDING RITUAL PURITY†

CHAPTER 11

Clean and Unclean Meats.‡ ^{1a}The Lord said to Moses and Aaron: ²Speak

to the Israelites and tell them: Of all land animals these are the ones you may eat: ³Any animal that has hoofs you may eat, provided it is cloven-footed and chews the cud. ⁴But you shall not eat^b any of the following from among those that only chew the cud or only have hoofs: the camel, which indeed chews the cud, but does not have hoofs and is therefore unclean for you; ⁵the rock hyrax,[§] which indeed chews the cud, but does not have hoofs and is therefore unclean for you; ⁶the hare, which indeed chews the cud, but does not have hoofs and is therefore unclean for you; ⁷and the pig,^c which does indeed have hoofs and is cloven-footed, but does not chew the cud and is therefore unclean for you. ⁸You shall not eat their meat, and you shall not touch their carcasses; they are unclean for you.

⁹Of the various creatures that live in the water, you may eat the following: whatever in the seas or in river waters that has both fins and scales you may eat.^d ¹⁰But of the creatures that swarm in the water or of animals that otherwise live in the water, whether in the sea or in the rivers, all those that lack either fins or scales are loathsome for you, ¹¹and shall always be loathsome to you. Their meat you shall not eat, and their carcasses you shall loathe. ¹²Every water creature that lacks fins or scales is loathsome for you.

¹³Of the birds,[¶] these you shall loathe; they shall not be eaten, they are loathsome: the griffon vulture, the bearded vulture, the black vulture, ¹⁴the kite, the various species of falcons, ¹⁵the various species of crows, ¹⁶the eagle owl, the kestrel, the

---

* [10:16–20] **Goat of the purification offering**: this is the people's purification offering of 9:3, 15. Since its blood is not brought into the sanctuary, then, according to 6:17–23, this is the type of purification offering which is to be eaten by the priests in a holy place. **Eleazar and Ithamar**: they burned the entire goat of the people's purification offering (9:15) instead of eating it in a sacred place (6:19) to remove ritually the sin of the community by the ingestion of the meat of the offering. Aaron's defense of this action of his sons is somewhat vague: he merely alludes to the loss suffered in the death of Nadab and Abihu, without giving an explicit reason for Eleazar and Ithamar's not eating the people's purification offering, as required.

† [11:1–15:33] Priestly legislation manifests two types of impurity or uncleanness: tolerated and prohibited. Prohibited impurity arises from various sins (e.g., 4:1–5; 5:2–3; 18:6–23; 20:2–5; Nm 5:13–14; 6:6–7). Tolerated impurity has three main sources: certain dead bodies (animal and human; cf. Lv 11 and Nm 19), various regular and abnormal genital discharges (Lv 12; 15), and diseases (specifically "scaly infection," chaps. 13–14). An additional tolerated impurity is that generated by the cult in order to rectify the effect of these impurities or sins (cf. chap. 4; 16:26, 28).

‡ [11:1–47] Apart from the introduction and conclusion (vv. 1–2a, 46–47), this chapter has three sections: (1) prohibitions against eating certain land, water, and air animals (vv. 2b–23); (2) consequences of contact with various animals (vv. 24–41); (3) a prohibition against eating small land animals, which is motivated by the requirement that Israel be holy as God is holy (vv. 41–45). These animals are impure only when dead. Cf. Dt 14:3–21.

§ [11:5–6] According to modern zoology, the rock hyrax (hyrax Syriacus) is classified as an ungulate, and the hare as a rodent; neither is a ruminant. They appear to chew their food as the true ruminants do, and it is upon this appearance that the classification in the text is based.

¶ [11:13–23, 30] **Birds**: the term is broader, including all animals that fly (including bats, v. 19, and flying insects, vv. 20–23). The identification of the various Hebrew names for these birds and reptiles is in many cases uncertain.

---

j. [10:17] Lv 6:18–19.

a. [11:1] Lv 27:11, 27; Gn 7:2–3, 8–9; Dt 14:3–21.

b. [11:4] Jgs 13:4, 7; Is 66:17; Ez 4:12–14.

c. [11:7] Prv 11:22; Is 65:4; 66:17; Mt 7:6; 8:30–32; Mk 5:11–16; Lk 8:32–33; 15:15–16.

d. [11:9] Jn 21:9–13.

LV

long-eared owl, the various species of hawks, ¹⁷the little owl, the cormorant, the screech owl, ¹⁸the barn owl, the horned owl, the osprey, ¹⁹the stork, the various species of herons, the hoopoe, and the bat.

²⁰The various winged insects that walk on all fours are loathsome for you. ²¹But of the various winged insects that walk on all fours you may eat those that have legs jointed above their feet for leaping on the ground; ²²hence of these you may eat the following: the various kinds of locusts, the various kinds of bald locusts, the various kinds of crickets, and the various kinds of grasshoppers.^e ²³All other winged insects that have four legs are loathsome for you.

²⁴You become unclean by the following—anyone who touches their carcasses shall be unclean until evening,^f ²⁵and anyone who carries any part of their carcasses shall wash his garments and be unclean until evening— ²⁶by all hoofed animals that are not cloven-footed or do not chew the cud; they are unclean for you; anyone who touches them becomes unclean. ²⁷Also by the various quadrupeds that walk on paws; they are unclean for you; anyone who touches their carcasses shall be unclean until evening, ²⁸and anyone who carries their carcasses shall wash his garments and be unclean until evening. They are unclean for you.

²⁹Of the creatures that swarm on the ground, the following are unclean for you: the rat, the mouse, the various kinds of lizards, ³⁰the gecko, the spotted lizard, the agama, the skink, and the chameleon. ³¹Among the various swarming creatures, these are unclean for you. Everyone who touches them when they are dead shall be unclean until evening. ³²Everything on which one of them falls when dead becomes unclean, including any article of wood, cloth, leather or goat hair—any article of which use can be made. It must be immersed in water and remain unclean until evening, when it again becomes clean. ³³Should any of these creatures fall into a clay vessel, everything in it becomes unclean, and the vessel itself you must break. ³⁴Any food that can be eaten which makes contact with water, and any liquid that may be drunk, in any such vessel become unclean. ³⁵Any object on which any part of their carcasses falls becomes unclean; if it is an oven or stove, this must be broken to pieces; they are unclean and shall always be unclean to you. ³⁶However, a spring or a cistern for collecting water remains clean; but whoever touches such an animal's carcass becomes unclean. ³⁷If any part of their carcasses falls on any sort of grain that is to be sown, it remains clean; ³⁸but if the grain has become moistened, it becomes unclean to you when any part of their carcasses falls on it.

^{39*g}When one of the animals that you could otherwise eat dies of itself, anyone who touches its carcass shall be unclean until evening; ⁴⁰and anyone who eats any part of its carcass shall wash his garments and be unclean until evening;^h so also, anyone who carries its carcass shall wash his garments and be unclean until evening.

⁴¹All the creatures that swarm on the ground are loathsome and shall not be eaten. ⁴²Whether it crawls on its belly, goes on all fours, or has many legs—any creature that swarms on the earth—you shall not eat them; they are loathsome. ⁴³Do not make yourselves loathsome by any swarming creature nor defile yourselves with them and so become unclean by them.ⁱ ⁴⁴For I, the Lord, am your God. You shall make and keep yourselves holy,[†] because

---

* [11:39–40] These animals create uncleanness, but are not prohibited as food (cf. 17:15–16). Priests who have a higher degree of holiness than other Israelites may not eat these animals (22:8; cf. Ez 44:31). Cf. Ex 22:30; Dt 14:21.

† [11:44–45] **Keep yourselves holy . . . you shall be holy**: a similar idea is expressed in 20:25–26. There, distinguishing between the animals is compared to God's distinguishing between the peoples and choosing Israel.

---

e. [11:22] Mt 3:4; Mk 1:6.
f. [11:24] Lv 5:2; 7:21.

g. [11:39] Lv 17:15–16; 22:8; Ex 22:30; Ez 4:12–14; 44:31.
h. [11:40] Lv 17:15; 22:8.
i. [11:43–44] Lv 20:25–26.

I am holy.[j] You shall not make yourselves unclean, then, by any swarming creature that crawls on the ground. [45]Since I, the LORD, am the one who brought you up from the land of Egypt that I might be your God, you shall be holy, because I am holy.

[46]This is the instruction for land animals, birds, and all the creatures that move about in the water, as well as any animal that swarms on the ground, [47]that you may distinguish between the clean and the unclean, and between creatures that may be eaten and those that may not be eaten.[k]

CHAPTER 12

Uncleanness of Childbirth. [1]The LORD said to Moses: [2]Tell the Israelites: When a woman has a child, giving birth to a boy, she shall be unclean* for seven days, with the same uncleanness as during her menstrual period.[a] [3]On the eighth day, the flesh of the boy's foreskin shall be circumcised,[†b] [4]and then she shall spend thirty-three days more in a state of blood purity; she shall not touch anything sacred nor enter the sanctuary till the days of her purification are fulfilled. [5]If she gives birth to a girl, for fourteen days she shall be as unclean as during her menstrual period, after which she shall spend sixty-six days[‡] in a state of blood purity.

[6§]When the days of her purification for a son or for a daughter are fulfilled,[c] she shall bring to the priest at the entrance of the tent of meeting a yearling lamb for a burnt offering and a pigeon or a turtledove for a purification offering. [7]The priest shall offer them before the LORD to make atonement for her, and thus she will be clean again after her flow of blood. Such is the ritual for the woman who gives birth to a child, male or female. [8]If, however, she cannot afford a lamb,[d] she may take two turtledoves or two pigeons,[e] the one for a burnt offering and the other for a purification offering. The priest shall make atonement for her, and thus she will again be clean.

CHAPTER 13

Scaly Infection.[¶] [1]The LORD said to Moses and Aaron: [2a]When someone has on the skin a mark, lesion, or blotch which appears to develop into a scaly infection, the person shall be brought to Aaron, the priest, or to one of the priests among his sons. [3]If the priest, upon examination of the skin's infection, finds that the hair on the infection has turned white and the infection itself appears to be deeper

---

* [12:2–5] The mother has two stages of uncleanness or impurity: the first where her uncleanness is as severe as during her menstrual period and is contagious to profane persons and objects (cf. 15:19–24), and the second where she does not contaminate persons and objects but is still impure to what is holy, such as the sanctuary (12:4) or sacrifices. The implication is that in the second stage she may resume sexual relations with her husband (which would be prohibited in the first stage according to 18:19).

† [12:3] Circumcision is the sign of the covenant between God and Israel (Gn 17:1–27) and allows full participation in the religious community (Ex 12:43–49; Jos 5:2–10). This command was fulfilled after Jesus' birth (Lk 2:21).

‡ [12:5] **If she gives birth to a girl ... sixty-six days:** while the longer period of uncleanness following the birth of a girl, compared to that following the birth of a boy, might reflect the relative disparity in social status between men and women in ancient Israel (and attested in other cultures), this is by no means certain. There is no simple correlation in the Bible between the worth of something and the degree of impurity it can occasion.

§ [12:6–8] Certain tolerated impurities (see note on 11:1–15:33) are strong enough to pollute the sanctuary and require purification offerings, including the parturient (see also 14:10–32; 15:13–15, 28–30). Cf. note on 4:3. Mary fulfilled the command of bringing sacrifices after the birth of Jesus (Lk 2:22–24).

¶ [13:1–14:57] These chapters deal with scaly or fungal infections (Hebrew ṣāraʻat). The older translation "leprosy" is misleading because ṣāraʻat refers to not just one but several chronic and enduring skin diseases in human beings. The disease known as "leprosy" (Hansen's disease) is probably not included among the conditions described in the chapter. Also the term ṣāraʻat refers to fungal growths in fabrics and on the walls of houses. The reason why these conditions, and not other diseases, were considered unclean may be that they were quite visible, associated with death (cf. Nm 12:9–12), and traditionally connected with punishment by the deity (Lv 14:34; Dt 28:27, 35; 2 Sm 3:29; 2 Kgs 5:26–27; 2 Chr 26:16–21).

j. [11:44] Lv 19:2; 20:7, 26; Mt 5:48; 1 Pt 1:16.
k. [11:47] Lv 10:10.

a. [12:2] Lv 15:19.
b. [12:3] Gn 17:12; Jn 7:22.

c. [12:6] Lk 2:22–24.
d. [12:8] Lv 14:21–22.
e. [12:8] Lv 1:14; Lk 2:24.

a. [13:2] Lv 22:4; Ex 4:6; Nm 5:2–3; Dt 24:8; 2 Sm 3:29; 2 Kgs 5:1, 3–7, 11, 27; Mk 1:40–45.

than the skin,* it is indeed a scaly infection; the priest, on seeing this, shall declare the person unclean. ⁴†If, however, the blotch on the skin is white, but does not seem to be deeper than the skin, nor has the hair turned white, the priest shall quarantine the afflicted person for seven days.‡ ⁵Should the priest, upon examination on the seventh day, find that the infection has remained unchanged in color and has not spread on the skin, the priest shall quarantine the person for another seven days. ⁶Should the priest, upon examination again on the seventh day, find that the infection is now faded and has not spread on the skin, the priest shall declare the person clean; it was merely a scab. The person shall wash his garments§ and so become clean. ⁷But if, after the person was examined by the priest and declared clean, the scab spreads at all on the skin, the person shall once more be examined by the priest. ⁸Should the priest, upon examination, find that the scab has indeed spread on the skin, he shall declare the person unclean; it is a scaly infection.

⁹When someone is afflicted with a scaly infection, that person shall be brought to the priest. ¹⁰Should the priest, upon examination, find that there is a white mark on the skin which has turned the hair white and that there is raw flesh in it, ¹¹it is a chronic scaly infection on the skin. The priest shall declare the person unclean without quarantine, since the individual is

certainly unclean. ¹²¶If the scaly infection breaks out on the skin and, as far as the priest can see, covers all the skin of the afflicted person from head to foot, ¹³should the priest then, upon examination, find that the scaly infection does cover the whole body, he shall declare the afflicted person clean; since the person has turned completely white; that individual is clean. ¹⁴But as soon as raw flesh appears, the individual is unclean; ¹⁵on observing the raw flesh, the priest shall declare the person unclean, because raw flesh is unclean; it is a scaly infection. ¹⁶If, however, the raw flesh again turns white, the person shall return to the priest; ¹⁷should the latter, upon examination, find that the infection has indeed turned white, he shall declare the afflicted person clean; the individual is clean.

¹⁸If a boil appeared on a person's skin which later healed, ¹⁹should now in the place of the boil a white mark or a reddish white blotch develop, the person shall be examined by the priest. ²⁰If the latter, upon examination, finds that it is deeper than the skin and that the hair has turned white, he shall declare the person unclean; it is a scaly infection that has broken out in the boil. ²¹But if the priest, upon examination, finds that there is no white hair in it and that it is not deeper than the skin and is faded, the priest shall quarantine the person for seven days. ²²If it has then spread on the skin, the priest shall declare the person unclean; it is an infection. ²³But if the blotch remains the same without spreading, it is merely the scar of the boil; the priest shall therefore declare the person clean.

²⁴If there was a burn on a person's skin, and the burned area now becomes a reddish white or a white blotch, ²⁵when the priest, upon examination, finds that the hair has turned

---

* [13:3] The symptoms of white hair and depth (perhaps a subcutaneous lesion) do not clearly correlate with known skin diseases or lesions. It may be that the symptoms are a hybrid ideal that do not reflect reality and are the result of priestly systematization. The same judgment applies to the conditions in vv. 10–11, 20, 25; cf. note on vv. 12–17.

† [13:4–8] The symptoms here involve a flaky patch of skin that spreads after one week or stays the same after two. This correlates with many skin diseases, such as psoriasis, seborrhoeic dermatitis, certain mycotic infections, patchy eczema, and pityriasis rosea.

‡ [13:4] **Quarantine . . . seven days**: unless lesions have unmistakable symptoms of scaly infection, time is needed to distinguish disease from a condition which is following the natural course of healing and remission. Cf. vv. 5, 21, 26, 27, 31, 33, 50, 54; 14:38.

§ [13:6] **Wash his garments**: even suspected scaly infections create some impurity, not just diagnosed infections (vv. 45–46).

¶ [13:12–17] This is not a paradox, namely where a limited lesion is impure but one that covers the whole body is pure. Rather, a white lesion that lacks ulcerated skin ("raw flesh") is pure, even if it covers the whole body. This formulation reflects priestly interest in systematization.

white in the blotch and this seems to be deeper than the skin, it is a scaly infection that has broken out in the burn; the priest shall therefore declare the person unclean; it is a scaly infection. ²⁶But if the priest, upon examination, finds that there is no white hair in the blotch and that this is not deeper than the skin and is faded, the priest shall quarantine the person for seven days. ²⁷Should the priest, upon examination on the seventh day, find that it has spread at all on the skin, he shall declare the person unclean; it is a scaly infection. ²⁸But if the blotch remains the same without spreading on the skin and is faded, it is merely the spot of the burn; the priest shall therefore declare the person clean, since it is only the scar of the burn.

²⁹*When a man or a woman has an infection on the head or in the beard, ³⁰should the priest, upon examination, find that the infection appears to be deeper than the skin and that there is fine yellow hair in it, the priest shall declare the person unclean; it is a scall. It is a scaly infection of the head or beard. ³¹But if the priest, upon examining the scall infection, finds that it does not appear to be deeper than the skin, though the hair in it may not be black, the priest shall quarantine the scall-stricken person for seven days. ³²Should the priest, upon examining the infection on the seventh day find that the scall has not spread and has no yellow hair in it and does not seem to be deeper than the skin, ³³the person shall shave, but not the scall spot. Then the priest shall quarantine the scall-diseased person for another seven days. ³⁴If the priest, upon examining the scall on the seventh day, finds that it has not spread on the skin and that it does not appear to be deeper than the skin, he shall declare the person clean; the latter shall wash his garments, and will thus be clean.

³⁵But if the scall spreads at all on the skin after the person has been declared clean— ³⁶should the priest, upon examination, find that the scall has indeed spread on the skin, he need not look for yellow hair; the individual is unclean. ³⁷If, however, the scall has remained unchanged in color and black hair has grown in it, the disease has been healed; the person is clean, and the priest shall declare the individual clean.

³⁸†When the skin of a man or a woman is spotted with several white blotches, ³⁹if the priest, upon examination, finds that the blotches on the skin are pale white, it is only tetter that has broken out on the skin, and the person therefore is clean.

⁴⁰When a man loses the hair of his head, he is simply bald on the crown and not unclean.^b ⁴¹So too, if he loses the hair on the front of his head, he is simply bald on the forehead and not unclean. ⁴²But when there is a reddish white infection on his bald crown or bald forehead, it is a scaly infection that is breaking out there. ⁴³If the priest, upon examination, finds that the infection spot on the bald area on the crown or forehead has the same reddish white appearance as that of a scaly infection of the skin, ⁴⁴the man has a scaly infection and is unclean. The priest shall declare him unclean; his infection is on his head.

⁴⁵‡The garments of one afflicted with a scaly infection shall be rent and the hair disheveled,^c and the mustache covered.^d The individual shall cry out, "Unclean, unclean!" ⁴⁶As long as the infection is present, the person shall

---

* [13:29–37] The symptoms in this unit may include either favus (a mycotic infection) or a protein deficiency syndrome (Kwashiorkor) where the hair may be fine and copper-red to yellow.

† [13:38–39] This may refer to vitiligo, where patches of the skin and hair lose pigmentation.

‡ [13:45–46] The symbolic association with death is found in the mourning activities in which those diagnosed with these afflictions engage: rending clothes, disheveling the hair, and covering the mouth. They are also excluded from the camp. Cf. examples of exclusion in Nm 5:1–4; 12:14–15; 2 Kgs 7:3–10; 15:5; 2 Chr 26:21. Persons with scaly infections must have been able to pollute others in the priestly system, though this is not stated. Hence, they must cry out "Unclean, unclean!" to warn others of their presence.

b. [13:40] 2 Kgs 2:23.
c. [13:45] Lv 10:6.
d. [13:45] Mi 3:7.

be unclean. Being unclean, that individual shall dwell apart, taking up residence outside the camp.*e*

Fungal Infection of Fabrics and Leather. [47]When a fungal infection is on a garment of wool or of linen, [48]or on the warp and woof of linen or wool, or on a hide or anything made of leather, [49]if the infection on the garment or hide, or on the warp or woof, or on any leather article is greenish or reddish, the thing is indeed a fungal infection and must be examined by the priest. [50]Having examined the infection, the priest shall quarantine the infected article for seven days. [51]If the priest, upon inspecting the infection on the seventh day, finds that it has spread on the garment, or on the warp or woof, or on the leather, whatever be its use, the infection is a harmful fungus; the article is unclean. [52]He shall therefore burn up the garment, or the warp or woof, be it of wool or linen, or any leather article which is infected; since it is a harmful fungus, it must be destroyed by fire. [53]But if the priest, upon examination, finds that it has not spread on the garment, or on the warp or woof, or on the leather article, [54]he shall give orders to have the infected article washed and then quarantined for another seven days. [55]If the priest, upon examination after the infection was washed, finds that it has not changed its color, even though it may not have spread, the article is unclean. You shall burn it with fire. It is a fray, be it on its inner or outer side. [56]But if the priest, upon examination, finds that the infection has faded after the washing, he shall cut it out of the garment, or the leather, or the warp or woof. [57]If, however, the infection again appears on the garment, or on the warp or woof, or on the leather article, it is still virulent and you shall burn the thing infected with fire. [58]But if, after the washing, the infection has disappeared from the garment, or the warp or woof, or the leather article, the thing shall be washed a second time, and thus it will be clean. [59]This is the instruction for a fungal*f* infection on a garment of wool or linen, or on a warp or woof, or on any leather article, to determine whether it is clean or unclean.

CHAPTER 14

Purification After Scaly Infection. [1]†The LORD said to Moses: [2]*a*This is the ritual for someone that had a scaly infection at the time of that person's purification.*b* The individual shall be brought to the priest, [3]who is to go outside the camp.*c* If the priest, upon inspection, finds that the scaly infection has healed in the afflicted person, [4]he shall order that two live, clean birds,‡ as well as some cedar wood, scarlet yarn, and hyssop be obtained for the one who is to be purified.*d* [5]§The priest shall then order that one of the birds be slaughtered over an earthen vessel with fresh water in it. [6]Taking the living bird with the cedar wood, the scarlet yarn and the hyssop, the priest shall dip them, including the live bird, in the blood of the bird that was slaughtered over the fresh water, [7]and then sprinkle seven times on the person to be purified from the scaly infection. When he has thus purified

---

† [14:1–32] The rites here are for purification from human scaly infections after recovery, not for healing (but cf. 2 Kgs 5:10–14).

‡ [14:4–7] The bird rite is also found for purifying a house from a fungus (vv. 49–53). The rite apparently removes impurity from the individual and, by means of the live bird, sends it away to unpopulated areas (v. 7). This is similar to the dispatch of a goat laden with sins on the Day of Atonement (16:21–22).

§ [14:5–7] The blood from the bird serves as a ritual detergent, much like the blood from the purification offering (see notes on 4:3). It is not a sacrifice, however, since it is not performed at the sanctuary. **Fresh water**: lit., "living water," taken from some source of running water, not from a cistern.

---

* [13:48] **Warp and woof**: it is possible that the nature of the weave allowed fungus to grow separately along warp or woof. Otherwise, this may refer to the yarns before they are woven together.

e. [13:46] Lv 14:3; Nm 5:2; 12:14–15; 2 Kgs 7:3–10; 15:5; 2 Chr 26:21; Mt 26:6; Mk 14:3; Lk 17:11–19.

f. [13:59] Lv 14:54–57.

a. [14:2] 2 Kgs 5:10, 14; Mt 8:4; 10:8; Mk 1:44; Lk 4:27; 5:14.
b. [14:2] Lv 14:48–53.
c. [14:3] Lv 13:46.
d. [14:4] Nm 19:6.

that person, he shall let the living bird fly away over the countryside.[e] [8]The person being purified shall then wash his garments, shave off all hair, and bathe in water,[*] and so become clean. After this the person may come inside the camp, but shall still remain outside his or her tent for seven days.[f] [9]On the seventh day this individual shall again shave off all hair, of the head, beard, and eyebrows—all hair must be shaved—and also wash his garments and bathe the body in water, and so become clean.

[10]On the eighth day the individual shall take two unblemished male lambs, one unblemished yearling ewe lamb, three tenths of an ephah of bran flour mixed with oil for a grain offering, and one log[†] of oil. [11]The priest who performs the purification ceremony shall place the person who is being purified, as well as all these offerings, before the LORD at the entrance of the tent of meeting. [12]Taking one of the male lambs, the priest shall present it as a reparation offering,[g] along with the log of oil, raising them as an elevated[h] offering before the LORD. [13]This lamb shall be slaughtered in the sacred place where the purification offering and the burnt offering are slaughtered, because the reparation offering is like the purification offering; it belongs to the priest and is most holy. [14][‡][i]Then the priest shall take some of the blood of the reparation offering and put it on the lobe of the right ear, the thumb of the right hand, and the big toe of the right foot of the person being purified.

[15]The priest shall also take the log of oil and pour some of it into the palm of his own left hand; [16]then, dipping his right finger in the oil on his left palm, he shall sprinkle some of it with his finger seven times before the LORD. [17]Of the oil left in his hand the priest shall put some on the lobe of the right ear, the thumb of the right hand, and the big toe of the right foot of the person being purified, over the blood of the reparation offering. [18]The rest of the oil in his hand the priest shall put on the head[j] of the one being purified. Thus shall the priest make atonement for the individual before the LORD. [19]The priest shall next offer the purification offering,[k] thus making atonement on behalf of the one being purified from the uncleanness. After this the burnt offering shall be slaughtered. [20]The priest shall offer the burnt offering[l] and the grain offering on the altar before the LORD. Thus shall the priest make atonement for the person, and the individual will become clean.

Poor Person's Sacrifices. [21]If a person is poor and cannot afford so much,[m] that person shall take one male lamb for a reparation offering, to be used as an elevated offering in atonement, one tenth of an ephah of bran flour mixed with oil for a grain offering, a log of oil, [22]and two turtledoves or pigeons, which the individual can more easily afford, the one as a purification offering and the other as a burnt offering. [23]On the eighth day of purification the person shall bring them to the priest, at the entrance of the tent of meeting before the LORD. [24]Taking the lamb of the reparation offering, along with the log of oil, the priest shall raise them as an elevated offering before the LORD. [25]When the lamb of the reparation offering has been slaughtered, the priest shall take some of its blood, and put it on the lobe of the right ear, on the thumb of

---

* [14:8] **Bathe in water:** This phrase occurs frequently in Lv 14–16 and is imprecise. It can refer to both ordinary and cultic washing. The context will determine the meaning. At this early period in Israel's history it is probably not a reference to cultic immersion in a Mikveh—a Second Temple period ritual.

† [14:10] **Log:** a liquid measure of capacity attested in the Bible only here. It is apparently equal in capacity to one-half liter.

‡ [14:14–17] The application of blood and oil here facilitates the movement of the person from the severely impure to the pure profane sphere; it reintegrates him or her into the community. Cf. 8:23–24.

---

e. [14:7] Lv 16:21–22.
f. [14:8] Lv 15:13, 28.
g. [14:12] Lv 7:1–10.
h. [14:12] Lv 7:30.
i. [14:14] Lv 8:23–24.

j. [14:18] Lv 8:12, 30.
k. [14:19] Lv 4.
l. [14:20] Lv 1.
m. [14:21] Lv 5:7, 11; 12:8.

the right hand, and on the big toe of the right foot of the person being purified. [26]The priest shall then pour some of the oil into the palm of his own left hand [27]and with his right finger sprinkle some of the oil in his left palm seven times before the LORD. [28]Some of the oil in his hand the priest shall also put on the lobe of the right ear, the thumb of the right hand, and the big toe of the right foot of the person being purified, where he had sprinkled the blood of the reparation offering. [29]The rest of the oil in his hand the priest shall put on the head of the one being purified. Thus shall he make atonement for the individual before the LORD. [30]Then, of the turtledoves or pigeons, such as the person can afford, [31]the priest shall offer one as a purification offering and the other as a burnt offering,[n] along with the grain offering. Thus shall the priest make atonement before the LORD for the person who is being purified. [32]This is the ritual for one afflicted with a scaly infection who has insufficient means for purification.

Fungal Infection of Houses. [33]*The LORD said to Moses and Aaron: [34]When you come into the land of Canaan, which I am giving you to possess, if I put[o] a fungal infection in any house of the land you occupy, [35]the owner of the house shall come and report to the priest, "Something like an infection has appeared in my house." [36]The priest shall then order the house to be cleared out before he goes in to examine the infection, lest everything in the house become unclean. Only after this is he to go in to examine the house. [37]If the priest, upon inspection, finds that the infection on the walls of the house consists of greenish or reddish spots[p] which seem to go deeper than the surface of the wall, [38]he shall go out of the house to the doorway and quarantine the house for seven days. [39]On the seventh day the priest shall return. If, upon inspection, he finds that the infection has spread on the walls, [40]he shall order the infected stones to be pulled out and cast in an unclean place outside the city. [41]The whole inside of the house shall then be scraped, and the mortar that has been scraped off shall be dumped in an unclean place outside the city. [42]Then other stones shall be brought and put in the place of the old stones, and new mortar obtained and plastered on the house. [43]If the infection breaks out once more in the house after the stones have been pulled out and the house has been scraped and replastered, [44]the priest shall come; and if, upon inspection, he finds that the infection has spread in the house, it is a corrosive fungus in the house, and it is unclean. [45]It shall be pulled down, and all its stones, beams and mortar shall be hauled away to an unclean place outside the city. [46][q]Whoever enters a house while it is quarantined shall be unclean until evening. [47]Whoever sleeps or eats in such a house shall also wash his garments.

[48][r]If the priest finds, when he comes to the house, that the infection has in fact not spread in the house after the plastering, he shall declare the house clean, since the infection has been healed. [49]To purify the house, he shall take two birds, as well as cedar wood, scarlet yarn, and hyssop. [50]One of the birds he shall slaughter over an earthen vessel with fresh water in it. [51]Then, taking the cedar wood, the hyssop and the scarlet yarn, together with the living bird, he shall dip them all in the blood of the slaughtered bird and the fresh water, and sprinkle the house seven times. [52]Thus he shall purify the house with the bird's blood and the fresh water, along with the living bird,

* [14:33–53] Discussion of fungi in houses is probably delayed until here because it deals with a case pertaining to living in the land (v. 34) as opposed to the foregoing cases which apply even in the wilderness. The rules on fabrics (13:47–58) apply to the tent dwellings in the wilderness.

n. [14:31] Lv 1:14–17; 5:7–10.
o. [14:34] Nm 12:9–15; 2 Kgs 15:4–5; 2 Chr 26:16–21.
p. [14:37] Lv 13:49.
q. [14:46–47] cf. Lv 15:10.
r. [14:48] Lv 14:2–9.

the cedar wood, the hyssop, and the scarlet yarn. [53]He shall then let the living bird fly away over the countryside outside the city. Thus he shall make atonement for the house, and it will be clean.

[54]This is the ritual for every kind of human scaly infection and scall, [55]and for fungus diseases in garments and houses— [56]for marks, lesions and blotches— [57]to give direction when there is a state of uncleanness and when a state of cleanness. This is the ritual for scaly infection.

CHAPTER 15

Sexual Uncleanness. [1]The LORD said to Moses and Aaron: [2†]Speak to the Israelites and tell them: When any man has a genital discharge, he is thereby unclean.[a] [3]Such is his uncleanness from this discharge, whether his body‡ drains freely with the discharge or is blocked up from the discharge. His uncleanness is on him all the days that his body discharges or is blocked up from his discharge; this is his uncleanness. [4]Any bed on which the man with the discharge lies is unclean, and any article on which he sits is unclean. [5]Anyone who touches his bed shall wash his garments, bathe in water, and be unclean until evening. [6]Whoever sits on an article on which the man with the discharge was sitting shall wash his garments, bathe in water, and be unclean until evening. [7]Whoever touches the body of the man with the discharge shall wash his garments, bathe in water, and be unclean until evening. [8]If the man with the discharge spits on a clean person, the latter shall wash his garments, bathe in water, and be unclean until evening. [9]Any saddle on which the man with the discharge

rides is unclean. [10]Whoever touches anything that was under him shall be unclean until evening; whoever carries any such thing shall wash his garments, bathe in water, and be unclean until evening.[b] [11]Anyone whom the man with the discharge touches with his unrinsed hands shall wash his garments, bathe in water, and be unclean until evening. [12]Earthenware touched by the man with the discharge shall be broken; and every wooden article shall be rinsed with water.

[13]When a man with a discharge becomes clean§ of his discharge, he shall count seven days[c] for his purification. Then he shall wash his garments and bathe his body in fresh water, and so he will be clean. [14]On the eighth day he shall take two turtledoves or two pigeons,[d] and going before the LORD, to the entrance of the tent of meeting, he shall give them to the priest, [15]who shall offer them up, the one as a purification offering and the other as a burnt offering. Thus shall the priest make atonement before the LORD for the man because of his discharge.

[16]¶When a man has an emission of semen, he shall bathe his whole body in water and be unclean until evening.[e] [17]Any piece of cloth or leather with semen on it shall be washed with water and be unclean until evening.

[18]If a man has sexual relations with a woman, they shall both bathe in water and be unclean until evening.

[19]**When a woman has a flow of blood from her body, she shall be in

---

§ [15:13] **Becomes clean**: i.e., when his discharge ceases. The rite that follows is for purification, not a cure; see note on 14:1–32.

¶ [15:16–18] Menstrual blood, semen, and other impurities in Lv 11–15 are considered "impure" either because they are force of life whose "loss" represents death or because, as uniquely human conditions, they are symbolically incompatible with the deity and the divine abode, the sanctuary. Lv 15:16 refers to a spontaneous nocturnal emission, and either because this marks life and death boundaries or because of its uniquely human (versus divine) character, any contact with it renders the object or person ritually unclean. Thus, in 15:18 it is not the marital act itself that is polluting, but only semen.

** [15:19–24] This is normal menstruation.

---

* [15:1–33] Sexual discharges may be unclean partly because they involve the loss of life fluids or are otherwise involved with phenomena at the margins of life and death.

† [15:2–3] The uncleanness here is perhaps a discharge of pus because of urethritis (often but not solely associated with gonorrhea).

‡ [15:3] **Body**: here a euphemism in the Hebrew for "penis."

a. [15:2] Nm 5:2.

b. [15:10] Lv 11:24–25, 27–28, 39–40; 14:46–47.

c. [15:13] Lv 14:8.

d. [15:14] Lv 12:8; 14:22.

e. [15:16] Ex 19:15; Dt 23:11–12; 1 Sm 21:6.

a state of menstrual uncleanness for seven days. Anyone who touches her shall be unclean until evening.[f] [20]Anything on which she lies or sits during her menstrual period shall be unclean. [21]Anyone who touches her bed shall wash his garments, bathe in water, and be unclean until evening. [22]Whoever touches any article on which she was sitting shall wash his garments, bathe in water, and be unclean until evening. [23]Whether an object* is on the bed or on something she sat upon, when the person touches it, that person shall be unclean until evening. [24]If a man lies with her, he contracts her menstrual uncleanness and shall be unclean for seven days;[g] every bed on which he then lies also becomes unclean.

[25]†When a woman has a flow of blood for several days outside her menstrual period, or when her flow continues beyond the ordinary period, as long as she suffers this unclean flow she shall be unclean, just as during her menstrual period.[h] [26]Any bed on which she lies during such a flow becomes unclean, as it would during her menstrual period, and any article on which she sits becomes unclean just as during her menstrual period. [27]Anyone who touches them becomes unclean; that person shall wash his garments, bathe in water, and be unclean until evening.

[28]†When she becomes clean from her flow, she shall count seven days; after this she becomes clean. [29]On the eighth day she shall take two turtledoves or two pigeons and bring them to the priest at the entrance of the tent of meeting. [30]The priest shall offer one of them as a purification offering

and the other as a burnt offering. Thus shall the priest make atonement before the LORD for her because of her unclean flow.

[31]You shall warn the Israelites of their uncleanness, lest they die through their uncleanness by defiling my tabernacle,[j] which is in their midst. [32]This is the ritual for the man with a discharge, or who has an emission of semen, and thereby becomes unclean; [33]as well as for the woman who has her menstrual period; or one who has a discharge, male or female; and also for the man who lies with an unclean woman.

CHAPTER 16

The Day of Atonement. [1]‡After the death of Aaron's two sons,[a] who died when they encroached on the LORD's presence, the LORD spoke to Moses [2]and said to him: Tell your brother Aaron that he is not to come whenever he pleases§ into the inner sanctuary, inside the veil,[b] in front of the cover on the ark, lest he die, for I reveal myself in a cloud above the ark's cover. [3]Only in this way may Aaron enter the inner sanctuary. He shall bring a bull of the herd for a purification offering and a ram for a burnt offering. [4]He shall wear the sacred linen tunic, with the linen pants underneath, gird himself with the linen sash and put on the linen turban.[c] But since these vestments are sacred, he shall not put them on until he has first bathed his body in water.[d] [5]From the

---

* [15:23] **An object:** the Hebrew is unclear. This translation means that even an object on the woman's unclean bed or chair can mediate uncleanness to another, but only if all the object touched is still on the bed or article sat upon, thus forming a chain of simultaneous contact.

† [15:25–30] This is menstruation outside the normal cycle or for periods longer than normal. A woman with a chronic blood flow was healed by touching the tassel of Jesus' cloak (Mt 9:20–22; Mk 5:25–34; Lk 8:43–48).

f. [15:19] Lv 12:2, 5; 2 Sm 11:4; Ez 36:17.
g. [15:24] Lv 18:19; 20:18; Ez 18:6.
h. [15:25] Mt 9:20–22; Mk 5:25–34; Lk 8:43–48.
i. [15:28] Lv 15:13–15.

---

‡ [16:1–34] This is the narrative sequel of the story in chap. 10. The ritual in chapter 16 originally may have been an emergency rite in response to unexpected pollution of the sanctuary.

§ [16:2] **Not to come whenever he pleases:** access to the various parts of the sanctuary is strictly controlled. Only the high priest can enter the most holy place, and only once a year. **The veil:** the Letter to the Hebrews makes use of the imagery of the Day of Atonement (in Hebrew *Yom Kippur*) to explain Jesus' sacrifice (Heb 9:1–14, 23–28). **Ark's cover:** the meaning of *kappōret* is not certain. It may be connected with the verb *kipper* "to atone, purge" (see note on v. 6) and thus refer to this part of the ark as a focus of atonement or purification.

j. [15:31] Lv 5:2–3; 22:9; Nm 19:13, 20.

a. [16:1] Lv 10:1–5.
b. [16:2] Lv 23:26–32; Nm 29:7–11; Heb 9:6–28.
c. [16:4] Lv 8:7; Ex 28:1–40.
d. [16:4] Lv 8:6.

Israelite community he shall receive two male goats for a purification offering and one ram for a burnt offering. [6]Aaron shall offer the bull, his purification offering, to make atonement* for himself and for his household. [7]Taking the two male goats and setting them before the Lord at the entrance of the tent of meeting, [8]he shall cast lots[e] to determine which one is for the Lord and which for Azazel.[†f] [9]The goat that is determined by lot for the Lord, Aaron shall present and offer up as a purification offering. [10]But the goat determined by lot for Azazel he shall place before the Lord alive, so that with it he may make atonement by sending it off to Azazel in the desert.

[11]Thus shall Aaron offer his bull for the purification offering, to make atonement for himself and for his family. When he has slaughtered it, [12]he shall take a censer full of glowing embers from the altar before the Lord, as well as a double handful of finely ground fragrant incense, and bringing them inside the veil, [13]there before the Lord he shall put incense on the fire, so that a cloud of incense may shield the cover that is over the covenant, else he will die. [14]Taking some of the bull's blood, he shall sprinkle it with his finger on the front of the ark's cover and likewise sprinkle some of the blood with his finger seven times in front of the cover.

[15]Then he shall slaughter the goat of the people's purification offering, and bringing its blood inside the veil, he shall do with it as he did with the bull's blood, sprinkling it on the ark's cover and in front of it. [16]Thus he shall purge the inner sanctuary[‡] of all the Israelites' impurities and trespasses, including all their sins. He shall do the same for the tent of meeting,[g] which is set up among them in the midst of their uncleanness. [17]No one else may be in the tent of meeting from the time he enters the inner sanctuary to make atonement until he departs. When he has made atonement for himself and his household, as well as for the whole Israelite assembly, [18§]he shall come out to the altar before the Lord and purge it also. Taking some of the bull's and the goat's blood, he shall put it on the horns around the altar, [19]and with his finger sprinkle some of the blood on it seven times.[h] Thus he shall purify it and sanctify it from the impurities of the Israelites.

The Scapegoat. [20]When he has finished purging the inner sanctuary, the tent of meeting and the altar, Aaron shall bring forward the live goat. [21]Laying both hands[¶] on its head, he shall confess over it all the iniquities of the Israelites and their trespasses, including all their sins, and so put them on the goat's head.[i] He shall then have it led into the wilderness by an attendant. [22]The goat will carry off all their iniquities to an isolated region.[j]

When the goat is dispatched into the wilderness, [23]Aaron shall go into the tent of meeting, strip off the linen vestments he had put on when he entered

---

* [16:6] **Make atonement**: the Hebrew verb *kipper* refers specifically to the removal of sin and impurity (cf. Ex 30:10; Lv 6:23; 8:15; 16:16, 18, 20, 27, 33; Ez 43:20, 26; 45:20), thus "to purge" in vv. 16, 18, 20, and 33, and more generally to the consequence of the sacrificial procedure, which is atonement (cf. Lv 17:11). "Atonement" is preeminently a function of the purification sacrifice, but other sacrifices, except apparently the communion sacrifice, achieve this as well.

† [16:8] **Azazel**: a name for a demon (meaning something like "angry/fierce god"). See note on 17:7.

‡ [16:16] **Inner sanctuary**: this refers to the most holy room (vv. 2, 11–15). **Trespasses, including all their sins**: the term for "trespasses" (Heb. *pesha'im*), which has overtones of rebellion, and the phrase "all their sins" indicate that even sins committed intentionally are included (such as when the sinner "acts defiantly," as in Nm 15:30–31). This complements the scheme found in Lv 4 (see note on 4:3): intentional sins pollute the sanctuary more and penetrate even further than inadvertent sins, namely to the most holy place. **The same for the tent of meeting**: this rite may be that found in 4:5–7, 16–18 where blood is sprinkled in the anterior room and blood is placed on the horns of the incense altar there. Cf. Ex 30:10.

§ [16:18–19] Thus a third locale in the sanctuary complex, the open-air altar, is purified. See the summaries in 16:20, 33.

¶ [16:21] **Both hands**: this gesture is for transferring sins to the head of the goat and is apparently different in meaning from the one-handed gesture that precedes the slaughtering of sacrificial animals (1:4; 3:2; 4:4; see note on 1:4).

---

e. [16:8] Jos 7:14–20; Acts 1:26.
f. [16:8] Lv 17:7.

g. [16:16] Lv 4:5–7, 16–18.
h. [16:19] Lv 4:25, 30, 34.
i. [16:21] Is 53:6; 2 Cor 5:21.
j. [16:22] Lv 14:7, 53; Is 53:11–12; Jn 1:29; 1 Pt 2:24.

the inner sanctuary, and leave them in the tent of meeting. **²⁴**After bathing his body with water in a sacred place, he shall put on his regular vestments, and then come out and offer his own and the people's burnt offering, in atonement for himself and for the people, **²⁵**and also burn the fat of the purification offering on the altar.

²⁶The man who led away the goat for Azazel shall wash his garments and bathe his body in water; only then may he enter the camp. **²⁷**The bull and the goat of the purification offering whose blood was brought to make atonement in the inner sanctuary, shall be taken outside the camp,*k* where their hides and flesh and dung shall be burned in the fire. **²⁸**The one who burns them shall wash his garments and bathe his body in water; only then may he enter the camp.

The Fast. **²⁹***l*This shall be an everlasting statute for you: on the tenth day of the seventh month every one of you, whether a native or a resident alien, shall humble yourselves* and shall do no work. **³⁰**For on this day atonement is made for you to make you clean; of all your sins you will be cleansed before the Lord. **³¹**It shall be a sabbath of complete rest for you, on which you must humble yourselves—an everlasting statute.

³²This atonement is to be made by the priest who has been anointed and ordained to the priesthood in succession to his father. He shall wear the linen garments, the sacred vestments, **³³**and purge the most sacred part of the sanctuary, as well as the tent of meeting, and the altar. He shall also make atonement for the priests and all the people of the assembly. **³⁴**This, then, shall be an everlasting statute for you:

once a year atonement shall be made on behalf of the Israelites for all their sins. And Moses did as the Lord had commanded him.

IV. HOLINESS LAWS

CHAPTER 17

Sacredness of Blood. **¹**The Lord said to Moses: **²**Speak to Aaron and his sons, as well as to all the Israelites, and tell them: This is what the Lord has commanded: **³†**Any Israelite who slaughters an ox or a sheep or a goat, whether in the camp or outside of it, **⁴**without first bringing it to the entrance of the tent of meeting to present it as an offering to the Lord in front of the Lord's tabernacle, shall be judged guilty of bloodshed‡*a*—that individual has shed blood, and shall be cut off*b* from the people. **⁵**This is so that such sacrifices as they used to offer in the open field the Israelites shall henceforth bring to the Lord at the entrance of the tent of meeting, to the priest, and sacrifice them there as communion sacrifices to the Lord.*c* **⁶**The priest will splash the blood on the altar of the Lord at the entrance of the tent of meeting and burn the fat for an odor pleasing to the Lord. **⁷**No longer shall they offer their sacrifices to the demons§ with whom they prostituted themselves.*d* This shall be an everlasting statute for them and their descendants.

⁸Tell them, therefore: Anyone, whether of the house of Israel or of the aliens residing among them, who

---

* [16:29] **Humble yourselves:** also v. 31. The idiom used here (Heb. *'innâ nephesh*) involves mainly fasting (Ps 35:13), but probably prohibits other activities such as anointing (Dn 10:3) and sexual intercourse (2 Sm 12:15–24). Such acts of self-denial display the need for divine favor. Fasting is often undertaken in times of emergency and mourning (cf. 1 Sm 14:24; 2 Sm 1:12; 3:35; cf. Mk 2:18–22).

k. [16:27] Lv 4:11–12; 6:23; Heb 13:11–13.
l. [16:29] Lv 23:27, 32; Nm 29:7.

† [17:3–4] Any animal slaughtered must be brought to the tent of meeting as an offering. This differs from Dt 12:15–28, which allows those living too far from the temple to slaughter an animal for food at home without offering it as a sacrifice.
‡ [17:4] **Guilty of bloodshed:** human beings and animals can incur blood guilt for killing human beings (cf. Gn 9:5–6); human beings can incur blood guilt for killing animals (see note on Lv 24:17–22).
§ [17:7] **Demons:** for Hebrew *śeʿîrîm*, lit., "goats." Like the demon Azazel (cf. 16:8, 10, 21–22), they dwell in the open country (17:5). Cf. Is 13:21; 34:14.

a. [17:4] Lv 24:18.
b. [17:4] Lv 7:20.
c. [17:5] Lv 3:1–2, 7–8, 13.
d. [17:7] Ex 34:15; Dt 32:17; 2 Chr 11:15; 1 Cor 10:20.

offers a burnt offering or sacrifice ⁹without bringing it to the entrance of the tent of meeting to offer it to the Lord, shall be cut off from the people. ¹⁰ᵉAs for anyone, whether of the house of Israel or of the aliens residing among them, who consumes any blood, I will set myself against that individual and will cut that person off from among the people, ¹¹since the life of the flesh is in the blood,ᶠ and I have given it to you to make atonement* on the altar for yourselves, because it is the blood as life that makes atonement. ¹²That is why I have told the Israelites: No one among you, not even a resident alien, may consume blood.

¹³Anyone hunting,† whether of the Israelites or of the aliens residing among them, who catches an animal or a bird that may be eaten, shall pour out its blood and cover it with earth,ᵍ ¹⁴since the life of all flesh is its blood. I have told the Israelites: You shall not consume the blood of any flesh. Since the life of all flesh is its blood, anyone who consumes it shall be cut off.

¹⁵Everyone, whether a native or an alien, who eats of an animal that died of itself or was killed by a wild beast, shall wash his garments, bathe in water, and be unclean until evening, and then become clean.ʰ ¹⁶If one does not wash his garments and bathe, that person shall bear the penalty.

CHAPTER 18

Laws Concerning Sexual Behavior. ¹The Lord said to Moses: ²Speak to the Israelites and tell them: I, the Lord, am your God.‡ ³You shall not do as they do in the land of Egypt, where you once lived, nor shall you do as they do in the land of Canaan, where I am bringing you; do not conform to their customs.ᵃ ⁴My decrees you shall carry out, and my statutes you shall take care to follow. I, the Lord, am your God. ⁵Keep, then, my statutes and decrees, for the person who carries them out will find life§ through them. I am the Lord.ᵇ

⁶¶None of you shall approach a close relative** to have sexual intercourse. I am the Lord. ⁷††You shall not disgrace your father by having intercourse with your mother.ᶜ She is your own mother; you shall not have intercourse with her. ⁸You shall not have intercourse with your father's wife, for that would be a disgrace to your father. ⁹You shall not have intercourse with your sister,‡‡ᵈ your father's daughter or your mother's daughter, whether she was born in your own household or born elsewhere. ¹⁰You shall not have intercourse with your son's daughter or with your daughter's daughter,§§ for that would be a disgrace to you. ¹¹You shall not have intercourse with the daughter whom your father's wife bore to him in his household,ᵉ since she, too, is your sister. ¹²You shall not

* [17:11] **To make atonement**: this is probably to be understood in the context of liability for shedding animal blood (cf. v. 4). Placing the blood on the altar exonerates the slaughterer from guilt for the killing. See note on 16:6.
† [17:13] **Hunting**: game animals are not permitted as offerings. One nonetheless has to treat the blood of these animals carefully by covering it with earth. Cf. Dt 12:16, 24.

‡ [18:2] **I, the Lord, am your God**: this declaration appears frequently elsewhere throughout chaps. 17–26, sometimes with a statement of God's holiness or his sanctifying activity. It emphasizes the importance of the laws and the relationship of the divine lawgiver to the people.
§ [18:5] **Find life**: in Dt 30:15–20 Moses sets before the people life and death. The alternatives are set out in detail in Lv 26 and Dt 28. Cf. Ez 20:11, 13, 21.
¶ [18:6–23] These laws deal with illicit sexual behavior. Lv 20:10–21 reiterates most of these cases, with penalties. Cf. also Dt 27:15–26; Ez 22:7–12. The ordering of the cases in Lv 18 seems to be: blood relatives (vv. 6–13), those related by marriage (vv. 14–18), then other cases (vv. 19–23).
** [18:6] **Close relative**: this refers to a blood relative and includes those not specifically mentioned in the list, such as one's own daughter and a full sister. **Have sexual intercourse**: lit., "to uncover nakedness."
†† [18:7–8] Cf. the story of Reuben lying with Bilhah, his father's concubine and Rachel's maid (Gn 35:22; 49:4).
‡‡ [18:9, 11] Cf. actual or possible marriage to a half sister in Gn 20:12 and 2 Sm 13:13.
§§ [18:10] Daughter incest is found in the story of Lot (Gn 19:30–38).

e. [17:10–14] Lv 3:17; 7:26–27; Gn 9:4; Dt 12:16, 23–24.
f. [17:11] Gn 9:4.
g. [17:13] Dt 12:15–16.
h. [17:15] Lv 11:39–40; 22:8.

a. [18:3] Lv 20:22–23.
b. [18:5] Ez 20:11, 13, 21; Gal 3:12.
c. [18:7] Lv 20:11; Dt 23:1; 27:20; 1 Cor 5:1.
d. [18:9] Lv 20:17; Dt 27:22.
e. [18:11] Lv 20:17.

have intercourse with your father's sister,[f] since she is your father's relative. [13]You shall not have intercourse with your mother's sister, since she is your mother's relative. [14]You shall not disgrace your father's brother by having sexual relations with his wife,[g] since she, too, is your aunt. [15]You shall not have intercourse with your daughter-in-law;*[h] she is your son's wife; you shall not have intercourse with her. [16]You shall not have intercourse with your brother's wife;†[i] that would be a disgrace to your brother. [17]You shall not have intercourse with a woman and also with her daughter, nor shall you marry and have intercourse with her son's daughter or her daughter's daughter;[j] they are related to her. This would be shameful. [18]While your wife is still living you shall not marry her sister as her rival and have intercourse with her.[k]

[19]You shall not approach a woman to have intercourse with her while she is in her menstrual uncleanness.[l] [20]You shall not have sexual relations with your neighbor's wife,‡[m] defiling yourself with her. [21][n]You shall not offer any of your offspring for immolation to Molech,§ thus profaning the name of your God. I am the LORD. [22]You shall not lie with a male as with a woman;[o] such a thing is an abomination. [23]You shall not have sexual relations with an animal, defiling yourself with it; nor shall a woman set herself in front of an animal to mate with it; that is perverse.[p]

[24]Do not defile yourselves by any of these things, because by them the nations whom I am driving out of your way have defiled themselves. [25]And so the land has become defiled, and I have punished it for its wickedness, and the land has vomited out its inhabitants.[q] [26]You, however, must keep my statutes and decrees, avoiding all these abominations, both the natives and the aliens resident among you— [27]because the previous inhabitants did all these abominations and the land became defiled; [28]otherwise the land will vomit you out also for having defiled it, just as it vomited out the nations before you. [29]For whoever does any of these abominations shall be cut off from the people. [30]Heed my charge, then, not to observe the abominable customs that have been observed before your time, and thus become impure by them.[r] I, the LORD, am your God.

CHAPTER 19

Various Rules of Conduct. [1]The LORD said to Moses: [2]Speak to the whole Israelite community and tell them: Be holy, for I, the LORD your God, am holy.¶[a] [3]**Each of you revere your mother and father,[b] and keep my sabbaths.[c] I, the LORD, am your God.

---

* [18:15] Judah had intercourse with his daughter-in-law Tamar (Gn 38), but did not know her true identity until her pregnancy was discovered.

† [18:16] This refers to cohabiting with one's sister-in-law not only while the brother is alive, but also after he is dead. Dt 25:5–10 allows for the marriage to the wife of a brother when that brother died without a male heir. Cf. Gn 38:6–14. It was the violation of this law of Leviticus which aroused the wrath of John the Baptist against Herod Antipas (Mt 14:4; Mk 6:18).

‡ [18:20] Adultery in the Hebrew Bible and the ancient Near East is intercourse between a married or betrothed woman and any male. In the Bible it is generally punishable by the death of both individuals (20:10; cf. Dt 22:22–27). Intercourse with an unmarried or unbetrothed woman is not prohibited but carries responsibilities and fines (cf. Ex 22:15–16; Dt 22:28–29). Cf. Lv 19:20–22.

§ [18:21] **Immolation to Molech:** the reference is to the custom of sacrificing children to the god Molech. Cf. Ez 16:20–21; 20:26, 31; 23:37. See note on Lv 20:1–5.

f. [18:12] Lv 20:19.
g. [18:14] Lv 20:20.
h. [18:15] Lv 20:12.
i. [18:16] Lv 20:21; Dt 25:5–10; Mt 14:3–4; Mk 6:18.
j. [18:17] Lv 20:14; Dt 27:23.
k. [18:18] Gn 29:27–28.
l. [18:19] Lv 15:24, 33; 20:18; Ez 18:6; 22:10.
m. [18:20] Lv 20:10; Ex 20:14; Dt 5:18; 22:22; Mt 5:27–30; Jn 8:4–5.
n. [18:21] Lv 20:2–5; Dt 18:10; 1 Kgs 11:7; 2 Kgs 16:3.

¶ [19:2] **Be holy, for I . . . am holy:** in the writings commonly attributed to the Priestly collection, Israel is called to be holy through obeying God's precepts (11:44–45; 20:7–8, 24–26; Nm 15:40–41). Cf. Dt 14:2, 21; 26:19; and Ex 19:6.

** [19:3–4] Cf. the Decalogue laws on revering parents (Ex 20:12; Dt 5:16), keeping sabbaths (Ex 20:8–11; Dt 5:12–15), and not making or worshiping idols (Ex 20:2–6; Dt 5:7–10).

o. [18:22] Lv 20:13; Gn 19:4–11; Jgs 19:22–30; Rom 1:27; 1 Cor 6:9.
p. [18:23] Lv 20:15–16; Ex 22:18; Dt 27:21.
q. [18:25] Lv 20:22.
r. [18:30] Lv 20:23; Dt 18:9.

a. [19:2] Lv 11:44.
b. [19:3] Lv 20:9; Ex 20:12.
c. [19:3] Lv 23:3.

[4]Do not turn aside to idols, nor make molten gods for yourselves.[d] I, the LORD, am your God.

[5]When you sacrifice your communion sacrifice to the LORD, you shall sacrifice it so that it is acceptable on your behalf. [6]It must be eaten on the day of your sacrifice or on the following day. Whatever is left over until the third day shall be burned in fire. [7]If any of it is eaten on the third day, it will be a desecrated offering and not be accepted;[e] [8]whoever eats of it then shall bear the penalty for having profaned what is sacred to the LORD. Such a one shall be cut off[f] from the people.

[9]*When you reap the harvest of your land, you shall not be so thorough that you reap the field to its very edge, nor shall you gather the gleanings of your harvest.[g] [10]Likewise, you shall not pick your vineyard bare, nor gather up the grapes that have fallen. These things you shall leave for the poor and the alien. I, the LORD, am your God.

[11]†You shall not steal. You shall not deceive or speak falsely to one another.[h] [12]You shall not swear falsely by my name, thus profaning the name of your God.[i] I am the LORD.

[13]You shall not exploit your neighbor. You shall not commit robbery. You shall not withhold overnight the wages of your laborer.[j] [14]‡You shall not insult the deaf, or put a stumbling block in front of the blind, but you shall fear your God. I am the LORD.

[15]You shall not act dishonestly in rendering judgment. Show neither partiality to the weak nor deference to the mighty, but judge your neighbor justly.[k] [16]You shall not go about spreading slander among your people; nor shall you stand by idly when your neighbor's life is at stake. I am the LORD.

[17]§You shall not hate any of your kindred in your heart. Reprove your neighbor openly so that you do not incur sin because of that person.[l] [18]Take no revenge and cherish no grudge against your own people. You shall love your neighbor as yourself. I am the LORD.[m]

[19]¶Keep my statutes: do not breed any of your domestic animals with others of a different species; do not sow a field of yours with two different kinds of seed; and do not put on a garment woven with two different kinds of thread.[n]

[20]**If a man has sexual relations with a female slave who has been acquired by another man but has not yet been redeemed or given her freedom, an investigation shall be made. They shall not be put to death, because she has not been freed. [21]The man shall bring to the entrance of the tent of meeting as his reparation to the LORD a ram as a reparation offering.[p] [22]With the ram of the reparation offering the priest shall make atonement before the LORD for the wrong the man has committed, so that he will be forgiven for the wrong he has committed.

---

§ [19:17–18] These verses form a unit and describe different attitudes and actions towards one's fellow Israelites. A separate passage is necessary to advise a similar attitude toward aliens (vv. 33–34). Cf. 25:39–46. The admonition at the end of v. 18 came to be viewed in Judaism and Christianity as one of the central commandments. (See Mt 22:34–40; Mk 12:28–34; Lk 10:25–28; cf. Mt 19:19; Rom 13:8–10; Gal 5:14). The New Testament urges love for enemies as well as neighbors (Mt 5:43–48; Lk 6:27–36; cf. Prv 25:21–22).

¶ [19:19] One reason why mixtures are prohibited seems to be that they are holy (see Dt 22:9, 10–11). Israelites are allowed mixtures in the wearing of fringes on the edges or corners of their clothing (Nm 15:37–41; Dt 22:12). Some mixtures are considered abominations (cf. Lv 18:23; Dt 22:5).

** [19:20–22] On adultery, see note on 18:20. Here it is not adultery in the technical sense since the woman is not free. A reparation offering is required as a penalty (see 5:14–26).

---

* [19:9–10] The Israelites maintain the poor in part by letting them gather unharvested portions of fields and vineyards. Cf. 23:22; Ru 2:1–10.

† [19:11–13] Cf. the Decalogue commandments against stealing (Ex 20:15; Dt 5:19), wrongly using God's name (Ex 20:7; Dt 5:11), and swearing falsely against another (Ex 20:16; Dt 5:20).

‡ [19:14] In Dt 27:18 a curse falls on the head of the one who misleads the blind.

d. [19:4] Lv 26:1; Ex 20:3–5; 34:17; Dt 5:8; 27:15.
e. [19:7] Lv 7:15–18.
f. [19:8] Lv 7:20.
g. [19:9] Lv 23:22; Dt 24:19–22.
h. [19:11] Ex 20:15–16.
i. [19:12] Ex 20:7; Mt 5:33–37.
j. [19:13] Dt 24:14–15.

k. [19:15] Ex 23:2–3; Dt 1:17; 16:19; Ps 82:2; Prv 24:23.
l. [19:17] Mt 18:15; Lk 17:3; Gal 6:1.
m. [19:18] Mt 5:43; 19:19; 22:39; Mk 12:31; Rom 13:9; Gal 5:14; Jas 2:8; 1 Jn 3:14.
n. [19:19] Dt 22:9–12.
o. [19:20] Dt 22:22–29.
p. [19:21] Lv 5:14–26.

23When you come into the land and plant any fruit tree there,[q] first look upon its fruit as if it were uncircumcised. For three years, it shall be uncircumcised for you; it may not be eaten. 24In the fourth year, however, all of its fruit shall be dedicated to the LORD in joyous celebration. 25Not until the fifth year may you eat its fruit, to increase the yield for you. I, the LORD, am your God.

26Do not eat anything with the blood still in it.[r] Do not recite charms or practice soothsaying.[*s] 27Do not clip your hair at the temples, nor spoil the edges of your beard. 28Do not lacerate your bodies for the dead, and do not tattoo yourselves.[†t] I am the LORD.

29You shall not degrade your daughter by making a prostitute of her;[u] otherwise the land will prostitute itself and become full of lewdness. 30Keep my sabbaths, and reverence my sanctuary.[v] I am the LORD.

31Do not turn to ghosts or consult spirits, by which you will be defiled.[w] I, the LORD, am your God.

32Stand up in the presence of the aged, show respect for the old, and fear your God. I am the LORD.

33When an alien resides with you in your land, do not mistreat such a one.[x] 34You shall treat the alien who resides with you no differently than the natives born among you; you shall love the alien as yourself; for you too were once aliens in the land of Egypt.[y] I, the LORD, am your God.

35Do not act dishonestly in using measures of length or weight or capacity. 36You shall have a true scale and true weights, an honest ephah and an honest hin.[‡z] I, the LORD, am your God, who brought you out of the land of Egypt. 37Be careful, then, to observe all my statutes and decrees. I am the LORD.

CHAPTER 20

Penalties for Various Sins. 1[§]The LORD said to Moses: 2Tell the Israelites: Anyone, whether an Israelite or an alien residing in Israel, who gives offspring to Molech shall be put to death.[a] The people of the land shall stone that person. 3[b]I myself will turn against and cut off[c] that individual from among the people; for in the giving of offspring to Molech, my sanctuary was defiled[d] and my holy name was profaned. 4If the people of the land condone the giving of offspring to Molech, by failing to put the wrongdoer to death, 5I myself will turn against that individual and his or her family, and I will cut off from their people both the wrongdoer and all who follow this person by prostituting themselves with Molech.

6Should anyone turn to ghosts and spirits and prostitute oneself with them,[e] I will turn against that person and cut such a one off from among the people. 7Sanctify yourselves, then, and be holy; for I, the LORD, your God,[f] am holy. 8Be careful, therefore, to observe my statutes. I, the LORD, make you holy.

* [19:26] **Recite charms . . . soothsaying**: methods of divination (cf. Gn 44:5, 15; Is 2:6; Ez 21:26–28). Legitimate means of learning the future or God's will were through the Urim and Thummim stones (see Lv 8:8), lots (see Lv 16:8) and prophets (cf. Dt 18:9–22; 1 Sm 28:6–7).

† [19:28] **Do not tattoo yourselves**: see note on Gn 4:15. This prohibition probably refers only to the common ancient Near Eastern practice of branding a slave with its owner's name as well as branding the devotees of a god with its name.

‡ [19:36] **Ephah**: see note on Is 5:10; **hin**: see note on Ez 45:24.

§ [20:1–5] The term Molech may refer to a deity, perhaps with an underworld association, and the activity forbidden here may be connected with divination. Cf. Dt 18:10; 2 Kgs 17:17; 21:6. In the kingdom of Judah the cult appears to have been practiced in the Valley of Hinnom, just outside Jerusalem on the west and south (2 Kgs 23:10; Jer 32:35).

q. [19:23] Dt 20:19–20.
r. [19:26] Lv 17:10.
s. [19:26] Dt 18:10; 2 Kgs 17:17; 21:6; 2 Chr 33:6.
t. [19:28] Lv 21:5.
u. [19:29] Lv 21:7, 14.
v. [19:30] Lv 19:3.
w. [19:31] Lv 20:6, 27; Dt 18:11; Is 8:19.
x. [19:33] Ex 22:20; 23:9; Jer 22:3; Mal 3:5.
y. [19:34] Dt 10:19.
z. [19:36] Dt 25:13–16; Prv 16:11; Am 8:5; Mi 6:10–11.
a. [20:2] Lv 18:21; Dt 12:31; 18:10; 2 Kgs 16:3; 17:17; 21:6; 23:10; Jer 32:35.
b. [20:3] Ez 23:39.
c. [20:3] Lv 7:20.
d. [20:3] Lv 15:31.
e. [20:6] Lv 19:31.
f. [20:7] Lv 11:44.

9 Anyone who curses father or mother shall be put to death;[*][g] and having cursed father or mother, such a one will bear the bloodguilt.[†] 10[‡]If a man commits adultery with his neighbor's wife,[h] both the adulterer and the adulteress shall be put to death. 11 If a man disgraces his father by lying with his father's wife,[i] the two of them shall be put to death; their bloodguilt is upon them. 12 If a man lies with his daughter-in-law,[j] both of them shall be put to death; they have done what is perverse; their bloodguilt is upon them. 13 If a man lies with a male as with a woman,[k] they have committed an abomination; the two of them shall be put to death; their bloodguilt is upon them. 14 If a man marries a woman and her mother also,[l] that is shameful conduct; the man and the two women as well shall be burned to death, so that shamefulness may not be found among you. 15 If a man has sexual relations with an animal,[m] the man shall be put to death, and you shall kill the animal. 16 If a woman goes up to any animal to mate with it,[n] you shall kill the woman and the animal; they shall both be put to death; their bloodguilt is upon them. 17 If a man marries his sister,[o] his father's daughter or his mother's daughter, and they have intercourse with each other, that is disgraceful; they shall be publicly cut off[§] from the people; the man shall bear the penalty of having had intercourse with his own sister. 18 If a man lies with a woman during her menstrual period and has intercourse with her, he has laid bare the source of her flow and she has uncovered it.[p] The two of them shall be cut off from the people. 19 You shall not have intercourse with your mother's sister or your father's sister,[q] because that dishonors one's own flesh; they shall bear their penalty. 20 If a man lies with his uncle's wife, he disgraces his uncle;[r] they shall bear the penalty; they shall die childless. 21 If a man takes his brother's wife, it is severe defilement and he has disgraced his brother;[s] they shall be childless.

22 Be careful to observe all my statutes and all my decrees; otherwise the land where I am bringing you to dwell will vomit you out.[t] 23 Do not conform, therefore, to the customs of the nations[u] whom I am driving out of your way, because all these things that they have done have filled me with disgust for them. 24 But to you I have said:[v] You shall take possession of their land. I am giving it to you to possess, a land flowing with milk and honey. I, the LORD, am your God, who have set you apart from other peoples. 25 [w]You, too, must set apart, then, the clean animals from the unclean, and the clean birds from the unclean, so that you do not make yourselves detestable through any beast or bird or any creature which creeps on the ground that I have set apart for you as unclean. 26 To me, therefore, you shall be holy; for I, the LORD, am holy,[x] and I have set you apart from other peoples to be my own.

27 A man or a woman who acts as a medium or clairvoyant[y] shall be put to

* [20:9] **Curses father or mother . . . put to death**: This is more than a simple expletive uttered in anger against one's parents. See note on Ex 21:17.

† [20:9–21] **Bloodguilt**: These penalties, beginning with cursing one's parents, reflect the concerns of a patriarchal society that the breakdown of one's relations with one's parents can lead to the breakdown of all other familial relationships, resulting in the breakdown of society.

‡ [20:10–21] See 18:6–23 and notes there. It appears that the inclusion of various penalties in 20:10–21 accounts for the different order of the cases here compared to the order found in 18:6–23. The reason why the offenses in 20:10–21 carry different penalties, however, is not clear. Perhaps the cases in vv. 17–21 were considered slightly less serious, being condemned but not criminally prosecuted.

§ [20:17] **Cut off**: see note on 7:20.

g. [20:9] Lv 19:3; Ex 21:17; Dt 21:18–21; Prv 20:20; Mt 15:4; Mk 7:10.
h. [20:10] Lv 18:20.
i. [20:11] Lv 18:8.
j. [20:12] Lv 18:15.
k. [20:13] Lv 18:22.
l. [20:14] Lv 18:17.
m. [20:15] Lv 18:23.
n. [20:16] Lv 18:23.
o. [20:17] Lv 18:9.
p. [20:18] Lv 18:19.
q. [20:19] Lv 18:12–13.
r. [20:20] Lv 18:14.
s. [20:21] Lv 18:16.
t. [20:22] Lv 18:25, 28.
u. [20:23] Lv 18:30.
v. [20:24] Ex 3:8, 17.
w. [20:25] Lv 11:2–47; Dt 14:4–20.
x. [20:26] Lv 11:44.
y. [20:27] Lv 19:31; Ex 22:17; Dt 18:11.